Legislations

V

PHRONESIS

A series from Verso edited by
Ernesto Laclau and Chantal Mouffe

There is today wide agreement that the left-wing project is in crisis. New antagonisms have emerged – not only in advanced capitalist societies but also in the Eastern bloc and in the Third World – that require the reformulation of the socialist ideal in terms of an extension and deepening of democracy. However, serious disagreements exist as to the theoretical strategy needed to carry out such a task. There are those for whom the current critique of rationalism and universalism puts into jeopardy the very basis of the democratic project. Others argue that the critique of essentialism – a point of convergence of the most important trends in contemporary theory: post-structuralism, philosophy of language after the later Wittgenstein, post-Heideggerian hermeneutics – is the necessary condition for understanding the widening of the field of social struggles characteristic of the present stage of democratic politics. *Phronesis* clearly locates itself among the latter. Our objective is to establish a dialogue between those theoretical developments and left-wing politics. We believe that an anti-essentialist theoretical stand is the *sine qua non* of a new vision for the Left conceived in terms of a radical and plural democracy.

Legislations

The Politics of Deconstruction

GEOFFREY BENNINGTON

VERSO

London · New York

First published by Verso 1994
© Verso 1994
All rights reserved

Verso
UK: 6 Meard Street, London W1V 3HR
USA: 29 West 35th Street, New York, NY 10001-2291

Verso is the imprint of New Left Books

ISBN 0 86091 414 3
ISBN 0 86091 668 5 (pbk)

British Library Cataloguing in Publication Data
A catalogue record for this book is available from the British Library

Library of Congress Cataloging-in-Publication Data
Bennington, Geoffrey
Legislations/Geoffrey Bennington.
p.   cm.
Includes bibliographical references and index.
ISBN 0-86091-414-3. — ISBN 0-86091-668-5 (pbk.)
1. Literature—Philosophy.   I. Title.
PN45.B422   1994
302.2'24—dc20   93-46858
CIP

Typeset by York House Typographic Ltd, London
Printed and bound in Great Britain by
Biddles Ltd, Guildford and King's Lynn

For Louis

Contents

Acknowledgements   *viii*
Introduction   *1*

PART I   REFUTATIONS

1   Deconstruction and the Philosophers (The Very Idea)
     (1988)   *11*
2   Demanding History (1983)   *61*
3   Not Yet (1981)   *74*
4   Outside Story (1983)   *88*
5   L'Arroseur Arrosé(e) (1988)   *99*

PART II   READINGS

6   The Perfect Cheat: Locke and Empiricism's Rhetoric
     (1984)   *119*
7   Aberrations: de Man (and) the Machine (1984)   *137*
8   'Ces petits *différends*': Lyotard and Horace (1987)   *152*
9   The Rationality of Postmodern Relativity (1986)   *172*
10   Spirit's Spirit Spirits Spirit (1990)   *196*
11   Mosaic Fragment: If Derrida Were an Egyptian . . . (1991)   *207*

PART III   OPENINGS

12   Towards a Criticism of the Future (1986)   *229*
13   Postal Politics and the Institution of the Nation (1986)   *240*
14   The Frontier: Between Kant and Hegel (1991)   *259*
15   Index (1988)   *274*

Index   *297*

Acknowledgements

All the chapters of this book, with the exception of the last, have been published previously: Chapter 1 in *Oxford Literary Review*, 10 (1988), pp. 73–130; Chapter 2 in D. Attridge, G. Bennington, and R. Young, eds, *Post-structuralism and the Question of History*, Cambridge: Cambridge University Press 1987, pp. 15–29; Chapter 3 in *Diacritics*, 12:3 (1982), pp. 23–32; Chapter 4 in *LTP*, 3 (1984), pp. 117–28; Chapter 5 in *New Formations*, 7 (1989), pp. 35–49; Chapter 6 in A. Benjamin, G. Cantor and J. Christie, eds, *The Figural and the Literal: Problems of Language in the History of Science and Philosophy*, Manchester: Manchester University Press 1987, pp. 103–123; Chapter 7 in L. Waters and W. Godzich, eds., *Reading De Man Reading*, Minneapolis: University of Minnesota Press 1989, pp. 209–222; Chapter 8 in A. Benjamin, ed., *Judging Lyotard*, London: Routledge 1992, pp. 145–67; Chapter 9 in *Journal of Philosophy and the Visual Arts*, 1990, pp. 23–31; Chapter 10 in D. Wood, ed., *Of Heidegger, Derrida and Spirit*, Evanston: Northwestern University Press 1993, pp. 82–92; Chapter 11 in D. Wood, ed., *Derrida: A Critical Reader*, Oxford: Basil Blackwell 1992, pp. 97–119; Chapter 12 in D. Wood, ed., *Writing the Future*, London: Routledge 1990, pp. 17–29; Chapter 13 in Homi K. Bhabha, ed., *Nation and Narration*, London: Methuen 1990, pp. 121–37; Chapter 14 in H. Kunneman and H. de Vries, eds., *Enlightenments*, Kampen: Kok Pharos 1993, pp. 45–60.

Thanks are due for permission to reprint the following copyright material in this book: Cambridge University Press and Johns Hopkins University Press for Chapter 2; University of Minnesota Press for Chapter 7; Routledge for Chapters 8, 12 and 13; Academy Editions for Chapter 9; Basil Blackwell for Chapter 11; Kok Pharos Editions for Chapter 14.

Every effort has been made to contact copyright holders of material included in this book.

Introduction

Someone comes and says something. Without really needing to think, I understand what is said, refer it without difficulty to familiar codes, would assign meaning and intention confidently if questioned about them, and possibly I even reply. This situation of 'communication', in its banality, is one in which nothing much happens: information may be transmitted, contact maintained, an order given and received, but nowhere is the established normality of language use or its associated 'forms of life' called into question.

Someone comes and says something. This time I do not quite understand, or am not entirely sure of having understood. Something in what is said or the manner of its saying jars, doesn't quite fit, seems perhaps to break a rule or transgress a norm, be it phonetic, grammatical, semantic, sociolectal, para-linguistic, behavioural. Something appears to have been meant or intended, but I am less confident than in the first case about what exactly it is. In this situation, something *has* happened: an event, however small, has occurred at the frontier of my linguistic competence or on the borders of the language-games I normally reckon to master. This border-incident, this event, may of course be trivial: people make grammatical and other mistakes all the time, and they can be, and often are, corrected by application of the existing rules: but sometimes the 'mistake' or the non-compliance with the rule is less obvious, harder to identify and casts the rule's confidence into doubt. This momentary 'violence'[1] is one in which an uncertainty opens up: maybe isn't just that this utterance breaks the rules – maybe this follows *other* rules, and if it does, might not those rules aspire to replace my own? Maybe these rules are *better* rules? Or is this a tricky attempt to talk me into something?

It is not hard to see that, contrary to the most widespread current ideology, the only communication worth the name takes place in this latter sort of situation. Something is communicated to me in a strong sense, or *there is* an event of communication, only when I do not have

1

immediately available to me the means to decode a transparent mess-age. This implies that there is communication only when there is a moment, however minimal, of non-understanding, of *stupidity* with respect to what is said. *Communication implies non-comprehension.* I am in a situation of communication with the other only when I do not understand what he, she or it says.[2] And this moment of stupid non-comprehension, taken to a limit, means that the space of communica-tion is most radically itself, most radically open to the coming of the other, when I am not even sure whether someone has come and said something. Was there even an utterance? Was there someone or something there? Communication takes place, if at all, in a fundamen-tal and irreducible uncertainty as to the very fact and possibility of communication.[3]

This 'violence' in communication means that the situation I am describing goes beyond local questions of language and meaning. Violence, as Walter Benjamin pointed out, is always an attempt to legislate, to lay down the law, just as any attempt to legislate is necessarily violent: and this situation is no exception. When someone (?) comes (?) and says (?) something (?), *I always might be facing a legislator*. The other, in so far as he, she or it *is* an other, always might be bringing me a new law. There is no real alterity unless the law I know is being cast into doubt.[4] The problem, which looks as though it ought in principle to precede all questions that might be asked about meaning, or about determinate ethical and political issues, is that of knowing whether I am faced with an other, therefore a legislator, or not.

For it always might be the case (nothing is a more common – political – experience: in fact, this just is the experience of the political) that the figure I take for a legislator is in fact a charlatan. It clearly *matters* whether I am faced with a legislator or a charlatan, but I have no means of making a confident decision between them: any decision of that sort would need to refer to an existing criterion, and thus foreclose the possibility that all my existing criteria are being chal-lenged by the other – which comes down to disallowing in advance the alterity of the other. Any *confident* claim to identify the legislator (or the charlatan) shows by its very confidence that it is wrong. No legislator ever could arrive and be recognized as such infallibly: the legislator *always* might be a charlatan, and the legislator or charlatan can be no more sure about this than anyone else.

Someone comes, and perhaps there is a saying of something. That someone here is me, for example, introducing a book of essays, which try to say something that cannot quite be contained in existing codes, definitions or rules. *Any* piece of writing, in so far as it has the ambition of saying something new, aspires to the sternness of legislation (and therefore, happily, inherits the levity and anxiety of the charlatan to lighten the solemnity of the law). A piece of writing more or less violently calls on the reader it always might not find to recognize it in a piece of legislation, appeals to that reader's responsibility to the law it tries to impose, and bows before his, her or its freedom to condemn the would-be legislator as a charlatan after all.

This moment at which the legislator always might be a charlatan (and to that extent always in a sense is, can never be shown not to be), just is the moment of the political, and it is irreducible because it is undecidable. This is why there is no end to politics. One of the contentions that runs through these essays – all, I realize after the fact, striving to describe in its paradoxical details the situation I have just sketched[5] – is that the critical appeal to 'politics' as a criterion of judgement *always* functions as an attempt to reduce just that situation, and therefore to reduce politics in the very act of invoking it. Another is that 'deconstruction' provides an access to it which is not provided elsewhere.[6]

Which implies that these are not just 'theoretical' essays about a variety of problems in philosophy, literary studies or even politics, but that they are *themselves* inscribed in a political situation.[7] This means, among other things, that all these texts are essentially *dated*: but this datedness, which no text can escape (every text is historical and bears the traces of its dates, even though – this is basis for a refutation of all historicisms, old and new – no text can be exclusively mastered by reference to any one or any finite set of dates, is readable only to the extent that it is perpetually escaping from its dates), is perhaps most clearly marked in the more or less polemical essays gathered in the 'Refutations' part of the book. These are not all particularly polite texts, and make no attempt to subscribe to a certain academic code which prescribes 'debate' as the appropriate form for criticism to take. Debate is pointless where errors are so frequent and serious. (This does not, of course, guarantee the accuracy and efficacy of the attempted refutation, which I must leave to the reader's judgement.) The undeniable indignation, bad temper and amusement which show through in at least some of these texts were inspired largely by the extraordinary ignorance and complacency which seemed to me to dominate critical accounts of deconstruction, and this in work which for other reasons came associated with a credibility or apparent legitimacy which I felt made the ignorance and complacency the more inexcusable. This apparent legitimacy has nothing to do with the (often very poor) quality of argument or knowledge displayed in the books I discuss, but with essentially political credentials gained elsewhere. The point of writing 'refutations' of such work is of course to correct, in a traditionally pedagogical spirit, errors which lead to a distorted presentation of, here, deconstruction: but also, more obliquely, to cast doubt on the political credentials presiding over and tolerating those errors. This is of course a violent operation, but that violence itself attempts to find a quasi-legitimacy by means of the following argument: authors such as Dews, Eagleton, Jameson and Ryan all appeal, in their criticisms of deconstruction, to the concepts of 'history' and/or 'politics'. These concepts function in their discourse as uncriticized and uncritical transcendental terms, which are supposed to justify criticisms coming down to the form: 'deconstruction has an unsatisfactory concept of history and/or politics', meaning – quite correctly – that deconstruction does not accept the transcendental concepts of history and politics invoked against it by these authors. But as the effort of deconstruction is precisely to question just such transcendental concepts, and more generally the transcendental position itself, then invoking them against it without further clarifying or modifying their status can *never* constitute a valid criticism. Because such authors think that it can and does, they do not feel the need to make any serious attempt to read the work they criticize, as I try to demonstrate.

The reactive approach to deconstruction (which is not of course limited to its opponents) is itself 'political' in the sense outlined in the first part of this Introduction, whether or not it explicitly invokes political arguments. The simple repetition of familiar metaphysical arguments (and using words like 'materialist' or 'social' or 'historical' or 'political' is of course no guarantee of escaping metaphysics, though it is often enough an excuse for assuming that such an escape has taken place, because of a sort of reversed transcendental illusion whereby these words seem to name something empirical or factical) comes down to the second version of the situation described above, in which the apparent non-coincidence of what is said with the available rules is interpreted as just a mistake, to be corrected. This attempt to enforce institutionalized rules (and there is no suggestion here that institutions and therefore rules are Bad Things, or could ever be simply avoided), even if it be done in the name of revolution (and more especially 'the' revolution) is fundamentally reactionary, and therefore profoundly *anti*-political, because it forecloses the possibility that the other be a legislator, and that possibility just is the possibility of the political as such. A quick measure of the failure of such criticism to be political is provided by the disastrous institutional effects of this so-called 'political' criticism, which programmes repressions, exclusions and misreadings of all sorts, quite independently of the intentions of any of the authors I have named.[8] A similar point could be made about a certain psychoanalytic reception of deconstruction, which has often relied on an unthought exclusionary institutionalization (psychoanalysis finding it notoriously difficult to think its own status as institution). In spite of a certain amount of noise to the contrary, deconstruction does not, and in principle cannot, give rise to institutionalization in the same way.

The philosophical case is more difficult. Deconstruction is not a philosophy even though it involves intensely philosophical moments. I try to show how the philosophical attempt to save deconstruction from the naiveties of 'political' or other positive approaches, though no doubt to be preferred (at the date at which I was writing, at least), always runs the risk of reinstating a philosophy of deconstruction which again closes off the opening to the other (and therefore to reading) which I have outlined. This risk is unavoidable, and because deconstruction comes as close as can be to philosophy, right up against it, the philosopher's tendency to misrecognize it inspires amused solidarity as much as criticism here.[9]

But if datedness is most obvious in these polemical pieces, it cannot be absent from the others. These I have divided into 'Readings' and 'Openings'. The essays grouped under the first rubric all attempt to read texts which seemed to me to pose more or less explicitly the problems evoked above. All do so under the aegis of work by Derrida and Lyotard which they also try, sometimes a little obliquely, to elucidate, in the margins of books I was writing at the same time.[10] Those grouped under the second rubric, usually more recent and in one case previously unpublished, attempt to move away from that slightly dutiful expository loyalty into more adventurous and nervous ground. I cannot state more simply than they the law they propose, nor of course guarantee its legitimacy.

BRIGHTON, SEPTEMBER 1993

Notes

1. See Jean-Jacques Lecercle, *The Violence of Language*, London: Routledge 1990.

2. I use 'he, she or it' less as a parodic exacerbation of the conventional 'he or she', than to mark the fact that it cannot be presupposed that the 'other' referred to here is necessarily human. This is an analytic consequence of the notion of the 'other'. See J-F. Lyotard, 'Avant-propos: de l'humain', in *L'Inhumain: causeries sur le temps*, Paris: Galilée 1988, pp. 9–15; translated by Geoffrey Bennington and Rachel Bowlby as *The Inhuman: Reflections on Time*, Cambridge: Polity Press 1991, pp. 1–7.

3. This refutes the general Habermasian analysis of communication as ideally and teleologically directed to understanding, and only accidentally or empirically affected by stupidity or non-comprehension.

4. I propose this as a radicalization of Davidson's ill-named 'principle of charity': the 'charity' I extend to the other must, in principle, be charitable enough to anticipate the

possibility that the other will sweep away all the principles I have, including the principle of charity itself. Charity in this displaced sense is the perpetual opening to the possibility that the other will teach me what charity really is, precisely by refusing my charity.

5. This is also true of my two non-expository books: *Sententiousness and the Novel* (1985), and *Dudding: des noms de Rousseau* (1991), both of which find a focus for this problem in *The Social Contract*.

6. The only strictly political thinking I am aware of that attempts to take deconstruction rigorously into account is that of Ernesto Laclau and Chantal Mouffe.

7. I have included in this volume the essays that seemed to me to pose these problems most clearly. Of the essays I have published, I have excluded from the book several texts written in French, some early essays in English, some very circumstantial or insubstantial pieces, some which were subsequently absorbed or reworked into other essays, and some papers which represent work in progress for a book on the concept of frontiers. Published work not included here is as follows: 'From Narrative to Text: Love and Writing in Crébillon *fils*, Duclos, Barthes'; *OLR*, 4:1 (1979), 62–81; 'The Field and the Fence', *OLR*, 4:2 (1980), 82–8; 'Reading Allegory', *OLR*, 4:3 (1981), 83–93; 'Réappropriations', *Poétique*, 48 (1981), 495–512; 'Les Machines de l'Opéra', *French Studies*, 36:2 (1982), 154–70; 'Theory: They or We', *Paragraph*, 1 (1983), 1–12; 'Sade: Laying down the Law', *OLR*, 6:1 (1984), 38–56; 'August: Double Justice', *Diacritics*, 14:3 (1984), 64–71; 'Lyotard: From Discourse and Figure to Experimentation and Event', *Paragraph*, 6 (1985), 19–27; 'Post', in David Kelley and Isabelle Llasera, eds., *Cross-References*, London: Society for French Studies 1986; 'Complexity without Contradiction in Architecture', *AA Files*, 15 (1987), 15–18; 'Outside Language', *OLR*, 11 (1989), 89–112; 'Deconstruction is Not What You Think' and 'Deconstruction and the Postmodern', in Papadakis, Cooke and Benjamin, eds, *Deconstruction: Omnibus Volume*, London: Academy Editions 1989; 'Not One', *Blank Page* 4, London: B4 Publishing 1990, unpaginated; 'Frontiers: Two Seminar Sessions', *OLR*, 14 (1992), 197–227; 'After the Event', *Columbia Documents of Architecture and Theory*, 1 (1992), pp. 147–58; 'Plus que parfait', *Le Contretemps*, 1 (1994). I have also excluded a number of unpublished conference papers.

8. In a spate of recent work which may appear to escape these strictures, Slavoj Žižek has urged the superiority of a Hegelian–Lacanian conceptuality over a deconstructive one for an understanding of politics (and indeed of everything else). Žižek argues that Hegal and Lacan really already are what Derrida would like to be (for short, non-totalizers), but that Derrida precisely isn't what he would like to be, but more like what he (Derrida) is supposed to argue Hegel and Lacan are (for short, totalizers). Apart from the need to maintain a pre-theoretical concept of authorial identity (without which this distribution of praise and blame would make no sense, and which is precisely not maintained in Derrida's work), and the need to explain endlessly to the slightly dazzled reader that Hegel and Lacan mean precisely the opposite of what they most obviously appear to mean (so that, for example 'absolute knowledge' precisely does not mean 'absolute knowledge', *and Žižek knows this*), Žižek's work in fact consistently confirms that Lacan and Hegel really do provide him with the very totalizing claim to knowledge he says they most radically unsettle, by treating history, politics and everything else as simply an endless fund of amusing *anecdotes* which can illustrate again and again just how right Lacan and Hegel always were and always will be. In Žižek's readings (though reading, as opening to the other/legislator, is in fact just what is most lacking here), Pascal, Hitchcock, Woody Allen, anti-Semitism, racial legislation in the USA, Kant, recent events in Eastern Europe, all turn out to be merely rather funny *instances* of what Lacan–Hegel has already said. In Žižek's account, the dimension of what I am calling 'politics' is radically foreclosed because nothing can *happen* that is not already recognizable, with a little interpretative *brio*, as the truth already given in (Žižek's presentation of) Hegal and Lacan.

9. This amused solidarity does not extend quite as far as Richard Rorty, who re-philosophizes Derrida precisely by trying to argue that the *good* Derrida just escapes transcendental philosophy, whereas there is also a *bad* Derrida who falls into the trap of putting up transcendental arguments. This crude binarism, and the illusion of choice it

offers, falls far short of Derrida's deployment of *quasi-transcendental* arguments: these are as good as they are bad in Rorty's terms, which are therefore radically indiscriminate.

10. *Lyotard: Writing the Event*, Manchester: Manchester University Press 1988; *Jacques Derrida* (in collaboration with Jacques Derrida), Paris: Seuil 1991; tr. Geoffrey Bennington, Chicago: University of Chicago Press 1993.

PART I

Refutations

1

Deconstruction and the Philosophers

(The Very Idea)

ha[1] (hah), int. expr. surprise, joy, suspicion, triumph, etc. [ME]
ha[2] (hah). See HUM v.
. . .

hah, int. & v.i. = HA[1,2]
ha ha (hah hah), int. repr. laughter
ha-ha (hah'hah), n. Sunk fence bounding park or garden. [F]
. . .

hum[1], v.i. & t.(-mm-). Make continuous murmuring sound, as of
bee, spinning top, etc.; make low inarticulate vocal sound, esp.
(usu.~& *haw or ha*) of hesitation; sing with closed lips; (colloq.) be
in state of activity, as *make things*~; (sl.) smell unpleasantly; (v.t.)
utter, sing, with closed lips. [ME, imit.; so MHG *hummen*]
hum[2], n. Humming sound esp. of hesitation (usu.~*s and ha's*),
applause, surprise, etc.; (sl.) bad smell. [imit.]
hum[3] (hem), int. expr. hesitation, dissent, etc.
hum[4], n. (sl.). Sham, hoax. [=HUMBUG]

The End

We knew it wouldn't last for ever. We 'literary critics' or even 'theorists'
had to move quickly while the going was good, make the most of our
chances, rush on excitedly, trying not to take too much notice of the
slow, heavy, inexorable tread of the law somewhere behind. The
philosophers were back there somewhere, tortoise to our hare. In 1986
their books came out.[1]

Not, of course, that we'd worried about the philosophers who
seemed to be too simply on our side: we knew clearly enough that
Rorty, for example, had got it all wrong, precisely because he didn't
want Derrida to be doing philosophy at all, but just to be telling
stories.[2] Others too had a silly idea of 'the literary' as liberating and
liberated, or else tried to pull Derrida into quarrels about other things,

calling him anti-foundationalist or fallibilist, sometimes even sceptic or relativist.[3] That never bothered us much – we knew that was wrong. Our problem was never with 'philosophers' who wanted to throw over philosophy for literature, nor with those who wanted to translate Derrida into analytic idioms (though we much preferred the latter). But we knew that we would get into trouble one day soon because of a paradox which became immediately obvious to anyone 'teaching' deconstruction (my first joke), and which Culler had formulated imperturbably in *On Deconstruction*: 'Derrida's own discussions of literary works draw attention to important problems, but they are not *deconstructions* as we have been using the term, and a deconstructive literary criticism will be primarily influenced by his readings of philosophical works.'[4] We had to get the 'philosophical' readings straight (who, in any case, could teach from something like *Signsponge?*), without being philosophers. It was all very well of Culler to sidestep this in an evasive footnote earlier in his book[5] – we had to do better than that. And turning to one of the sources of information indicated in that footnote (assuming we hadn't been secretly weeping over the text in question for some time already), we found stern warnings of things to come. Gasché's much-quoted 'Deconstruction as Criticism' told us what we feared: that we were philosophically naive or at least 'untrained'[6] (we had been doing our best to catch up with some reading on the side, be fair). This was chastening in the extreme. Not, of course, that *we* had ever really been guilty of the confusions Gasché so severely denounced, though we all knew someone who was. But as reproaches went, there was a disturbing difference between these and the sort we had got used to from the moralists such as Said or Jameson or Eagleton,[7] who simply kept getting it wrong about reference or history or the political or the real (best not even mention the Lacanians),[8] and who could be easily enough refuted, however volubly they repeated their charges. Putting them right kept us going happily enough (though tended to give some people the unfortunate idea that something they kept calling a 'debate' was going on, or, even worse, that talk of 'agendas' was in order). This was different, and something of a threat: which of us was going to deny the force of at least most of Gasché's demonstration? Far from being someone we could laugh at and put right, Gasché clearly *knew better*. And there must be others too who knew their three H's[9] better than we did and would be following soon enough. Maybe we'd do better to stop talking so loud about 'Western Metaphysics' and get back to poems – but we'd learned enough meantime to see that *that* sort of opposition wouldn't hold, and that any such move, especially if seen as a turning from theory to practice (as in Norris's New Accents book, which thus makes its first mistake in its subtitle, but also as in Ulmer, say)[10] was going badly wrong somewhere – to say nothing of the fact that if we went back to poems we might have to teach with *Signsponge* after all.

And then we felt fairly secure after all in the sense that none of the effects (as we say) of Derrida's work was to put in question (as some others say) the generic distinction of philosophy and literature – so we could assume that no one could simply take Derrida away from us (sympathy we felt for that participant at the 1980 Cerisy conference, admitting in the final session that he had feared to come, lest his 'petit Derrida intérieur' get taken away from him; relief when he claimed this hadn't happened).[11] We also had a good hunch that Derrida made notions such as authority and 'mastery' difficult, so perhaps need not be unduly alarmed by Gasché's opening remark in his book that 'to judge Derrida's writings as literary – to exclude them from the sphere of "serious", that is, philosophical discussion, or to recuperate them for literary criticism – is a feeble attempt to master his work, one that cannot do justice to the complexity of the Derridean enterprise' (p. 1). And when Irene Harvey, in the 'Open Letter to Literary Critics' which opens *her* book (and we indeed spent some time wondering whether there was some play on the 'open' here, for how could such a 'letter', printed as here, be other than 'open' in the normal sense?) 'insists' 'that justice has not yet been done to the seriousness of Derrida's project' (p. x), we nodded at the repetition of the question of justice and noted the absence of scare-quotes around the notion of the serious and wondered what to make of that.

But we knew this was stalling: we cared about doing justice to this work, and we took it desperately ' "seriously" '. We knew, again with Culler, that any simple denial of mastery to Derrida's work would be foolish,[12] and that our own efforts to teach that work depended on our ability to master it in some significant sense. Something similar had held for Gasché's insistence in 'Deconstruction as Criticism' on 'the necessity of restoring [deconstruction's] rigorous meaning against its defenders as well as against those who argue against it' (p. 182) (we wondered here about clever things happening in the redoubled 'against' in this syntax): we knew immediately, too comfortably, that there was a funny smell about this type of restoration (especially when we read 'Restitutions', and got stuck trying to translate its subtitle):[13] but we weren't so stupid as to think some such move wasn't sometimes necessary – we ourselves had to invoke some such notion to avoid the 'liberalism' of which we were so often accused, and which would be an accurate label if we were liberal to the point of not arguing that the accusers were just wrong. However much we hummed and ha'd at a certain relentlessness and brutality of the writing of these people so much less literary than us, *n'est-ce pas?* (and although this is true of Harvey and Gasché, who expound Derrida and philosophy with undertaker's *gravitas* and many a stylistic solecism, to the point of provoking an irrepressible hilarity in the reader, no such preliminary comfort is available in Llewelyn's short, complex, funny and eccentric book), we knew that in the circumstances such aestheticism on our part would be rather vulgar. There is no alternative but to take these books *philosophically*: the tortoise is upon us at last. In the closing 'Chronology' section of Norris's recent *Modern Masters* volume on Derrida, we are told that these three books (which exhaust 1986 in the list) 'all of which address [Derrida's] *philosophical* concerns' (emphasis Norris's) 'mark a decided shift in the Anglo-American response to his work'. No escape (especially, perhaps, for Norris, hare to everyone's tortoise).[14]

Don't get us wrong. Of course we're delighted with these excellent books. After years of warning students off almost *all* secondary reading on Derrida, it's a relief to have these books to turn to. We had in any case been arguing for years for the *'philosophical'* importance of Derrida's work, often enough with philosophers. This didn't necessarily make us happy with literary critics' attempts to get philosophical with Derrida: we admit to wincing a bit at Barbara Johnson's presentation of deconstruction as 'a form of critique' in her introduction to her translation of *Dissemination*,[15] and we always thought there was something a bit iffy about Culler's use of Nietzsche on cause and effect in *On Deconstruction*.[16] So we're delighted with these books for knowing their philosophy and teaching us some of it. But secretly delighted too that, with the possible exception of Llewelyn, these philosophical presentations, in their acute sense of our philosophical naivety, end up displaying their own philosophical naivety – which consists precisely in their being too philosophical (naivety itself: 'the type of the comic that stands nearest to jokes').[17] Perhaps there is no simple way to avoid this – and especially not be being *less* philosophical. The fact remains that all three books are reductive in specific and different ways: Harvey comes round to an anthropologization of Derrida which is based on odd misreadings of parts of the *Grammatology* and returns us to the subject of all things; Gasché wants to place Derrida in a History of Philosophy in which he will not be contained (Llewelyn is canny enough to be suspicious of such a desire (p. 82)); Llewelyn reduces to various forms of 'semiology' the objects of Derrida's readings.

Addresses

All three books are unphilosophical enough (as books of philosophy usually are) to show a concern for their address or destination. In the

case of Gasché and Harvey, this is very much determined by the
(supposedly) predominantly 'literary' reception of Derrida in the
United States, by that increasingly tiresome scapegoat, so-called 'so-
called American deconstruction'. Llewelyn is rather different again,
setting up a complex situation by pointing to measured similarities
between Derrida and the later Wittgenstein, Derrida and Peirce,
Derrida and Quine, with the claim that 'this will assist those of us who
come to Derrida with the philosophical ethos predominant in English-
speaking countries to feel less like innocents abroad' (p. xi): but that
'us' is treacherous (as always: the 'we' used in our own writing is
difficult enough – to avoid misplaced anxieties, we recommend that it
be read throughout as used in its modestly so-called 'Royal' form), for
Llewelyn himself, who ought grammatically to be the only indubitable
member of the group to which it refers, clearly escapes that group, and
can tell the others that 'We have not seen it all before', and that recent
anglophone philosophy is in any case more 'Continental' than it knows
(ibid.). (A welcome claim, this: analytic philosophers habitually
manage to grasp that part of Derrida's work that overlaps with theirs,
dismiss the rest on various grounds, and then express surprise that
when you get down to Derrida's real 'views' or 'beliefs' [Llewelyn's
book is not exempt from these rather touching idioms], they turn out
to be what you've always thought anyway.)

Such a stress on address, destination and the question of context
which cannot be separated from them is of course strictly Derridean,
as all three authors know: Llewelyn quotes to this effect from the
opening of 'La différance' on the question of opening (p. 38), and
Harvey and Gasché both quote at least part of a famous passage from
the 'Question of Method' section of the *Grammatology* (though only
Gasché explicitly thematizes 'method' as such (pp. 121–4)), and which I
quote first in what Norris's chronology refers to judiciously as Spivak's
'landmark' translation:[18]

> We must begin *wherever we are* and the thought of the trace, which cannot not
> take the scent into account, has already taught us that it was impossible to
> justify a point of departure absolutely. *Wherever we are*: in a text where we
> already believe ourselves to be.[19]

(We have often wondered what landmark-readers have made of this
reference to scent: it might be thought, for example, that this passage
gives some needed support to Ulmer's insistence on the importance of
the sense of smell in Derrida[20] – but in fact he quotes it only in his
Preface, omitting the 'not' after 'cannot' (p. xiii), which would create
some difficulties for his thesis were it not, alas, only a misprint. The
French text of this 'motto' (Ulmer, op. cit.) runs as follows:

> Il faut commencer *quelque part où nous sommes* et la pensée de la trace, qui ne peut pas ne pas tenir compte du flair, nous a déjà enseigné qu'il était impossible de justifier absolument un point de départ. *Quelque part où nous sommes*: en un texte déjà où nous croyons être. (p. 233)

'Quelque part où nous sommes' is literally 'somewhere where we are', which is perhaps less definite and singularizing than 'wherever we are'; 'en un texte déjà où nous croyons être' is a little strange, but the 'déjà' definitely does *not* qualify our belief: literally, 'in a text already where we believe we are'; 'flair' in the context of 'trace' certainly refers to the sort of scent that hounds might be on or might have lost (maybe this was always clear) – but simply 'flair' might have been a safer translation ('Selective instinct for what is excellent, paying, etc.' (COD)). For more details, see Volume 1 of our forthcoming *Some Errors in the Published Translations of the Works of Jacques Derrida* (Volume 7 will be devoted to *The Truth in Painting*).

Harvey quotes this passage at the beginning of a sub-section entitled ' "Le Fil conducteur" ' (pp. 24–8), suggests that this notion of a 'fil conducteur' 'is always Derrida's point of departure for his deconstructive projects', and yet manages to end the same paragraph with the statement that 'we must begin at the beginning'. Lest this last injunction be thought a joke in the circumstances (a reading perhaps encouraged by the specification of that beginning as 'the opening of deconstruction', which leaves the question, precisely, open), the next paragraph states that, 'As deconstruction moves towards the text of its choice, it approaches armed with certain goals or intentions' (p. 25): the notions here of 'moving towards', 'approach', 'choice', 'goals' and 'intentions' are all extremely problematical. This is not a purely verbal question (nothing in Derrida is), and Harvey's later finding difficulties with Derrida's ascription of 'intentions' to Nietzsche (p. 198: 'he considers Nietzsche to have "intended" (a strange word for the Derridaen [*sic*] discourse) to speak of the *différance* . . . ') is in its way just as problematic. Derrida does indeed constantly use the word 'intention' in his earlier work, of himself and of the authors being read, but not in a way that would lend itself to Harvey's description, which is, as we shall have occasion to verify, rather intentional and goal-oriented in general. (Llewelyn has a helpful gloss of Derrida's remarks about intention in 'Limited Inc.' (pp. 72–3).) Further, the notion of a *fil conducteur*, the metaphorical possibilities of which Harvey spends a long time glossing, is, despite Derrida's extensive use of the term, much less a Derridean than a Kantian notion, which is also at least once the object of an explicit distancing criticism by Derrida. This makes us suspect that Harvey is unwise to make of the *fil conducteur* such a *fil conducteur* for her reading.[21]

Gasché, more cautiously and accurately (Gasché's book is almost unfailingly accurate and reliable), quotes the same passage (without the troublesome bit about flair), quite rightly suggests that this means that deconstruction 'proceeds in a radically empiricist manner' (p. 170; see too Gasché's comments on this on pp. 80 and 186, which show him quite able to deal with the obvious objection based on a passage in *De la grammatologie* just prior to the famous quotation about where to start, namely that deconstruction only looks 'empiricist' from within the closure of metaphysics), and shows that the lack of an absolute starting-point does not leave us in the grip of the arbitrary and the subjective or wilful, linking this statement to Derrida's invocation of 'a certain historical necessity' (ibid.). He might well have referred to an earlier moment in the same work when Derrida, discussing his use of the word 'trace', says that 'If words and concepts receive meaning only in linkings of differences, one can justify one's language, and the choice of terms, only within a topic and a historical strategy' (p. 102 [70]); and of course we none of us need reminding that 'strategy' for Derrida is to be thought of as a strategy 'without finality'.[22]

This almost, but not quite, pragmatic insistence by Derrida (compare with Peirce quoted by Samuel Weber: 'There is but one state of mind from which you can "set out" – namely, the very state of mind in which you actually find yourself at the time you do "set out"';[23] Derrida is not of course talking about his or anyone's state of mind here, though he is sometimes moved to do so[24] on the impossibility of any absolutely justified starting point is, in its simplicity, the source of untold problems to his expositors. Whence, in the end, our hilarity. For if Derrida has no absolutely justifiable starting-point, nor do those expounding his thought: Llewelyn solves the problem by putting fairly independent and cross-referenced chapters in a more or less arbitrary order, and suggests the possibility of reading them in an order different from that in which they are printed (p. xiii); Harvey and Gasché are committed to a semblance of ordered philosophical exposition, and although they attempt to recognize the essential limits of such an enterprise, they are in fact caught up in it like a subtle bird-lime.

The reasons for this are perhaps best explained in *Glas*, where Derrida, having watched the departure from the critical forum of all types of critic, describes in an 'example of the reading-advice I am constantly erasing' how he 'decapitates' metalanguage, 'or rather plunge its head back into the text to extract it again regularly, for the interval of a breath taken . . . ' (neither Harvey nor Gasché does anything with *Glas*: Llewelyn, who makes more use in general of the later texts, quotes it with no great fuss, thus helping at long last to give the lie to prevailing myths about *Glas* (which the recent *Glassary* will only reinforce, in spite of its explicit protestations, and despite Derrida's claim that, 'contrary to the rumor and to what some would like you to believe, in [this] book there is not one single *pun*'[25] – (cf. too Norris's silly description of it as 'Joycean', in a note which then suggests the book has to do with Derrida's early idea [in the *Origin of Geometry* introduction] that 'thinking must in some sense choose' between the quest for univocity and that of (Joycean) equivocality:[26] in fact, Derrida's point is precisely that no such choice is possible in so far as each paradigm is infiltrated by the other – the same goes for the famous 'two interpretations of interpretation' passage at the end of 'Structure, Sign and Play'[27] – but then Norris seems to know this too in so far as he implicitly chides Derrida's American readers with assuming that Derrida has made the second, 'Joycean' choice: but it is Norris who starts off by describing *Glas* as univocally Joycean. The point about *Glas*, which is not *essentially* different from any other text by Derrida, is that it presents a certain original and extreme tension or torsion or *stricture* of the univocal and the equivocal, and thereby is subject to a stricture in terms of its explicability. But this is true of all Derrida's texts, and of all texts: being able to understand this question of differential stricture (worked out most fully in the 'Spéculer . . . ' section of *The Post Card* and the 'Restitutions' essay of *The Truth in Painting*,[28] as well as in *Glas* itself) and its relationship with a thought of *structure* seems to us one of the more promising ways of going about reading Derrida – it is disappointing and significant that none of these three books ever thematizes stricture at all: Harvey's section called 'The Structure of *Différance*' (pp. 203–44) begins by recognizing problems in using the term structure, but persists (although the 'Economy' of the book's title should already have disrupted structure); Gasché's use of the term 'infrastructure' only escapes the same problems on a very generous reading.

Context

These questions of address and destination, of starting-points and strategy of exposition are clearly bound up with Derrida's thinking on context. According to the argument with Austin and then Searle, there are only ever contexts (and this is the sense of the earlier 'dans un texte déjà') but no context is saturable or exhaustively determinable.[29] Llewelyn usefully contrasts the force of this with post-Fregean thinking in the analytical tradition which, 'Having been persuaded that the name has meaning only in the context of a sentence . . . has gone on to teach that it has meaning only in the context of an entire form of life' (p. 112), only to hang on to the 'dream' of being able to totalize and determine the form of life in question. Derrida's double argument about context and the necessary possibility of grafting away from context into other contexts effectively undermines that dream. It is perfectly reasonable to read Derrida's entire output as working between the attachment to and detachment from context or rather, for again this is a differential stricture, as exploiting the economy of forces of detachment and the forces of attachment, depropriation and re-appropriation, letters never quite arriving, arguments never quite understood. Harvey and Gasché also explore this argument in some detail. Harvey's explication here is particularly useful:

> Where does a context begin or end? Derrida will say always – in context. Quite simply, the notion of *context as such* cannot and indeed does not [hum] exist. There is no such thing as a context-in-general, by definition. Yet the term exists as such. So one must define context as such always according to the context (p. 239).

Reapplying this type of argument to Derrida's own texts, however, Harvey and Gasché are motivated, in the first instance at least, more by attachment than detachment. Gasché in particular is concerned that literary criticism has culpably taken Derrida out of his proper philosophical context, into which he must be returned if understanding is to be achieved. Late in his book, for example, insisting against stupid literary people that the 'general text' is not a particularly literary notion, he writes:

> Needless to say, [if we had the time and energy, we would list all of Gasché's slightly weary comments of this type, which all imply to his chosen addressee, 'if only you weren't so ignorant I wouldn't have to go into this (again)'] if the notion of the general text is to become an operative concept of literary criticism at all, its function in Derrida's debate with Husserlian phenomenology and Heidegger's philosophy cannot simply be overlooked. The context of this debate alone makes the general text a significant term, and determines its specific features and implications. No mere invocation or magical conjuration of this term can make up for the indispensable reconstruction of its actual context (p. 293).

This insistence on context is a leitmotif of Gasché's book, and the putting into context is always presented as an antidote to epidemic and probably contagious misconceptions (although we fear, with some indirect support from Llewelyn (pp. 39 and 82), that this antidote will be a *pharmakon*). This does seem, in certain contexts, to be entirely justified. For example, Gasché thinks that a common misunderstanding of deconstruction (all our friends think this) is that it consists in the neutralization of contradictory concepts or 'textual strata' that the reading has unearthed: Gasché links this to the idea of 'self-deconstruction' which is indeed widespread, and in fact this is one of the few serious blunders of Culler's book:[30] Llewelyn opens his Preface by apparently falling into the same trap by arguing that the texts Derrida reads 'dis-seminate themselves' or 'de-construct themselves' (p. x), but ends the same Preface by saying, 'let us be clear from the start [this being precisely what was anything but clear at the start], when Derrida refers to the deconstruction or dissemination of something, the "of" marks a genitive which is both objective and subjective' (p. xiii: this could be linked to the later discussion of 'the middle voice', pp. 90–4), and proceeds, devastatingly, as follows:

> The suspicion that antagonistic positions or opposite concepts are identical arises from a neglect of the historical and pragmatic aspects of the contexts in which they are expressed. [A certain literary-critical revenge might be exercised on that 'expressed', with some help from 'Limited Inc.'.[31]] Only through such a simplification or reduction of this context . . . is such a dramatization of antithetical positions of criticism possible. By neglecting the pragmatic and historical context of the utterance of what is dramatized in such a manner as to cancel it out, the criticism in question reveals its origins in Romantic (as well as, in a certain interpretation, Idealist) philosophy. (p. 139: those checking our references will see that we have significantly excised the word 'ideologies' from within this quotation, and cut it short just before the word 'ideology' again; there might be a point to be made about context here.)

Gasché's Chapter 7 opens with the need to contextualize in the sense of establishing a 'conceptual filiation' of 'deconstruction' in terms of its 'antecedents' ('Abbau' and 'Destruktion') in Husserl and Heidegger (of whom Harvey says, absolutely mysteriously, 'the fact that they are historical antecedents of Hegel is of little significance here' (p. 107)), and in fact this particular type of 'contextualization' determines Gasché's project as a whole, which tries to situate Derrida in terms of (a particular reading of) 'the' philosophical tradition, and specifically in terms of a particularly powerful modern inflection of that tradition in terms of reflection. 'Deconstruction as Criticism' had already taken its stand against so-called deconstructive literary criticism for confusing deconstruction and reflection – this book wants to set up a tradition of philosophy as a philosophy of reflection and then show how Derrida exceeds reflection. Whence the stress on context. The problem with this approach is its particular determination of context as history as 'filiation': Gasché's commitment to seriousness, contextualizing and the philosophical tradition leads him to provide, in his first section, an anything-but-Derridean history of the philosophy of reflection (first was Descartes, then came a man called Kant, then two you might not have heard of, called Fichte and Schelling, then a really very important one, Hegel . . . [who does he take us for?], and eventually some modern German people who sound *terrible*.[32] This is the context. To set it up, Gasché is obliged to forget everything about reading he (and some literary critics) might have learned from Derrida, so that Derrida can appear in this dismal procession in his rightful place, and no sooner. If Gasché anticipated on a Derridean reading of the history of philosophy he would already be breaking the rules of contextualization he has set himself (but that such rules can always be broken is one of Derrida's essential points, which has inevitable retroactive effects on 'history' (via the familiar 'always already' operator) and should prevent Gasché from getting away with it). Gasché must have some sense of this problem: on pp. 64–5 he argues that 'Total dialectical mediation as it characterizes absolute reflection is, in principle, of unequalled superiority', and suggests rather warily that its bad reputation is due to certain 'aberrational consequences to which it has led' – it is not entirely clear how in his perspective he could ever account for the possibility of such aberrations.

   This is not all. A necessary corollary of this particular reductive form of contextualization is that when we do finally arrive at Derrida, Gasché has largely to shift abruptly from attachment to detachment, and *de*-contextualize Derrida's thought. The point is that not only in his explicit reflection on signatures, events, contexts and dates,[33] but in his own practice of contextual stricture we have described with the help of *Glas*, Derrida necessarily escapes the type of simple naming and dating that Gasché must presuppose in his account. To the extent (and Llewelyn has a nice play on this type of expression in Derrida (p. 45)) that Derrida decapitates metalanguage or stuffs its head into the flow of the object-text, to the extent that the genitive is both subjective and objective (i.e. neither), then it is entirely misleading to suggest that 'Derrida' or 'Derrida's thought' *happen* in the simply linear historical way that Gasché has to assume. This severely philosophical presentation relies on a pre-philosophical (or maybe all too philosophical) notion of history, which is quite as debilitating as the 'Romantic' aberrations of the literary critics he is chiding with such authority. Further still, if it is true that that aberration was linked to a certain ignorance of historical context and produced a 'suprahistorical criticism that pretends to speak from a position free of ideology' (there's one of the ones that got away), then we must assume that Gasché has no such pretension and that his view of history must come from somewhere historically specific – it's just embarrassing that that view is pre-Derridean and in fact essentially Hegelian. There is really no way that Gasché can understand in this perspective the fact that Derrida's descriptions of the supplementary structure of history should be worked out in and through Rousseau, that real pre-Kantian, post-Hegelian 'antecedent' of Hegel. The same type of point could be made for practically any of the texts Derrida reads (this is the point of the 'Plato's signature is not yet complete' remark, quoted by Llewelyn (p. 89), which implies that the *double* movement of the argument about context (attachment/detachment; stricture) always already fouls up Gasché's reductive determination of it).

Whence the effect of decontextualization: Gasché is committed to a vision of philosophers 'doing' philosophy, thinking in terms of what they have inherited from 'the tradition', never essentially engaged in 'actively' *reading* the tradition, as is Derrida. It is a horrible philosophical travesty of Derrida to present his work as essentially coming out in the form of ideas, thoughts or even arguments at the end of the digestive tract of history. So Gasché's extremely useful (the question would be whether the price paid in naivety and hilarity balances that usefulness in the restricted economy of academic exchange) exposition of Derrida's 'infrastructures' contains, as the (luminous) explication of the re-mark gets under way, the following aside, of great moment for us:

> As in our previous analyses, I shall discuss this infrastructure in abstraction from the rich context in which it is produced within Derrida's work. Consequently, I shall not take advantage of the examples of the re-mark, such as the fan, the blank, or the fold in the work of Mallarmé, on which Derrida relies in formulating this general law. (p. 218)

What's this? Abstraction? From context? Fan, blank and fold as *examples*? What's going on here? This is just the mirror-reflection (ha ha) of Gasché's previous insistence on context. The point of Derrida's work would be that, as usual, there is no question here of a *choice* between that sort of context and that sort of abstraction, between doing philosophy and reading (philosophical) texts, between Gasché and, say, Descombes.[34]

Gasché knows all this too. Arguing a little later that in a complex way Derrida is in some sense continuing (as much as criticizing) Husserl's project of a 'pure logical grammar', Gasché interpolates the following remarkable paragraph before proceeding with his exposition, apparently unaware of the effects his last sentence should have on his entire project:

I should add a brief note on Derrida's indebtedness to Husserlian phenomenology. Not infrequently one hears the opinion that Husserlian phenomenology is a dead end and that, consequently any attempt to continue the questioning of that philosophy is doomed to failure from the start. . . . [We indeed heard this opinion uttered just the other day, and immediately turned to the opiner, saying:] As far as Derrida is concerned, his relation to Husserl is at least threefold. First, it is a relation, to use Granel's words, to 'simply the greatest philosopher who appeared since the Greeks'. To put it differently, it is a relation to the philosophical as a battle of gods and giant about being (*gigantomachia peri tes ousias*), as Plato calls it in *Sophist*, as well as to the philosophical in all its technical and thematic richness. [Something a bit funny about this first reaction, which begins like a prize-giving and goes on to sound like something out of Harold Bloom.] Second, Derrida's relation to Husserlian thought is radically critical of the metaphysical implications of the project of phenomenology itself, as has been amply documented. Third, it is a continuation and radicalization of a number of motifs in Husserl's own works that are capable of unhinging the major metaphysical themes at the center of his philosophy, such as the idea of a primordial axiomatical grounding, the ideal of deductivity in general, the idea of evidence, and the idea of the idea itself. Yet to contend, as I do here, that Derrida continues Husserl (and this is true of his relation to Heidegger as well) precisely on those issues that foreground the classical ethico–theoretical decisions constitutive of philosophy as philosophy is also to say that such a continuation is at the same time a decisive break with the idea of tradition, continuity, Oedipality, and so on. Indeed, the motifs in question are of such a nature that they themselves are radically more fundamental than the possibility of continuity, and since, moreover, they cannot be developed *within* the philosophical discourse as such, their continuation is possible only from a perspective that is marginal with respect to the history of philosophical development. *From this standpoint, the fact that Derrida may have discovered these motifs in Husserl's works is, in a certain way, radically contingent* (p. 246, our emphasis of last sentence).

One consequence of this is that Gasché's own placing of Derrida in a tradition dominated by reflection is *also* contingent. Derrida himself has been as careful as possible to determine his 'object' very broadly as 'the metaphysics of presence' (of which the 'metaphysics of reflection' is a particular, 'modern' inflection), aiming to secure the possibility of dealing with 'the greatest totality'.[35] Gasché implies that in some way Derrida is wrong about this, that reflection is what he's really after: he quotes *Dissemination* on this, and he might have added a moment in 'Pas' pointed out by Llewelyn (p. 74):

Giving no order, receiving no order from the law of laws, from the order of language, giving none because it receives none, 'Come' exchanges nothing, it says nothing, shows, describes, defines, states nothing, at the moment it is

pronounced, nothing that is something or somebody lending or communic-
ating themselves. It doesn't even call someone who would be there before
the call. To say that it calls the call, that it calls *itself* would be more accurate
so long as no specular reflexion is heard here. . . . For the same reasons,
which I should like to pronounce clearly, simply, in limpidity, 'Come', which
is not an order, is no more a prayer, a request, a desire. Although it makes
all these modes possible, it is not for all that anterior to them, upstream like
a transcendental origin, pure and for itself like a primitive word or an *a
priori*. It is each time a singular event on condition of a 'Come', each time
unique but eternally repeated . . . [36]

Kant

We winced, we said, at Barbara Johnson's description of deconstruction as critique, if only because it made the students recalcitrant and
less ready to believe us that 'critique' was a word they used (sometimes,
alack, as a verb, which goes with debates and agendas) far too much out
of excitement. 'Critique' is also notoriously slippery between a Kantian
sense and a Marxist inflexion of that sense. Here she is:

> Deconstruction is a form of what has long been called a *critique*. A critique of
> any theoretical system is not an examination of its flaws or imperfections. It
> is not a set of criticisms designed to make the system better. It is an analysis
> that focuses on the grounds of that system's possibility. [Best now take a
> deep breath and read the next sentence quickly, for despite its return to the
> question of beginnings, it is really part of an introduction to Barthes's
> *Mythologies* which has strayed into the wrong text here.] The critique reads
> backwards from what seems natural, obvious, self-evident, or universal, in
> order to show that these things have their history, their reasons for being
> the way they are, their effects on what follows from them [?!] and that the
> starting point is not a (natural) given but a (cultural) construct, usually blind
> to itself. For example, Copernicus can be said to have written a critique of
> the Ptolemaic conception of the universe. (p. xv)

'Grounds' of possibility and the reference to the 'Copernican Revolution' lead us rapidly enough to Kant. We think there has been a general
sense that Hegel is the one to get at, and Hegel is still big for Gasché,
but oddly enough it seems that it is Kant who provides the language for
discussing Derrida. It is true that all three authors duly explain that
deconstruction in some sense 'exceeds' the Hegelian dialectic (see
Harvey, pp. 76–7; Llewelyn's idea that 'On the scale of continuity-
discontinuity Bataille's transgression and Derrida's displacement are
somewhere between a Hegelian transmissive Aufhebung and a Bache-

lardian or Kuhnian intermissive break (*coupure*) (p. 12; cf. p. 46 and further discussion on p. 84) is perhaps best not taken too literally – talk of discontinuity is not much help in relation to Derrida (cf. too Harvey (p. 8), wrong, we think, about historicity)); by far the most useful discussion of deconstruction and dialectic is provided by Gasché's analysis of the Platonic *symploke*, weaving together opposites on the basis of a prior violent exclusion of non-oppositional differences. In principle at least the difference of deconstruction from the dialectic is simply enough formulated in terms of a resistance to the determination of difference as opposition which gets the dialectic going[37] (if we were hoping to amuse here, we would quote criticisms of Derrida's thinking on the grounds that it is 'undialectical', as if that automatically disqualified it). But it seems as though the philosophical stake of writing a philosophical book on Derrida might be much more that of showing why his work is *not* the Kantian-type transcendental philosophy which the most sympathetic construal of Johnson's description of *critique* would make it. The challenge to any philosopher attempting to present Derrida's work is that of explicating why the 'conditions of possibility' discovered by that work are always also simultaneously 'conditions of impossibility' (roughly: what makes it possible for a letter to arrive at its destination necessarily includes the possibility that it might go astray; this necessary possibility means that it never completely arrives; or, what makes it possible for a performative to be brought off 'happily' necessarily includes the possibility of recitation outside the 'correct' context; this necessary possibility means that it is never completely happy),[38] and what effects this has on thinking. All three of our authors duly spend time explicating conditions of (im)possibility, with varying degrees of clarity and accuracy (e.g. Gasché, pp. 174–5, 289, 308; Harvey, pp. 68, 202; Llewelyn, pp. 80, 98).

This tendency to turn to Kant as a means of setting off what Derrida is doing is most clearly exemplified in Harvey's book. She is able to state, for example, that unlike Heidegger, Derrida 'does not rely on the "essential" in his analysis, but on what Kant called "the conditions of the possibility of things"' (p. 185: Gasché also identifies Heidegger's attachment to essentiality as a point of difference with Derrida (pp. 119–20)). The 'Introduction' to her book in fact opens with a recognition of apparent similarities between Kant's 'program' and Derrida's, and the announcement of an attempt, despite these appearances, 'to radically distinguish Derrida's project from Kant's' (p. 3: we have already noted difficulties around terms such as 'project' in Harvey's description). (The gesture here is not so different from that of Derrida himself at the beginning of 'Freud and the Scene of Writing', locating and then dissipating merely apparent ways in which deconstruction might be thought of as a psychoanalysis – that other 'Copernican Revolution' – of Western Metaphysics.)[39] A first move here is to argue that Derrida might be considered to be doing a 'critique of critique' (p. 6), showing the conditions of possibility of Kant's critique. But this can only be a first move, in so far as critique is always a digging for foundations, a search for firm ground on which the edifice of metaphysics might subsequently be (re)built, and the point is that deconstruction is not even a metacritique in this sense.[40] And Harvey duly ends her Introduction with the question of impossibility raised above: Kant is obliged to stop with a notion of 'constitution' he cannot question further; Derrida goes on to show that anything like a constitution is made possible and impossible by *différance*:

> That which leads Kant to rely on the notion of *constitution* (*Beschaffenheit*) as such, which cannot be known further . . . is that which Derrida aims to reveal the *conditions of the possibility of* and in turn, necessarily, the conditions of the – more rigorously speaking – impossibility of [it cannot of course be more rigorous to talk *simply* of conditions of impossibility which on their own wouldn't get very far]. [*Différance*] is not a centre or a ground for Derrida but the ungrounded ground of ground, or that which allows for the constitution of the notion of ground itself and in turn for the notion of constitution itself – Kant's ultimate ground (p. 20) (cf. Gasché's more precise though more cumbersome explanation (pp. 100, and 157 for Derrida's replacement of 'constitution' by 'inscription' after early acceptance of the language of constitution or production), and Llewelyn's usefully perplexed account (p. 63)).

Llewelyn ends his paragraph on this point by quoting (as he does more than once) Derrida quoting Husserl saying that 'for this all names are lacking': no one here is going to pretend that this lack is a provisional misfortune to be got over by a little more inventiveness, and this essential lack of a proper name for the groundless ground of grounds is one reason for the inevitability of approaching deconstruction via the analogy of critique, and for the almost intolerable tension of deconstruction which prevents such an approach ever being 'the truth'.

Gasché especially struggles with this tension and, casting in his lot with the dignity of the philosophical (which he clearly does not find funny at all, unlike Derrida and the rest of us) puts his money on what he calls 'infrastructures'. This term is supposed to do the work we are looking for:

> An infrastructure is not what is called a ground in traditional philosophical language. It is, on the contrary, a nonfundamental structure, or an abyssal

structure, to the extent that it is without a bottom. . . . Infrastructures are
not deeper, supraessential origins. If they are said to ground origins, it
must be added that they unground them at the same time. Infrastructures
are conditions as much of the impossibility as of the possibility of origins
and grounds. (pp. 155,161)

Gasché justifies his privileging of this term from Derrida himself:
somewhat to our surprise, because it is hardly a common word in
Derrida's writing. Yet Gasché is prepared to claim that 'the very
concept of infrastructure, as the *formal rule* that each time regulates
differently the play of the contradictions in question, is an intrinsic
part of [Derrida's] original contribution to philosophy' (p. 142). Here
again, as with reflection, it would appear that Derrida gets it slightly
wrong about his own work, which would on this account be more or
less secretly ruled by a low-profile 'concept', produced as a 'transformed concept of "infrastructure"', as Derrida says in *Positions*, in a
transformation which Derrida 'has never explicitly outlined' (p. 147),
but which Gasché is generous enough to outline for him and us
together.[41]

'Infrastructure' is, then, the 'concept' which will on Gasché's account
go down in *Noddy's History of Philosophy* with the name 'Derrida'
attached to it. This is all rather strange: even on Gasché's own account,
this cannot be a concept at all. The 'cases' 'subsumed' under this
'concept' are called by names such as 'Trace', '*Différance*', 'Supplementarity' and 'Re-Mark' (see Gasché's wonderfully clear expositions of
these in his Chapter 9: we're all for clarity): these are not names of
concepts, but of what Gasché calls 'philosophical quasiconcepts'
(p. 156; cf. p. 172 for an unexplained extra hyphen). These quasiconcepts have no proper name, as Gasché knows very well: they are
not entities, but are preontological, prelogical, presemantic. The name
they are given (and here we return to the questions about beginnings
and contexts) cannot name anything like an essence, but is borrowed,
'strategically', from the discourse being read (this is the same structure
as the 'decapitation' quoted from *Glas*, where the name 'decapitation',
consequently enough, is borrowed from the context of Genet's texts
for the occasion).[42] We take it that this is familiar to all readers of
Derrida, and that there is no need to explain again why it is simply a
mistake to assume that this signals some unfortunate or culpable
collusion with what we should all be trying to denounce or overthrow.
(Though, oddly enough, Gasché himself gives an incomplete account
of the retention of the name 'writing': Derrida explains that he keeps
to the term because writing was always determined as the signifier of a

signifier; that's what he argues all signifiers are, and that's why he retains the term.[43] Gasché gets a bit tangled up here, saying merely, '*Writing* is thus a phantom name for the structural *X*, despite the fact that it is very different from what has always been called writing. What makes it susceptible to being named *X* is that, within the discourse of metaphysics, it marks the repression of *X* and therefore essentially communicates with it' (p. 167; cf. the similarly truncated account on p. 275). This is too simple an account, and would scarcely motivate the retention of the word. At least Gasché avoids the error made by Christopher Norris on this point: in both his books he clearly confuses the *parole* of the *parole/langue* couple with that opposed to writing, and appeals to a vague analogy between the system of *langue* and the common conception of writing which confuses everything in the very inaccurate account of the earlier book, and clouds the much more secure exposition of the later.[44] (We are of course aware from previous *Oxford Literary Review* experience that even to hint that Norris has got things wrong is an unpardonable crime of elitism committed against the generous populism of the 'prestigious' *New Accents* series and the principle that accessibility excuses inaccuracy.)[45] While on the *langue/parole* question, it is worth noting Llewelyn's questioning of the necessity of anything as complicated as '*différance*' to escape the notorious problem of priority between *langue* and *parole* (why not just say they are equiprimordial?), and the slightly unsatisfactory sidestepping of the problem posed by an apparent *non sequitur* in Derrida's argument – if *non sequitur* there be at this point, it is certainly vulnerable to logical objection, and it will not do to appeal to Derrida's notion of athetic writing to suggest that such objections are inappropriate or illegitimate. Differential stricture again: Derrida's texts are all written in tension with logic – they do follow recognizable argumentative structures up to a point, and this is true of the argument about *langue* and *parole*. Descombes also suggests that there is some confusion in Derrida's account of this. (See my 'Outside Language', *Oxford Literary Review*, Vol. 11 (1989), pp. 189–212.)

But if the 'irreducibly plural' and only partially systematizable 'general system' of these infrastructures is thus shot through with resistance to conceptual determination (which implies that each Derridean reading is something of an event, rather than just another example of a general law), then it seems difficult to regard the general term 'infrastructure' as a concept too. Some of the problems of attempting to do so appear later in Gasché's book, around the explication of metaphoricity, and why there is nothing specifically literary about Derrida's exploration of it:

Metaphoricity, because of its structure and the problems it accounts for, is thus not to be confused with its empirical (philosophic or literary) homo-logue. In Derrida's sense, metaphoricity is a structure of referral that accounts for the possibility and impossibility of the philosophical discourse, yet not insofar as this discourse may be construed as literary (sensible, fictional, and so on) because of its inevitable recourse to metaphor and poetic devices,[46] but insofar as it is a general discourse on the universal. The literary dimension of the philosophical text is by nature incapable of pointing to, let alone accounting for, this constituting nonorigin of philo-sophy. Seen in this perspective, metaphoricity is a transcendental concept *of sorts*. Although it is likely that the term I propose will meet with a good bit of disapproval, I shall call metaphoricity a *quasitranscendental*. With *quasi-* I wish to indicate that metaphoricity has a structure and a function similar to transcendentals without actually being one. [This last sentence is one of those that occasion our occasional hilarity: this description would give the quasitranscendental metaphoricity a metaphorical relationship with 'actual' transcendentals, even though presumably it makes any such relationship possible: this priority of the quasi consistently doubles up Gasché's exposi-tion, and its reader.] (p. 316)

Now in fact Gasché has used this notion of the quasitranscendental earlier, with no such precautions, and it seems a perfectly good word to us (much better than infrastructure, at any rate, which is the one he should be apologizing for): in this earlier occurrence, Gasché writes, 'Arche-writing is *only*, if one may say so, the quasitranscendental synthesis that accounts for the necessary corruption of the idealities, or transcendentals of all sorts, by what they are defined against, and at the very moment of their constitution' (p. 274; this is, *mutatis mutandis*, the structure which motivates Derrida's later quarrel with Heidegger's assumption that the 'essence of technology is not technological', and could have motivated a Derridean refutation of Althusser's assump-tion that the concept of history is not historical).[47] This quasitranscen-dental ensures that *all* transcendentals are 'only' quasitranscendentals, being originarily contaminated by what they transcend. This is the decapitation again, the radical empiricism, the impossibility of abstrac-tion from context, of having a true starting-point, of determining Derrida's terms as concepts. Just as the philosophical urge of Gasché's book leads him to abstract from context none the less and to screw down the possibility of detachment from context with his other hand, so here he is led to gather up this dispersed plurality of strictly limitedly transcendentalizing terms by abstracting from them a single concept called 'infrastructure' which it is Derrida's contribution to philosophy to have invented. That this ought not to be possible is ensured by the quasi- itself, the always interrupted movement of transcendence, which Gasché explicates admirably at several points, and nowhere more so than where he argues that 'the re-mark is the structure that accounts for the possibility of all transcendental or theological illusions . . . ' (p. 218), of which illusions Gasché's notion of infrastructure as concept would be a particularly refined example.

Transcendence and Finitude

We can sharpen up all these points by linking transcendence and finitude, as Derrida has since his earliest work. The 'interrupted movement' just mentioned, for example, appears in 'Signature, Event, Context', in the discussion of the necessary possibility of the absence of any empirically determined addressee in general: 'And this absence is not a continuous modification of presence, but a rupture of presence, the "death" or possibility of the "death" of the addressee inscribed in the structure of the mark (it is at this point, I note the fact in passing, that the value or the "effect" of transcendentality is necessarily linked to the possibility of writing and "death" thus analysed).'[48] And the derivation of 'I am mortal' and eventually 'I am dead' from 'I am' will be remembered as one of the more striking feats of *La Voix et le phénomène*.[49] The paradox would be that the movement of transcendence is set in motion by the necessary possibility of my death, but the effect of that movement, traditionally, is to determine my being as essentially immortal, subject to death only accidentally.

Gasché links this insistence on finitude to Nietzsche, Dilthey and the early Heidegger, only to argue that such an insistence does not really successfully break with a philosophy of the subject (pp. 84–5). But as usual, according to the tension we have already identified, the simplicity of this type of contextualizing is complicated later. For example, discussing the links between iterability and idealization, most clearly laid out by Derrida in 'Limited Inc.', Gasché writes, quite correctly, 'Although iterability as such is the *becoming* of intelligibility and ideality, the very possibility of repetition as the root of truth also prohibits truth from ever becoming *itself*. Iterability, without which the ideality on which truth is based could not be achieved, is at once [i.e. simultaneously or, as Harvey always puts it, with a preciosity rather touching in view of general brutality of her writing, *à la fois*] the death of truth, its finitude' (p. 215). Or again, analysing the structure of auto-affection, Gasché again gets it right: 'interiority, however successfully produced in auto-affection, appears to be dependent on structures of finitude; a certain outside inhabits this interiority, which is thus prevented from fully coinciding with itself. Yet without the impurity of this outside, a self could not even hope to aim at coinciding with itself'

(p. 233). Indeed, everything we have said about context seems to be to do with this question: discussing questions of closure and trans-gression, Gasché affirms, again quite rightly, that 'The excess or transgression of philosophy is, therefore, decided at the margins of the closure only, in an always strategical – that is, historically finite – fashion' (p. 169). And yet, in the closing pages of his book, in the context of the description of metaphoricity as quasitranscendental already quoted, Gasché refers to Derrida's 'persistent critique of the notion of finitude' (because he wants to distinguish Derrida's 'quasi-transcendental' from what he calls Heidegger's 'finite transcendental') without providing any references at all for this apparently startling idea. Finitude as an essential part of the explication of conditions of (im)possibility, yet also (only) part of a tradition and the object of Derrida's 'critique'? Are we dealing with two different notions of finitude here? But why doesn't Gasché (or at least his index) make that clear? As the understanding not only of Gasché's book but also of one of the most enigmatic statements in the whole of Derrida ('Infinite différance is finite', *La Voix et le phénomène*, p. 114 [102]) would seem to depend on some clarification of this question, we had better take our time. This is still all about death and transcendence, and suggests a nexus of Kant, Heidegger and Derrida which may well not fit easily into Gasché's historical schemes.

Harvey is a help here, thematizing the problem as that of death rather than that of finitude. Her misreading of what is at stake here (for it is demonstrably a misreading, as we shall show, and not a matter for differences of opinion) will clarify the issue. A sense of what is to come is given early in her book, when she suggests, still working with her general sense of deconstruction as a teleological activity, that in so far as deconstruction is to be thought of as the 'origin' of *différance* (i.e. the 'practice' of deconstruction in some sense 'produces' *différance* as its result), then 'beyond Derrida [as usual, this beyond turns out to be extremely dispiriting], we suggest, the structure of deconstruction as the *origin* of *différance* and as the telos of deconstruction (with meta-physics playing the role of mediator, in the Hegelian sense, here) entails a "subjective" process of recovery or revelation' (p. 87). This idea is then provisionally dropped as still 'pre-Heideggerian', but returns later to dominate the closing parts of Harvey's reading. A glimpse of the particular deviation involved here comes in the explica-tion of the 'necessary possibility of my death' argument which we have seen to be essentially bound up with the question of transcendentality, and is driven by a legitimate and necessary concern for what becomes of the *idiomatic* in a system which appears to cross out any constituting subjectivity. Harvey begins by weakening somewhat the force of

Derrida's argument by insisting on the 'my death' part and neglecting the corollary involving the necessary possibility of the death of any empirically determined addressee in general, with the result that the argument is taken to imply an essentially public ('for others') quality of meaning (p. 195: 'Sense or meaning is thus essentially public or collective . . . '; cf. p. 223: 'As we have shown, meaning is for Derrida ultimately a *collective* affair'; our quarrel is with the 'essentially' and the 'ultimately'): this is not simply false, though already a slightly humanistic version of Derrida, for whom, it will be remembered, the trace precedes even such distinctions as human/animal and animate/inanimate, with the clear implication that there is nothing specifically 'human' (even if collective) about meaning.[50] Making meaning a function of intersubjectivity rather than simply subjectivity might be good enough for sociologists or Habermas, but not for us. Harvey does also recognize this, by insisting (there is an awful lot of insisting in her book) that the question of the idiomatic in some sense transgresses a simple notion of humanity into the realm of animality and/or the sacred. Unfortunately, however, the discussion of animality is completely vitiated by Harvey's taking as Derrida's own statement what is in fact his reconstruction of what he calls, immediately before the passage she quotes, a 'still living myth' (Harvey, p. 167 and n19, referring to *De la grammatologie* p. 344 [242]; Harvey proceeds to find it 'ironic' that Derrida should hold such a view of animality, and ties herself in knots for a while getting him back out of the trouble he was never in: see too on animality pp. 180–1 and 201, and 196 for the convergence with the sacred, still on the basis of the same type of misreading, which will return).

This question of the idiomatic returns a little later in the context of a slightly curious argument which moves from the recognition of the 'unnamability' of *différance* and a repeated insistence on the (relative) context-specificity of Derrida's various 'nicknames' for *différance* (which, as Harvey rightly says, is itself already a nickname) (ibid.), to a sense that all these nicknames might none the less be taken to designate 'a certain *concept* of *différance* which transcends specific situations, circumstances and texts' (p. 212). The argument here, rather as in Gasché, appeals to the force of detachment and abstraction from context, indeed recognized by Derrida,[51] as a way of re-philosophizing deconstruction whenever it appears to be escaping: the point being that Derrida does not simply respect the purely nominal unity of a text as secured by its author's signature, but is happy to find Platonic moments in, say, Freud. This would imply that the 'context-specificity' of a particular nickname elaborated while reading Freud must carry with it a *force de rupture* with respect to that context. This structure is of course what provides the pretext for critics of Derrida to complain on the one hand that he spends inordinate amounts of time picking at the tiniest textual details while on the other making everything the same 'from Plato to NATO', as one of the twentieth century's major Marxist aestheticians puts it,[52] wittily. Having made this necessary point (which just is the (interrupted) movement of transcendentality which Gasché tends to immobilize; this is, rather, though still not satisfactorily thought as such, a movement or *devenir-transcendental*) which would appear to be leading toward a reconceptualizing and proper-naming of the 'concept' which Derrida's nicknames never quite name, Harvey suddenly veers back to proper names of authors, and asks the following question which is unfortunately syntactically undecipherable:

> Nevertheless is it possible, according to Derrida's own 'system of interpretation', to view the differences between 'supplement', *'différance'*, 'reserve', 'trace' and 'writing', for example, as related only to the proper name of the author which, as we know, no longer legitimately houses its ultimate authority? (pp. 212–13)

The argument now proceeds as follows: Derrida suggests that the relationship between the nicknames (or infrastructures, or quasitranscendentals) is itself ruled by the play of 'différance' (and this fact – which Gasché recognizes – that one such name can describe the relationship of all is another example of decapitation, re-mark and interrupted transcendence which will always prevent Gasché from being correct in calling 'infrastructure' a concept). In the play of *différance* (or supplementarity), there is an indefinite substitution of signifiers which never comes to rest in a transcendental signified. As Derrida says early in *De la grammatologie*, without a transcendental signified, the difference between signifier and signified cannot be rigorous (p. 33 [20]). A 'signified' is just a signifier positioned by other signifiers *as* a signified; the signified is 'always ready in the position of a signifier' (p. 107 [73]); once there is strictly speaking no signified, there is strictly speaking no signifier either (p. 32n9 [324n9]) (and, still worth recalling, no question of a 'materiality of the signifier': see pp. 20, 45 and 138 [9–10, 29, 91] for the reasons). This argument, which Harvey does not recall quite in this form at this point, is briefly invoked by Derrida in the much later discussion of incest in Rousseau, which is the (largely forgotten) context of Harvey's discussion: even the prohibition of incest is not an origin or fundamental signified, even though, *in the economy of Rousseau's text*, it is presented as the unnamable origin, 'the first supplementarity which allows in general the substitution of signifier for signified, signifiers for other signifiers' (p. 376). The paradox for a conventional reading of Rousseau is that this 'origin' is unthinkable in terms of presence; for once he prescribes that the signified or represented (the mother) *not* be made present against its usurping and dangerous supplements, signifiers or representatives (other women), then the value of presence no longer holds at the basis of the system which consistently valorizes presence none the less. This basic prohibition which is the 'origin' of society and language in Rousseau's description is thus no origin because already a substitution: all of Rousseau's subsequent suspicion about signs and representation, and his general demand that the thing itself be brought forward in its unmediated presence, are undermined by this 'first' supplementarity. As Derrida says, showing how even Rousseau's system does not escape the general argument against the transcendental signified, 'there is a point in the system at which the signifier can no longer be replaced by its signified, which has as its consequence that no signifier can be, purely and simply' (p. 376).

Harvey does not quite re-establish this context, as is always possible. But that this be always possible and sometimes recommendable does not of course mean that any handling of context will do (see *De la grammatologie*, p. 227 [158]). Derrida, in a passage Harvey quotes, goes on to argue that this point of non-replacement is also the 'point of orientation' for the whole system, 'the point where the fundamental signified is promised as the end point of all the referrals, and escapes as that which would, in the same blow, destroy the whole system of signs' (p. 376). Language points to this point and in so doing forbids it: this just is the structure of desire ('our indestructible and mortal desire') which is thus, following an argument by now familiar, made possible by that (spacing, supplementarity) which also makes its fulfilment impossible (cf. the famous statement earlier in *De la grammatologie*: 'Without the possibility of *différance*, the desire for presence as such would not find its breathing-space. Which means simultaneously that this desire carries within it the destiny of its non-fulfilment. *Différance* produces what it forbids, makes possible the very thing it renders impossible' (p. 206). (Repetitive, isn't it? As Harvey puts it in the single funniest sentence in any of these books, 'If one asks it what it means, it just goes on repeating the same thing over and over again, we repeat' (p. 194: if we had the time and competence, we would write a stylistic study of the (repetitive) use of the closing (first-person plural) performative verb in Harvey's sentence structure).)

All of this to be able to discuss Harvey's deviation around the question of the idiom. For by not respecting context here, forgetting perhaps that the calculation of the differential stricture of the movements of attachment and detachment is always an *event* to be negotiated in its singularity, too confident in her argument that the 'nicknames' can always break with their context, she jumps in with the following gloss of the 'point of non-replacement', having preceded the quotation by the suggestion that this is 'the locus of the signified as such, it would seem', and urgent in its string of rhetorical questions:

> What is this 'point of non-replacement' for Derrida, which is also the 'point of orientation'? The non-replaceable, non-representable, which allows for representation and replacement; indeed the play of *différance* itself. Do we not here have the idiom, the subject, the writer, the non-authorised authority, the illegitimate father, who in fact has never left his text? Do we not have the 'madness' which reason thinks it has excluded from the house of being or language itself? Do we not have that intrinsically unsayable, the point of the non-blink of the eyes in that face of the other which is also our own, which we know has never left us? We might indeed be in the Abyss, and it may indeed be in us, as Derrida says; and there may indeed be an intrinsic and inextricable relation of signifier and signified, but does this not also translate, at this point of non-return, of non-replaceability, non-representability, and non-substitutability, into the relation of author to text? . . . Is it not this that Derrida himself has pointed towards throughout his work? (pp. 213–14)

To which the answer is: no. (Or at least, not all of these things.)

But Harvey, not to be deterred, proceeds to claim that this 'point which does not exist' 'could only be the me of my writing', the 'non-existence' of which would be the recognition of inscription: 'it is the "me", as the subject of metaphysics, as the thrown Dasein [which are surely not quite the same thing], who is tossed into a relation of submission to the very thing he would command – the text of life itself' (p. 214; the 'he' here reminds us of Spivak's daft insistence on assigning the structure of necessary-possibility-of-absence-of-author to male authors, on the grounds that Derrida has almost exclusively written about men).[53] Again, this is not simply wrong, but partial and limiting and humanistic.

These problems occur in part because Harvey tends to take commentary on Rousseau as assertion by Derrida [54] (although we might accept Llewelyn's claim that 'Nowhere in his variations, Schubertian in their length and subtle modulation, on Rousseau's *Essay on the Origin of Languages* does Derrida enunciate a thesis on the origin of languages *in propria persona*' (p. 47) only if we understand that this does *not* necessarily imply that everything Derrida enunciates is simply in Rousseau's *persona*). The same problem recurs and accentuates the inflection of Harvey's argument we are attempting to follow. Glossing Heidegger on being-towards-death, Harvey recalls the moment of her analysis we have just shown to be incorrect, and now explicitly calls the point of non-substitution 'the subject' (p. 231). To shore up this argument, Harvey now says that, according to Derrida, death is the 'master-name' of the supplementary series (and again finds it strange that Derrida should appeal to a 'master-name' at all: this recurrent need to invoke irony or strangeness might have prompted some doubts as to the accuracy of the readings – luckily our literary sensitivity, sharpened up by having to deal with the intricacies of free indirect discourse in Flaubert, prevents us from getting such things wrong).[55] She goes on to find Derrida ventriloquizing Rousseau on art and music. This is in fact again a reconstruction of the logic of Rousseau's thinking rather than a claim made by Jacques Derrida, for whom there are no master-names in this manner. This does not mean that all of Harvey's statements about death are wrong, but that at the very least she introduces an unnecessary pathos into a thinking which is not pathetic in this way. Life-death for Derrida is again a question of differential stricture, and death is not a question of 'the ultimate menace', as Harvey is forced to think (p. 232), nor is it simply the *telos* of all life, however devious life's approach to it (p. 234). The detour is *already* death as much as it is life; if 'life [is] death deferred', this is not to be read as meaning simply that 'Just as all metaphysical oppositions turn into their opposites [presumably meaning the *terms* of all metaphysical oppositions] over time and space which is writing, so too life becomes death for Derrida' (p. 234) [gosh] – and Harvey in fact knows and says all this too in these confusing pages, well enough to undermine completely her own claims about anchoring the system in something called a subject, or Dasein, or life, or death.

All of which is still entirely within the problem of understanding the apparent Kantianism of the appeal to conditions of (im)possibility, and the attendant problems of finitude, death and (quasi)transcendentality. We have not yet brought in other Kantian words and themes which are quite essential to what is going on here: this is all difficult and we might always yet throw over this type of philosophical patience, who knows, in favour of the immediate seductions of poetry or revolutionary politics. After all, as philosophers go, Kant was really *bourgeois*, and was more or less delegated by his class to tighten up on a nasty individualism under threat, wasn't he?[56] But Idea of Reason, Transcendental Aesthetic, Transcendental Imagination are lurking here in these three books, and we cannot deny their importance easily (especially their importance in poetry and revolutionary politics). Here, linking on to what we have been worrying away at, is Llewelyn quoting 'The Ends of Man' (written, notoriously, in May 1968, when all the rest of us were out in the streets, why weren't you?):

It could be shown that at every stage of phenomenology, and notably each time recourse to the 'Idea in the Kantian sense' is necessary, the infinity of the *telos*, the infinity of the end rules the power of phenomenology. The end of man (as factual anthropological limit) announces itself to thought from the end of man (as determined opening or infinity of a *telos*). Man is what has a relation to his end, in the fundamentally equivocal sense of this word. Since always. The transcendental end can appear to itself and be deployed only on condition of mortality, of a relation to finitude as origin of ideality. The name of man has always been inscribed in metaphysics between these two ends. It has meaning only in this eschato-teleological situation. (*Marges*, p. 147; Llewelyn, p. 36; tr. mod.)

This summary of a whole tradition of thinking will help. The transcendental movement makes sense only in the case of a finite being; my finitude makes (im)possible my transcendence. I think, therefore I am, and before you know it I'm essentially an immortal thinking substance, though only the possibility of my death makes this possible and thus impossible. Again, my finitude is a condition of my experience, conceived as a basic passivity with respect to an already-existing world: this situation could not hold for an infinite being. That experience has transcendental conditions of possibility. Finitude and transcendence go hand in hand: this is Heidegger's demonstration in *Kant and the Problem of Metaphysics*. Space and Time, Transcendental Aesthetic. But Derrida's writing as *espacement* (a spatial word with a perfectly current temporal usage in French) precedes space and time as *their* condition of possibility. Gasché and Harvey both point to the possibility, briefly raised in *De la grammatologie*, of thinking of Derrida as providing a more rigorous or originary transcendental aesthetic than either Kant or Husserl. This is an attractively daunting reading for us literary people for whom these matters (especially time) are almost entirely mysterious.[57] Derrida seems to provide some support for this type of reading at the beginning of the 'Hinge' section of *De la grammatologie*, for example.[58] But much later, Derrida shows how the space-time 'produced' by the trace cannot be thought along the lines of Kantian or Husserlian transcendental aesthetics or kinaesthetics (pp. 410–11 [290–1]). Harvey runs through this argument in the 'Postface' to her book; Gasché first sees in Derrida's hint a sign of the temptation to talk still in terms of constitution in early work which we have noted, and which may be partially what leads Harvey astray. But later, discussing spacing (which we think he limits too closely to space), he wants no nonsense at all about Derrida writing a new transcendental aesthetic: 'As should be obvious at this point [get that?], this cannot possibly be the case. Spacing is not a form of (pure) intuition that structures a subject's experience of the world. . . . The notion of spacing as the condition of possibility of sensible and intelligible, or ideal, space undercuts the very possibility of a self-present subject of intuition or of universal and absolute experience' (p. 201) (and under-cuts equally, he might have added, quoting these pages from the *Grammatology*, 'the origin myth of an uninhabited world' (p. 411 [291]).

Llewelyn is more inclined towards the Kant of the Transcendental ('productive') Imagination: still Heidegger's Kant, this. (Gasché dis-cusses the Transcendental Imagination in the historical part of his book, very much in the perspective of Hegel's Kant (pp. 29ff)). Llewelyn says that 'There is much to recommend interpreting some of Derrida's writings as a reworking of Kant's analysis of the productive imagination *à partir de* Heidegger's re-working', and immediately adds, rather mysteriously, 'That Derrida expresses a low opinion of the explanatory power of appeals to the imagination goes some way to confirm this' (p. 116). Although no reference is given for this 'low opinion', we assume that Llewelyn means a passage early on in 'Force and Signification' where Derrida indeed suggests that critics appeal too easily to a notion of the imagination, and then glosses Kant, affirming that in spite of differences, the First and Third *Critiques* are talking about *the same* imagination, and proceeds to track the 'origin' of that imagination in what we can now see to be an early sketch of the notion of *différance*.[59] In Heidegger's reading of Kant, it is this same transcendental imagination which is the groundless, abyssal root of transcendence and of pure thought in general, the 'origin' even of sensory intuition. In Heidegger's reading, the transcendental imagina-tion is essentially temporal, and Llewelyn goes on to suggest that Kant's treatment of the threefold temporal synthesis (which he is clearly himself reading through Heidegger) can provide a 'somewhat similar temporal structure' to that at work in Derrida, and which Llewelyn has just set apart from Husserlian and Hegelian time and history and linked to Freud's *Nachträglichkeit* (p. 117). Heidegger's fundamental argument, which Llewelyn recalls rather allusively, is that the order of syntheses given by Kant, of apprehension in intui-tion, then of reproduction in imagination, then of recognition in the concept, is misleading. Heidegger argues first of all that pure appre-hension (which produces the now as such, as opposed to empirical intuition which aims at such and such an entity present now) is already a mode of the transcendental imagination. The second synthesis, of pure reproduction, must distinguish the series of nows and preserve a past now for recall now. As this is in fact a necessary condition for an experience of any now at all (*Critique of Pure Reason*, A101–2), Llewelyn is able to argue that this would imply a sort of originary delay (the production of the present in some sense depending on its reproduction): 'In the beginning was the begun, the always already there of a temporality that cannot be traced as one traces a line, cannot be traced' (p. 117). At first sight this does not seem quite to be Heidegger's point, however (not that Llewelyn is necessarily pretending that it is). Just as previously Llewelyn thought that Derrida was making an unnecessary fuss about the question of priority of *langue* and *parole*, and that it was sufficient to think of them as equiprimordial, so here it looks as though we can say to Llewelyn that the same holds of the first two synthesis, in what Heidegger calls their 'originary unity'.[60] Except that in moving into the third synthesis, which Heidegger is very keen to demonstrate as formative of the future, he indeed allows Llewelyn's point: there is, transcendentally speaking, an absolute past prior to any present which alone ensures the unity of that present.[61] Heidegger's question about the third synthesis is, however, that of what ensures the unity of the present and that 'past' if not an advance, futural determination towards that unity as identity. Heidegger, of course, in a way Derrida would be suspicious of, would like to make of that futurity an 'original' time which would be of a piece with his notion of authenticity as analysed in terms of Being-towards-death: Llewelyn does not here insist on this, but moves into the third synthesis as follows:

> The transcendental concepts that condition empirical concepts include the concepts of the three analogies, substance, cause and reciprocity. These are respectively analogies of the permanence of time, that is, time itself, and of the temporal modalities succession and coexistence. Inevitably, if temporality and the constructions of the schematism of imagination that is the milieu between intuitive perception and conception are congenitally contaminated by delay and relay, if what Kant calls self-affection is infected by the primary secondariness at which he himself hints, then the concepts of substance and cause and reciprocity which are for Kant the bounds of sense will only be theoretical and fictive 'effects' of an aboriginal dream-time where representation is older than presentation and presence is perpetually postponed. (p. 118)

Which would seem to imply something very similar to Levinas's point about Derrida, namely that Kant's Idea of Reason, which is not a concept of the understanding because of the impossibility of conceptual validation through intuition, is already at work in the concept and the understanding, that the evidence of present intuition, rigorous reliance upon which will preserve us, in so far as is possible, from transcendental illusion (i.e. treating the Idea as though it were a concept of the understanding) *is itself a transcendental illusion*.[62]

So not a new transcendental aesthetic, but a radical appeal to something like the transcendental imagination which would account, in an essentially Heideggerian way, for the (im)possibility of intuition and conceptuality? We can find some further support for such a reading in a passage from 'La Pharmacie de Platon', arguing that the *pharmakon* is neither simple nor composite, but 'rather the prior milieu in which is produced differentiation in general, and the opposition between the *eidos* and its other; this milieu is *analogous* to the one that later will, subsequent to and according to the decision of philosophy, be reserved for transcendental imagination, that "art hidden in the depths of the soul" ' (p. 144 [126]). This passage is signalled by Gasché (pp. 151–2), arguing that his infrastructures are 'instances of an intermediary discourse, concerned with a middle in which the differends are suspended and preserved' (we think 'intermediary' is still misleadingly dialectical here, though Gasché takes due care to insist that these are not 'third terms that eventually initiate solutions in the form of speculative dialectics' (ibid.): Derrida's 'milieu' can safely be translated as 'milieu' in such contexts, something like a 'solution' in the liquid sense, from which the 'differends' never quite crystallize out. This general milieu, which is that of the 'same' which is not identical, allows for infinitely more subtle degrees and varieties of difference than dialectical thinking). But if this *milieu* of *différance*, almost of 'transcendental dispersion',[63] is the deconstructive *analogon* of the Transcendental Imagination, what of the Idea of Reason quoted above that might, it would seem, gather all together again, at least in a teleological perspective, and provide precisely the articulation of possibility and impossibility we are looking for, in a sort of generalized 'illusion' which could not be measured against any sort of truth?

The quotation from 'The Ends of Man' above links the Idea to phenomenology, and it is indeed in the 'early' analyses of Husserl that Derrida makes frequent reference to it. This is an extremely delicate question which will return us to finitude: put bluntly, a very common misconception of what Derrida is about, which Levinas's comment runs the risk of reinforcing, could lead to a version of deconstruction which assumes that *différance* just is the postponement to infinity of the Kantian Idea.[64] This misconception would be encouraged by the insistence on finitude we have so far been inclined to accept.

Harvey makes quite persistent use of 'the Idea in the Kantian sense' in her own account of deconstruction: the remarks about the 'fil conducteur' lead her almost necessarily to wonder whether the 'goals' or 'intentions' she ascribes to deconstruction are to be thought of as such Ideas (and thereby essentially unreachable – so the 'deconstruction of metaphysics' could never in principle be achieved) (p. 25). She is quite rapidly able to argue that this is certainly the case with grammatology (which would refute Ulmer, for example,[65] though we are inclined to think that grammatology is always already impossible in a more radical manner than an Idea of Reason), and goes on to assert that this is also true of the 'detachment from metaphysics' (p. 73). This would appear a reasonable enough description (and is certainly useful for us when we need to argue against over-hasty sociologizings of Derrida, which assume that *différance* or 'play' are supposed to be proposals for living and then get indignant because they appear unrealistic – this sort of error[66] makes us sorely tempted to treat Derrida as doing transcendental philosophy, if only to avoid time-consuming argument) were the Idea not also the object of Derrida's analyses. When she comes to address these analyses, there is a necessary complication. On the one hand, a notion she has been using as an operative concept for her own analysis reappears as an object for the object of her analysis (and in fact an object for her object's object). On the other, as this is the point at which the possible complicity between Derrida and that object (here, Husserl) is addressed (as it was by Gasché, and we remember the problems raised by a certain 'radical contingency' interfering with a model of filiation and tradition), then we are returned to questions of metalanguage and decapitation. This complication infiltrates Harvey's syntax and produces 'The final thrust of the deconstruction of Husserl involves a certain recognition by Derrida of that which he admits Husserl recognized' (p. 85). This 'thrust' is the well-known moment at which Derrida asserts that the whole system of Husserl's 'essential distinctions' turns out to be purely teleological. Derrida's argument, it will be recalled, is that on the one hand, phenomenology as a whole is grounded in the privilege of the 'living present'; but on the other, as what is (purely) thought under this concept is determined as ideality (i.e. permitting of infinite identical repetition) as opposed to factuality, then the living present is *in fact* infinitely deferred, and thus itself has only an *ideal* status. The possibility, for example, of the objective replacement of subjective expressions is for Husserl an ideal, but one which is infinitely distant, and from which, therefore, we are in fact infinitely removed. 'As the ideal is always thought by Husserl in the form of the Idea in the Kantian sense, this substitution of ideality for non-ideality, of objectivity for non-objectivity, is *infinitely deferred*'. This *différance*, says Derrida, just is that of the difference between ideality and non-ideality. In this situation, the possibility of making the essential distinctions Husserl demands (notably between indication and expression in the context of *La Voix et le phénomène*) is *also* infinitely deferred. Whence the slightly tricky aporia Derrida discovers. *In fact*, the distinctions are not respected, because their possibility is infinitely deferred; *en droit*, in principle, at the end of the infinite deferral, they disappear because their maintenance depends on the maintenance of a distinction between fact and principle, which distinction disappears in the Idea, which promises principle *as* fact. Once again (we re-repeat), 'their possibility is their impossibility' (*La Voix . . .* , p. 113 [101]). Derrida suggests that this would imply that Husserl never really tried to derive difference as secondary to presence, though he nonetheless also does do so.

Harvey takes this recognition to mean that in some sense deconstruction borrows its *telos* and origin from phenomenology (p. 85), and to do this she has to assume that the 'aporia' located by Derrida just is a description of the 'Idea in the Kantian sense' (p. 86), which it is not, being rather an interruption of progress to the Idea. This leads her to suggest a 'principle of principles' for deconstruction, namely ' "no practice is every totally faithful to its principles" ' which depends, in its banality, on this misreading. (Derrida scholars who recognize that Harvey's formulation is a (near) quotation from *De la grammatologie*, p. 59 [39] will again note the effects of decontextualization.) Even though Harvey goes on to say that only *différance* makes the Idea in the Kantian sense possible (p. 89), she here significantly forgets the corollary of impossibility, and her general attachment to teleological explanation in fact commits her to a view of *différance* as Idea. Yet Derrida goes on:

> This appearing of the Ideal as infinite *différance* can only be produced in a relation to death in general. Only a relation to my-death can make appear the infinite *différance* of presence. At the same stroke, compared to the ideality of the positive infinite, this relation to my-death becomes an accident of finite empiricity. The appearing of infinite *différance* is itself finite. Given this, *différance*, which is nothing outside this relation, becomes the finitude of life as essential relation to self as to one's death. *Infinite* différance is *finite*. It can therefore no longer be thought of within the opposition between finitude and infinity, absence and presence, negation and affirmation. (p. 114 [102])

For however useful the stress on finitude, the danger is that it re-inforces a view of infinity which is, precisely, metaphysical. Gasché usefully recalls (p. 179) Derrida's refusal of a classical account of the impossibility of totalization on the grounds of the empirical finitude of man, faced with the inexhaustible richness of experience it can never master. The problem with the insistence on finitude, however useful it can appear (even for Gasché, as we have seen) is that it tends to reinforce the claims of the transcendental and the teleological, via the 'Idea in a Kantian sense', at least read in a certain (Husserlian) manner. There are several points in *De la grammatologie* to disallow such a reading.[67]

Whence, again, Gasché's use of 'quasitranscendental'. It is now clear that it would be wrong to consider this as a sort of failed transcendental, as an unfortunate expedient forced upon us by a sort of sober pragmatism against the wilder hopes of the metaphysicians, as our own borrowing of the notion of decapitation from *Glas* might suggest.

And it is in fact in *Glas* that some of Derrida's most explicit statements about the transcendental are to be found, though none of our three authors quotes them. Here, for example, in a discussion of Hegel on Antigone and the role of the sister in general:

> And what if the unassimilable, the absolutely undigestable played a fundamental role in the system, an abyssal role rather, the abyss playing a quasitranscendental role and allowing there to be formed above it, like a sort of effluvium, a dream of appeasement? Is it not always an element excluded from the system that assures the space of possibility of the system? The transcendental has always been, strictly, a transcategorial, what could not be received, formed, finished in any of the categories internal to the system. The system's vomit. (pp. 171–183a; 210–227a [151–162a])

Even to present this as an *interrupted* movement towards, as we have tended to do, is no doubt still too teleological and ideal. Here again, attention to stricture and striction would help, and *Glas* is again the place to look:

> Striction no longer allows itself to be circumscribed as an ontological category, nor even as a category at all, not even a trans-category, a transcendental. Striction – what serves to think the ontological or the transcendental – is thus *also* in the position of a transcendental trans-category, transcendental of a transcendental. . . . There is no choice to be made here: whenever a discourse is made *against* the transcendental, a matrix – striction itself – constrains the discourse to place the non-transcendental, the outside of the transcendental field, the excluded, in a structuring position. The matrix in question constitutes the excluded as the transcendental's transcendental, as simili-transcendental, as transcendental contra-band. The contra-band is *not yet* dialectical contradiction. It necessarily becomes it, to be sure, but its not-yet is not-yet teleological anticipation, which means that it never becomes dialectical contradiction. It *remains* something other than that which, necessarily, it is to become. (pp. 272a; 340–1a [244a])

Gasché suggests all too briefly that Heidegger's 'finite transcendentals' constitute Being as Being understood and interpreted (pp. 316–7), and are still bound to *logos* and logic. The quasitranscendentals, however, are not 'situated within the traditional conceptual space that stretches from the pole of the finite to that of infinity', but 'are at the border of the space of organized contamination which they open up'. We dis-locate the traditional space by a radicalized appeal to finitude, but in the 'second' moment that finitude is reinscribed, like all the other terms. Similarly, the quasitranscendentals do not respect the distribution of empirical and transcendental (see too p. 151), and

> By dislocating the opposition of fact and principle – that is, by accounting for this conceptual difference *as* difference – the quasitranscendentals, instead of being more radical, seem to be characterised by a certain irreducible erratic contingency. (p. 317)

This contingency (as usual the word will not quite do, but we are wary of a common tendency around deconstruction to bewail the inadequate or metaphysically usurped language available, the weary sigh of the deconstructionist for whom language is too coarse and vulgarized to do the trick: this would again be to fall too simply into finitude and the Idea.[68] The old names with which deconstruction works are not provisional stand-ins in view of a perfected new language to come: the necessary imperfection of these words means they are just fine as they are, nothing could do better *this time*; paradoxically enough, there will be no substitute for these incomparable supplements)[69] will recall that which Gasché recognized contaminating the filiation of Derrida from Husserl, and which we suggested disrupted any simple historical placing of Derrida as the latest or last philosopher of the tradition. This 'contingency' guarantees that despite Gasché's necessary insistence on deconstruction's 'mimicry' (and mockery) of philosophical systematicity, Derrida's work is less a system than a series of impure 'events'. In the context of his own salutary doubts as to the possibility of placing Derrida in the History of Western Thought (p. 82), Llewelyn quotes from *La Carte postale* an avowal of a longing for presence, proximity, proper meanings and wonders how we could ever decide whether 'Derrida' could truly have intended such things. Llewelyn's point is that such a question seems impertinent, and we could say it is a dramatization of the necessary possibility, entertained elsewhere in *La Carte postale*, that Derrida might always be writing the opposite of what he thinks or 'believes'. We are more inclined to take such sentiments literally, and argue against anybody that deconstruction really is a thinking of and for the present, for now, *en ce moment même*.[70] This will help to negotiate the pathos of past and future which deconstruction also inevitably generates.[71] In so far as deconstruction scans the rhythm[72] of our decapitation or going under, then the emergence towards concept or Idea which these three books unequally espouse is a partial moment of that moment, helping us to get our breath before the plunge, certainly, but largely leaving us to take that plunge alone.

The Beginning

The problem around the 'Idea in the Kantian sense' inevitably opens the question of ethics, where, almost by definition, our real interest lies: Derrida's persistent location of '*ethico*-theoretical' decisions at the root of supposedly purely theoretical concerns (see *La Voix et le phénomène*) is proof enough of that. The Idea links pure reason and the faculty of judgment (via the sublime) to the practical reason (which Heidegger would also want to ground in the transcendental imagination (op. cit., §30)), but we now know this would still fall within the structure of finitude. If we are right to suggest that Derrida interrupts the movement toward the Idea, and paradoxically plunges us back into the 'present' and the 'empirical', then clearly our ethics and politics are changed too. The free community of rational beings can no longer simply be invoked, even regulatively, to orient our ethical and political judgment, nor can its various surrogates. But freedom, quaintly enough, is nevertheless what Derrida is all about. The paradox of traditional political thinking of all colours would be that by taking its model from conceptual thinking, it projects freedom as a state at the end of a progress ideally oriented by calculable and programmable laws. Freedom is ejected from now except in the negative form of unforeseen obstacles.[73]

Interestingly enough, our three books have little to say here to help us; Gasché never broaches the question at all, despite the demand that justice be done to Derrida. Llewelyn (focusing explicitly on 'sense', of course), says little more, and although both briefly mention Levinas in the context of a questioning of classical ontology, neither points out that in Levinas what is 'otherwise than being or beyond essence' (Llewelyn, p. 41, referring of course to the title of Levinas's 1974 book) is bound up with the ethical. Harvey does examine the question more closely: first in the course of her explication of Derrida's 'trace', in its 'profound though subtle differences' with that of Levinas (pp. 169–74), but more importantly in a return to the 'point of orientation' of the system, which we have seen to be the prohibition of incest in Rousseau, and which Harvey mistakenly tries to make the point of the subject or author in Derrida. Now, however, she links this point to the (im)possibility of ethics. Although this is still in part an anthropologizing description about the socialization of the child '(in all of us)' (p. 226), Harvey quite rightly links this question to Derrida's writing 'beyond good and evil' as the 'non-ethical opening of ethics'. Treading carefully around the pitfalls of Harvey's description, we can pick out a valuable argument relating back to the idiomatic and the singular: the point being that the ethical is radically 'particular' (Harvey's term,

p. 227; we prefer 'singular'), and therefore bound to an always particular context. (We would want to argue that this return to the question of context implies that these books, addressing us explicitly in context, are already thereby engaged in an 'ethical' relation.) Which implies that any generalization of an 'ethics in general' or 'ethics as such' or 'ethics itself' is already unethical. This can be linked to Derrida's comments on Lévi-Strauss in *De la grammatologie*, where the giving of proper names, the 'suspension of the absolute vocative' (p. 164 [112, which gives 'vocative absolute']) is called the originary violence of language. Whence the familiar (im)possibility. This is presumably basically the impossibility of a philosophical ethics which is, whether in Kantian or, apparently, Levinasian form, always still subordinate to ontology determined in terms of presence.

There is no question of going into these questions here, although they are the questions that matter to us.[74] Let us end with the beginning, the 'literary', the 'Introduction' to *Parages*, whose *motifs*, in-citations and solli-citations,

> lead back to places where, the criteria of decidability ceasing to be ensured, a decision can, finally, engage.
> And the event take place. More than once. . . .
> . . . ventures beyond the too-well-received divides between performative speech and constative speech, into those environs where a border line begins to tremble. It regularly undecides itself, between the event of citation, in advance divisible and iterable, and the desire of the coming itself, before any citation. But the event – meeting, decision, call, nomination, initial incision of a mark – can only come about from the experience of the undecidable. Not the undecidable which still belongs to the order of calculation but the other, which no calculation could ever anticipate. Without this experience, would there ever be the chance of a step taken [*franchi*]? A call for the event (*viens*)? a gift, a responsibility? Would there be any other thing, any other cause then causality? Would not everything be delivered over to the programme? (pp. 12,15)

Of course we have been insufficiently (and therefore excessively) philosophical in our reading of Derrida, and have much to learn from these books, however excessively (and therefore insufficiently) philosophical they all are too. It happens in our case that we have learned most of what we understand of events, citation, doubling (and even decapitation and hilarity) from 'literary' texts (for the sake of economy, from *Le Rouge et le noir* alone).[75] But there is no linear scale here with a literary end and a philosophical end:[76] at their best, all three of these books know this well enough. Gasché's point is that in thinking we were being literary (or psychoanalytical, or linguistic, or rhetorical) we were in fact being excessively, and therefore insufficiently, philosophical:

this is the point of many of Derrida's essays, of course.[77] But the sternness of the rebuke (which can also provoke our hilarity, as here), however justified by the perhaps extraordinary amount of rubbish talked for and against Derrida and deconstruction, might always rephilosophize what, by going through philosophy to its edges (we are tempted to say its ha-ha), is also, by that fact, the least philosophical discourse imaginable. Harvey's third 'open letter', to Derrida himself, recognizes the unrealized *telos* of her own work as a 'philosophy of deconstruction' that Derrida himself would reject (p. xiii); Gasché's Introduction carefully sets at a distance this risk he also acknowledges to be inevitable and necessary; Llewelyn characteristically ends best, on the double affirmation which is the object of some of Derrida's most recent work,[78] and which is also a call to the other, 'we repeat'. And to Llewelyn, adding to Derrida's 'Amen amen, *oui oui*' his own 'hear hear' (p. 123), we add, with an eye on 'Pas' and 'Two words for Joyce', our own perplexed 'now, now', polite 'come come', and mild 'ha ha'.

Notes

1. Rodolphe Gasché, *The Tain of the Mirror: Derrida and the Philosophy of Reflection*, Cambridge: Harvard University Press 1986; Irene E. Harvey, *Derrida and the Economy of Différance*, Bloomington: Indiana University Press 1986; John Llewelyn, *Derrida on the Threshold of Sense*, London: Macmillan 1986. Page references to these three works will be given in the text. No attempt is made here to do justice to Stephen Melville's interesting but rather wayward *Philosophy Beside Itself: Deconstruction and Modernism*, Minneapolis: Minnesota University Press 1986, which will, however, occasionally reappear in the notes. Gillian Rose's *Dialectic of Nihilism: Post-Structuralism and Law*, Oxford: Blackwell 1984, and Peter Dews's *Logics of Disintegration: Post-Structuralist Thought and the Claims of Critical Theory*, London: Verso 1987, both of which contain 'philosophical' discussion of Derrida, are not discussed here, despite some egregious misunderstandings and tendentious misrepresentations: see Chapter 5 below. Of course, we were not unaware of other philosophers taking an informed interest in Derrida, but who have not (yet) taken the risk of writing books about him: this is dedicated to Andrew Benjamin, Robert Bernasconi, Jay Bernstein, David Krell and David Wood, in the hope that they will forgive our philosophical naivety.

2. See especially 'Philosophy as a Kind of Writing', in *Consequences of Pragmatism*, Brighton: Harvester 1982, pp. 90–109 [in Harvey's bibliography (p. 273), this article is attributed to a certain Richard Rotry, and called 'Philosophy as a King of Writing'], and his contribution to the *Against Theory* 'debate' ('Philosophy Without Principles', in W.J.T. Mitchell, ed., *Against Theory: Literary Studies and the New Pragmatism*, University of Chicago Press 1985, pp. 132–8), where he seems (p. 135) prepared to concede to Searle the *philosophical* points in his exchange with Derrida, which can only be an unusual reaction, even among analytical philosophers. As a preliminary index of the changes in Christopher Norris's (and therefore many others') accounts of deconstruction, it is worth noting that in his New Accents volume, *Deconstruction: Theory and Practice*, London: Methuen 1982, Norris finds a 'fine lucidity' in Rorty's account (pp. 128–9), whereas in his Modern Masters volume, *Derrida*, (London: Fontana 1987, he is rightly critical (pp. 150–5): this turn seems to be brought about by Norris's essay, 'Philosophy as a Kind of Narrative: Rorty on post-modern liberal culture', in *The Contest of Faculties: Philosophy and Theory after Deconstruction*, London: Methuen 1985, pp. 139–66. Norris writes copiously,

fluently and with every appearance of plausibility in his regularly produced books: we think this makes criticism of his errors the more important, though are aware that such criticism will, for the same reason, appear churlish and ungenerous. Let us say immediately that the Modern Masters volume is much more secure in every respect than the New Accents, as will become clearer in these notes: none the less, even the Modern Masters book tends to place Derrida within entirely classical polarities with a philosophical end and a literary end, for example, or a rational end and an irrational end, or an Enlightenment end and a post-modern end, and, within the terms of these polarities, which are never really questioned as such, remain content to argue that Derrida is in each case nearer the former end *than you think*, the 'you' thus positioned being either the literary critic with all his/her familiar naiveties and rash enthusiasms, or the philosopher with all his/her prejudices. The book does at least urge, even if it is very far from demonstrating, the philosophical 'seriousness' of Derrida's work, and its 'ultimately ethical nature' (p. 230: on a strict reading, none of the words in this last formulation is acceptable). Readers of the latter part of the book are also, unfortunately, likely to be misled whenever Norris himself translates from the French: sometimes he helpfully provides the French words in question, so that on p. 205, for example, anyone can see that 'structure destinale' cannot really be translated as 'structural destiny', and, on p. 201, that 'program of indoctrination' is perhaps a *little* strong for 'institution d'enseignement'. But no such help is available on, for example, p. 197, where Norris's rendering is 'One can understand this Declaration as a vibrant act of faith, as an hypocrisy indispensable to any political, military, or economic *coup de force*, etc., or, more simply, more economically, as the deployment of a tautology: in so far as this Declaration has a meaning and an effect, there must be a final, legitimizing instance'. An accurate translation of the French text (from *Otobiographies: L'Enseignement de Nietzsche et la politique du nom propre*, Paris: Galilée 1984, p. 27 [not p. 9, as Norris has it]), would give: 'One can understand this Declaration as a vibrant act of faith, as an hypocrisy indispensable to a politico-militaro-economic etc. *coup de force* or, more simply, more economically, as the analytic and consequent unfolding of a tautology: for this declaration to have a meaning and an effect, there must be a last instance'. Perhaps these are only nuances: in the preceding chapter, however, Norris is led to attribute to Derrida a surprising degree of sympathy with 'Oxford philosophy', on the basis of a quotation from *La Carte postale de Socrate à Freud et au-delà*, Paris: Aubier-Flammarion 1980, p. 108, where he translates the word *ingénuité* as 'ingenuity' (p. 197) – it does, of course, mean 'ingenuousness' or 'naivety'.

3. For Derrida as anti-foundationalist, see Rorty again and Stanley Fish's 'Consequences' in the *Against Theory* volume (pp. 106–31 (p. 112)); for deconstruction as scepticism, see Norris, *Deconstruction* (p. xii): 'Hume saw no way out of his sceptical predicament, except by soothing the mind with careless distractions . . . . Deconstruction is likewise an activity of thought which cannot be consistently acted on – that way madness lies – but which yet possesses an inescapable rigour of its own'. See too pp. 127–8, where Derrida's supposed scepticism is seen as better than others because he had to work hard to get to it. The whole book has a sense of deconstruction always about to run off uncontrollably into 'madness', and can give only extrinsic and accidental reasons why it does not. In *The Contest of Faculties*, pp. 216–7, Norris again refers to 'the sceptical rigours of deconstruction' and suggests further that 'Deconstruction is simply the most hard-pressed and consequent of relativist doctrines applied to questions of meaning, logic and truth': but it would seem that this would be only a relative relativism, not to be confused with the 'unbridled relativism', or the 'relativist euphoria' that would apparently characterize 'absolute' (?) relativism. (We imagine entries in a latter-day *Dictionnaire des idées reçues*: 'Relativism: always unbridled (see scepticism)'; 'Scepticism: always thoroughgoing (see relativism)'.) The account in his Modern Masters volume limits itself to Derrida's 'vigilant scepticism as regards deconstructive "method" ' (p. 20), and later suggests (we think) that Derrida is not simply a sceptic nor a simple opponent of scepticism. But in any case Derrida is neither a sceptic nor a relativist, nor simply an anti-foundationalist, and fallibilist could only be a very partial description.

4. Jonathan Culler, *On Deconstruction: Theory and Criticism after Structuralism*, London: Routledge & Kegan Paul 1983, p. 213. Norris, *Derrida*, p. 21, suggests, to the contrary,

that as part of their 'desire to annex deconstruction as a kind of anti-philosophy', literary critics show a 'strongly marked preference for those texts where the deconstructive groundwork (so to speak) is very largely taken as read, and where Derrida most thoroughly exploits the resultant opportunities for experiments in style' (the subsequent complication of the terms of this description does not alter its empirical falsity).

5. Culler, p. 85n. The note reads: 'I will not attempt to discuss the relationship of Derridian deconstruction to the work of Hegel, Nietzsche, Husserl and Heidegger. Gayatri Spivak's introduction to *Of Grammatology* provides much useful information. See also Rodolphe Gasché, "Deconstruction as Criticism". See too Culler's footnote 1 to p. 227 for a general reflection on how both defenders (including Gasché) and opponents of deconstruction tend to make a distinction between 'original' and 'derivative' versions of deconstruction.

6. Rodolphe Gasché, 'Deconstruction as Criticism', *Glyph* 6 (1979), pp. 177–216: we are naive and ridiculous on p. 178 and 'untrained' on p. 183.

7. Edward Said, 'The Problem of Textuality: Two Exemplary Positions', *Critical Inquiry*, 4 (1978), pp. 673–714; Fredric Jameson, *The Prison-House of Language: A Critical Account of Structuralism and Russian Formalism*; Terry Eagleton's remarks on Derrida, which it seems safest to describe as in a constant process of historical transformation, are spread across his *Walter Benjamin or Towards a Revolutionary Criticism* (London: Verso 1981), and especially the chapter, 'Marxism and Deconstruction', pp. 131–42; *Literary Theory: An Introduction* (Oxford: Blackwell 1983) and *Against the Grain: Essays 1975–1985* (London: Verso 1986). In a note to her 'Love Me, Love my Ombre, Elle', *Diacritics* 14:4 (1984), pp. 19–36 (p. 21n4), Spivak refers to these three authors and links them to M.H. Abrams in more than one way: she also suggests that what she calls a 'powerful continuist misreading of Derrida' (whatever that means) in Perry Anderson's *In the Tracks of Historical Materialism* (London: Verso 1983) is 'worth more careful scrutiny'. However, only quite brief scrutiny is required to show that Anderson's comments about Derrida are all wrong – see for example his claim on p. 42 that Derrida, somehow both still on a common path and 'marking the post-structuralist break', 'rejected the notion of language as a stable system of objectification, but radicalized its pretensions as a universal suzerain of the modern world, with the truly imperial decree, "there is nothing outside of the text", "nothing before the text, no pretext that is not already a text". The Book of the World that the Renaissance, in its naïveté, took to be a metaphor, became the last, literal word of a philosophy that would shake all metaphysics': it would be hard to believe Anderson had read the books he is quoting from, were it not for the fact that he gives careful references. On p. 46 he assumes that Derrida unproblematically espouses the Nietzsche option at the end of 'Structure, Sign and Play', despite Derrida's careful statement that no such choice is to be made (*L'Ecriture et la différence* (Paris: Seuil 1967), pp. 427–8; tr. Alan Bass (London: Routledge & Kegan Paul 1978) p. 293: 'I do not believe that today there is any question of *choosing*'): Norris has a brief discussion of this point in *Derrida*, pp. 139–41, but omits to quote this clear statement (see too note 26, below); on p. 50 Anderson is unable to understand the complexity of Derrida's statements on history and historicity other than by forcing them into a schema whereby 'A total initial determinism paradoxically ends in the reinstatement of an absolute final contingency', and then calling this an 'irony'; on p. 54, intent on presenting Derrida as destroyer, he claims that 'Structurality, for Derrida, is little more than a ceremonious gesture to the prestige of his immediate predecessors', and then quotes the same bit of 'Structure, Sign and Play' to the same effect as before (compare the discussion of structurality by Gasché (pp. 145–7) to get a sense of what's actually going on). In the 'Foreword' to his book, Anderson recognizes a debt to Peter Dews, and says that the latter's forthcoming work 'will soon render these pages more or less obsolete' (p. 8): as Dews's book makes all the same mistakes, we assume that it is also the source of Anderson's careful references, and deserves priority. Dews's work had made Anderson's obsolete before being published, and Anderson returns the favour by repeating concisely in advance the errors it takes Dews much longer to get through. As each book thus pre-empts the other and renders it obsolete, it is strictly speaking unnecessary to read either. Even Eagleton feels obliged to take Anderson to task for what he politely

calls his 'seriously one-sided approach to his topic' (*Against the Grain*, pp. 94–5), but does so with a view to making a very simplistic distinction between 'left' and 'right' deconstruction, whereas we do not think that the 'politics of deconstruction' can be dominated in this manner. The very prevalent approach which is prepared to countenance deconstruction only in so far as it might be 'useful' within a previously defined political strategy (for bringing about socialism, say) is already denying itself any real understanding of Derrida's work, the politics of which is much more challenging and complex.

8. The standard case would be that presented by Barbara Johnson's justly ubiquitous 'The Frame of Reference: Poe, Lacan Derrida', *Yale French Studies*, 52 (1977), pp. 457–505; reprinted in various forms in her volume *The Critical Difference: Essays in the Contemporary Rhetoric of Reading* (Baltimore: Johns Hopkins University Press 1980) in Geoffrey Hartman, ed., *Psychoanalysis and the Question of the Text* (Baltimore: Johns Hopkins University Press 1978); Robert Young, ed., *Untying the Text: A Post-Structuralist Reader* (London: Routledge & Kegan Paul 1981). See Derrida's reaction to Johnson's attempt to find Lacan already saying what Derrida was supposedly trying and failing to say in *La Carte Postale de Socrate à Freud et au-delà* (Paris: Flammarion 1980), pp. 162–4 (tr. Alan Bass (Chicago: University of Chicago Press 1987), pp. 149–51, and especially p. 164 [151] on the status of 'dissemination' as 'one of the words, among so many others, to lead on beyond any "last word" [in English in the text]', and as not a 'master-word'. For this type of operation, see too Shoshana Felman, *Le Scandale du corps parlant: Don Juan avec Austin ou la séduction en deux langues* (Paris: Seuil 1978), and Culler's judicious remarks in *On Deconstruction*, pp. 118n4 and 261. Gregory Ulmer's essay 'Sounding the Unconscious' in *Glassary* (Lincoln and London: University of Nebraska Press 1986) takes *Glas* to be in some sense about the Unconscious, and aims to show 'how psychoanalysis in general, and Lacan specifically, make possible the kind of critique of self-presence mounted by Derrida' (p. 37). This he attempts via a parallel between Derrida on inner speech and Lacan's discussion of Schreber: we can do no more here than add a reference, which Ulmer seems to forget, to Derrida's own parallel between 'hearing-oneself-speak' and Schreber, in 'Qual Quelle: Les sources de Valéry', in *Marges: de la philosophie* (Paris: Minuit 1972), pp. 327–63 (p. 354) [tr. Alan Bass (Brighton: Harvester 1982), pp. 273–306 (298)], and to suggest that whatever the interest of the parallel, to claim that 'what Lacan learns from Schreber about the operations of the Unconscious in language is the same lesson that Derrida puts to work in the formation of the theory and practice of the text' (p. 43) is, apart from the repetition of the theory/practice error, to elide the most interesting questions. Jacqueline Rose has some suggestive remarks on Derrida in the Introduction to her *Sexuality in the Field of Vision* (London: Verso 1986), pp. 18–23, but we think misreads Derrida: on the 'pulsion du propre' (p. 20) at least by taking commentary of Freud for assertion of a thesis by Derrida; by assuming that Derrida's 'endless dispersal of subjectivity' (ibid.) is an attempt simply to get rid of the subject once and for all; and by assuming a 'psychic' account must be given of the 'logos's' 'forgetting' of *différance*. It is striking that none of our three philosophical books finds it necessary to devote more than the briefest of passing references to Lacan. Melville's book does go into these problems at length, and suggests interesting criticisms of Johnson and Felman – this falls outside the limits of our discussion.

9. i.e., Hegel, Husserl, Heidegger, said by Descombes to dominate French philosophy from 1933–60, then to be replaced by the three 'masters of suspicion', i.e. Marx, Nietzsche and Freud, (*Le Même et l'autre: Quarante-cinq ans de philosophie française (1933–1978)* (Paris: Minuit 1979), p. 13 (tr. *Modern French Philosophy* (Cambridge: Cambridge University Press 1980), p. 3]).

10. Gregory L. Ulmer, *Applied Grammatology: Post(e)-Pedagogy from Jacques Derrida to Joseph Beuys* (Baltimore: Johns Hopkins University Press 1985). Ulmer's basic premise, which he supports by quoting Culler (see note 4, above) on the tendency of literary critics to rely on Derrida's 'philosophical' texts (p. xi), is that Derrida 'deconstructs' philosophical texts and 'mimes' literary and artistic ones (p. x), which is false, and that the term 'Grammatology' can be used to cover both of these aspects of Derrida, which is also false. Ulmer is confident that 'grammatology' is somehow 'beyond' deconstruction, and he also suggests that, for example, *La Carte postale* is 'an anti-book awaiting relief by a

Writing beyond the book. Or, to put it another way, it is a work of theoretical grammatology which contains the script for an *applied* grammatology' (p. xiii). (Norris ventures to use 'applied deconstruction' to suggest a general shift in Derrida's work towards 'wider political bearings', in his concern with question of teaching and the institution of the University (p. 13).) Although this approach, and the peculiar violence it works on Derrida's own usage of the term 'grammatology', do not of course prohibit Ulmer from saying some interesting things, we are sure these opening remarks are quite mistaken. See too the concise delimitation of these problems in David Carroll's excellent *Paraesthetics: Foucault, Lyotard, Derrida* (New York and London: Methuen 1987), pp. 199n5 and 202n18.

11. Jean Maurel, recorded in Philippe Lacoue-Labarthe and Jean-Luc Nancy, eds, *Les Fins de l'homme: à partir du travail de Jacques Derrida* (Paris: Galilée 1981), p. 695. See too in the same volume, apart from many excellent papers, the opening discussion as to the validity of the 'philosophical' status Nancy and Lacoue-Labarthe want to give the conference (pp. 16–17).

12. Jonathan Culler, 'Jacques Derrida', in John Sturrock, ed., *Structuralism and Since* (Oxford: Oxford University Press 1979), pp. 154–80 (p. 155).

13. 'Restitutions of the Truth in Pointing [pointure]', in *The Truth in Painting*, tr. Geoff Bennington and Ian McLeod (Chicago: University of Chicago Press 1987), pp. 255–382.

14. Norris, *Derrida*, p. 245. This idea of a sudden 'decided shift' betrays a somewhat Lentricchian view of history.

15. Jacques Derrida, *Dissemination*, tr. Barbara Johnson (London: Athlone Press 1981), pp. viii and xv. See note 40, below, for explicit statements to the contrary.

16. Culler, pp. 86–8.

17. Sigmund Freud, *Jokes and their Relation to the Unconscious* (Pelican Freud Library, Vol. 6) (Harmondsworth: Penguin Books 1976), p. 240.

18. Norris, *Derrida*, p. 243.

19. *De la grammatologie* (Paris: Editions de Minuit 1967), p. 233; tr. Gayatri Chakravorty Spivak as *Of Grammatology* (Baltimore and London: Johns Hopkins University Press 1976) p. 162. All subsequent references will be given in the text, in the form p. 233 [162], and we follow this convention for references other than the first to other works by Derrida. We have consistently retranslated, not always because of inaccuracies in the published versions, but also because of a general desirability for different possible translations to be suggested.

20. See Ulmer, pp. 55–7 and 94–7: Ulmer's whole approach is attractively off-beat, but it is rather improbable to suggest that 'Grammatology . . . is a strategy of cognitive evocation, modeled on the effect of olfaction' (p. 97). See too Llewelyn, pp. 119–20, also picking up on Derrida's discussion of disgust in Kant, in 'Economimesis', in S. Agacinski et al., *Mimesis des articulations* (Paris: Aubier-Flammarion 1975), pp. 57–93; tr. R. Klein, *Diacritics*, 11:2 (1981), 3–25.

21. We do not suggest that Derrida never uses or exploits this term: to take only a recent example, in *De l'esprit: Heidegger et la question* (Paris: Galilée 1987) tr. Geoff Bennington and Rachel Bowlby, (Chicago: University of Chicago Press 1989), p. 23, Derrida refers to an earlier piece of work on Heidegger in which 'I distinguished four *fils conducteurs*'. See too *De la grammatologie*, p. 228 [159, translated as 'guiding line']. And of course there is much play on *fil* and *fils* in *Dissemination*. But we should be wary of making it an important or vital Derridean concept, if only because in 'Limited Inc.' Derrida suggests it is a term for the 'classical philosopher' (Supplement to *Glyph*, 2 (1977), p. 73; tr. Samuel Weber, *Glyph*, 2 (1977), pp. 162–254 (p 244). See too *Glas* (Paris: Galilée 1974, p. 26a, rpt. Denoël Gonthier, 1981, I, 26a); tr. John P. Leavey, Jr and Richard Rand (Lincoln and London: University of Nebraska Press 1986), 19a: 'I shall also try not to transform love and the contradiction of familial affect into a privileged *fil conducteur*, or even into a *telos* or regulating ideal. It is the test which interests me, not success or failure'. We take it that Gasché's use of *fil conducteur* in the context of his discussion of the Platonic *symploke* (p. 97) is a witticism. For a Kantian usage, see for example his 'Idea for a Universal History from a Cosmopolitan Point of View', tr. B. Nisbet, in H. Reiss, ed., *Kant's Political Writings* (Cambridge: Cambridge University Press 1970), p. 42, and §5 of

the Introduction to the *Critique of Judgement*, where the essentially teleological nature of the guiding thread is clear. See Lyotard's commentary in *Le Différend* (Paris: Minuit 1983), pp. 234–5. In similar vein, Melville uses the term 'project' (pp. 4 and 60); but see Derrida's reply to our question using the unfortunate formula 'deconstructive enterprise': 'I will insist that there is no such thing as a deconstructive *enterprise* – the idea of a project is incompatible with deconstruction. Deconstruction is a situation. Of course, sometimes it takes the shape of a project, of a text signed by somebody and so on. But what we call deconstruction in its academic or in its editorial form is also a symptom of deconstruction at work everywhere in society and the world; so the "enterprise" is not the essential thing in deconstruction' ('Of Colleges and Philosophy', in *Postmodernism*, ICA Documents 4&5 (1986), pp. 66-71 (p. 69).) Reinscribing the *fil conducteur* according to these strictures would take us back to the notion of flair, on to the notion of *frayage*, and involve a passing refutation of Harvey's idea that 'deconstruction, if properly understood, walks through the text and, if improperly understood, leaves its tracks behind it' (p. 35): it is not difficult to find evidence for the idea that leaving tracks is precisely what deconstruction tries to do – see for example *De la grammatologie*, p. 90 [61], on the leaving of a track as condition of not falling back into pre-critical naivety. See too, tying up these threads, the opening reflections of 'La Pharmacie de Platon'.

22. 'Why does one still call *strategic* an operation which in the last instance refuses to be commanded by a teleo-eschatological horizon? To what point is this refusal possible and how does it negotiate its effects? Why must it negotiate them, up to and including this why itself? Why would *strategy* refer to the *play* of the strategem rather than to the hierarchical organization of means and ends? etc. These questions will not be reduced so quickly' (*Positions* (Paris: Minuit 1972), pp. 95–6; tr. Alan Bass (Chicago: University of Chicago Press 1981), p. 70). There are certainly affinities to be sought in Kant's *Zweckmässigkeit ohne Zweck* of the third *Critique*, usually translated into French as 'finalité sans fin': but before you take this as confirmation of what is taken to be a culpable 'aestheticism', please take the time to read Derrida's discussion in 'The Sans of the Pure Cut', in *The Truth in Painting*, pp. 83–118. This probably relates to our discussion of 'the Idea in the Kantian sense' later in the text.

23. C.S. Peirce, *Collected Papers* (Cambridge, Mass. 1934) Vol. 5, p. 416); quoted in Samuel Weber, 'The Limits of Professionalism', *Oxford Literary Review*, Vol. 5, Nos 1–2 (1982), pp. 58–74 (p. 65).

24. As, for example, in 'The Principle of Reason: The University in the Eyes of its Pupils', in *Diacritics*, 13:3 (1983), 3–20, p. 5 on state of mind while preparing a lecture. On the 'auto' or 'otobiographical' in Derrida, see Llewelyn, p. 89, and Gasché, p. 331n18 for brief comment, and Claude Lévesque and Christie V. McDonald, eds, *L'Oreille de l'autre: otobiographies, transferts, traductions; Textes et débats avec Jacques Derrida* (Montréal: VLB 1982) [a revised form of Derrida's major contribution appears as part of his *Otobiographies: L'Enseignement de Nietzsche et la politique du nom propre* (Paris: Galilée 1984)].

25. *Glas*, p. 132b; 162b [115b]. Also quoted by Leavey in his piece 'This (then) will not have been a book . . . ', in *Glassary*, p. 36. See too, a little later in *Glas*, the argument ending, 'The death-agony of metalanguage is thus structurally interminable. But as effort and effect. Metalanguage is the life of language: it always flaps like a bird caught in a subtle lime' (p. 148b; 182b [130b]; see too 186b 231b [165b]). The notion of decapitation also appears in *Positions* (p. 62 [45]); cf. too the end of 'Hors-Livre' and the beginning of 'La Double séance', in *La Dissémination* ['Outwork' and 'The Double Session' in *Dissemination*].

26. Norris, *Derrida*, p. 243: see too p. 46 for a comparison of *Glas* and *Finnegans Wake*. Compare the more cautious and helpful comment made by Vincent Leitch (*Deconstructive Criticism: An Advanced Introduction* (London: Hutchinson 1983), p. 205): '*Glas* bears to critical discourse a relation like that which *Finnegans Wake* holds with the novel'. In the New Accents book, Norris suggests that 'Within Derrida's writing there runs a theme of utopian longing for the textual "free play" which would finally break with the instituted wisdom of language. It is a theme that emerges to anarchic effect in some of his later texts' (p. 49). Apart from the fact that this could not be a theme, it is clear that by definition what Norris here misleadingly calls 'free play' cannot be an object of desire as

such, but is what makes desire possible. Ulmer also makes a mistake about this: 'while Derrida has always seen the difference between literary and philosophical styles as representing alternative theories of language – ever since his first book, in which he opposed Husserl to Joyce and declared his preference for the latter – his decision to write in a fully experimental style himself came after 1968' (p. xi): apart from the tendentious before/after division which is of extremely limited relevance to Derrida's work, as Llewelyn's impressive ranging across the whole range of texts shows (cf. too Gasché, p. 4), this repeats the type of mistake Anderson makes about choosing: although Derrida does, in the *Origin of Geometry* Introduction, pose the appearance of a choice between a 'Husserlian' and a 'Joycean' option (p. 103 [102]), he goes on to show that these are not at all exclusive alternatives. If it were at all possible to find the expression of a 'preference' here, it could in fact only be for Husserl (see p. 107 [104]), although the impression of a 'preference' for Joyce (as if preference were what was at stake here) might just have been gathered from Derrida's later summary in 'Two Words for Joyce', tr. Geoff Bennington, in Derek Attridge and Daniel Ferrer, eds, *Post-Structuralist Joyce: Essays from the French* (Cambridge: Cambridge University Press 1984) pp. 145–59 (p. 149) (the French text is to be found in *Ulysse Gramophone: Deux Mots pour Joyce* (Paris: Galilée 1986), pp. 15–53). See too Marian Hobson's refutation of Ulmer on this point, in 'History Traces' in Attridge, Bennington and Young, eds, *Post-Structuralism and the Question of History* (Cambridge: Cambridge University Press 1987), pp. 101–15 (p. 115, n9). We assume that the 'literary', 'Joycean' reading of *Glas* was encouraged by Geoffrey Hartman's *Saving the Text* (Baltimore and London: Johns Hopkins University Press 1981): see our brief review in *French Studies*, Vol. 36, No. 3 (1982), 365–6. We should probably add that it is not at all our aim here to endorse Hartman's claim that 'Derrida tells literary people only what they have always known and repressed' (p. 23).

27. See note 7, above, and Samuel Weber's commentary in 'Closure and Exclusion', *Diacritics*, 10:2 (1980), 35–46.

28. 'Spéculer – sur "Freud" '. In 'Love me, Love my Ombre, Elle' (see note 7, above), Spivak takes the translator (Ian McLeod) of an early fragment of this as 'Speculations – on Freud' (*Oxford Literary Review*, 3:2 (1978), 78–97) to task for 'miss[ing] the point of the infinitive and of giving Freud as a citation' (p. 23n7). We can now reveal that the typescript from which the translation was made, before the publication of *La Carte postale*, bore the title 'Spéculations – sur Freud'. On stricture, see Marian Hobson, 'History Traces', p. 108.

29. See especially *Marges*, p. 381 [320].

30. The notion even merits an entry in Culler's index: neither active nor reflexive uses of the verb 'to deconstruct' will really do, as Melville half realizes at the end of his book (pp. 152–3: Melville accepts these strictures when applied to the literary text, but not when applied to what he calls 'criticism', which he takes Derrida to be espousing as the task of philosophy (p. xxvii): his claim that 'the impulse to criticism is the impulse to make of or find in finitude a positive achievement' (p. 153) betrays a basic humanism which limits Melville's understanding of Derrida). Llewelyn usefully invokes Heidegger's *Gelassenheit* and *Seinlassen* to get out of simple active/passive oppositions (p. 93). In Gasché's 'Deconstruction and Criticism', de Man is made to look guilty of the same mistake; in his later ' "Setzung und Übersetzung": Notes on Paul de Man' (*Diacritics*, 11:4 (1981), pp. 36–57), however, it appears that de Man's notion of allegory would prevent this type of accusation. As none of the three books here explicitly discusses the relationship of Derrida and de Man (except for a brief comment by Gasché to the effect that 'no-one was more aware than Paul de Man' of the fundamental 'discrepancies' between 'deconstructionist criticism' and 'Derrida's philosophical enterprise' (p. 3)), I shall not go into the question here (except to point out that no such sense of a radical discrepancy emerges from Derrida's *Mémoires: for Paul de Man*, tr. Cecile Lindsay, Jonathan Culler and Eduardo Cadava (New York: Columbia University Press 1986)). Again, Melville goes into the question quite fully.

31. See 'Limited Inc.', p. 38 [205]. Gasché would quite rightly immediately retort with *Positions*, p. 45 [33]: 'The representation of language as "expression" is not an accidental

prejudice, but a sort of structural lure, what Kant would have called a transcendental illusion'.

32. Gasché has some slightly confusing remarks on this historical context in his Introduction, which might be taken to suggest that we are being a little unfair: 'I discuss Derrida's philosophy in terms of the criticism to which the philosophical concept of reflection and reflexivity has been subjected. The reasons for this choice are clearly circumstantial. Indeed the dominant misconception of Derrida is based on the confusion by many literary critics of deconstruction with reflexivity. . . . Yet my history of the critique of reflection . . . is not a straightforward history. . . . Hegel's speculative criticism of the philosophy of reflection is given what some may consider inordinate importance. But Part I is intended not as a total history of that problem, but merely as an oriented history that serves as a theoretical prelude to the systematic exposition of Derrida's thought. . . . In spite of my contention that Derrida's philosophy *must* be related to the modern history of the concept of reflection and to the criticism it has drawn, I seek primarily to bring into view Derrida's debate with the traditional paradigms of philosophy in general' (pp. 5–6, my emphasis). One feels the 'circumstantial' slipping away.

33. Apart from 'Signature, événement, contexte' and 'Limited Inc.', see especially *Signéponge/Signsponge*, tr. Richard Rand (New York: Columbia University Press 1984), and, on dates, *Schibboleth: pour Paul Celan* (Paris: Galilée 1986), tr. in G. Hartman and Sanford Budick, eds, *Midrash and Literature* (New Haven: Yale University Press 1986), pp. 307–47.

34. Descombes takes Derrida to think that history is already over, and that there is nothing more to say, and no more philosophy to do, only reading and re-reading (*Le même et l'autre*, p. 162 [137–8]: this is clearly linked to Descombes's argument, in the Introduction to his *Objects of all Sorts: A Philosophical Grammar*, tr. L. Scott-Fox and J. Harding (Oxford: Blackwell 1986: the Introduction does not appear in the original French version (Paris: Minuit 1983)), that French philosophy in general has become dominated by the method of immanent critique (pp. 3–4), and to his claim, in 'Les Mots de la Tribu' (*Critique*, 456 (1985), 418–44; this text was written to present to a French audience the 1984 Johns Hopkins Franco-American 'Case of the Humanities' conference) that 'the textual model has been overexploited. . . . The textual model is exhausted' (p. 443). These and other arguments by Descombes will be the object of analysis and refutation in *Oxford Literary Review*, Vol. 11 (1989).

35. *De la grammatologie*, pp. 67–8 [45–6], where the argument is that in general analysis of the treatment of writing by the tradition will ensure the possibility of 'broaching the de-construction' of this 'greatest totality', 'the concept of episteme and logocentric metaphysics'. Harvey quotes this on p. 87 of her book, but cuts the quotation to omit the 'broaching', thus turning 'deconstruction of metaphysics' too simply into a *telos*.

36. Jacques Derrida, 'Pas', *Gramma*, 3–4 (1976), 111–215 (pp. 118–19); reprinted in *Parages* (Paris: Galilée 1986), pp. 19–116 (pp. 26–7).

37. For a concise statement by Derrida, see *Positions*, p. 55 [40–1]: 'If there were a definition of *différance*, it would be, precisely, the limit, the interruption, the destruction of Hegelian sublation everywhere it operates': see too 59–61 and n6 [43–4 and n13], *La Dissémination*, p. 12n5 [6n] and 280n45 [248n], also referring to *De la grammatologie*, p. 40 [25]. Melville also takes Hegel's *Phenomenology* to provide a 'primary context' for Derrida (p. 37), but at several other points in his book acknowledges the importance of a Kantian dimension (e.g. pp. xxvii and 164n13). The resistance to the determination of difference as contradiction also informs Derrida's discussion of sexual difference in *Eperons: les styles de Nietzsche* (Paris: Flammarion 1978), especially p. 75n1 [tr. Barbara Harlow as *Spurs* (Chicago: University of Chicago Press 1979)], in *Glas*, especially pp. 127–31a; 155–61a [110–14a], and 'Geschlecht: différence sexuelle, différence ontologique' (in *Psyché. Inventions de l'autre* (Paris: Galilée 1987), pp. 395–414, tr. in *Research in Phenomenology*, 13 (1983), pp. 65–83). See too the concise statement in reply to Jacqueline Rose in 'On Colleges and Philosophy', p. 71: 'My point is not against sexual difference. It's against the transformation, the identification of sexual difference with sexual binary opposition'. None of the three books goes into this question (despite the importance

accorded it by Derrida), apart from the briefest of commentaries by Llewelyn (pp. 86–7) in a section rather misleadingly entitled 'The Gender of Truth' (pp. 83–70); Harvey briefly shows some interest in Kant's sexual metaphors (pp. 16–19), but then drops the question, so we shall too.

38. If we were concerned here to articulate Derrida and analytical philosophy, then the necessary possibility of not succeeding in referring might well be the point of contact. Derrida's argument would say that as failure to refer is a structural or necessary possibility, then that failure inhabits and infects every act of reference, however apparently successful. Llewelyn has some interesting reflection on the questions analytic philosophy might ask of this argument (pp. 64–6); and we are grateful to Michael Morris for suggesting that an analytical philosopher's answer to Derrida's (rhetorical?) question, 'What is a success when the possibility of failure continues to constitute its structure?' (*Marges*, p. 385 [324]) is simply, 'It's a success'. This logic of the necessary possibility is easy to get wrong: Norris's discussion of the 'postal' writing in *La Carte postale* suggests two different systems, one in which letters arrive, another in which they do or might not (*Derrida*, pp. 192–3) – the point is rather that this is the *same* system, and missing that point violently separates conditions of possibility and conditions of impossibility: but they are the *same* conditions. We wonder whether some confusion around the difference between *two* systems and *one double* system is not at the root of some of David Wood's perplexities about Derrida: in 'Following Derrida' (in John Sallis, ed., *Deconstruction and Philosophy* (Chicago: Chicago University Press 1987), pp. 143–60), he takes Derrida to be exploiting *two* strategies around the question of the possibility of the escape from metaphysics: one involves staying in, the other stepping out (see p. 149) – we think this is the *same* duplicitious strategy, rather than two different ones. The whole problem of the value of the non-identical same-in-*différance* in Derrida would be worth careful study and elucidation.

39. In *L'Ecriture et la différence*, pp. 293–5 [pp. 196–8].

40. For digging and foundations, see for example Kant's preface to the first edition (1790) of the third *Critique*, tr. James Creed Meredith (Oxford: Clarendon Press 1928), p. 5. See too Derrida's commentary in *La Vérité en peinture*, pp. 47–8 [39–40]. The difficulty of accurately describing deconstruction as critique can perhaps be measured by Derrida's comment in 'Lettre à un ami japonais' (in *Psyché*, pp. 387–93 [tr. in Bernasconi and Wood, eds, *Derrida and Différance* (Warwick: Parousia Press 1985), pp. 1–8]), p. 390 [pp. 4–5]: 'No more is [deconstruction] a critique, in a general sense or in a Kantian sense. The instance of *krinein* or *krisis* (decision, choice, judgement, discernment) is itself, as is all the apparatus of transcendental critique, one of the essential "themes" or "objects" of deconstruction'. Or, 'deconstruction is not a critical operation, the critical is its object; deconstruction always bears, at one moment or another, on the confidence given the critical, critico-theoretical, that is to say, deciding instance, the ultimate possibility of the decidable; deconstruction is deconstruction of critical dogmatics' ('Ja, ou le faux-bond', *Digraphe*, 11 (1977), pp. 83–121 (p. 103); quoted in Leitch, p. 205); the reference to the decidable here suggests that Norris's reading (in the context of 'the principle of Reason') of deconstruction's being a 'certain interpretation of undecidability' which 'continues to operate within the problematics of representation and the subject-object relation' (*Derrida*, p. 162), is wrong.

41. There can be no strictly Derridean justification for the exhorbitant privilege Gasché gives to the term 'infrastructure' which, despite all his precautions, carries precisely the sedimentations of ground and foundation he is anxious to avoid. Derrida's most obvious use of the term, in the third of the *Positions* interviews, would suggest that it is engaged in an immediate context to an even greater extent than his other terms: 'But conversely, what is perhaps being currently reconsidered, is the form of closure that used to be called "ideology" (a concept no doubt to be analysed in its function, its history, its provenance, its transformations), the form of the relations between a transformed concept of "infrastructure", *if you like*, of which the general text would no longer be the "effect" or "reflection"*, and the transformed concept of the "ideological" ' (p. 125 [90]); my emphasis on 'if you like', which Gasché excises from his quotation of the passage (p. 147). It is hard to see in this a very strong invitation, and Gasché's rather proud claim

that 'The notion of infrastructures has not yet been picked up by any of those who have written on Derrida' (p. 7) might not signal such perspicacity on his part after all. In *Positions*, the note added (by the editors of *Promesse* for the first appearance of this interview) to the asterisk in the above quote quotes *De la grammatologie* saying simply, 'Now we know that these exchanges pass only through language and text, in the infrastructural sense we now accord this word' (p. 234 [164]): but this adjectival usage scarcely justifies Gasché's nominalization of such a loaded term.

42. See also note 25, above.

43. *De la grammatologie*, p. 16 [6–7]: 'Not that the word "writing" ceases to designate the signifier of the signifier, but it appears in a strange light that "signifier of the signifier" ceases to define accidental redoubling and fallen secondariness. To the contrary, "signifier of the signifier" describes the movement of language: in its origin, certainly, but one already has the premonition that an origin whose structure is spelled out thus – signifier of signifier – carries itself off and effaces itself in its own production. The signified here functions always already as a signifier . . . '. See too pp. 46 [30], 63 [43], and 65 [44] for further hints.

44. Norris's New Accents volume gives the puzzled reader no sense at all of why Derrida should have kept the term 'writing', except out of provocation and loose analogy, informing misleading approximations such as, 'What is repressed [in Saussure], along with "writing" in its common or restricted sense, is the idea of language as a signifying system which exceeds all the bounds of individual "presence" and speech' (p. 27: the second part of this sentence is really quite a novel reading of Saussure), or '. . . showing that writing cannot be reduced to its normal (i.e. graphic or inscriptional) sense. As Derrida deploys it, the term is closely related [but how?] to that element of signifying *difference* which Saussure thought essential to the workings of language. Writing, for Derrida, is [but why??] the "free play" or element of undecidability within every system of communication' (p. 28); these claims will never make anyone understand why 'Writing is that which exceeds – and has the power to dismantle – the whole traditional edifice of Western attitudes to thought and language' (p. 29). This precise moment in the Modern Masters volume is equally obscure: 'It may then become clear how the individual speech-act (*parole*) presupposes a grasp of those signifying contrasts and relationships which make up the structure of language as a whole (*la langue*). Speech, that is to say, is already inscribed in a differential system which must always be in place before communication begins. And this system is very like writing, in the sense that written signs have traditionally been thought of as marks of difference, supplementarity and non-self-present meaning' (p. 92), leaving the student in the position of Hjelmslev, of whom Derrida says in *De la grammatologie* (p. 89 [60]), 'He would not have understood why the name writing remained to that X which becomes so different from what one has always called "writing".'

45. We are indebted for our understanding of Norris's early misunderstandings to Nick Royle's excellent review, 'Nor is Deconstruction', *OLR*, 5:1–2 (1982), 170–7. In a review of this whole issue of *OLR* (*Literature and History*, 10:1 (1984), 134–6), in the course of which he confides in the reader, as a serious-minded and above all concerned person, that he failed to get very far with the extracts of *Signsponge* also published in it, because he 'kept thinking about the women of Greenham Common, and decided life was too short', Terry Eagleton (himself thoroughly upbraided in Norris's book), attacks Royle's 'esoteric possessiveness' and general elitism in what he describes as a 'rather shabby review' (p. 135). We admit to the suspicion that the (very common) equation of complexity and elitism betrays the real (and, in every sense, *pathetic*) elitism of equating the popular and the simple.

46. This 'rhetoricizing' view is in fact the general matrix of all the mistakes in Norris's earlier book (and the basis for his critique of Eagleton), and also appears in Norris's *The Deconstructive Turn: Essays in the Rhetoric of Philosophy* (London: Methuen 1983), specifically on p. 35: '. . . rhetoric (or "writing" in Derrida's terminology)': for a clear statement of different intent in the later book (which could almost be a quotation from Gasché), see *Derrida*, p. 22: see too pp. 82, 108 and 170 for comments which can be taken as criticism of his own earlier work. This again marks a shift from his earlier thinking: *The*

Deconstructive Turn has a 'Methodological postscript: deconstruction versus interpretation' (pp. 163–73), which is precisely concerned to argue against Gasché's 'purism'.

47. For the question of technology, see *De l'esprit*, p. 26. This type of insistence should make it clear that the 'quasi' here affecting transcendentals is not to be confused with Habermas's usage in *Knowledge and Human Interests*, tr. J. Schapiro (London: Heinemann 1972), pp. 194–5, discussed in Garbis Kortian, *Metacritique: The Philosophical Argument of Jürgen Habermas*, tr. John Raffan (Cambridge: Cambridge University Press 1980), pp. 105–8, and devastated by Gillian Rose, *Hegel Contra Sociology* (London: Athlone 1981), pp. 34–6, who shows that Habermas's 'quasi-' marks a relativizing, naturalistic limitation on the transcendental: this is quite unlike Derrida's thinking, as could be shown by tracking the similarities of Habermas's argument with Foucault's 'historical *a priori*', which escapes none of the problems raised by Derrida's 'Cogito et histoire de la folie' (*L'Ecriture et la différence*, pp. 51–97 [31–63]). A starker sense of how little Habermas can understand Derrida is given by the former's ill-informed and loose arguments in *The Philosophical Discourse of Modernity* (Cambridge: Polity Press 1988).

48. See *Marges*, p. 375 [316].

49. For 'I am mortal', see *La Voix et la phénomène* (Paris: PUF 1967); tr. David B. Allison (Evanston: Northwestern University Press 1973), pp. 60–1 [54–5]; for 'I am dead', see ibid., pp. 107–8 [96–7].

50. See *De la grammatologie*, pp. 68–9 [47]. Cf. too *La Dissémination*, p. 90 [80–1].

51. This is the problem raised in the 'Question de méthode' section of *De la grammatologie* with respect to Rousseau (pp. 230–1 [160–1]), and more especially in the earlier 'Introduction à l'époque de Rousseau' (pp. 145–8 [97–100]).

52. Terry Eagleton includes himself in a list of the century's major Marxist aestheticians in *Walter Benjamin . . .*, p. 96, and uses 'Plato to NATO', among other occurrences, on p. 141 of the same book.

53. Spivak, 'Love me . . . ', p. 19 and n1. This sort of thing makes us glad for the transcendentalizing Gasché. We would always recommend preference of the transcendental over the anthropologizing reading of Derrida, were it always possible to tell them apart.

54. We only insist on those moments of misreading which affect the general argument as we are following it: there are others; on p. 70 Harvey takes the phrase '*In fact*, but also for *reasons of essence*' to imply an equation or coincidence of fact and essence; on p. 94 she goes into a Heideggerian-toned 'interrogation' of Derrida's question from 'The Supplement of Copula', 'Is philosophic discourse ruled', providing the French, 'Le discours philosophique est-il réglé?' to make sure we've got it right: but the immediate context of this in fact shows Derrida asking 'the classical question: is philosophical discourse ruled – to what point and according to what modalities – by the constraints of language?' (*Marges*, p. 211 [177]), which is hardly the same question, and shows an exploitation of detachability from context which might have been pointed out in a 'philosophical' presentation; on pp. 119–20 she blows an excellent presentation of the argument for a certain ideality of the signifier by concluding, falsely, that 'the essence of the "pure" signifier is always already a signified'; we have seen her attribute Derrida's gloss on Rousseau's view of animality to Derrida himself, and find it 'ironic' that Derrida should think this; she does the same with childhood on p. 223, and with history and evil on p. 224. We do not mention examples of misreading induced by reliance on inaccurate translations, which can be found especially on pp. 59 (relying on translation of 'l'on serait en droit' as 'it is *right*') and 159.

55. Derrida's essay 'Une Idée de Flaubert: La lettre de Platon' (*Psyché*, pp. 305–25) happily recognizes an essential link between philosophy and Flaubertian stupidity.

56. This is the substance of Eagleton's argument directed against Lyotard's recent use of Kant, in a paper delivered to the IAPL 'Writing the Future' conference, University of Warwick, 1986.

57. For a notable exception, see T.J.A. Clark, 'Time After Time: Temporality, Temporalization', *OLR*, 9 (1987), 119–35.

58. 'Origin of the experience of space and time, this writing of difference, this tissue of the trace allows the difference between space and time to be articulated, to appear as

such in the unity of an experience (of a "same" lived experience on the basis of a "same" body proper).' *De la grammatologie*, pp. 96 [65–6].

59. *L'Ecriture et la différence*, pp. 15–16 [7]. For the imagination as a complex point of proximity between Kant and Hegel, see 'Le Puits et la pyramide: introduction à la sémiology de Hegel' (*Marges*, pp. 81–127 [69–108]), pp. 89–91 [78–9]. See too Melville, p. 51–2. Harvey, (pp. 142–6) having duly quoted Kant, again rather perilously uses the analysis of imagination in Rousseau out of context to stand for Derrida's thought. Derrida discusses the imagination in Husserl in *La Voix et le phénomène*, pp. 48–9 [43–5].

60. Martin Heidegger, *Kant and the Problem of Metaphysics*, tr. James S. Churchill (Bloomington: Indiana University Press 1962), §33, point b).

61. This is also explicitly Derrida's point about the 'originary passivity' of parole, in *De la grammatologie*, p. 97 [66].

62. Emmanuel Levinas, 'Jacques Derrida: Tout Autrement', in *Noms Propres* (Montpellier: Fata Morgana 1976; rpt. Paris: *Le Livre de Poche* 1987), pp. 65–75. This text is the object of an extensive unpublished commentary by Simon Critchley. The question of the future in Derrida is complex, and we fear that Norris (*Derrida*, pp. 140–1, on the end of 'La Structure, le signe et le jeu') mistakes the problem here. See too David Krell, *Intimations of Mortality* (Penn State University Press 1986), and our own 'Towards a Criticism of the Future', Chapter 12 below.

63. See '*Geschlecht*', p. 412 [81].

64. It may well be that, along with their readings of Levinas, their uses of 'the Idea in the Kantian sense' would be a promising place to start a reading of Derrida with Lyotard. We cannot begin that here.

65. Ulmer (see note 10, above) thinks that Grammatology is applicable and thus can and does already exist.

66. See, for a typically robust example of this widespread type of reaction, Allon White, 'Bakhtin, Sociolinguistics and Deconstruction', in Frank Gloversmith, ed., *The Theory of Reading* (Brighton: Harvester 1984), pp. 123–46 (p. 140): 'The luxury of "endless deferral" is only available to those who play with themselves in the abstract idealist realm of "language". The real social difference of heteroglossia in fact puts a swift end to the unmotivated "*différance*" of Derridean discourse: Derridean "*différance*" evaporates once you move from "langue" to "parole", or from competence to performances'. See Robert Young's criticisms in 'Back to Bakhtin', *Cultural Critique*, 2 (Winter 1985–6), 71–92 (pp. 80–3). Derrida would reply in fairly straightforwardly phenomenological terms to this type of criticism: 'One often sees the descriptive practice of the "human sciences" mix up, in the most seductive confusion (in all senses of seductive), empirical inquiry, inductive hypothesis and intuition of essence, without any precaution being taken as to the origin and function of the propositions put forward' (*L'Ecriture et la différence*, p. 189n1 [316n46]). The same type of argument rules out in principle the rather simplistic appeal to political or 'historical' 'grounds' which informs all of Eagleton's discussion, and, for example, Colin MacCabe's comments on Derrida in his Foreword to Gayatri Chakravorty Spivak, *In Other Worlds: Essays in Cultural Politics* (New York and London: Methuen 1987), p. xi, where, after an unintelligible half-sentence summary of Derrida's 'rigorous forms of analysis', MacCabe goes on: 'Derrida elaborated this work in the context of Heidegger's meditation on Being and in an attempt to recapture the revolutionary potential of a series of the key texts of literary modernism – Mallarmé, Artaud, Joyce, a project which found its rationale in the situation of France in the 1960's . . . that period . . . was in large part a reaction both to the sudden advent of consumer capitalism under De Gaulle and the widely perceived exhaustion within the French Communist Party.' The extent to which the confusion evident in such a description has informed most non-'deconstructionist' accounts of deconstruction is one of the reasons for our delight in these philosophical books; and if this is anything like what 'historicizing' deconstruction means, give us 'American deconstruction' any time.

67. The difficulties here are played out between the assertion on the one hand that 'Death is the movement of *différance* in so far as it is necessarily finite' (p. 206 [143]), and, on the other, that if the 'power' of *différance* were to become infinite – which its essence

excludes *a priori* – life itself would be reduced to an impassive, intangible and eternal presence: infinite *différance*, God or death' (p. 191 [131]). See too pp. 99 and 108 (68 and 73]. Infinite *différance* is the same as no *différance*, and this is why both ends of this 'scale' can be called both God and death. *Différance* thus exceeds description in terms of finite and infinite and necessarily generates paradoxes and aporias when approached in the language of metaphysics. This also implies the necessary interruption of the Idea in the Kantian sense and its relation to the transcendental, and suggests that the most important thing about the conclusion to Derrida's *Origin of Geometry* Introduction, 'Transcendentale serait la Diffrence' (p. 171 [153]), is the tense of the verb.

68. 'The notion of totality always refers to the essent [*l'étant*]. It is always "metaphysical" or "theological" and it is in relation to it that the notions of finite and infinite get their meaning' (*L'Ecriture et la différence*, p. 207 [141]). In a note appended to this statement, Derrida refers to Henri Birault's demonstration that Heidegger progressively abandons the appeal to finitude as too onto-theological, and adds the following, which leaves the question of the relationship between Derrida and Heidegger as mysterious as ever: 'A thinking which wants to go to its own furthest extent [*au bout d'elle-même*] in its language, to the furthest extent of what it is aiming at under the name of originary finitude or the finitude of Being, ought therefore to abandon not only the words and themes of the finite and the infinite but, what is no doubt *impossible*, all they command in language (in the profoundest senses of this word). This last impossibility does not mean that the beyond of metaphysics and onto-theology is barred to all access [*impraticable*]; it confirms the necessity that this incommensurable overflowing push off from within metaphysics. A necessity clearly recognized by Heidegger. It marks clearly that only difference is fundamental and that Being is nothing outside the essence'. (pp. 208–9n2 [317–8n70]). Compare the slightly mysterious avatars of the reference to Birault (in the absence of reference to this note of Derrida's), in Gasché's 'Joining the Text: From Heidegger to Derrida' (in Arac, Godzich and Martin, eds, *The Yale Critics: Deconstruction in America* (Minneapolis: University of Minnesota Press 1983), 156–75 (174n4)), and in his book, pp. 316–7. It is unclear to us, in view of Derrida's note, how Gasché can take Derrida's 'persistent critique of the notion of finitude' (p. 317) as 'proof' that his quasitranscendentals are not finite whereas Heidegger's transcendentals are. It seems a mark of final impatience that the term 'critique' should reappear here on the penultimate page of Gasché's book. In both the article and the book, Gasché pins the essential difference between Heidegger and Derrida to the latter's 'passage to the order of discourse of philosophy' ('Joining the Text', p. 173), or 'inquiry into the conditions of the possibility and impossibility of the logic of philosophy as a discursive enterprise' (*The Tain of the Mirror . . .* , p. 317). Even though Gasché includes in his notion of discourse 'the conceptual, rhetorical, argumentative, and textual order of philosophy as the thought of unity' (ibid.), this appeal to discourse would appear to fall back short of all the earlier insistence, against the literary appropriation of Derrida, on the non-empirical and non-phenomenologizable nature of Derrida's 'text'. We are far from sure that the difference between Heidegger and Derrida can be specified so rapidly.

69. There may of course be strategic or economic grounds for preference among terms: see in 'Cartouches' Derrida's dropping of (what just happens to be) the term 'contingent' for the term 'lot' (*La Vérité en peinture*, pp. 230 and 275 [200 and 239]), the second of these words provoking a reference to chance (contingency?) and necessity (lot?). Beware of the common mistake of assuming that Derrida shifts his terms simply because of a sense that they are going stale and that a change would be good. *Supplement*, for example, is as good a term today for the reading of Rousseau as it was in 1967: the temporality of its rightness is that of the text, not of simple chronological time.

70. See Derrida's second essay on Levinas, 'En ce moment même dans cet ouvrage me voici', in *Psyché . . .* , pp. 159–202 (translation Ruben Berezdevin, forthcoming).

71. On this question of pathos, see the exchange between Derrida and Lyotard transcribed in *Les Fins de l'homme*, pp. 311–3.

72. For a discussion of Being as rhythm in Heidegger and Mallarmé, see Gasché, 'Joining the text . . . ', p. 162, and see also Derrida, for example *La Dissémination*, pp. 204–5 and n3, 293, 312 and n64 [178 and n4, 251, 276 and n76] and, implicitly at

least, *L'Ecriture et la différence*, pp. 334–5 [226], and in the discussion of the fort/da game in *Spéculer* . . . . One of the many 'chances' of Derrida's extraordinary 'Mes Chances' (*Tijdschrift voor Filosofie*, 45e Jaargang, Nummer 1 (1983) 3–40; tr. in Smith and Kerrigan, eds., *Taking Chances: Derrida, Psychoanalysis, and Literature* (Baltimore: Johns Hopkins University Press 1984), pp. 1–32) is that it refers to Heidegger's reference to Democritus's *rhythmos* (p. 14 [9]). Rhythm, inseparable from stricture, is also everywhere in *Glas*: see, provisionally, pp. 174b; 216b [154b].

73. See 'Mes Chances' for perhaps the most extended discussion of this question. We might risk the provisional claim that for Derrida necessity is that there be chance. We are quite sure that this is where to start addressing questions of freedom and ethics in Derrida: these questions also involve questions of the event and of literature: see 'Mes Chances', p. 22 [extremely inaccurately translated, p. 16].

74. We think that all of this is compatible with the excellent but still very preliminary piece by Robert Bernasconi, 'Deconstruction and the Possibility of Ethics', in *Deconstruction and Philosophy*, pp. 122–39: see especially the last sentence of the text: 'But we find the ethical enactment above all in the way deconstruction ultimately refuses to adopt the standpoint of critique, renouncing the passing of judgements on its own behalf in its own voice' (p. 136) – here the 'ultimately' is vital.

75. The place of hilarity in *Le Rouge et le noir*, as 'hilarious performative reading', has been admirably shown by Ann Jefferson, 'Stendhal and the Uses of Reading: *Le Rouge et le noir*', in *French Studies*, Vol. 37, No. 2 (1983), pp. 168–83.

76. See *Parages*, p. 10, saying of the 'place' mentioned in the passage quoted above, 'they leave no chance, and no right can be recognized in them to any divide between literature and philosophy. A proposition which does not forbid, and on the contrary requires new and rigorous distinctions, a whole redistribution of spaces (be it said to those who would wish to take find their advantage from this proposition, all sorts of advantages and they are always those of confusion)'.

77. Notably 'Le Facteur de la vérité' (in *La Carte postale*), and 'Le Supplément de copule' and 'La Mythologie blanche' (in *Marges*).

78. This theme of the double affirmation is elaborated in a number of recent pieces: see for example the end of 'Pas', the essay 'Ulysse Gramophone', and the piece in memory of Michel de Certeau ('Nombre de Oui', in *Psyché* . . . , pp. 639–50).

2

Demanding History

History is demanding.

It is difficult, it makes demands. Saying that it 'makes demands' implies that history can be positioned as the sender, the *destinateur*, of prescriptive sentences, sentences the addressee and referent of which can vary.

History is also demanded.

Here history is no longer the sender of prescriptions, but their referent: this time sender and addressee are variable. A third possibility would make of history the addressee of a demand, that, for example, it deliver up its meaning or its secrets, leaving sender and referent unspecified.

Of these three possibilities, the first, in which history makes the demands, could be used to explain the writing and delivery of this paper: if I gave this type of justification, I would position myself (or, more accurately, would be positioned by the text) as history's addressee, and my 'subject' would be positioned as the referent of the demand. Anecdotally, this would mean that history prescribed, or seemed to prescribe, that in the current 'conjuncture', I, or whoever else heard the demand, should consider something like 'history and deconstruction'. This scene is immediately complicated, however, in that 'history', which in this hypothesis or story is the sender of the prescription, reappears in the position of referent. History said 'Talk about me'. And if one accepted, with Jean-François Lyotard, that the meaning, the *sens*, of a sentence constitutes a fourth pragmatic 'pole' or 'post',[1] and if it were decided that the *sens* could also be named as 'history', then the complication would have spread.

Further, if the simplicity or propriety of the name 'history' were to be questioned, in other words if it were to be positioned as addressee and referent of a new demand (a demand as to its meaning in these pragmatic scenes), and it were to be shown that neither that addressee nor that referent were stable, but divided (at least into the standard

61

ambiguity according to which 'history' names both a specific discourse
and the referent of that discourse); and if then the word were itself
'historicized' and the specificity of that 'specific' discourse were shown
to be problematic (with respect to the division between 'truth' and
'fiction', for example), then the reapplication of these divisions to each
occurrence of the word 'history' in all the possible permutations of the
pragmatic scene would generate a proliferation of possibilities, each of
which would in some sense inhabit all the others, and all further
sentences, such as these, which attempted to position as their referent
one or more of the pragmatic possibilities thus generated.

The specific pragmatic 'scene' I want to consider is extracted more
or less violently from this set of possibilities. A variation on the second
of the three 'primal' scenes with which I began is what I shall discuss at
greatest length. Here history is not the sender of the demand, but only
its referent: an unspecified sender says, 'Talk about history', to an
unspecified addressee. The scenario I want to look at is one in which
the sender of that prescription is something that might be called 'the
Left', or possibly 'Marxism' (as for example in Jameson's *Political
Unconscious*, the first two words of which are simply, 'Always historicize!'),[2] and the addressee something that might be called 'post-
structuralism', and especially 'deconstruction'. So I'm inflecting and
condensing the title of the book for which this essay was written: *Post-
Structuralism and the Question of History* becomes something like 'The
Left puts the question of History to Deconstruction' or 'The Left
demands History of Deconstruction'. The working hypothesis is that
the sender of the prescription would like post-structuralism and
especially deconstruction to 'come clean' about history: and that this
would also involve coming clean about historical materialism, about
Marxism, and thereby about the sender of the prescription.

This still involves a certain number of worrying presuppositions,
notably that the proper names occupying the two poles of the pragmatic scene not occupied by 'history' (i.e. the poles of sender and
addressee) are any more stable than it. 'Deconstruction' may seem to
have a more precisely locatable referent than 'post-structuralism', but
is none the less not an unequivocal name for a unified movement. Even
if (as is largely the case here) that name is used as a metonym for
'Derrida's work', the unity presupposed is only guaranteed by the
fragile promise of a signature. But if the scenario I have set up is not
entirely fictitious, then my excuse comes from the demand for history
itself, in so far as 'the Left' or 'Marxism' tends to presuppose some such
unity, and indeed to hypostatize it in the name 'deconstruction*ism*'.
The last of the three names involved in the scenario is no less unstable,
as my hesitation between 'the Left', 'Marxism' and 'historical material-

ism' suggests. Here again the justification is given less by my foisting a false unity on what is clearly a heterogeneous and conflictual movement, than by the desire of most of the identifiable atoms in that movement to represent the whole, to secure the unity of a body or the rights over a legacy.

The scenario is not entirely a fiction, and might therefore be described as itself 'historical'. Terry Eagleton's recent book on literary theory chides Derrida's work for being 'grossly unhistorical',[3] and elsewhere, in an often-repeated joke, of making history seem the same all the way from 'Plato to NATO'. This, along with the charge of 'idealism' (as for example in Coward and Ellis's *Language and Materialism*),[4] is fairly standard of Left reactions, and I'm not going to provide any detailed documentation of it here. Nor am I going to attempt to make out a case for the inaccuracy of this type of charge, although it would not be difficult to construct an argument showing that deconstruction, in so far as it insists on the necessary non-coincidence of the present with itself, is in fact in some senses the most historical of discourses imaginable. Nor would it be difficult to argue that deconstruction escapes the hold of the idealism/materialism opposition. I shall also try to resist the temptation of denouncing a very general tendency to present the operation of deconstruction as a 'critique' (of Western Metaphysics, say), of assuming that 'logocentrism' is just another word for 'idealism' (this in attempts to 'save' Derrida, or some of him, for or by materialism), and of thinking that, in Derrida's usage, 'writing' and 'text' mean the same as what others call 'discourse'.[5] Instead, I shall narrow down the scenario still further and consider something like the (hi)story of the 'Left's' engagement with deconstruction, especially with respect to its own representations of history. This restriction will seem only the more excessive in that I shall appeal to only a very small part of the available evidence, ignoring notably almost all the recent American work on the subject (and particularly Michael Ryan's recent book *Marxism and Deconstruction*),[6] and concentrate on recent work by Terry Eagleton, whom I take to be the British Marxist who has most clearly *taken on* deconstruction, in both senses of the expression 'to take on'.

But even if these simplifying assumptions reintroduce a fictive element into the historical scenario, they are not entirely unmotivated: for if the demand for history is made along the lines of this scenario, and if the Left would indeed like 'deconstruction' to 'come clean', this is motivated by a concern for its own unity and propriety. The assumption of, or desire for, a unity of 'Marxism' or 'the Left' is quite constant in the most incompatible elements which would locate themselves as 'Left' or 'Marxist'. If 'the Left', or that shifting and unstable consensus called 'Marxism', wants an answer to its question or obedience to its demand, then this is in the interests of its own constitution (or institution) *as* 'the Left' or 'Marxism'. It seems necessary to be able to *locate* deconstruction in terms of the polarities of 'Right' and 'Left', or 'Idealism' and 'Materialism', or, more precisely, to be able to 'appropriate' it (it seems to be characteristic of Marxism to assume at least the *possibility* of an 'appropriation' of a type of discourse which has expended not inconsiderable energy undermining the notion of 'appropriation') to incorporate it, or else, if the question remains unanswered or the demand unmet, to reject or expel it. If deconstruction were to come clean (which would already imply some notion of appropriation) then it would be easier to decide, from a given position in the topological space of 'the Left', whether the apparently radical and subversive nature of deconstruction is truly or only apparently radical and subversive (the nature of the truly radical and subversive being largely pre-comprehended), to see which bits might be taken on board and used, and which denounced or ignored.

The metaphorics of 'coming clean' and of 'appropriation' here are in themselves paradoxical, given a pervasive and contrary metaphorics of dirt and baseness in Left discussions of history. Jameson talks about the 'ash-can' of history, for example, to which non-recuperable remains of non-dialectical theories will at some point have to be consigned.[7] Or in one of the best essays in the recent *Re-Reading English* volume, Tony Bennett wants to disrupt E.M. Forster's ideal and timeless reading room with 'the muddied boots of history'.[8] Eagleton, in the book on Benjamin,[9] talks about materialists' 'grubby hands', and of prising open ideological encirclement 'in order to allow a whiff of history to enter and contaminate the aesthetic purity of its premisses' (pp. 109 and 89). And again, in the recent *Literary Theory* book, he refers to Northrop Frye's desire to keep literature 'untainted by history' (p. 92), away from the 'sordid "externalities" of referential language' (p. 93).

Of course the use of language such as this is a rhetorical ploy, involving a strategic use of a certain representation, which I think is largely justified, of the language of the other, the 'enemy', the idealist. But the link it suggests between history and what is low (which should probably have to be referred to Marx's claim to have 'inverted' Hegel's dialectic, to have pulled the claims of the spirit down to their material conditions; and referred too, of course, to the metaphorics of base and superstructure) is complicated if it is reapplied to the history of Marxism (materialism, the Left), not necessarily in the extreme and non-specific language of the 'purge', but in the image which might be constructed of Marxism as a body. In Eagleton's *Benjamin* book there is the following characterization of Eliot's 'tradition':

> Eliot's tradition is a self-equilibrating organism extended in space and time, eternally replete but constantly absorptive, like a grazing cow or the Hegelian Idea. Perhaps it is most usefully visualized as a large, bulbous amoeba, whose pulsating body inflates and deflates, changes colours, relations and proportions, as it digests. (p. 54)

What such a description leaves out (and in leaving it out it is doubtless true to the discourse it describes) is any notion that a body not only absorbs but also excretes: add that function, and the characterization will do as a description of the 'body' of 'Marxism', which both secures and compromises its unity and integrity as a body by ingesting and expelling or excreting, leaving behind it a trail of what it was in the form of the waste-product, the *déchet*, the dropping. The history of what Marxism itself expels as its own 'deviations' (due to absorption of foreign bodies) or its own 'vulgar' versions (generated by internal or intestinal malfunctions), could persuasively be read, in eminently materialist terms, as a history of digestion and eventually of shit. Marxism as a history of digestion would of course have to begin with the digestion of Hegel, which is probably not yet complete: remember a famous letter from Engels on this.[10] Deconstruction has not yet been digested by the Left, I think, although there is a certain amount of rumbling in the intestines as the useful and nourishing is separated from the rubbish or roughage: but take as an example of what could be its fate a comment Althusser made on his own 'structuralist' deviation from the line, in his *Eléments d'Autocritique*: 'Et c'est sans doute à cette occasion que le sous-produit circonstantiel de ma tendance théoriciste, le jeune chiot du structuralisme, nous a filé entre les jambes.'[11] The history of 'Marxism', which is of course not necessarily identical with the history demanded by Marxism, can be read in these terms: and the link with what it denounces and rejects as 'vulgar' versions of itself is not far away.

There are many forms of ingestion and appropriation, and they all imply a concomitant expulsion. They range from what may seem to be 'merely verbal' borrowings of the term 'deconstruction' (used by, for example, Raymond Williams, to mean simply 'decoding' or 'decipherment' in an attack on some forms of semiology),[12] elsewhere to refer to any form of radical questioning or analysis (as in Peter Widdowson's presentation of the *Re-Reading English* volume),[13] sometimes explicitly connected with questionable accounts of what Derrida is reputed to say and with what's right or wrong with it (as in Catherine Belsey's *Critical Practice*[14] or Peter Brooker's essay in *Re-Reading English*[15]).

Let me return from this brief detour (which will have left its own remains) to the pragmatic scenario I sketched out a moment ago. The motivation for this scenario can, as I said, be found or constructed in the two words which open Jameson's *The Political Unconscious*, and which are, simply enough, 'Always historicize!' This is the demand. Jameson goes on to qualify it with a sentence which is no longer prescriptive but descriptive or constative, describing this primary prescription as 'the one absolute and we may even say "transhistorical" imperative of all dialectical thought'.[16] This description again complicates the pragmatic scene: the descriptive qualification of the prescription precludes that prescription's subsequent reappearance as the referent of a repeated version of itself. You can't historicize the prescription which demands that you *always* historicize. This limitation seems to be a necessary qualification of any apparently radical historicizing position, if infinite regress is to be avoided.[17] It is a version of this limitation that allows Althusser to claim that the concept of history is not itself historical (although his reasoning in support of that claim is more than dubious).[18] It also seems reasonable to suppose that this primary prescription requires its transcendental or 'transhistorical' status if it is to ground anything like a *theory*. This is also, broadly speaking, the position of Eagleton's *Criticism and Ideology*,[19] where it becomes clear that the demand for history and its transhistorical rider describe the strategy of appealing to a 'last instance' and a 'last analysis': in *Criticism and Ideology* this demand is also the claim for science, and what science finds in the last instance is history, the 'ultimate object' of the text (p. 74), the 'source and referent' of signifying practices (p. 75), literature's 'ultimate signifier' and 'ultimate signified' (p. 72). This transcendental position for history is confirmed when Eagleton writes, 'ideological space is curved like space itself, and history lies beyond it as only God could lie beyond the universe' (p. 95). History has to be saved against 'the notion that the text is simply a ceaselessly self-signifying practice', which 'stands four square with the bourgeois mythology of individual freedom' (p. 73).

It is clear that since *Criticism and Ideology*, Eagleton has been retreating from its general scientism. In the *Walter Benjamin* book, for example, he describes historical materialism as a 'rhetoric' (p. 112). But that same book retains the desire to save history, in some form, from deconstruction and textuality, still seen as homologous with bourgeois liberalism (p. 138). However, if the chapter in which this denunciation of deconstruction is made can be read as a gesture of expulsion, there is plenty of evidence in the rest of the book of ingestion and appropriation, and this is nowhere clearer than in Eagleton's reflections on the relationship of history to narrative and textuality, within which the double gesture of ingestion and expulsion is repeated.

This discussion is preceded by a warning, based on a consideration of Benjamin's essay, 'The Story-Teller': Eagleton sees this essay as 'something of an embarrassment to those who would press [Benjamin] unequivocally into the service of an anti-narrational "textuality", enlist him in the ranks of those modernists or post-modernists for whom narrativity is no more than the suspension and recuperation of an imaginary unity' (p. 60). The important word here is probably 'unequivocally', and if 'equivocality' is treated as a first step towards dissemination and textuality, then Eagleton might be said to dramatize such a move in his writing, for the pages that follow are indeed far from unequivocal. A first step here links the storyteller to the figure of the collector (the link being established through a play on the notion that the story is a *collective* genre), and the collector is already a textualizer; 'The collector is a modernist in so far as he or she breaks with the suave schemas of the museum catalogue in the name of a fiercely idiosyncratic passion that fastens on the contingent and unregarded. Collecting is in this sense a kind of creative digression from classical narrative, a "textualising" of history that reclaims repressed and unmapped areas' (p. 61). A brief consideration of quotation, in which signifiers are 'torn from their signified and then flexibly recomposed to weave fresh correspondences across language' (p. 65), leads to the direct discussion of history and of the narrative/textuality alternative.

The ambivalence of the approach is further complicated in that it is not always clear what exactly the referent of the argument is here; whether it is 'Marxism', 'historical materialism' or 'history (itself)' which is to be described as either narrative or text. Eagleton begins the discussion by allowing that Marxism appears at first 'to take up its rank among the great narrative constructs of history' (pp. 63–4), where the duplicity of the genitive already leaves open the possibility of seeing Marxism as a way of constructing history as a narrative, or else as a more or less local narrative construct within history. Eagleton's mildly parodic sketch of this version of history (or Marxism, or historical materialism) as 'the mighty world-historical plot of humankind's primordial unity, subsequent alienation, revolutionary redemption and ultimate self-recovery in the realm of communism' (p. 64) could well be read as a pastiche of Jameson. Here Eagleton consigns the authority for this type of reading to Marx's 'early writings', and will draw firstly on the *Grundrisse* and subsequently on the *18th Brumaire* to counter it (the latter said to contain 'the seeds of a theory of historical textuality' (p. 68): no reference is made here to Mehlman's *Revolution and Repetition*,[20] but, characteristically of the strategy of ingestion and expulsion, the book is later roundly criticized by Eagleton (p. 162)). The text cited from the *Grundrisse* pushes towards an apparently 'genealogical' account of history, although Eagleton finds in the text 'a symptomatic maladjustment here between figure and discourse, a shadowy fault-line along with Marx's text might be deconstructed' (p. 65). This possibility of deconstruction (and there is no reason to think that the word is not used in a Derridean way) *already* opts for the 'text' rather than the narrative: but what is so far recognised as text is Marx's text, not history 'itself'. On the other hand, it is not easy to see how that referent could still reasonably be described as other than textual if the writing which 'theorizes' it (in fact to the extent that it is a text this theory cannot *simply* be a 'theory' in a strong sense of that word) is described as textual. But there are tensions in Eagleton's account, in that he is wary of any such generalized textuality, and wants to reconcile what textuality he concedes with a certain narrativity, which he cannot do without, as we shall see: this limited acceptance of textuality enables Eagleton to avoid the 'great human adventure' naiveties of a Jameson, [21] but the retention of narrativity generates a number of political problems.

But before this restitution of a measured narrativity, Eagleton looks more closely at the notion of textuality. Now there is an inversion, in that it is history 'itself' which becomes a sort of full-blown text in the form of a heterogeneous excess over the now only *limited* textuality of the Marxist discourse which is none the less seen as 'producing' that text of history in its heterogeneity. The 'heterogeneity' of history is adduced (and again this could be read against Jameson) against 'those who draw on the past for their utopias' (p. 68), and who thereby '[subdue] the heterogeneous movement of history to the enthralment of an *eschaton*' (p. 68). This type of teleological or eschatalogical construction of history allows the text describing or theorizing the text of history to be in excess of the text of history it describes or theorizes: in Marx's words, which Eagleton quotes, it allows 'the phrase to go beyond the content'. Against this, Eagleton writes that 'for Marxism, however, [note how Eagleton carries out this operation of appropriation on Marxism too: what he is going to claim is of course not true of all Marxism or of all Marxisms] the "text" of revolutionary history is not foreclosed in this way: it lacks the symmetrical shape of narrative, dispersed as it is into a textual heterogeneity ("the content goes beyond the phrase") by the absence around which it turns – the absence of an *eschaton* present in each of its moments' (pp. 68–9). This provokes what seems to me to be an important conclusion, namely that 'The authority of socialist revolution . . . is not to be located in the past, least of all in the texts of Marx himself, but in the intentionality of its transformative practice, its ceaseless "beginning"' (p. 69).[22] This non-narrative but multiple and heterogeneous history is supported a little later by the observation that 'it is of crucial importance that the founding economic document of Marxism [meaning of course *Capital*], unlike that of Christianity, is not a narrative' (p. 69: it is not clear how this antithesis works in view of the fact that the Bible is not an 'economic document', or at least not in the restricted sense of 'economic' used here).

So 'revolutionary history' is a text. But what is 'revolutionary' about it is *not* the textuality of history, but, oddly enough, a reinstated version of narrative. By writing history as text, Eagleton has moved towards a position which he has consistently linked to bourgeois liberal pluralism. At this point he seems to be claiming that history is not a narrative but a text, and that Marxism too is not a narrative but a text. This is clearly too much text, and narrative now starts to reclaim some of its rights. In fact this reclaiming has already begun to the extent that the history which is described as a text is 'revolutionary history', in so far as the notion of 'revolution' presupposes narrative. So between the text quoted above on 'ceaseless beginning' and the odd antithesis of *Capital* and the Bible, Eagleton draws back from the textual position:

> This is not to reduce socialist revolution to a form of liberal pluralism. The aim of such politics is to abolish commodity production by the institution of workers' self-government, an aim involving the planned, exclusive 'narratives' of revolutionary organisation. (p. 69)

So Marxism now becomes a text of limited plurality (rather like the 'parsimonious plural' of classical narrative as described by Barthes in *S/Z*), which has what Eagleton calls an 'ironic' relationship with the · historical 'text', in so far as the Marxist narrative inevitably forecloses the now excessive (and in itself not foreclosed) 'textual' heterogeneity of history. The problem with this positioning is that the historical text is in fact projected as a *telos* (or an *eschaton*, to use Eagleton's term) by a narrative of revolution. History will only really be a text once it has become a narrative. Or, history is really a text but we pretend that it is a narrative. Or, the textuality of history exceeds narratives (even those of socialist revolution), and as that cannot be allowed to happen, then narratives must be restored.

Eagleton negotiates this nexus by marking a return to Jameson. First, he quotes *The Prison-House of Language* to equate the 'always already' of Derrida's text with the quite different question of the priority of material conditions over consciousness in Marxism. Eagleton himself finds this parallel a little too 'symmetrical' but lets it pass. Then he shifts to Althusser's own account of different historical times (referring to this as a 'deconstructed image of history') which he invokes as a sort of textuality. He does not recall that this particular 'textuality' is limited by the horizon of the social 'totality' in Althusser, and that it is heavily dependent on the science versus ideology distinction which the notion of textuality calls into question. Finally, he returns to the later Jameson to reinstate narrative as the unavoidable feature of ideology (ideology here in an Althusserian sense from which Eagleton again takes a purely gestural distance in a note), as an 'indispensable fantasy'. And here, perhaps unavoidably, the bad old political side of Althusser resurfaces, for it turns out that this 'indispensable fantasy' is indispensable to the proletariat's identity as a revolutionary class, and something that the 'we' who know better (who have somehow got science and can write the theory of their naive narratives) do well not to disturb. Here is the argument:

> The insertion of the subject into an ideological formation is, simultaneously, its access to a repertoire of narrative devices and conventions that help to provide it with a stable self-identity through time. We know ['we' the privileged subjects of knowledge and science] that the 'truth' of the subject has no such stable self-identity; the unconscious knows no narratives, even though it may instigate them. But this is not to argue that narrative is merely 'illusory', any more than we ['we' again] should chide the working-class movement for nurturing its mighty dramas of universal solidarity overcoming the evils of capitalism [the construction of this subject called 'the working-class movement' and of the 'mighty dramas of universal solidarity' are perhaps themselves fantasies of the other subject, the subject of knowledge and science]. And just as the individual subject is permitted [permitted, presumably, by 'us'] to construct for itself a coherent biography, so a revolutionary or potentially revolutionary class [the notion of the 'revolutionary class' *presupposes* the type of narrative fantasy which it is here supposed to account for] creates, across the structurally discontinuous social formations identified by Marxism, that 'fiction' of a coherent, continuous struggle which is Benjamin's 'tradition'. (p. 73)

It seems likely that the slightly sinister political implications of this position are a source of some worry to Eagleton, as he immediately needs to underline that this fiction 'is not a *lie*', and to argue that there are *some* continuities in real history, that they are not all simply 'mapping fantasies'. On the one hand, it is not at all clear what relevance this claim for a partial truth (as *adequatio*) for narratives can have, and on the other the claim that there are 'real' continuities could only ever be substantiated by writing more narratives and telling more stories: the politically most favourable logic to be drawn would seem to be that what counts is the *effectiveness* of such little stories, which are in any case no longer anything like 'mighty dramas' – but then 'we' would have no job left to do, as the pretence of science and the subsequent indulgence for proletarian fantasies would be meaningless. The claim to be able to discern the real continuities and thus to ground those fantasies at least partially in 'truth' depends simply on the illusion of an intelligentsia as subject of science to stand outside and above that reality and those fantasies. This is on its own terms not at all a historical or historicizing position: to rehistoricize *this* fantasy would be to see in it a story on the same level as others in the text, and to abandon any transcendental horizon, and with it, any notion of *telos, eschaton,* guarantees and dialectics.

Eagleton's strategy with respect to history and textuality seems no more satisfactory in his two most recent books. In *The Rape of Clarissa*[23] the double gesture returns: deconstruction is expelled along with the character Lovelace, who becomes a 'post-structuralist precursor', writing 'post-structuralist fictions' in a 'deconstructive style' (pp. 46, 61, 83), and although Richardson himself is an 'engagingly modern deconstructionist' (p. 22), Clarissa has to be saved from modern deconstruction, in the name of history. Eagleton warns that no reading which ignores the 'historical necessity' of the bourgeoisie's 'moral closure' (against the 'deathly dissemination' of the 'profligate force of the aristocratic pen and penis' (p. 84)) can 'fail to be moralistic' (ibid.). The success of Eagleton's own avoidance of this trap can perhaps be judged by his reference to Lovelace as 'this pathetic character' with a 'crippling incapacity for adult sexual relationship' (p. 63), or, in an aside on modern popular romantic fiction, references to 'such degraded fiction', its 'monstrously debased form' and its 'diseased impulse to transcendence' (p. 37).

Eagleton again takes on deconstruction in the most recent book, that on Literary Theory, and marks a double movement in this field of tension. On the one hand, there is a move back to simple narratives: Eagleton is concerned to write the narrative history of the rise of English studies in this country, to write 'the narrative of post-structuralism' (p. 148), here simplistically seen as 'born of' May 1968 (p. 142),[24] and even to write the narrative history of literary theory in general: 'The story of modern literary theory . . . is the narrative of a flight' from the realities of experience, and so on (p. 196). But against this move, a newly stressed notion of discourse as a question of power and strategy moves against the narrativizing tendency displayed by the book as a whole, and suggests that the narratives be read neither as the materialist truth of the matter, nor as a 'mapping fantasy' allowing Eagleton to live out his position with respect to the real conditions of his existence, but simply as a pragmatically determined move designed to obtain certain effects. This shift (already in fact anticipated in the *Benjamin* book's remarks on rhetoric) moves us far from any claim for science and last instances: 'It all depends on what you are trying to do, in what situation' (p. 211). This is perhaps why Eagleton now talks of 'political' and no longer 'revolutionary' criticism. The new emphasis seems to be on local situations and interventions nowhere subordinated to a centralizing agency or a master-narrative: 'There are many goals to be achieved, and many ways of achieving them' (p. 212). And although liberal pluralism is still liberally denounced, he asserts that 'radical' critics are also 'liberal' with respect to what texts or cultural practices should be looked at, and 'pluralists' about questions of theory and method (pp. 210–11). 'Structuralism, semiotics, psychoanalysis, deconstruction, reception theory and so on: all of these approaches, and others, have their valuable insights which may be put to use' (p. 211). Feminism and Marxism are privileged with respect to this series, but only by their absence: this absence is still worrying because it could easily become transcendence, a position beyond the game in which the moves constituted by other theories are played. And in a sense this type of transcendence is *already* implied by the (violent) serialization of those other theories, the suggestion of their ideal equivalence as instruments, or rhetorical strategies.[25] That this is all still ultimately subordinated to a great narrative of history is made clear in the book's closing paragraph, an allegory which runs as follows: '*We* know that the lion is stronger than the lion-tamer, and so does the lion-tamer. The problem is that the lion does not know it. It is not out of the question that the death of literature may help the lion to awaken' (p. 217). Here 'we' are again, outside the scene, all-seeing and knowing. We try to tell the lion that it is strong, that it should leap, roar, bite and devour: it opens one eye and yawns, recognizing another tamer when it sees one.

Notes

1. Lyotard's most rigorous formulation of these four 'posts' is to be found in *Le Différend*, Paris: Minuit 1984, (tr. Georges van den Abbeele, Minneapolis: University of Minnesota Press 1988). This paper was written for the *OLR*/Southampton conference in 1983 – I have not attempted to modify the text to take account of more recent work, which would not, however, lead to me make substantial changes to the argument.

2. Fredric Jameson, *The Political Unconscious*, London: Methuen 1981, p. 9.

3. Terry Eagleton, *Literary Theory: an Introduction*, Oxford: Basil Blackwell 1983, p. 148.

4. Rosalind Coward and John Ellis, *Language and Materialism*, London: Routledge & Kegan Paul 1977, p. 126.

5. For a generous sample of this sort of nonsense, see Michael Sprinker, 'Textual Politics: Foucault and Derrida', *Boundary* 2, 8 (1980), 75–98.

6. Michael Ryan, *Marxism and Deconstruction: A Critical Articulation*, Baltimore and London: Johns Hopkins University Press 1982. I have discussed this book in a review article, 'Outside Story', Chapter 4 below.

7. Jameson, *The Political Unconscious*, p. 10, and see too 'Marxism and Historicism', *NLH* XI, 1 (1979), 41–73 (p. 48). For some criticisms of Jamesons's positioning of rival theories with respect to Marxism, see my 'Not Yet', Chapter 3 below.

8. Tony Bennett, 'Text and History' in *Re-Reading English*, ed. Peter Widdowson, London: Methuen 1982, pp. 223–36 (p. 223).

9. Terry Eagleton, *Walter Benjamin, or Towards a Revolutionary Criticism*, London: New Left Books 1981.

10. Engels, letter to Conrad Schmidt, 1 November 1891: 'Ohne Hegel geht's natürlich nicht, und der Mann will auch Zeit haben, bis er verdaut ist.'.

11. Louis Althusser, *Eléments d'Autocritique*, Paris: Hachette 1974, p. 53.

12. Raymond Williams, *Marxism and Literature*, Oxford: Oxford University Press 1977, pp. 167–8.

13. 'Introduction: The Crisis in English Studies', *Re-Reading English*, pp. 1–14: 'deconstruction' is used on pp. 7 and 8.

14. Catherine Belsey, *Critical Practice*, London: Methuen 1980. Belsey describes deconstruction as simply 'the analysis of the process and conditions of [the text's] construction out of the available discourses' (p. 104), suggests that 'the object of deconstructing the text is to examine the *process of its production*' (ibid.), and finally says that 'to deconstruct the text . . . is to open it, to release the possible positions of intelligibility, including those which reveal the partiality (in both senses) of the ideology inscribed in the text' (p. 109).

15. Peter Brooker, 'Post-Structuralism, Reading and the Crisis in English', *Re-Reading English*, pp. 61–76. This essay is explicitly concerned to 'appropriate' bits of post-structuralism for a collective subject pre-comprehended as made up of good historical materialists (p. 72). Brooker finds Derrida's thinking 'patently unmaterialist', his 'conception of history . . . confined to the history of western philosophy', his 'deconstructive procedure . . . imperfectly dialectical offering no guarantee of progressive acceleration and transformation'. Etc. It would be worth following the desire for *guarantees*, but not much else.

16. Jameson, *The Political Unconscious*, p. 9.

17. For a classic *reductio ad absurdum* of radical historicism, see Leo Strauss, *Natural Right and History*, Chicago: Chicago University Press 1953, pp. 9–34.

18. See for example Louis Althusser, *Lire le Capital*, 2 vols, Paris: Maspéro 1966; republished in Petite Collection Maspéro, 4 vols, I, pp. 46 and 132. For some criticism of the validity of the reasoning, see E.P. Thompson, 'The Poverty of Theory', in *The Poverty of Theory and Other Essays*, London: Merlin Press 1978, pp. 193–397 (pp. 223–5): this reference should not be taken to imply general agreement with Thompson's attack on Althusser.

19. Terry Eagleton, *Criticism and Ideology*, London: New Left Books 1976.

20. Jeffrey Mehlman, *Revolution and Repetition*, Berkeley and Los Angeles: University of California Press 1977, which makes brilliant use of the same text by Marx to put forward just such a reading of history.

21. See Chapter 3 below for some rather bad-tempered comments on this aspect of Jameson.

22. The reference here is to Edward Said, *Beginnings: Intention and Method*, Baltimore and London: Johns Hopkins University Press 1975, and is acknowledged by Eagleton (p. 68n144).

23. Terry Eagleton, *The Rape of Clarissa*, Oxford: Basil Blackwell 1982.

24. In a later piece in the *TLS*, Eagleton no longer sees post-structuralism as the child of 1968, but suggests that 'structuralism and the student movement were the prodigal children of the same distraught father' ('The Critic's New Clothes' *TLS*, 27 May 1983, p. 546). These explanations are really equivalent in their weakness.

25. The situation recalls Jameson's equally 'liberal' picture of a 'market-place' in which theories compete and where Marxism wins because it is *also* the transcendent measure of value. See 'Not Yet', p. 76 below.

3

Not Yet*

Ni le coup ni le pas ne sont ici d'un trait indivisible.
(Jacques Derrida, *La Carte postale de Socrate à Freud et au-delà* Paris:
Aubier-Flammarion 1980, p. 278)

*A constant injunction in Jameson: reckon the place of the analyst into the
analysis. When I analyse Jameson, is my place defined geographically,
politically, or in the topology of some scheme of intellectual or institutional
sites? Am I writing in (or from?) Oxford, Paris, 'poststructuralism', writing
out of (or into?) ambition, indignation, admiration, or a combination of
obscure and unpayable debts? The place has certainly to be reckoned with,
but can it be reckoned, recognized, determined and labeled? No doubt: but
perhaps not yet. Play the move first, then find out which rules have been
followed, and which broken. The best moves neither follow nor break rules,
but displace the rules and their place. Failing that, I have tried to cheat,
advancing, obliquely, a piece called 'Lyotard': this is less a real move than
an advertisement or an* avertissement *for a move that might be played
here (where?) one day. In chess terms, I read a position in which 'Lyotard' is
a threat: a move which has not yet been played, but which looks (to a player or
a kibitzer, either of whom might be a patzer) like a good one.*

Wholes

Jameson's task has been to urge on the American critical public the
need to become aware of the virtues of dialectical thought, and
ultimately to persuade them of the excellence of a Marxist theory and
practice of interpretation: *Marxism and Form* (Princeton: Princeton
University Press 1971), and *The Prison-House of Language* (Princeton:

---

*This chapter was originally published as a review of Fredric Jameson, *The Political
Unconscious: Narrative as a Socially Symbolic Act*, London: Methuen 1981.

74

Princeton University Press 1972) were the first moves in this strategic enterprise, and *The Political Unconscious* continues their critical use and presentation of contemporary continental thought, elaborating in the first part of the work a theory of dialectical interpretation, and in the second defending and illustrating that theory. In doing this, Jameson contrives to confront a good number of the issues that have seemed important to contemporary critical practice.

And first of all, that very separation between theory and practice, an opposition which the book would like to exploit and transcend. In his Preface, Jameson says that he would be 'content to have the theoretical sections of this book judged and tested against its interpretive practice' (p. 13), but immediately recognizes the difficulty of any appeal to the theory/practice dichotomy. There is an 'uneasy struggle for priority between models and history, between theoretical speculation and textual analysis' (p. 13), but this struggle can be dialectically resolved:

> These two tendencies – theory and literary history – have so often in Western academic thought been felt to be rigorously incompatible that it is worth reminding the reader, in conclusion [this is the conclusion of the Preface] of a third position which transcends both. That position is, of course, Marxism, which, in the form of the dialectic, affirms a primacy of theory which is at one and the same time a recognition of the primacy of History itself. (p. 14)

Of course. Of course 'of course', and the capital H in History, are the traces of a polemical stance which Jameson is anxious to assume: but this stance is itself not simple nor, and this is welcome, *purely* polemical. Jameson is not indulging in what Jean-François Lyotard would call a *délire interprétatif*, is not merely searching out the traces in other critics of unconscious adhesion to 'idealism', 'bourgeois ideology' or whatever. The position of the proposed Marxist hermeneutics is double, and this is of some importance. The strategy might be described as one of disengaged engagement, and involves, at this meta-level of the book's presentation, a complex articulation of levels which produces two metaphorical strings, only the first of which is clearly that of polemics. Here, *in* a field of hermeneutics (and we shall have to wonder about the possibility of fencing that field and of making holes in the fence), there is war: 'Interpretation is not an isolated act, but takes place within a Homeric battlefield, on which a host of interpretive options are either openly or implicitly in conflict' (p. 13). Here the Marxist 'act' represents one option among others, competing against others. The competition produces the second series of metaphors, and here the place of conflicting interpretations is unified as a marketplace,

and the competition becomes economic: Marxism competes here as a
commodity among others, but simultaneously transcends the competition and provides a standard for the judgement of its own performance. What Jameson calls the metacommentary allows him to evaluate
other commentaries, to judge their economic performance against
Marxist commentary:

> The retrospective illusion of the metacommentary thus has the advantage
> of allowing us to measure the yield and density of a properly Marxist
> interpretive act against those of other interpretive methods – the ethical,
> the psychoanalytic, the myth-critical, the semiotic, the structural and the
> theological – against which it must compete in the 'pluralism' of the
> intellectual marketplace today. I will here argue the priority of a Marxian
> interpretive framework in terms of semantic richness. (p. 10)

Marxism has a place in the market, but also puts other 'rival' commod-
ities in their place: this means that as method it cannot remain in the
market, and this is its ultimate privilege over other methods. Competing on the terms it does, it has no need to compete, in so far as
'Marxism is here conceived as that "untranscendable horizon" that
subsumes such apparently antagonistic or incommensurable critical
operations, assigning them as undoubted sectoral validity within itself,
and thus at once cancelling and preserving them' (p. 10). Marxism as
commodity and as measure: pure gold.

  The advantages of this position are considerable, in that Jameson
has not (yet) to settle scores with rival methods (he suggests that this is,
ultimately, necessary), which are not (yet?) to be 'triumphalistically
consigned to the ashcan of history' (p. 10). The strong point here is
that we should not see texts as coming before us in some sort of
innocence, but as already read and interpreted – reading a text
involves engaging with these previous interpretations. The opening
injunction of the book, 'Always historicize!', applies primarily to the
'interpretive categories or codes through which we read and receive
the text in question' (p. 9); the way in which this is to be carried out is
made clear in a later formulation.

> One of the essential themes of this book will be the contention that Marxism
> subsumes other interpretive modes or systems; or, to put it in methodolo-
> gical terms, that the limits of the latter can always be overcome, and their
> more positive findings retained, by a radical historicizing of their mental
> operations, such that not only the content of the analysis, but the very
> method itself, along with the analyst, then comes to be reckoned into the
> 'text' or phenomenon to be explained. (p. 47)

Jameson is arguing that interpretation involves the allegorical 'rewriting [of] a given text in terms of a particular interpretive master code' (p. 10), and that the master codes of the rival methods can themselves be rewritten in terms of their historical situation. The psychoanalytical master code of desire must thus be rewritten in terms of the conditions of possibility of its emergence, which 'become visible, one would imagine, only when you begin to appreciate the extent of psychic fragmentation since the beginnings of capitalism' (p. 62), and the 'Language-itself' master code of structuralism becomes possible with language's 'structural abstraction from concrete experience' (p. 63). In this rewriting of rewritings, we might look for Jameson's *own* master code, and call it History. But Jameson cannot accept such a positioning of History as merely 'one optional code among others' (p. 101): that would be to limit him to polemics, to refuse the transcendental horizon. If that horizon is to be accepted, then History has to be placed outside and beyond textuality, as something which can, to be sure, only be approached through discourse, but which is, 'in itself', not discursive. If, through his own discursive approaches to History as 'absent cause', Jameson is able to use it as a sort of code of codes, this is only in so far as its otherness blocks the possibility of further, infinite rewriting: History becomes the ground of all activities of writing and coding as such.

Narrative, history, interpretation, History: we shall have to return to the systematic articulation of these privileged operators of the metacommentary. First it will be as well to look briefly at what Jameson does with his method, and to see which other critical gestures he subsumes under it. Despite a lengthy discussion of Althusser, and references to Lacan, Derrida, Lyotard and Deleuze–Guattari (I shall return to that discussion and those references), the two methods or models Jameson puts to most work are both taken from classical structuralism. The first is the proposition from Lévi-Strauss that 'the individual narrative, or the individual formal structure, is to be grasped as the imaginary resolution of a real contradiction' (p. 77): the second is Greimas's rectangular model of the 'elementary structure of signification', to be used here not as a universal account of thought or language, but to 'model ideological closure' (p. 83): the semiotic rectangle 'maps the limits of a specific ideological consciousness and marks the conceptual points beyond which that consciousness cannot go, and between which it is condemned to oscillate' (p. 47). Both of these elements were present in the earlier books (see *Marxism and Form*, pp. 383–84, and especially *Prison-House*, pp. 161–8); here, however, they are given much fuller elaboration, and specifically set to work within Jameson's own theoretical model for interpretation, which consists of three 'concentric frameworks' or 'distinct semantic horizons' (p. 75). The three interpretive essays which form the second part of the book work through these three circles, moving, as it were, from history to History. Thus the essay on Balzac seeks out the specific 'real contradiction' to which an individual text (*La Vieille Fille*) projects its imaginary resolution: at the second level or circle, the piece on Gissing treats the text as the *parole* of the *langue* of a 'collective class-discourse', and works at the level of the ideologeme (in this case, that of *ressentiment*): the third level, corresponding to the discussion of Conrad, is bounded by the 'ultimate horizon of human history as a whole' (p. 76), conceived as the 'whole complex sequence of the modes of production' (p. 76). It is no accident that these three essays form a sort of narrative of the passage from the nascent capitalism struggling with the ideological survivals of the Ancien Régime in Balzac's day (a certain freedom of narrative modalization remaining here, in that the bourgeois 'individual subject' and its narrative concomitant in the 'point of view' had not yet been invented), through the reification of Gissing's 'moment', where the subject too is reified and the novelist 'limited to something like an indicative mode' (p. 196) to Conrad, whose moment is that of the 'breakdown of realisms' (p. 207), and of the passage to what Jameson refers to as 'high modernism', our moment: it is worth quoting the final passage of the essay on Conrad to show how the narrative of Jameson's book is also the narrative of the possibility of its eponymous concept:

> After the peculiar heterogeneity of the moment of Conrad, a high modernism is set in place which it is not the object of this book to consider. The perfected poetic apparatus of high modernism represses History just as successfully as the perfected narrative apparatus of high realism did the random heterogeneity of the as yet uncentered subject. At that point, however, the political, no longer visible in the high modernist texts, any more than in the everyday world of appearance of bourgeois life, and relentlessly driven underground by accumulated reification, has at last become a genuine Unconscious. (p. 280)

It would, I think, be pointless to rehearse the detail of Jameson's analyses, which are undoubtedly rich and dense, either with the churlish aim of quarrelling over details, or with the aim of holding up samples for admiration (although there is much to admire). Although, or because, the book is forceful and persuasive, I shall attempt to resist persuasion, to return to some of these privileged operators of Jameson's method, to re-turn them (for I take this to be a necessary, if far from sufficient, operator of any deconstructive reading) against the text which puts them to work, in the hope of constituting something of the system of the 'not yet', which provides a sort of logic for *The Political Unconscious*.

History means Hegel, and Hegel means totality and plenitude: the fall from plenitude means narrative and history and hermeneutics, and these all mean Utopia and the return of plenitude. All of this means guilt, which again means interpretation and narrative and nostalgia. All of this was first set in place in *Marxism and Form*. Here is Hegel:

> The impossibility of the Hegelian system for us is not a proof of its intellectual limitations, its cumbersome methods and theological super-structure; on the contrary, it is a judgement on us and on the moment of history in which we live, and in which such a vision of the totality of things is no longer possible. (*Marxism and Form*, p. 47)

This 'no longer' (which of course goes with the 'not yet'; but that coupling is still in Hegel) is the trace of the fall, and there are many more such traces in *The Political Unconscious* itself, references to 'our particular fallen reality' (p. 24), or 'the appalling rate and degree of dehumanization in modern society' (p. 251n), or a discussion of Conrad's attempt to

> conjure back the older unity of the literary institution, to return to that older concrete social situation of which narrative transmission was but a part, and of which public and bard and storyteller are intrinsic (although not necessarily visible or immediately present) components: such literary institutions, once genuine or concrete forms of social relationships, have long since been blasted by the corrosive effects of market relations, and, like so many other traditional, organic, precapitalist institutions, systematically fragmented by that characteristic reorganizational process of capitalism which Weber described under the term rationalization. (p. 220)

Interpretation depends on such a fall in order to have any work to do, but also depends on the fall's not being total or irremediable: we must not have fallen so far as to have lost all possibility of contact with the lost plenitude; we can perhaps climb back up again on the basis of 'real work' (although the theoretical work is perhaps also fallen with respect to 'genuine manual labour': see p. 45), or the 'lived richness of daily life' (p. 30). So although 'a Marxian conception of our relationship to the past requires a sense of our radical difference from earlier cultures' (p. 75n), the Marxian hermeneutic must ensure that that distance is not too radical, that we can get back to 'the living idea beneath the layers of dead language' (*Marxism and Form*, p. 84). The condition for such a hermeneutic is a certain unity, which is a narrative unity:

> Only Marxism can give us an adequate account of the essential mystery of
> the cultural past, which, like Tiresias drinking the blood, is momentarily
> returned to life and warmth and allowed to speak, and to deliver its long-
> forgotten message in surroundings utterly alien to it. This mystery can be
> reenacted only if the human adventure is one . . . These matters can
> recover their original urgency for us only if they are retold within the unity
> of a single great collective story; only if, in however disguised and symbolic
> a form, they are seen as sharing a single fundamental theme – for Marxism,
> the collective struggle to wrest a realm of Freedom from a realm of
> Necessity. (p. 19)

The unity of the transcendental narrative of History is essential to
Jameson's project, and determines its every move. The problem will be
not to collapse the texts to be interpreted too soon onto this unity, and
this is one side of the 'not yet'. Other Marxist criticisms (Goldmann is
the principal target here) have been too hasty with their homologies
and their various forms of causality: Jameson's 'not yet' defers this sort
of mapping, writing longer hermeneutical narratives, and demonstrates the need for more and more subtle mediations (the selection of
which will be strategic, in terms of the text to be read), but the *telos* is
the same, namely to 'restore, at least methodologically, the lost unity of
social life, and demonstrate that widely distant elements of the social
totality are ultimately part of the same global historical process'
(p. 226).

It is this *restorative* element in Jameson's writing which generates the
need for the discussions of Althusser, in that Jameson evidently needs
to rescue a *telos* for History and the possibility of mediations from
Althusserian strictures. Here Jameson attempts a partial reinstatement of the notion of 'expressive causality' (and, less importantly for
his work, of 'mechanical causality') against Althusser's critique. The
first move in this attempt involves the reinscription of these two modes
of causality 'within the object', as 'local laws within our historical reality'
(p. 34). This is essentially the same gesture as that which reinscribed
rival interpretations of texts in the object of study for Marxist hermeneutics. On the other hand, this 'object' would appear to involve a sort
of collective subject: the allegorical narratives grounded in a notion of
expressive causality 'reflect a fundamental dimension of our collective
thinking and our collective fantasies about history and reality' (p. 34).
However, *within* this gesture of retention, Jameson also wants to retain
the critique of it implied in Althusser's notion of 'structural causality',
so that he can still criticize interpretations which get through their
mediations too soon. No simple model of levels, then, with a 'determination in the last instance' by a mode of production conceived in
purely economic terms. In Jameson's reading of Althusser, the mode

of production is not a level among others but the structure itself, in so far as it is 'nowhere empirically present as an element, it is not part of the whole or one of the levels, but rather the entire system of *relationships* among those levels' (p. 36). This emphasis on relationships is powerful and necessary, and allows Jameson's theory to transcend problems of static classification (a social class, for example, becomes not a closed entity but something defined only in its conflictual relationships with other classes): the temptation to project 'pure' taxonomic spaces seems averted by the insistence that the various modes of production are themselves never pure, never present. Rather several modes are said to coexist at any given moment, and Jameson radicalizes this suggestion of Poulantzas's by theorizing it as permanent 'cultural revolution': 'texts emerge in a space in which we may expect them to be crisscrossed and intersected by a variety of impulses from contradictory modes of production all at once' (p. 95).

This side of the 'not yet', then, prevents interpretive foreclosure at the level of the individual fantasm (Balzac), in so far as that fantasm is mediated through the structure of the family to the level of conflictual class-discourses; at that level too (Gissing) in so far as contradictions at this level result from the trace of the level of the modes of production, and even, apparently, at this final level, by the refusal to allow any given mode to be present to itself at any moment. This structure of deferrals would appear to suggest that in stressing plenitude and the fall above I was simply giving in to my own 'délire interprétatif', and uncharitably quoting out of context apparently nostalgic references which would be no more than a theoretically innocent residue, or what Jameson himself calls 'the shorthand of philosophical idealism' (p. 13). But even if we have been able to pursue the 'not yet' thus far, we must stress that the deferrals are not, and in Jameson's theoretical structure, cannot be, those of *différance*, but must be deferrals in view of an eventual totalization: for where there is *différance* there is no hermeneutics. In *The Prison-House of Language* Jameson criticized certain forms of structuralism for giving rise to an infinite regression which never sought to 'buckle the buckle' and come to rest in Truth (*Prison-House*, p. 208), and here the 'not yet' undergoes what Jameson himself would no doubt wish to term a 'dialectical reversal', but which I suspect is rather an unrelieved aporia. The 'absent cause', History (the particular 'Grand Zéro' – Lyotard – of Jameson's book), which can only be approached 'through its prior textualization', is in fact here given a prior textualization in that it becomes, despite Jameson's provisos, the projected *telos* of Jameson's own narrative, his own 'imaginary resolution of a real contradiction'. The 'absent cause' is not always already absent, but simply *not yet* present in its own essential transparency. This is the avowed Utopian side to Jameson's narrative, although we might feel that the story ends rather *en queue de poisson* with a reference to an 'as yet untheorized object – the collective' (p. 294).

Holes

This untheorized object is called upon to do a lot of silent work in the text, and is notably, often in footnotes, used in Jameson's containment of what he calls the contemporary 'Nietzschean and anti-interpretive current' in France. The proper names he associates with this current are those of Foucault, Derrida, Kristeva, Baudrillard, Deleuze–Guattari and Lyotard. We can, I think, ignore Jameson's attempt to neutralize the force of this (heterogeneous) work through the suggestion that these writers, in their attack on hermeneutics, are in fact projecting new hermeneutic 'methods' of their own. It is clear that to describe deconstruction (at least in Derrida's use of the term) or Lyotard's 'libidinal economy' as hermeneutic methods (p. 23n) is not to respect the strong sense of 'hermeneutics' that Jameson is concerned to defend in *The Political Unconscious*. What is more serious is the attempt to subsume such writing under the Great Narrative itself, again according to the logic of the 'not yet': the Marxist metacommentary can recuperate this work by describing it as 'essentially psychoanalytic', concerned with 'the experience of the subject in consumer or late monopoly capitalism' (p. 124) and then, through a shuffling of descriptives and prescriptives (a different type of analysis would show how this slippage between descriptives and prescriptives generates theory as narrative, dialectic as the 'dialectic of enlightenment', which Adorno and Horkheimer, just like Jameson after them, could only mime in their analysis), by reinscribing it along the road to the collective:

> For Marxism, indeed, only the emergence of a post-individualistic social world, only the reinvention of the collective and the associative, can concretely achieve the 'decentring' of the individual subject called for by such diagnoses; only a new and original form of collective social life can overcome the isolation and monadic autonomy of the older bourgeois subjects in such a way that individual consciousness can be lived – and not merely theorized – as an 'effect of structure' (Lacan). (p. 125)

It would of course be tempting here to turn Lacan back against Jameson, and to see, in this projection of a 'new' collective which is yet 'reinvented', the flight of the lost object of desire: but no doubt such an analysis could itself be accommodated into Jameson's narrative, which we might begin to suspect of sharing that 'windless closure' he ascribes to 'formalisms'. Or against the wholeness preceding our fall, we might arm ourselves with Baudrillard's demonstration of the nostalgic irreality of use-value, or attempt to slash across Jameson's 'unity of a single great collective story' (p. 19) with some of Lyotard's non-dialectical negatives: 'There are no primitive societies . . . There is no whole body . . . There is no libidinal dignity' (*Economie Libidinale*, Paris: Minuit 1974, pp. 133, 137, 138). But even if Lyotard might be more effective here than Lacan (criticized by Lyotard for allowing the subject, despite its decentring, a certain meta-unity in language – just as Jameson gathers up that decentring in the collective to come), he would probably *not yet* escape enclosure through the 'local validity' or the 'not yet' arguments we have seen at work.

Indeed, Jameson, makes it as difficult as possible to question these arguments in favour of totality by restating them in terms of the different political situations of France and the United States, and specifically of the different positions of the political 'Left' in the two countries. Whereas in France the traditional left parties are seen as just one more centralized totalizing instance to be fragmented, in the USA, according to Jameson, that fragmentation is the Left's problem:

> The privileged form in which the American Left can develop today must therefore necessarily be that of an alliance politics; and such a politics is the strict practical equivalent of the concept of totalization on the theoretical level. In practice, then, the attack on the concept of 'totality' in the American framework means the undermining and the repudiation of the only realistic perspective in which a genuine Left could come into being in this country. (p. 54n)

Americans be warned. *In practice*, this is not a very nice way of silencing or neutralizing Americans (and maybe Englishmen publishing in 'the American framework'), and of reducing the French to their national boundaries. Any attempt I might therefore make to undermine Jameson's argument with quotations from Lyotard is automatically labelled as politically irresponsible. If Jameson's narrative promise of collectivity might be analysed in terms of his own analysis of Balzac's fantasm, then here it is tempting to reapply the ideologeme of *ressentiment* as analysed in the essay on Gissing. Here Jameson suggests that our distance from that particular ideologeme can allow us to see:

> that this ostensible 'theory' is itself little more than an expression of annoyance at seemingly gratuitous lower-class agitation, at the apparently quite unnecessary rocking of the social boat. It may therefore be concluded that the theory of ressentiment, wherever it appears, will always itself be the expression and the production of ressentiment. (p. 202)

It is not difficult to imagine an analysis in which Deleuze, Derrida and the rest would have begun the 'slave uprising in ethics' (p. 201), to which Jameson's reaction would constitute the annoyance at this rocking of the dialectical boat, and my reapplication of the term, in deliberate violation of the sort of historical controls Jameson would require, an expression of my own annoyance at his suggestion of my irresponsibility. The point about such a use of *ressentiment* would not merely be that of accepting a certain hermeneutic irresponsibility, but also of suggesting that what Jameson *himself* finds the most striking thing about *ressentiment*, namely its 'unavoidably autoreferential function' (p. 202) *already* guarantees its refusal to be contained in the type of historical narrative Jameson is writing.

Perhaps it is not yet time for this sort of suggestion. Maybe we can take another step, *un pas encore*, with Jameson's problematic, accepting the injunction to 'historicize', along with the seriousness that entails, by questioning the status of the mode of production. As we have seen, Jameson invokes this concept at the widest of his three concentric circles, but refuses to use the notion of mode in a static classificatory way. At this widest level of interpretation, the 'text' to be studied is that provided not by a given mode, but by the specific form of the 'permanent cultural revolution' at the period in question. The relative strength of this view must be stressed. But it is not unproblematical, in that it still relies for its articulation on the possibility of describing, even if only as theoretical constructs, the individual modes whose progression, however complex, constitutes history. Jameson's brief remarks on feminism (pp. 99–100) are perhaps enough to suggest that his use of the concept of 'mode of production' is difficult, and it is interesting that in a broadly sympathetic discussion of Jameson's book, Terry Eagleton has suggested this as a limitation ('The Idealism of American Criticism', *New Left Review*, 127 (1981) 63). But the point at which the use of the concept of 'mode of production' is the most problematical is at the end of the book, where Jameson wants to ground his claim for the need of a 'positive' Utopian (and not just negative and demystificatory) side to the Marxist hermeneutic. Here Jameson is concerned to appropriate for Marxism Durkheim's view of religion as the symbolic affirmation of the unity of the collectivity: suitably purged of its conservatism and subject-oriented tendencies this view, and Rousseau's vision of the *fête*, will 'know their truth and come into their own', precisely when the collectivity comes. We should note immediately that this proleptic celebration of collective auto-affection involves an end to the conflict of the modes of production, and that Jameson projects this back onto Durkheim and Rousseau, who are thus, in an important sense, dehistoricized. Secondly, the positive use of Durkheim within a Marxist problematic is crucial here, in that Jameson needs it to explain how his hermeneutics is not going to be simply demystificatory and negative, but an affirmation of the Utopian vocation of all 'cultural artefacts'. Without the final horizon of unity and totality, then the 'vast unfinished plot' (p. 19) of the Marxist story will *remain* unfinished and undirected, and the earlier annex- ation of Lévi-Strauss and the mechanisms of wish-fulfilment mere methodological convenience with no transcendental justification: in short, unless Jameson can situate Durkheim's theory of religion within what he would call a properly Marxist framework, then he will be left, on his own terms, practising either 'mechanical' or instrumental analy- sis, or else 'relax[ing] into the religious or the theological, the edifying and the moralistic' (p. 292). Now the point of contact between Durk- heim and Marxism is here provided by Marx's notorious 'Asiatic mode of production'. Jameson recognizes that this is a difficult and contested concept, and indeed the 'conception of social unity expressed in the "body of the despot"' (p. 295), which is Marx's here, calls up again the second of the Lyotardian negatives quoted above. More importantly in the immediate context, Jameson recognizes that the Asiatic mode of production has been the object of criticism from other Marxists, but sidesteps their attempt to expunge the concept from Marxism by insisting that 'the *problem* of the symbolic enactment of collective unity is inscribed in that problematic by Marx himself at this point, whatever solution may ultimately be devised for it' (p. 296). 'Marx himself': another 'whole body'? Does Marx's own inscription of the Asiatic mode necessarily situate it as a problem in the problematic? What would be the status of a Marxist's expulsion of Marx's 'own' problem from that problematic?

The traces of the attempted expulsion of this problem (its dismissal as a false problem) are largely relegated to references in the footnotes. One of these references is to Hindess and Hirst's book, *Pre-Capitalist Modes of Production* (London: Routledge & Kegan Paul 1975), which is credited with developing a 'powerful critique' of the Asiatic mode (p. 295n). Hindess and Hirst are also concerned to prevent the type of annexing of Durkheim which Jameson is proposing, and a new foot- note quotes them. Here is the footnote in full:

> Speaking of an analogous view of religion in contemporary Marxist anthro- pology, Hindess and Hirst observe: 'Meillassoux clearly interprets the collective hunt as performing the function of a collective ritual serving to reinforce collective sentiments. Such positions may have a place within a Durkheimian problematic of forms of ritual and social cohesion but it has nothing whatever to do with Marxism' (Hindess and Hirst, *Pre-Capitalist*

Modes, p. 55). One is tempted to add: in that case, too bad for Marxism! (p. 296n)

I shall not attempt to analyse the gestures of inclusion and exclusion going on in this text, although such a rhetorical analysis would of course be necessary if we were here concerned to reinscribe the problems of the body, the corpus and so on. But it may well be that the implications of the work of Hindess and Hirst are indeed 'too bad for Marxism', or at least for the type of Hegelian Marxism here defended by Jameson. For in subsequent work, Hindess and Hirst cast doubt not only on the concept of the Asiatic mode of production, but on the concept of 'mode of production' *as such*, and with it, those of 'society', 'social totality', concepts which sit on the unquestioned horizon of Jameson's book. In *Mode of Production and Social Formation* (London: Macmillan 1977), and in the two-volume work written with Anthony Cutler and Athar Hussein, *Marx's Capital and Capitalism Today* (London: Routledge & Kegan Paul 1977–8), almost all of the major Marxist concepts with which Jameson is working are displaced within the framework of a generalized critique of epistemology. Whatever the value of that critique, the detail of which I am not going to rehearse here, it is clear that if the mode of production is no longer a coherent concept, then all the other mainstays of Jameson's 'untranscendable horizon', which he calls Marxism, are equally undermined. The Necessity of History, the unity of classes, the pretensions of a 'genuine Left', of the proletariat or of its 'organ of consciousness, the revolutionary party' (p. 283) to achieve transparency: despite the undoubted pathos of these notions and the apparatus they set in place, they will not stand up to the type of internal reading of Marxism operated by Hindess and Hirst, and will function only as what Lyotard calls 'a pretext for an apparatus to capitalize the desire for revolution' (*Economie Libidinale*, p. 126).

Once the privileged operators of Jameson's method have been called into question in this way, then the unity of his great narrative cannot be sustained, and we can begin to doubt its capacity to accommodate and neutralize other types of intervention. The category of narrative is crucial to Jameson, who sees in it (it is here that the reference to the 'shorthand of philosophical idealism' is made) 'the central function or *instance* of the human mind' (p. 13). If we reject this *faith* in narrative, then there are important consequences for political practice on the one hand (some of these are suggested in the conclusion to *Marx's Capital and Capitalism Today*), and on the other, for the enterprise of interpretation itself. If, as Lyotard has suggested in recent work (*La Condition postmoderne*, Paris: Minuit 1979), we can no longer give credence to the various 'Grands Récits' (of which Jameson's type of Marxism would be a privileged example), then we must displace the whole notion of hermeneutics. Critical activity would then become an activity of vigilant local strategic intervention ('strategic' only if we can think of strategy in Derrida's sense of a 'strategy without finality'), the equivalent of what Lyotard in a discussion of justice formulates as follows:

> it is no longer a question of reflecting on what is just and what is unjust within the horizon of a social totality, but, on the contrary, within the horizon [the French allows 'sur l'horizon'; 'within' still implies the totality] of a multiplicity, or of a diversity. (J.-F. Lyotard and J.-L. Thébaud, *Au Juste*, Paris: Bourgeois 1979, p. 167)

Against Jameson's hermeneutic, which grounds criticism in a transcendental unity, I here then suggest the need to recognize the 'pagan' situation of a Lyotard. My own insistent, and I hope irritating, use of Lyotard in an American context largely ignorant of his work, would stand as a *figure* of the type of intervention here advocated. Naturally, this allows a certain violence, and a certain irresponsibility: this violence and irresponsibility are not arbitrary, but calculated to disrupt totalizing and systematizing narratives. This is a terrorist activity, perhaps, but directed against a different sort of Terror.

4

Outside Story

Marxists have persistently reproached deconstruction with not taking their thought seriously, and those they would call 'deconstructionists' have largely ignored the reproach, perhaps because it could so easily be returned to its sender.[1] What has been most conspicuously absent from the various Marxist attempts to dismiss or appropriate deconstruction (these two apparently opposed gestures in fact forming a system the rules for which could be formalized)[2] is, in general, any serious acquaintance with the object to be dismissed or appropriated. Michael Ryan's book is important and valuable less for its attempt to gather what circumstantial evidence there is that Derrida 'really is' a Marxist or Communist, or to show that early 'uninformed' notions about Marx are rectified in Derrida's later texts,[3] than because it shows ample evidence of a serious reading of Derrida's work and of an attempt to grasp its difficult implications.

Too often the presuppositions of a certain Marxism have condemned it to a paranoid policing of the frontiers which attempt to guarantee the property or propriety of its name or title, and the suspicion this implies has denied it in advance the very possibility of reading Derrida: it is, then, more than welcome that Michael Ryan has, in principle and declared intention at least, *opened* the frontier of Marxism to the effects of a text which rigorously questions the values of property, propriety and appropriation that have previously been used in an attempt to contain that text. This 'openness' of Ryan's book allows it to entertain the possibility that any unity or closure implied by proper names in general, and therefore by the proper names which appear in its title, will be called into question by the progress of the argument, of the 'articulation' announced in the subtitle. One inevitable consequence is that the use of the term 'Marxism' becomes problematical, with implications that it is difficult to calculate, and that Ryan's book cannot be expected to dominate.

This possibility of a non-propriety of the proper names that make up the proper name of the book is, apparently, recognized by Ryan from the opening pages of his Preface, in which both Marxism and deconstruction are split. Marxism divides into the 'scientific' and the 'critical' deconstruction, familiarly, into 'American deconstruction' and 'the work of Jacques Derrida' (p. xiii). The articulation or 'alloy' to be attempted (ibid., but of course these two terms are far from synonymous) involves only the second term of each pair: 'scientific' Marxism is excluded because 'it interprets the world in one way at all times', and is thus closed and 'metaphysical', and (most) 'American deconstruction' is dismissed because it is 'too far removed from the concerns of marxism' (ibid.). This aggression against 'American deconstruction' must of course be linked to the local situation in which Ryan's book is written and published, and is part of the political importance it has with respect to the American academy. It also raises difficult questions, both with respect to the accuracy of the (now commonplace) accusations made against 'the depoliticized and aestheticist propensities of the importers' of deconstruction (p. 103), and for any attempt to decide to what extent a 'conjunctural' analysis of the book could ever account for its 'political' claims and effects. One immediately welcome *use* of the attack on the so-called 'Yale School' is to suggest that those Ryan calls 'leftists' might be a little less hasty in their dismissal of deconstruction, and also that 'deconstruction' need not be the name merely for a type of literary analysis. (Ryan conspicuously does not discuss literary texts.)

On the other hand, in so far as Ryan himself tells us that 'deconstruction teaches one to attend to gestures of exclusion' (p. 3), it might be worth wondering to what extent these simple prefatory divisions and exclusions could *themselves* be read deconstructively,[4] for if deconstruction does indeed question the propriety of so-called proper names (this questioning being bound up with its attention to exclusion, which is precisely what produces effects of property and propriety), it does not suggest that they can (or ever could) simply be abandoned, or that their effects are negligible: it is indeed essential to recognize that neither 'Marxism' or 'deconstruction' functions univocally, but the move from that recognition to a summary carving-up of the fields they are habitually used to enclose is not unproblematical.

This move does, however, allow the book to begin, and it would be churlish to criticize it if its practical or political expediency (and Ryan would probably want to claim no more – but no less – for it than this)[5] were absolutely clear. But in fact the apparently simple topology set up by the trenchant divisions of the Preface does not (and cannot) remain simple, and symptoms of this failure or impossibility can be read in the text. Almost inevitably, 'critical Marxism' implicitly claims the privilege of being '(real) Marxism', in so far as in Ryan's reading Marx is a critical Marxist (Engels, especially Lenin, and Althusser got it wrong): and Derrida's work (or at least the 'major works', which Ryan, again not unproblematically, assigns to the period 1968–75) is 'real deconstruction', to the extent that, as Ryan puts it, 'Derrida . . . still holds copyright on deconstruction' (p. 108). Property thus returns *à qui de droit*, and at more than one point the book hovers on the edge of a mere confrontation (and no longer an articulation or alloy) of the renewed propriety of 'Derrida' and 'Marx', a confrontation which might never be able to move beyond the (important) statement that 'Derrida is not Marx, but . . . ' (p. 57).

The topology of the Preface is troubled further by Ryan's positioning of his own enunciation. Explicitly and even aggressively, he does not attempt to write from the *point* of the articulation (the point at which (critical) Marxism and (Derrida's) deconstruction would be both joined and separated), at which the discourses to be articulated and eventually alloyed would each open onto and into the other, but from a position he situates as being on the (in)side of critical Marxism. Still within the Preface, he writes: 'I have attempted to explain certain aspects of Derrida's work which can be used *within* critical marxism . . . at times, it is not even an accurate account, because my purpose has been to interpret Derrida in a way that is politically useful to nonfrancophile activists' (p. xiv, my emphasis). The persistent danger that the promised 'articulation' will become annexation is nowhere more evident than in an anecdotal claim that Ryan 'began to see that deconstruction could be used as a mode of marxist political criticism' (p. xvi): the tension between this type of declaration and the description of the book as 'an attempt to develop a new form of analysis which would be both marxist and deconstructionist' (p. xv) is never resolved.

This complication does not exhaust the increasingly difficult topology of the book. For if it now seems that deconstruction is being partially imported into critical Marxism (which would thus suffer from a lack, even if that lack might sometimes be seen as no more than an inability to name what it has always been doing as . . . deconstruction), then elsewhere it is rather Marxism which is imported into a deconstruction which is the subject of the lack: 'My first critique would be that deconstruction lacks a social theory and that this is not an extrinsic or accidental oversight but an intrinsic fault' (p. 35),[6] Derrida's work must be *supplemented* by that social theory (see p. 46).

This location of an 'intrinsic fault' in deconstruction is made possible by the systematic functioning of a broader reading-grid which, however admirable its (avowedly and inevitably partial) presentation of

Derrida's questioning of philosophical oppositions, itself depends on a number of such oppositions. It would, for example, place deconstruction in a series of terms which would include words like 'philosophy', 'logic', 'the academy', 'the scholarly', and so on, and mark this series negatively with respect to a valorized series involving terms such as 'politics', 'the pragmatic', 'social relations', etc.[7] Despite its intention to 'alloy' these two series (to show, for example, that the philosophical is always already political, and vice versa), Ryan's text constantly re(in)states this type of opposition which, despite declarations to the contrary, could easily enough be tracked to the opposition of the speculative and the practical, the contemplative and the active, theory and praxis.[8] The 'intrinsic fault' of deconstruction is that it is already situated on the wrong side of this opposition: it is too philosophical, too academic, and so on. The axiological appeal of this retained opposition (retained by or as something stronger than Ryan's declarations) is, primarily, or ultimately, underpinned by the opening paragraph of the book's Introduction, which states that despite the possibility of articulation, there is 'one fundamental way' in which Marxism and deconstruction 'cannot be related': this is because deconstruction is philosophy whereas Marxism is not; Marxism 'names revolutionary movements' (p. 1). This stark opposition is followed, without transition, by a sentence which states simply: 'Millions have been killed because they were marxists; no one will be obliged to die because s/he is a deconstructionist' (ibid.).

It is not immediately clear what status to accord this affective dignity granted by the pathos of terror and death: but it *is* clear that this problem is in itself one of the 'philosophical' problems of 'the political'. It introduces, among other things, a sense of urgency which the traditional, serene image of philosophy cannot easily accommodate, and which communicates a certain tone to Ryan's book as a whole. In this sense, the political is *in a hurry* compared with philosophy, and in so far as Ryan's book is presented as being primarily 'political' (both in that this is a political intervention in a local pragmatic scene, and that it argues consistently and persuasively against any classical Marxist subordination of the political to the economic), it would seem possible to justify his own hurry and even impatience in such terms. One of the typical signs of this impatience-as-mark-of-political-urgency is, implicitly at least, a tendency to put to one side Derrida's later, reputedly more 'playful' writings as 'increasingly difficult, self-referential, and esoteric' (p. xiv).[9] The corollary of this is, paradoxically enough, an attachment to the earlier, reputedly more 'philosophical' texts, from which 'theses' can apparently be extracted, rephrased and restated, and against which the more 'playful' writing can either be ignored, or else re-appropriated as somehow exemplary or illustrative of those theses. It would seem that the urgency of the political requires as its other a quite traditional conception of philosophical writing, which it can hope to take up and use.

This position will commit the reader of Derrida's work to a language which can state the supposed theses extracted from that work only at the price of ignoring or repressing (as, for example, difficult, self-referential and esoteric) the *effects* of those same theses, in which, however, even supposing that they can rigorously be isolated *as* these and strictly described in a thetic mode, the writing marginalized as playful is already inscribed.[10] One serious effect of this on Ryan's book is that, just as his prefatory division of Marxism and deconstruction into their respective subsets invited a deconstructive reading, so here the location of lacks and supplements cannot strictly pretend to dominate Derrida's writing, in so far as it falls short of the discussion of lacks and supplements in *Of Grammatology*. It would seem, then, that (still in the terms of the topology proposed by the Preface), Ryan's writing from 'within' critical Marxism blinds his text to the necessary possibility of its availability to deconstructive reading. It could be argued that this is not an extrinsic or accidental oversight, but an intrinsic fault.

The use of a language which, in presenting Derrida's work, falls short of its implications, is common enough in the discussion of deconstruction, and is in any case hardly to be avoided. What is specific in this relationship of languages in Ryan's book is its inscription as political – for Ryan's aim is not merely to discuss the politics of deconstruction, but to do so politically. The link this sketches out between a certain sense of urgency, a certain type of language, and 'the political', reacts on the possible opening of (an already 'open', 'plural') Marxism to deconstruction, and reinstates a certain, specific closure – the 'within', precisely, of critical Marxism. The complications gener-ated here reactivate all the questions of property and propriety raised above, and which Ryan never openly questions with respect to the enunciation of his own discourse. But the symptoms of such complica-tions are visible in the envisaged possibility of 'applying' deconstruc-tion to Marx's (own, proper) text or corpus 'itself'. The problems this raises of political expediency, of philosophical responsibility, and even of *secrecy* as a form of the political, are crucial to any reading of Derrida which wishes to define itself primarily in political terms.

The possibility of something like a deconstruction of Marx's text is addressed explicitly at one point in the book, at the end of a chapter which argues persuasively for a deconstructive approach to the Marx-ist opposition of the economical and the political. Ryan attacks the 'metaphysics' of the economical (of 'determination in the last instance', and so on), which he sees as characteristic of 'scientific' Marxism, and writes in his concluding paragraph that 'any critical pertinence deconstruction might have in this regard seems best attained through applying it to that metaphysics' (p. 102). (At this point it might seem that the promised 'articulation' of Marxism and deconstruction in fact resolves into the use of the latter as a means of *dis*articulating certain aspects of the former.) The tense moment that follows is worth quoting in full:

> This is not to say that there are probably not areas in Marx's text that could benefit from deconstructive analysis; what political interests such an analysis would serve would need to be laid out in advance. My interest here has been to read Marx in such a way that the implicit opposition his text offers to the metaphysics of scientific marxism becomes evident. And, ultimately, because I believe Marx and Derrida, critical marxism and deconstruction, are on the same side, I have not tried (nor do I see the value of trying) 'to deconstruct' Marx's text. The critical validity of marxism does not depend on the sanctity or inviolability of that text. And the relation between deconstruction and marxism can take more critically helpful (less scholarly) forms, as I shall now argue. (ibid.)

End of chapter. This passage raises a number of crucial questions.

1. If 'the critical validity of marxism does not depend on the sanctity or inviolability of [Marx's] text', then, simply, *why not* 'deconstruct'? What is there to lose in such an operation? What is the tribunal of political expediency that decides that it is best to keep Marx's text out of deconstruction's hands? The problem is the more acute in that it is suggested that areas (but which areas?) of Marx's text would 'benefit' from the exercise. The trouble is caused, perhaps, by the requirement of a prior political guarantee: it is not clear that deconstruction can give any such guarantee, but it may well be that this inability to predict the effects of work carried out is *itself* a form of the political, which the (metaphysical) desire for guarantees is worried by, and shortcircuits.
2. Can one in fact *decide* (politically, for example), to 'deconstruct' a text or not? Ryan's scare-quotes around the verb perhaps mark the awareness of a problem here. The scenario or pragmatic scene of such a decision would imply (a) a (voluntarist) *subject* of deconstruction, and (b) an *object* of deconstruction locatable and identifiable as a signed text. Neither of these premises is unproblematical, and both tend to reinforce some notion of a whole body of Marx's text,

to be protected from an incursion by a deconstruction here situated as external to that text, whereas, in Derrida's terms, deconstruction is not applied to the 'inside' of a text from a position simply describable as 'outside' that text.

3. Even supposing that one *could* decide 'to deconstruct' or not in such simple terms, and assuming that the prior location of Marx and Derrida as being 'on the same side' were an immediately convincing reason *not* to attempt the deconstruction, rather than a motive for feeling that the solidarity of 'the same side' would encourage the operation, then this prior location of 'sides' in a game or struggle (for Ryan would not wish this to be a neutral topology, but a conflictual relationship of forces) implies a simplification and even singularization of games or struggles the plurality of which Ryan elsewhere strongly (and rightly) affirms. This implication would lead (a) to a new closure of the critical Marxism earlier characterized as 'the provisional tag for a plurality of movements' (p. xiii), and (b) suggest a reduction of the heterogeneous field of 'the political' to something more like, simply, 'politics', a unitary field with simple 'sides' in which equally unitary subjects could emerge by virtue of having *a* political position. It would be difficult to reconcile this monolithic or 'molar' conception of the political with Ryan's important (and even overoptimistically plural or 'molecular') insistence on 'undecidability' and 'seriality', not to be dominated by any transcendent paradigm. It seems likely that this type of (here largely implicit, but at other points in the text, especially those specifically 'political' in intent, overt) attachment to the notion of the subject, which seems to characterize the most critical forms of Marxism,[11] is both what separates Marxism 'proper' from what it labels and expels as 'post-Marxism', and also what proves most resistant to anything like an 'alloy' with deconstruction.

This *explicit* protection of Marx's text, with all the difficulties it entails, also covers an *implicit* protection of Marxism, which takes too many forms and involves too many – no doubt largely unconscious – ruses to be followed in full detail here. Briefly, a double gesture is again involved, and this is a version of the double gesture of exclusion and appropriation mentioned above. For example, by writing that 'deconstructive philosophy' is 'a critique of idealist theories of meaning and of consciousness in language philosophy' (p. 2), Ryan, on the one hand, reduces the complex specificity of the operation of deconstruction by describing it as a 'critique' – the acknowledgement at one point that deconstruction 'also questions the position of critique' (p. 34) cannot in itself rewrite all the very numerous descriptions of deconstruction *as* critique. And on the other hand, he reduces the 'object' of deconstruction (which Derrida calls 'Western metaphysics', '(phal)logocentrism', and so on) first to the regional concerns of 'language philosophy', and second to the area of 'idealism'. In fact, deconstruction is not to be contained within 'language philosophy' if its claims are to be taken at all seriously, and 'idealism' is not simply synonymous with a term such as 'logocentrism'. Elsewhere, indeed, Ryan offers slightly different descriptions, which simply narrow things down to other regions: thus, 'Brutally summarised the deconstructive "revolution" consisted of questioning some of the most treasured mainstays of bourgeois philosophy, both in its idealist (Continental phenomenological) as well as its positivist (Anglo-American) mode' (p 33: here deconstruction is allowed beyond 'idealism', but only at the price of a reduction of its field to 'bourgeois philosophy'), or, discussing Derrida's insistence on difference and alterity against the claims of 'the property or ownness of what seems self-identical or unique', 'Derrida elaborates upon this insight at the level of philosophical argument and successfully wields it to demolish certain foundations and strategies of bourgeois philosophy and social science . . . ' (p. 35: here deconstruction is allowed (ambiguously) beyond 'philosophy', but is still held within the 'bourgeois').

This type of limitation allows the solidarity of Marxism and deconstruction to appear greater than it might in fact be, while allowing the former to retain a special field of effectivity denied to a deconstruction carefully ghettoized in regions pre-defined by Marxism. The unity of this complex of gestures with the 'protection' of Marxism is clear, in so far as within the field assigned to it, and from which deconstruction is, at first, excluded (while simultaneously being reproached for not venturing into that field, for this is the same 'intrinsic fault' noted above), Marxist words and concepts are allowed to circulate unquestioned.

The notion of value can be taken as an example of this. Reading from Derrida the idea that although 'an absolute or whole truth is indeterminable', 'truths are possible . . . and such truth is often plural' (p. 38), Ryan is able to argue that the theories of value proposed by Marx and by Sraffa are 'both true'. This simply glosses over the fact that the determining value of 'labour' in Marx's account (as a force outside the system to be accounted for, but animating that system, like God in Newtonian cosmology) is heavy with metaphysical resonances, which Sraffa's intra-systemic account avoids, in principle at least. Elsewhere, Ryan maps Derrida's concern with relationality and 'radical alterity' (this latter a dangerous formulation out of context) onto Marx's account of exchange-value:

> If there is a notion of 'radical alterity' in Marx of the sort that Derrida thinks exceeds the traditional philosophical definition of truth, it is the thematic of relationality. Exchange value is a relation that is never present as such. It is of the nature neither of a subject, because it belongs to the socio-economic system, nor of a substance, because it is produced by difference and relations. The relational definition of the world destroyed the idealist pretensions of theory . . . (p. 34; see too p. 16).

So far, so good: the analysis of exchange-value in Marx links him closely to Derrida, and the argument progresses to allow Ryan to affirm, at the end of his paragraph, that 'Marx, like Derrida, thus undoes two presuppositions of idealism: the distinction between mental and manual, and between theory and practice' (ibid.). But in thus superimposing the two texts, Ryan does not question the function of Marx's analysis of on the one hand *use*-value, and on the other labour, which ground Marx's analysis of exchange, both theoretically and axiologically, in something very like a 'nature', as *arche* and *telos* of the analysis.[12] When use-value *does* resurface a little later in the analysis, it manages to be close to Derrida too, by implication, when 'dissemination' is made synonymous with 'production and circulation without exchange' (p. 41). Dissemination in Derrida does not, however, function as a positively marked term in opposition to 'relationality' or 'différance', and so the proportional analogy suggested by Ryan is untenable.

This type of articulation or 'alloy', then, does not stand up to inspection. Showing this is perhaps just the sort of 'logical' (rather than 'practical' (see p. 120)) or 'scholarly' (rather than 'critically helpful' (p. 102)) activity that Ryan is concerned to avoid. He would, I think, recognize the tendentious character of some of his readings, but argue precisely that this is part of what makes his book political. And indeed there is much to admire in the more immediately political parts of the book, analysing among other things American foreign policy, the structure of the University, and liberalism (chapters 6 and 7, pp. 117–58). But what is needed here (as in much recent Marxist work which stresses 'the political') is a much more refined and differentiated notion of what the political might involve. There is a danger that, whatever the intention, proclaiming the importance of the political/ practical/active over the academic/theoretical/contemplative in a book produced by a University press and read almost exclusively by academics, will become no more than a rhetorical gesture of self-congratulation, and a loose usage of the claim to 'deconstruct' these two series of terms and concepts can support this confusion. It is not difficult to sympathize with Ryan's concern at certain aspects of 'deconstruction' in the United States, and to support his desire to disturb those aspects. But here that properly local 'political' move is grafted onto a quite different invocation of the political in the text (notably the quite extensive use of the work of Antonio Negri and the notions of subjectivity and autonomy) which, *in that local situation at least*, is more than vulnerable to the reading strategies of the type of work it is aimed to disturb. In this sense, the political desire signalled by the note of urgency discussed above is in fact shortcircuited by its inscription in the same local situation, which can comprehend such gestures easily enough. A little pressure applied to this problem will allow a paradoxical formulation: Ryan's very insistence on a given notion of the political politically limits the political interest and effectivity of his book.

The problems raised by this paradox are considerable. A prerequisite for any attempt to address them seems to be abandonment of any global and totalizing notion of 'the political' – and the desire to unify the indeterminate number of 'political' positions or situations under a name such as 'Marxism' can only aggravate the difficulties. 'Deconstruction' as a name can evidently produce the same effect, although it has the advantage of carrying with it fewer sedimented connotations, and could more easily be abandoned. But 'deconstruction' can name 'the political' only improperly or, better, can only name the impropriety of the political in its dispersion. This is evidently not a comfortable position, if only because it cannot be thought of adequately as *a* position.[13] On the other hand, it does not imply some purely 'local' or 'tactical' field, or what Ryan over-hastily welcomes as the possibility of a 'seriality without paradigm'.[14] The iterability of writing (here, empirically, the fact that I read Ryan's book outside the 'local situation' in which it intervenes, and, no longer empirically, the fact that the possibility of my reading it outside that situation is a *necessary* possibility of its publication) unsettles simple appeals to 'locality' just as surely as it disturbs any simple totalization of localities.

In this respect, it would be necessary to return yet again to Ryan's opening distribution of his field, and to wonder if 'American deconstruction' and 'Scientific Marxism' can be dismissed so easily. The work of a de Man cannot rapidly be put aside once the desire for political simplicity, or politics as a desire for simplicity, is questioned. The resulting complexity for an enterprise such as Ryan's need not be the cause of regret or lamentation: the affirmation of such complexity *is* deconstruction as politics – indefinitely.

Notes

1. Reviewing Michael Ryan, *Marxism and Deconstruction: A Critical Articulation*, Baltimore and London: Johns Hopkins University Press 1982.

2. For further discussion, see Chapter 2.

3. For the circumstantial evidence, see pp. xiv–xv; for Derrida's 'early, uniformed mistake' about Marx, see p. 46, where the presentation is somewhat tendentious.

4. As in the reading of the relationship between Derrida's work and 'American deconstruction' put forward by Jonathan Culler in *On Deconstruction: Theory and Criticism after Structuralism*, London: Routledge & Kegan Paul 1983, pp. 120 and 227–8.

5. p. xiv: 'My concern has been more pragmatic than scholarly.'

6. See too p. 63: 'Marxism thus adds a missing dimension to deconstruction by extending it into social and political-economic theory.'

7. This type of opposition can be read at work on, for example, pp. xiv, 56, 63, 78, 82, 102, 116, etc.

8. In a characteristic way, Ryan tends to *declare* rather than *show* that the distinction between theory and practice is untenable or undecidable: see for example pp. 14 and 34. It is none the less basic to the book's organization, and not, as Ryan would perhaps claim, simply retained *sous rature* out of strategic considerations.

9. Ryan does none the less use a 'later' text such as 'Limited Inc.', and a text such as 'Scribble' (Introduction to Warburton, *Essai sur les hiéroglyphes*, Paris: Aubier-Flammarion 1978; tr. in *Yale French Studies*, 58 (1979), 116–47), eminently 'serious' and 'political' in character, would have been worth attention. In general, there is no simple division of Derrida's texts into 'early' and 'late'. (This was written in 1983: there are of course many subsequent texts which would belie the early/late distinction Ryan appeals to here.)

10. See Derrida's 'Punctuations: The Time of a Thesis', in A. Montefiore, ed., *Philosophy in France Today*, Cambridge: Cambridge University Press, pp. 34–50 (pp. 42 and 44–5).

11. Ryan does acknowledge that 'critical marxists such as Negri excessively privilege subjectivity' (p. 91), without however seeming to question the associated notions in such as Negri of autonomy, self-management, etc. It is however welcome that he is suspicious of the invocation of Lacan, which has recently allowed Marxists to shore up their notion of the subject with some theoretical sophistication: see Ryan's discussion, pp. 104–12.

12. Ryan would not accept this assertion: see pp. 60–1 for the claim that Marx in fact deconstructs the nature/culture opposition. The argument is not entirely convincing.

13. The plural title of Derrida's *Positions* is one indication of this. Althusser's book of the same name (Paris: Editions Sociales 1976) would provoke a somewhat different reading.

14. Ryan privileges this notion in his presentation of deconstruction, without however invoking the text in which Derrida most fully discusses these terms ('Cartouches', in *The Truth in Painting*), except to dismiss it as one of his 'autobiographical reviews of Parisian art displays' (p. 43). Derrida never in fact suggests that a pure escape from the paradigm is possible, nor therefore a pure escape into seriality.

5

L'Arroseur Arrosé(e)

How are we to explain the many oversights and errors in these two books?[1] Both show an at least defensibly broad knowledge of the authors they analyse (though Gillian Rose is prepared to pontificate on Deleuze's relation to Nietzsche without apparently knowing that Deleuze has written a book on Nietzsche, and accuse Derrida of a 'naive' reading of Hegel without apparently having read Derrida's most extensive analysis, in *Glas* – and Peter Dews, who knows most of the texts, does not care to pursue Lyotard beyond the seventies, for reasons we shall see), and both include patches of intelligent and even sometimes quite clever writing. The problem must lie elsewhere, and the gross inaccuracies of detail and unfairnesses of presentation must be due to some other cause. It is not hard in such circumstances to suspect that a desire is at work: in both books, however different they are in scope, tone and strategy, this desire is to belittle, discredit and expel (most of if not all of) a bad object called in both cases 'post-structuralism'. In both cases, this expulsion involves an attempt to demonstrate that it's been said before (in German), and/or that it's wrong, and been left behind as at best an intermediate point along the way. Defending Germany (essentially a philosophical *tradition* for both authors) against France (essentially mere *fashion*) in this way (without ever thematizing the difficult question of philosophical nationality), both books manage to be peculiarly and dispiritingly English: Rose often seems to ground her arguments in a never elucidated notion of 'concrete historical situations' which almost any of the authors she discusses (starting with Kant) might have made more problematic; Dews, in an equally opaque notion of politics which is all too recognizable as the British Left's excuse for not wanting to think very hard. Both books more or less explicitly force the thinkers under discussion into a dialectical machinery which not surprisingly turns out to be allergic to them, and both are more or less consonant with the premises of that new unhappy positivist doxa known as 'cultural politics'. The confrontation of the two books produces a bizarre result: Dews's apparently well-informed and plausible work turns out to be the more reductive; Rose's demonstrably ill-informed and violent discussions engage with real issues. I shall concentrate on their discussions of Derrida, where the stakes are highest, and the misunderstandings and injustices most blatant.

Dews states his political rationale in his Preface, which tells a nice little – and undoubtedly sincere – story of an initial troubling encounter with post-structuralism: 'I was struck by the power and inventiveness of post-structuralist thinking, while simultaneously being disturbed by an awareness that many of its implications ran counter to my most deeply held political convictions' (p. ix). The book is the record of a long and hard-won escape from seduction – the depth of conviction is preserved against the initial *admiratio*, and the politics emerges on the side of theory and logic: 'Over the years, I have tried to work through this tension theoretically, in the belief that the logic of disintegration can ultimately be resisted on logical grounds' (ibid.). Logic is, then, on the side of political conviction and will see us through. This logical insistence is supposed to distinguish Dews's book from the purely 'moral' grounds from which the politics of post-structuralism have been attacked from both left and right (pp. xv–xvi): Dews will aim to give us a basically logical rather than moral politics: I would want to say that the attacks by Graff and Eagleton, which Dews takes as his examples of what to avoid, are political moralism rather than moral politics (which is of course what we all want) – but also that the pretension to establish a logical politics inevitably collapses into moralism anyway: for the claim to occupy ethical ground with cognitive truth (as too in Rose's constant implicit claim to know the Law) means merely that the ethical is squeezed into a situation where all it can do is hallucinate its own demise.

The reader, prepared with this comforting set-up and the good read it promises, is surprised to be almost unable to proceed beyond a section entitled 'The Politics of Deconstruction' in the first chapter of the book: for where Dews can apparently hold together politics and logic, Derrida is not allowed to have a politics precisely because politics and logic don't mix. This wonderfully aberrant section moves through the following points: (1) a repetition of the now traditional misreading of the end of 'Structure, Sign and Play', which assumes Derrida is simply urging on us a 'Nietzschean' Dionysianism; (2) a recognition that 'from the early 1970s onwards, Derrida makes more persistent – and undoubtedly sincere – attempts to link the theoretical activity of deconstruction [which is not in fact essentially a theoretical activity] up with more directly political engagements and practices' (pp. 34–5);

(3) an example of the beginner's error of conflating 'text' in Derrida's sense with 'discourse', and the concomitant complaint that Derrida's description of institutions as involving 'forces' and 'antagonisms' implies a 'politically necessary recognition of a non-textual reality' (p. 35) (this naturally taken as contradicting Derrida's best-known dictum about 'nothing outside the text' – it might just be worth suggesting, as a corrective, a quick look at 'Force and Signification' and 'Différance', though any other text will do); (4) the following attempt at a refutation: 'given that institutions are traversed by relations of force, it is difficult to see how deconstruction could be applied to them [to correct the error involved in this notion of "application" it might just be worth reading "Letter to a Japanese Friend", though any other text will do]. For deconstruction is centrally concerned with exposing the mechanisms whereby texts generate effects of meaning and truth while, at the same time, undermining them – in other words, with logical contradictions. Political antagonisms, however, cannot be reduced to logical contradictions' (p. 35). Reading breaks down here, in perplexity or laughter: Dews can apparently work out his political convictions and antagonisms logically, but Derrida apparently can't make any transition from the logical to the political, because of essentially incompatible features of these two domains. The logic of logic is therefore that it can communicate with politics when it suits me, but not otherwise. Whence the suspicion of moralism. Leaving aside the fact that it is quite mistaken to limit deconstruction to the search for logical contradiction (what delimits the *logos* cannot be entirely confined by logic), it is clear that, according to Dews's own 'logic', this contradiction between his description of his own work and that of Derrida leaves it completely undecidable whether the book is thereby duly rendered 'political' or not. It can only be political if it's logical, but it can't be logical if it's political: given how much is at stake, the best conclusion for everybody here must surely be that it's neither.

Derrida suggests that 'coherence in contradiction expresses the force of a desire': and the desire here is strong enough to dictate all sorts of large and small inaccuracies of presentation the better to make out the politico-logical case. For example, a few pages after the passage just quoted (which is less a passage than an aporia in the strict sense), Dews, on the basis of three examples of which the least one can say is that they do not immediately establish the point he wants to push, makes the astonishing claims that Derrida 'must argue that certain concepts have a necessary content which cannot be modulated by the uses to which they are put', and that 'Throughout Derrida's work it is possible to find pronouncements on the "essentially" metaphysical content of certain concepts' (p. 37). No references are given for this last sentence: even if it were possible – and perhaps Dews simply lost a record card – to find such pronouncements (as opposed to the idea that philosophical terms bring with them a load of metaphysical baggage which cannot simply be stipulated out and which is difficult to displace, which is a quite different claim, and which could rapidly be demonstrated by an analysis of Dews's (metaphysical) use of a term such as 'content' here), it might have seemed opportune even to an opponent of Derrida's thinking to quote the perfectly accessible and well-known remark in *Positions* that: 'I have never thought that there were concepts which were metaphysical in themselves. Moreover no concept is itself and consequently is not, in itself, metaphysical',[2] or, at the end of 'Signature, Event, Context': 'Each concept . . . belongs to a systematic chain and itself constitutes a system of predicates. There is no metaphysical concept in itself. There is work – metaphysical or not – on conceptual systems.'[3] Dews has read these well-known texts, in at least a minimal sense of 'read': that he clearly hasn't read them in any stronger sense implies he has been able to read practically nothing of Derrida, none of whose work would be conceivable without the possi-bility (and here we really are dealing with a necessity, with 'necessary possibility') of displacing conceptual networks and exploiting resources left uneasily dormant in metaphysical determinations.

This almost total misunderstanding and misrepresentation of Der-rida could be illustrated at many points, which all interconnect. Dews is concerned, for example, to argue that Derrida is 'determined to prevent any contamination between the empirical and the transcend-ental' (p. 18): this very peculiar idea, which Dews supports in a lengthy summary of Derrida's 'critique' of Merleau-Ponty (this 'critique' occu-pies about three pages of Derrida's first book, the *Introduction to Husserl's Origin of Geometry*, and consists in no more than a correction of Merleau-Ponty's misreading of certain aspects of Husserl's thought) is evidently linked to the claim that Derrida, unlike most post-Hegelian philosophers, 'continues to evade the exposure of thought to the contingency of interpretation, and the revisability of empirical know-ledge' (p. 37), whereas for Dews, following Adorno and Habermas, 'Philosophical concepts must be challenged and transformed in a confrontation with the results of concrete investigations, whether these take the form of empirical science or some other form' (p. 36). It is not at all clear from the context (even expanding that context to mean the whole of Dews's book) what this 'other form' is supposed to be: it seems to me that it would describe quite precisely the activity of deconstruction it is trying to attack. For it is in fact Dews who is maintaining, through his stupefyingly banal dialectic, the distinction between the empirical and the transcendental which is shown in

deconstruction both to have no ultimate transcendental validity and to
resist over-hasty attempts to confuse the distinction (such as that of
Merleau-Ponty in the context discussed above): deconstruction is,
despite the best efforts of Dews not to read, eminently describable
(with Gasché) as a 'radical empiricism' which exposes to contingency
and historicity (this is why deconstruction is less a theory than a series
of events) in a way which Dews's quite unquestioned notion of 'knowledge' will never understand, however many internal and empirically
inspired revisions of that knowledge the philosopher supervises. To
argue that deconstruction 'cannot learn from its objects' (p. 37) is to
assume quite unwarrantedly, that deconstruction *has* objects (and is
therefore a subject or the activity of a subject) after the fashion of
interpretation or critique: but this is to presuppose the very relation
that deconstruction is trying to unsettle.

Dews's own 'concrete' input, which I assume we are supposed to take
as exemplary of the positions for which he argues, takes two forms:
one an attempted genealogy of Derrida's work in the tradition of
German Idealism; one a sort of socio-historical description which is, I
imagine, supposed to give some 'empirical' edge to the book as a whole,
but which in fact functions as an unthematized transcendental.

The first of these strands argues that Derrida is not really new, and
that the essential aspects of his thinking are already contained in
German Idealism, and notably Fichte and Schelling. The form of this
argument is familiar and also to some extent informs Gillian Rose's
book. It presupposes that Derrida's work, identifiable as a set of theses,
happens at the end of an essentially linear history: both books assume
that that work claims to operate some sort of break with that history,
and endeavour to show that in fact no such break occurs. Even without
questioning those assumptions, the form of the attempted demonstration is not of itself very convincing: as Kant says in the *Prolegomena*,
'Men who never think independently have nevertheless the acuteness
to discover everything, after it has been once shown them, in what was
said long since, though no one could ever see it there before.'[4] But as
the premises about history upon which such remarks are inevitably
based are at the very least questioned in Derrida's work (though never
by those who trumpet the demands of history), and as deconstruction
happens 'in' Plato or Rousseau as much as 'in' Derrida (the scare-
quotes signalling that the relation of text to signature is a question not
to be prejudged), then it is unclear what points are to be scored in this
type of demonstration. We can be sure that there is confusion somewhere when it is possible for Dews to argue that Derrida thinks he's
doing something new when in fact he's repeating the tradition,
whereas Descombes, for example, takes Derrida to think there's

nothing new to be done, and all we can do is repeat the tradition – the suspicion is that both these claims are wrong, or at least invoke an insufficient understanding of repetition ('iteration alters: something new takes place').[5] In any case, however interesting Dews's expositions to those of us not very familiar with Fichte and Schelling, the attempted parallels fail on their own terms, even assuming that Fichte and Schelling are accurately presented here, because they are based on the assumption that what Derrida means by *différance* just is Absolute Difference (p. 27), whereas the point is that *différance* by definition resists any such absolutizing of difference: the 'track' which Derrida's reading attempts to leave in the text (p. 24) is also the trace of that resistance, which is why Dews is wrong to claim that 'this track can only be the mark of speculation' (ibid.). The violent reduction of *différance* to Absolute Difference makes it easy for Dews to operate dialectical exchanges with the notion of absolute identity which are unfortunately beside the point. This could be illustrated at any number of points, but perhaps never more clearly than where Dews attempts to argue that Derrida's account of supplementarity (which he rather misleadingly assimilates to 'the movement of the signifier' (see too p. 110 for an equally inaccurate presentation) – this much more Lacanian emphasis – 'signifier' is not a Derridean term – serves its purpose in the book, as we shall see) is formally identical to Fichte's account of an infinite regress of reflection (which it is not: supplementarity is neither progressive nor regressive): Dews claims that Derrida's description is unable to account for any emergence of meaning at all, but this would only be the case if *différance* were absolutized in a manner which Derrida explicitly disallows. Because Dews works within entirely metaphysical pairs he can only see the question of meaning within alternatives of determinacy or indeterminacy, whereas Derrida's work on iterability, for example (notably in the exchange with Searle), is able to account for the economy of determinacy and indeterminacy ('economy' here marking the fact that neither term is absolutizable) in a way which avoids the inevitable aporias of other accounts.

Dews, however, having set things up as we have seen, inevitably finds Lacan's account (which really is describable within the terms of the tradition) more understandable, and I should say that the presentation of Lacan seems to me to be the most valuable part of his book. Its value lies not only in its generosity of presentation, but in the way the account of Derrida's thinking is shown *a contrario* to be so insufficient. The crux of Dews's decision to follow Lacan at least in this first part of his book is, of course, the subject (here, as usual, always more or less confused with the human individual). Giving due consideration to Lacan's notion of the 'fading' of the subject, which he takes to prove 'how remote the Lacanian subject is from the notions of self-presence and self-identity denounced by Derrida' (p. 100), Dews promptly shows that it is not so remote at all, but merely pushed down a level or two, to become 'an underlying principle of the very transformation of self-identity, no matter how elusive this principle might be' (p. 101: the sub-ject just is what underlies transformation, and whether it be determined as conscious, unconscious or, elusively, as 'elusive' changes little here). When Derrida, locally and provisionally, defending the coherence of Husserl's thought against Merleau-Ponty's over-hasty attempt to confuse the *a priori* and the factical, suggests in a formally identical manner that the determination of difference must take place on the basis of an underlying intuition of sameness (and Dews might also have invoked Derrida's local and provisional defence of the coherence of Husserl's thinking against Levinas's hasty leap to 'absolute alterity'), Dews condemns him for excluding history and empiricity: when, having shown that the distributions on which a philosophy of the subject depends are indeed undermined by historicity (which is not *in* history), Derrida locates in Lacan an attachment to just those distributions, Dews condemns him for destroying the subject, despite careful statements by Derrida to the effect of 'situating' the subject rather than destroying it.

Dews's entirely linear view of thinkers' 'careers' also pushes him into the claim that only after the confrontation with Lacan has Derrida 'been obliged' to admit, at least implicitly, that he was wrong, and start talking about singularity and the idiom – whereas the question of singularity is of course the object of Derrida's discussion at least from 'La Parole soufflée' (1965), first published ten years before the piece on Lacan, is raised as a problem in the *Grammatologie* (1967), and is also the object of treatment in terms of proper name and signature, in an effort to talk of singularity without falling back into a philosophy of the subject, in *Signéponge*, first a conference paper from 1975, the same year as the piece on Lacan. Maybe Derrida realized his mistake very quickly; maybe even before he made it. Dews contrives, against the most obvious facts, to present this situation as a before (Derrida destroys the subject) and an after (Derrida repents), and then to condemn the repentance for not being complete enough. The pressure of this type of linear account can produce comic effects: Dews claims that Derrida is in decline after 1975, but generously concedes that some good Derridean work was done thereafter: his example is of Lacoue-Labarthe and Nancy's *Le Titre de la lettre*, which dates from 1973.

This example will already give some idea of what to expect from the second of the strands which are supposed to illustrate the acceptance by philosophy of empirical input and the revisability of knowledge.

This second strand, which I have somewhat ennobled by calling it
'socio-historical', plays a vital role in constituting Dews's object under
the title of 'post-structuralism'. This is no longer, we are told in the
Introduction, a 'living force' in France (whatever that means), and, at
the beginning of Chapter 1, that 'this designation cannot be understood in a strictly chronological sense' (p. 1): and yet a certain chronological emphasis is maintained because of what Dews calls 'public
consciousness' upon which there 'dawned' 'the possibility of a theoretical advance beyond structuralism' (p. 2). This type of entirely journal-
istic 'history' provides the frame for all the discussions in the book, no
doubt giving some vague 'socio-historical' credibility to the project or
some 'context' for the logical resistance the quality of which we have
already sampled. This is a history of a philosophical scene with heroes
and a demanding public, where what counts is success and influence
and the defeat of rival stars. This strand mingles happily enough with
the first, apparently more serious, type of analysis in terms of philosophical tradition. Derrida's success, in the intellectual climate of the
late 1960s (p. 4), for example, is attributed to a use of the French
tradition (positivism to structuralism (p. 3)) against the German ('to
which he belongs' (p. 5)), and vice versa – this double manoeuvre
creating the impression or illusion of radical breaks all over the place.
When this type of apparently serious grounding in tradition is not
invoked, however, the effect is quite comical. For example, with no
apparent sense of the circularity of the account, Dews tells us with
Lentricchean seriousness that 'it is no accident' that Lacan and Derrida
'gained their first wide popular acclaim' (the roar of the crowd) at
around the same time: because the 'time was ripe' (p. 92). But then
Lacan surged ahead while Derrida waned (after the 'hectic wordplay
of *Glas*' (p. 93): this almost obligatory type of description of *Glas*
suggests that Dews hasn't read it either), and couldn't even reconquer
his public with involvement in the GREPH: 'it can be no accident',
Dews repeats, that this is when Derrida published his major attack on
Lacan. Nor is it an accident that Lacan's 'success . . . persisted undimi-
nished until his death' (p. 94): this is not just to do with institutional
resources, charisma, mesmeric lectures (ibid.) – for we are not dealing
here with 'simply an external phenomenon of fashion' (p. 93): oh no –
the point is that Lacan really *is better*, providing 'precisely what a public
no longer satisfied with the philosophically inadequate formulas of
structuralism would be looking for: a theory of the subject which no
longer took the form of a philosophy of consciousness' (p. 94). Consumer culture. Customer always right. Lacan delivers goods. Derrida:
weak product, poor marketing, bad customer relations: no wonder it
doesn't sell. In the ruthless world of the intellectual marketplace, he

was competing with Lacan, and just never could get his act together 'in what must be considered the central area of their common concern: the relation of language and meaning to subjectivity and consciousness' (ibid.: this assertion is debatable at the very least). Buy Lacan, 'nuanced and discerning' (p. 94): the public says yes.

It is something of a mystery what such descriptions (there are others, all couched in this vague and unreflected *Zeitgeist* language) are doing in the book. There is presumably an underlying assumption here (common enough in Britain at the moment) that what gets called 'cultural history' (or cultural politics) has final legitimacy in accounts of literature and thought. I fear (I hope) that even self-proclaimed cultural historians would not recognize Dews's sketches as the sort of thing they want to do: but even if they did, this would not alter the fact that even the most informed and subtle cultural history cannot account for its own historicity, which is precisely the level of the questions posed by Derrida and Lyotard, and even (more obscurely) Foucault and Lacan. Cultural history may lay some claims to understand 'post-structuralism' *as a cultural phenomenon* — but what matters about the thought of the authors identified with that movement cannot by definition be explained at that level. Dews's book perpetuates the commonest of errors (encouraged by, precisely, an uncontrolled confusion of empirical and transcendental argument) by assuming that history, in the very simplest sense, has the last word. This in fact entails a surreptitious transcendentalizing of history and is fundamentally obscurantist (and, again, moralistic) in effect if not intention. Dews would no doubt want to re-historicize *these* remarks by linking them to what he calls the 'curious restoration climate' in the current French philosophical scene, 'in which the need is felt to protect philosophy from a supposedly diminishing relation to the human sciences' (p. xiv): but this is not an argument about a hierarchy of values, simply a demand for clarity and rigour, respecting elementary distinctions without which the worst confusion sets in — distinctions which, as with many of the features Dews wants to locate in specific datable moments, in fact pervade the work of Derrida and Lyotard (at least) from the beginning.

This type of narrative account, whatever its essential limitations, does seem more plausible when applied to Foucault and Lyotard, Dews's two other principal objects of discussion. Their work does indeed seem more easily divisible into periods or phases, and May 1968 seems a reasonable date to use for some orientation. Dews uses May '68 as what it seems kindest to view as a convenient fiction: the 'events' showed that structuralist-style descriptions could not account for change in social structures: 'Social systems are both imposed by

force from above – they embody relations of *power* – and are adhered to
or rejected from below – they are invested or disinvested with *desire'*
(pp. 110–11) – Foucault and Lyotard, there you have it.

I do not intend to dwell on the detail of the exposition of Lyotard
and Foucault, much of which is useful enough. Foucault is much more
Dews's sort of thing (however severe his criticisms) because much of
Foucault's own work betrays the sorts of confusion of the philosophical
and the historical which we have seen to inform Dews's whole
approach, and which allows his comparisons with the Frankfurt school
to seem more interesting here. It is significant, however, that Dews's
account of *Discours, figure* and some contemporaneous texts of Lyotard's, simply accepts as correct Lyotard's criticisms of Derrida,
whereas they are in general based on a misunderstanding, parallel to
Dews's own, of the status of Derrida's term 'text'. Lyotard's book is
among other things (as Dews recognizes) a devastating critique of the
linguisticism to which Lacan is certainly prone, but it is mistaken to
attribute such a linguisticism to Derrida too. Lyotard's notion of
'difference' in *Discours, figure* is to what he calls 'opposition' not unlike
what Derrida's *différance* is to any determinate difference, and is
certainly not in opposition to it. If any motif justifies the term 'post-
structuralism' beyond its cultural sense, it is a defence of difference
from its automatic determination – in dialectical style (see Hegel's
discussion of Absolute Difference in the *Greater Logic*) – as opposition
and contradiction. If Dews had pursued Lyotard's work as far as *Le
Différend* (1983), he might have been able to show that the notion
developed in that book of a 'presentation' which is never present
maintains important emphases from *Discours, figure* while being manifestly consonant with Derrida's *différance*. It is also a little strange that
Dews devotes discussion to a somewhat unhappy article of Lyotard's
on the notion of alienation in Marx (pp. 128–9 and 201–2), but
nowhere so much as mentions the violent and scandalous discussion of
Marx in *Economie libidinale*, which would certainly have deserved
attention in any 'historical' presentation (not to speak of impact on the
'public'), nor the calmer discussion in *Le différend*, which would cast
some doubt on the logical politics Dews seems to want. Similarly, the
political ideas propounded around the time of *Discours, figure* are
indicted by Dews for what he calls 'an elementary bad faith' because
they do not 'outline any intended alternative order' (p. 131), with no
mention of the fact that the very form of this reproach is the object of
subsequent analysis and refutation, especially *Le Différend*, but already
in *Economie libidinale*, if we must accept Dews's periodizations. Lyotard's more general sense of 'politics' as an endless task of judging in
absence of a Law to certify what judgement is 'correct' (and thereby in

absence of the debilitating effects of all politics conceived within the horizon of the sublation of the political, as all dialectical politics are), has the inestimable advantage of not fantasizing, projecting and prescribing an *order* at all, without in any way thereby being the 'anarchy' whose spectre is reported to be looming whenever Right or Left finds it needs more than three ideas to think with.

More generally, Dews is concerned to put all these authors into a dialectical fairy-story whereby an initial 1960s 'idealism' of language in Derrida and even Lacan is challenged by the non-discursive 1970s (desire, power). This supposedly 'second phase' of post-structuralism is taken to be justified in its criticisms of the first (though Lacan's eccentric position here still needs to be explained), and when its claims are shown to be wanting (Foucault retreating into a 'residual natural-ism' (p. 169) of 'the body and its pleasures', Lyotard spurning *Economie libidinale* in *Au Juste*, where, on the basis of a loose remark contrasting *logos* and *lexis*, compounded by his own tendentious transcription of *logos* as simply 'reason', Dews feels able to detect 'the death-knell of post-structuralism' (p. 219)), Dews can confidently pronounce the whole big bad thing dead and point us towards Habermas in his conclusion. We have seen how this story dictates the quite ridiculous treatment of Derrida and the decision to stop discussion of Lyotard at a certain point. It remains to mop up Lacan with Habermas, which is done by arguing that Lacan has no distinction between the symbolic and social orders, and the job is done. Again, everything Dews takes from Habermas in his Conclusion is vulnerable to arguments in the later Lyotard against the general privilege accorded here to the cognitive dimension of language, as if it could be taken for granted – but it is precisely around this point that the important ethical and political questions need to be raised. Nothing that Dews quotes from Habermas in these closing pages suggests that the latter's magic concept of intersubjectivity will solve these problems: it is all very well for Habermas (as Dews presents him here, but *The Philosophical Discourse of Modernity* is in fact rather worse) to claim that the 'alternative' of transcendental and empirical falls away at this point – this is only so because the transcendental problems involved in saying 'ego stands in an interpersonal relationship, which allows him or her to relate to him- or herself as a participant in an interaction from the perspective of the other' (quoted pp. 240–1) are assumed to have been solved, but the embarrassed mix of transcendental ('ego') and empirical ('him or her') language suggests that the solution to those problems is simply presup-posed. Of course a great many areas of thought ('sociology' in a broad sense) have to presuppose such a solution if they are to get any work done, but that does not mean they provide one. Dews suggests that

Derrida gets nowhere here, because of an 'inability to provide anything other that a repudiation of the philosophy of the subject, which
continues to share its fundamental premises' (p. 241): but the unavoidable conclusion is that it is Habermas and Dews who continue to share
those premisses by waving the flag of intersubjectivity, whereas Derrida's use of the quasi-concept of the trace, and his dialogue with
Levinas, promise some understanding instead of this obscurantism
shored up only by vague and self-righteous appeals to politics. The
basic problem is summarized in a remark on Lyotard, quite extraordinary for its hesitancy, given how much of Dews's argument hangs on
this point, from the penultimate paragraph of the book: 'it is surely
implausible to suggest that repression can be attributed purely to the
nature of language as such, rather than largely resulting from the
rigidification of language under specific institutional pressures'
(p. 241) – be that 'largely' ever so large, the residue it leaves and cannot
explain (and this residue alone makes the rest possible, has, indeed,
'transcendental' effects) may, perhaps, be worth attention.

It is a surprising pleasure to re-read Gillian Rose's very fierce book
after Dews, although again the problems are many and strange. After
a first part to which we shall return, the strategy here, directed against
Deleuze, Derrida and Foucault, is to spray out page after page of
accusation in the hope that some of it will stick – large parts of these
chapters read as though Rose has simply transcribed into her text
exasperated notes written in the margin while reading rather distract-
edly. It is often difficult to sense more of an argumentative direction
than that, and the effect is peculiarly amusing: clearly *nothing* these
authors have ever said is right. As with so much criticism of the authors
claimed (never by themselves, I think) to be 'post-structuralist', many
of the objections raised here are directed against positions which the
authors in question have never held, and some of them repeat arguments against such positions which those authors have or would have
accepted without difficulty. The general form of these moments (see
especially in the Introduction and Conclusion (pp. 5 and 208)) is that
Rose foists on to her objects claims about surpassing and overcoming
which are couched in the very language which the authors in question
are trying, more or less patiently and successfully, to question obliquely. No such obliquity for Rose, who strides in waving her red pen,
underlining and crossing out and giving about a D+ to the poor
candidates, who really should try harder. On p. 175 she misreads a
passage from Foucault to find in it a 'tone of indictment', but never
apparently reflects that this might describe her book as a whole.

The worst, reactive, impulse is to do the same to her, and produce a
simple list of the worst blunders. This is tiresome but not entirely

avoidable, and, as always, would require much more time and space than did the original errors. Let me simply borrow the red pen for a sentence, to say that *every page* of the Derrida chapter contains serious errors of presentation of Derrida's thought about, for example, law, writing, metaphor, Rousseau, Hegel and Heidegger. These errors range from a practice of selective quotation which can affirm that statements in the *Grammatologie* about Heidegger are made about Hegel (p. 139), can replace the word '*Aufhebung*' with the word 'writing' in a quotation from *Writing and Difference* (p. 163), and severely cut remarks about mathematization and materialism in *Positions* (p. 164), through the misapprehension that the *Grammatology* is a 'critique of ancient and modern natural law' (p. 132), a history of writing (p. 135), and an attempt to prove Rousseau wrong and reserve all insight for Derrida himself (p. 137), to general misapprehensions as to the terms 'writing' and 'metaphoricity' (pp. 147 and 165), and simple ignorance of texts which her own perspective would make vital reading ('Plato's Pharmacy', *Glas*). (Substantive points which rely on errors of detail in published translations also appear on pp. 140, 147 and 148–9, but I write these in black rather than red.)

The extreme density of occurrence of these sometimes quite gross and sometimes quite minor errors (which tend to come down to an extreme violence of decontextualization imposing all but intolerable demands of vigilance on the critical reader and contrasting oddly with some of the apparent care shown in reading in Part I of the book, which is occasionally almost deconstructive in its quality of attention) makes this a difficult book to discuss. And yet it is pursuing a theme of immense importance with a sense of the philosophical stakes involved which is certainly not to be dismissed. The story Rose tells is one of a repetition since Kant of what she calls with rather little explanation 'the antinomy of law', which is roughly the split in the law between description and prescription (redescribed on p. 17n30 as 'juridical' and 'litigious' for reasons that maybe beg some questions), regularity and ruling (but also generality and particularity, freedom and necessity, value and validity, subjecthood and subjection: the links between these various formulations are never clarified, and at one point, perhaps under pressure of this proliferation, she refers to antinom*ies* of law): in Kant the mysteries of the categorical imperative and of the 'usurpatory concept' of freedom function in her reading rather like what Derrida (unfavourably quoted on this by Rose on p. 135) would call a blind spot or vanishing point which organizes the textuality of the whole Kantian system and, by extension, of transcendental philosophy in general. By checking the analogically juridical terminology of Kant's three *Critiques* against the definitions provided in the *Metaphysical*

Elements of Justice (and there is an unfortunate lack of methodological justification for this reliteralization of a juridical terminology in the *Critiques* which those texts can in principle allow for as providing analogical presentations – can we be sure that that language, irreducible though it may be, can so simply be explicated on the strength of the *Elements*, a doctrinal and no longer critical text?), Rose is able to argue that the whole tribunal of Reason is rooted in an ultimately unjustifiable claim the legal title of which cannot be satisfactorily established. Whence the unfortunate retreat of law and the general Kantian *quaestio quid juris* into mystery and unknowability. The book then simply tracks what it claims is a repetition of this failure to know the law through the schools of Marburg and Heidelberg and on to the post-structuralists: chapters habitually end by asserting that the thinkers discussed remain in thrall to this antinomy (assuming it to be singular), perpetuating the law's unknowability with varying degrees of dangerousness while pretending to have got beyond it – thus on Heidegger (pp. 65 and 83, where he 'keeps the commandments of the Torah from us' – the suggestions linking Heidegger and Judaic thinking in this chapter might well contribute to the current exchanges around Heidegger and Nazism, and compared perhaps essentially with Lyotard's recent *Heidegger et 'les juifs'* (Paris: Galilée 1988)); on Deleuze (p. 108); on Lévi-Strauss (p. 130); on Derrida (p. 168); and Foucault (p. 207).

What will save us from this fate is, improbably enough, a certain sociology, or so it seems at first. Rose is very upset to find that Foucault 'discredits sociology but uses its central concepts and theses, smuggling in the main sociological recasting of the question of law' (p. 200), and generally takes post-structuralism to task for 'eschewing the sociological alternative to metaphysics' (p. 5). Most clearly, perhaps, the claim is made in the Conclusion that sociology inherited these problems from (a correctly interpreted) Hegel (break off here and read her earlier, admirable, *Hegel Contra Sociology* to find out what that correct interpretation involves) and Nietzsche: 'Socio-logic relieved transcendental logic of that unending trial of reason by taking the persons of the law out of the critical court-room and recasting them as social actors, by taking rights and obligations and treating them as status and role, by turning juridical things into social interaction' (p. 211). This is of course of a piece with the stern demand made for location in concrete historical situations: Kant's best efforts, we are told, lead to no more than a rededuction of Roman Law (p. 22), and the Kingdom of Ends of his practical philosophy is solidly grounded in the basic distinction of Roman private law between persons and things, a distinction which cannot be formalized or idealized in the way Kant requires. Kant's claims about autonomy are thus undermined by an irreducible heteronomy in the form of the historically specific categories of Roman Law. All that post-structuralism does is to repeat a merely apparent transcendental enigma that is resolvable into the right sort of historical description.

But this is to give Rose's book a rather crude positivist look it does not in fact quite always have. And this also means that sociology is not what will save us from post-structuralism – for sociology is itself in thrall to the law: 'Sociological repetition of structure and action arises from its status as the jurisprudence of actor and obligation; it may be that we have become so accustomed to thinking that law blinds us to the social that we overlook how socio-logic blinds us to law' (p. 211). But this then leaves us in a curious situation of uncertainty which takes the point and edge off the knife that Rose has been trying to stick into post-structuralism all through her book. For these last comments are pretty much the sorts of reproach we levelled at Dews, and it is interesting that Rose takes implicit distance from Dews's two winners, Adorno and Habermas, in her final paragraph, and that the only explicit reference the book makes to either of these thinkers is a footnote (p. 80 n19) suggesting Adorno was wrong about Heidegger (and in *Hegel Contra Sociology*, Habermas is given very short shrift). And we also tend to nod with agreement when Rose asserts that the unanswered question of the 'law',

> founds the idea of method we still revere and grounds the oppositions which still condition us – metaphysics and science; theory and practice; freedom and necessity; history and form. The discovery that the form of reason and the form of law imply each other did not become the occasion [in this book] to devise a reformed Kriticismus, but to acknowledge the complexity of our continuing witness which went on to divulge further strata of litigious experience disciplined even by the forms of intuition, space and time, themselves. (pp. 211–12)

It seems that sociology won't be able to help much with this, unless, but it seems unlikely, Rose is urging that we just have to give up trying either to answer the question of the law or to escape from the law, and get on writing history or anthropology.

It seems rather that the anger and injustice of much of the book is to do with what the 'post-structuralists' say about Hegel: for Rose would claim that their readings of Hegel are just as violent and unjust as I am suggesting hers are of Derrida et al. The crux is this: for Rose, 'dialectical history is multiple and complex', not, as its critics claim, 'unitary and simply progressive' (p. 3). But post-structuralism would not disagree with that – more with the way that multiplicity and complexity are handled. Again, the section on Absolute Difference in the *Greater Logic* would be a good place to start showing how Hegel, purporting to get opposition and contradiction out of diversity and difference, is in fact already determining diversity and difference as opposition and contradiction in a way which is certainly complicated, but which is as teleological and therefore as unitary as anyone could wish.

Rose is determined to show that Hegel survives post-structuralism, and spends long pages arguing that Derrida has got him all wrong. Thus for example, 'Derrida claims that his "displacement" of Hegelian language is "both infinitesimal and radical"', when it is, in effect, predictable and knowable within the Hegelian system' (p. 161), or 'It is Derrida's writing which produces a restricted economy within the more general economy' (p. 162); it looks to Rose as though Derrida is relying on a conventionally 'conservative' or reactionary reading of Hegel, but in the end, 'He produces not a reactionary or a revolutionary reading of Hegel but a naive one' (p. 163). This 'naivety' seems to involve taking too 'literally' (i.e. not speculatively, Hegelianly enough) Hegelian themes such as Absolute Knowledge, teleology, contradiction, *Aufhebung*, dialectic, history, Spirit, and so on. If I understand Rose's purportedly non-traditional reading of Hegel (break off here and re-read *Hegel Contra Sociology*), the reappropriative element is less marked than Derrida pretends (she thinks Derrida misunderstands Hegel's copula as stating the very abstract identity it is splitting, and takes Derrida's designation of Hegel as the first thinker of writing to imply a wholly traditional concession to a radicality of 'method', without unfortunately explaining this very clearly). The implication is that Derrida sets up a reductive, reappropriative Hegel to make his own 'supplementarity' look more original. Derrida does not recognize himself in the mature Hegel's work on difference, and when he attempts to find something going on in an early text, he gets it wrong, overlooking 'how differente beziehung is, for Hegel, above all a relationship since from the perspective of differance no relationship can be known' (pp. 160–1).

There are a number of ways that these points might be countered. We already know for example, that this last claim is false: 'from the perspective of différance' (which is not a 'perspective') relationships may be known but not absolutely known, and absolute knowledge does not organize the scene, even if we allow with Rose that absolute knowledge is 'never finished' (p. 162). The easiest way to counter the accusation around the speculative proposition is to read the left-hand column of *Glas* without getting in a panic about 'hectic wordplay'. We might look too, for example, to Lyotard's demonstration in *Le différend* that the whole movement of the speculative dialectic depends on the presupposition of the operator of the Result (which is not therefore a result, to the extent that it is presupposed), which drags diversity into opposition, contradiction and sublation. Or turn to Michel Serres's argument at the beginning of the first volume of *Hermès*[6] for understanding the dialectic as an unnecessarily reductive operation compared with a network-model. Or François Laruelle's recent and rather daunting discussion of 'philosophies of difference' in their difference, precisely, from dialectical thinking.[7] These references would of course require extensive analysis. The point, however, is simply that what Rose and Dews both call 'post-structuralism' is, in so far as it has common preoccupations, an extremely modest and even minimal thinking which questions the maximal hetero-tautological movement which, whether Rose likes it or not, determines in principle Hegel's thinking, however many details one may find which cause trouble for this movement, and however long one dwells over that trouble as what in fact keeps the movement moving. That it be possible to demonstrate the 'logic' of the 'general economy' on the basis of Hegel in no way contradicts this, but is predicted by a thinking of difference, which the dialectic never can quite reduce, but cannot quite tolerate either. No one is trying to deny that this is all very close to Hegel, right up against him. But the remainder, the text (in all its senses) is just what Rose cannot read, as her indiscriminate practice of quotation shows. That we condemn this practice as unjust and unfair shows, of course, that we are still involved with the law – but where Rose sees us nihilistically perpetuating that law's unknowability, we see her extraordinarily violent and intolerant pretension to know it and lay it down as precisely the source of her worst injustice.

In her Introduction, Gillian Rose suggests that 'When Philosophy visits Boethius in the imperial prison, when Rousseau brings Sophie along to complete Emile's personality, when Zarathustra goes to visit her with his whip, it is at the crux of gender that philosophy – love of wisdom – the republic, and the legal fictions of personality explode' (p. 6). Read *Glas* to see if Derrida would disagree: but then wonder which, of that book and *Dialectic of Nihilism*, claims for itself the phallogocentric arrogance of the Law.

Notes

1. Reviewing Peter Dews, *Logics of Disintegration: Post-Structuralist Thought and the Claims of Critical Theory*, London: Verso 1987; and Gillian Rose, *Dialectic of Nihilism: Post-Structuralism and Law*, Oxford: Blackwell 1984. Page references will be given in the text.

2. Jacques Derrida, *Positions*, Paris: Minuit 1972, pp. 77–8.

3. Jacques Derrida, *Marges – de la philosophie*, Paris: Minuit 1972, pp. 392–3.

4. Immanuel Kant, *Prolegomena to any Future Metaphysics that will be able to come Forward as Science*, tr. P. Carus, revised by James W. Ellington, Indianapolis: Hackett Publishing Company 1977, p. 18.

5. Jacques Derrida, *Limited Inc.*, Paris: Galilée 1990, p. 82.

6. Michel Serres, *Hermès I: La Communication*, Paris: Minuit 1969.

7. François Laruelle, *Les Philosophies de la différence: Introduction critique*, Paris: PUF 1986, describes difference as being 'the principal problematic which will give its dominant colour to twentieth-century philosophy as "history" and the "dialectic" did for the nineteenth' (p. 7).

PART II
Readings

6

The Perfect Cheat: Locke and

Empiricism's Rhetoric

The title of this paper is derived from a famous and much-quoted passage in Book III of Locke's *Essay Concerning Human Understanding*,[1] in which rhetoric is denounced:

> If we would speak of Things as they are, we must allow, that all the art of Rhetorick, besides Order and Clearness, all the artificial and figurative application of Words Eloquence hath invented, are for nothing else but to insinuate wrong *Ideas*, move the Passions, and thereby mislead the Judgment; and so indeed are perfect cheat . . .[2]

The chapter in which this denunciation appears is entitled 'Of the Abuses of Words', and the passage on rhetoric ends that chapter, being the last of the 'abuses' Locke lists. The chapter follows that dealing with the 'Imperfections' of words, and its object is distinguished from such Imperfections in that whereas the latter are, in principle at least, faults of language itself rather than of its users, the former, the abuses, involve what Locke calls '*wilful Faults and Neglects*', of which men are 'guilty'[3]. 'Imperfections' involve problems which are properly epistemological, 'Abuses' problems which are rather moral and political in nature. The chapter on these abuses is followed by one devoted to suggested 'remedies' to both imperfections and abuses, and these remedies attempt to minimize the imperfections and eradicate the abuses through a purification, in the sense of an expurgation or an expulsion. Locke will not attempt to reform language in general, although the reasons for not attempting such a reform are not themselves so much philosophical as practical and even worldly, based at once on a measure despair with 'Men' and on a disapproval of the 'vanity' such a reform would imply on the part of a reformer, and motivated by the eminently worldly fear of appearing 'ridiculous'.[4] He will try to expel abuse from, and reduce the effects of imperfection in, not the whole of language, but the area of philosophy, the domain of those '*who* pretend *seriously* to *search after*, or maintain *Truth*',[5] or, as the section on rhetoric has it, the place 'where Truth and Knowledge are concerned'.[6] Philosophy should thus be an enclave of clarity within the 'world' (the 'world', as the writings on education tell us, being the place of deceit, desire and the novel), and should establish and maintain frontiers against encroachment from that other space, while restraining itself, with a certain regret, from making forays or crusades into that space. For example, discussing the redoubtable problems posed by the 'Names of *Substances*', Locke says that conformity of these names with things 'as they exist' is 'absolutely necessary in Enquiries after philosophical Knowledge, and in Controversies about Truth', and continues:

> And though it would be well too, if it extended it self to common Conversation, and the ordinary Affairs of Life; yet I think, that is scarce to be expected. Vulgar Notions suit vulgar Discourses: and both, though confused enough, yet serve pretty well the Market, and the Wake. Merchants and Lovers, Cooks and Taylors, have Words wherewithal to dispatch their ordinary Affairs; and so, I think, might Philosophers and Disputants too, if they had a Mind to understand, and to be clearly understood.[7]

Or, in the same vein: 'the Market and Exchange must be left to their own ways of Talking, and Gossippings not be robb'd of their ancient Privilege . . .'[8]

It is worth noting immediately, although for the moment I do no more than note, that this tolerant division of discursive space and the peaceful topology it implies is troubled by Locke's persistent implication that the creation of too closed a space for philosophy can lead to the sterile wrangling of the Schools, and the concomitant desire, voiced in his 'Epistle to the Reader', to make philosophy 'fit' and 'capable' 'to be brought into well-bred Company, and polite Conversation', this 'bringing' of Philosophy 'into' the 'world' going with a certain incursive violence marked in the project to 'break in upon the Sanctuary of Vanity and Ignorance', in the 'Service of Humane Understanding'.

Leaving aside this trouble and violence, it would seem at first that the more benign picture of discursive spaces sketched above is valid in the particular 'abuse' of language constituted by rhetoric. For in discussing this case, Locke admits the existence of discourses 'where we seek rather Pleasure and Delight, than Information and Instruction',[9] and in such discourses would seem to allow, a little grudgingly, the *figurative Speeches*, and allusion in Language' which he condemns in philosophy. Such uses of language are 'laudable or allowable' (it is worth pondering the value of the 'or' in this formulation), in 'Harangues and popular Addresses', but are 'wholly to be avoided' in 'all Discourses that pretend to inform or instruct', and, further, 'where Truth and Knowledge are concerned, cannot but be thought a great fault, either of the Language or Person that makes use of them'.[10] So rhetoric is, perhaps, acceptable in its place, and that place is not philosophy; there is a frontier to be respected and policed. But, on the other hand, it would seem that despite a show of tolerance, philosophy only constitutes this frontier by transgressing it and by occupying provisionally, as a sort of pre-emptive strike, the ground of rhetoric itself. For the value of the 'laudable or acceptable' compliment condescendingly paid to rhetoric in its place is doubtful, given the prior condemnation of rhetoric's general aim to 'insinuate wrong *Ideas*, move the passions, and thereby mislead the Judgment'. Rhetoric's status as 'perfect cheat' is a *general* fault of rhetoric *as such*, which is thus really deprived of any legitimate ground at all. Its ground is in principle already that of illegitimacy, of planned deceit rather than simply error.

This status of rhetoric can be clarified by comparison with a passage in which Locke is condemning the abuse involved in using words inconsistently in reference to collections of simple ideas;

> Words being intended for signs of my *Ideas*, to make them known to others, not by any natural signification, but by a voluntary imposition, 'tis plain cheat and abuse, when I make them stand sometimes for one thing, and sometimes for another; the wilful doing whereof, can be imputed to nothing but great folly, or greater dishonesty. . . . If Men should do so in their Reckonings, I wonder who would have to do with them? One who would speak thus, in the Affairs and Business of the World, and call 8 sometimes seven, and sometimes nine, as best served his Advantage, would presently have clapp'ed upon him one of the two Names Men constantly are disgusted with. And yet in Arguings, and learned Contests, the same sort of proceeding passes commonly for Wit and Learning: but to me it appears a greater dishonesty, than the misplacing of Counters, in the casting up a Debt; and the cheat the greater, by how much Truth is of greater concernment and value, than money.[11]

Despite obvious analogies, the difference between this type of 'plain cheat' and rhetoric's 'perfect cheat' is perhaps the following. This 'plain cheat', along with other abuses listed in the chapter, is worth denouncing in these terms because it can be remedied by a sort of intellectual and ethical hygiene: the 'Errors and Obscurity', the 'Mistakes and Confusion',[12] and the moral turpitude their use can imply can be avoided by applying the remedies Locke puts forward in Chapter XI. But rhetoric, the 'perfect cheat', is introduced and expelled in this single section, given neither detailed discussion nor detailed remedies. There is no need, says Locke, to list the various 'artificial and figurative application of Words Eloquence hath invented', because that is already the job of rhetoric *itself*, and is thus *already* in the domain of the cheat. Nor is there any need to suggest remedies to rhetoric, as there is in the case of the other imperfections and abuses. Rhetoric is not an imperfection, it is *perfect* cheat; and if it is abuse, it is not a local and corrigible abuse, but a counter-move to Truth and Knowledge *in general*. Further, following an apparently non-philosophical reasoning similar to that used against any project to reform language in general, Locke states that although philosophy can deplore rhetoric, it cannot pretend to eradicate it, because rhetoric, concerned to 'move the Passions', is itself the *object* of a passion, of love. The passion that rhetoric-as-deceit moves is already the passion *for* rhetoric-as-deceit:

> 'Tis evident how much Men love to deceive, and be deceived, since Rhetorick, that powerful instrument of Error and Deceit, has its established Professors, is publickly taught, and has always been had in great Reputation: And, I doubt not, but it will be thought great boldness, if not brutality in me, to have said thus much against it. *Eloquence*, like the fair Sex, has too prevailing Beauties in it, to suffer it self ever to be spoken against. And 'tis vain to find fault with those Arts of Deceiving, wherein Men find pleasure to be Deceived.[13]

The artful, feminine perfection of the 'cheat' of Rhetoric is such as to avoid having 'clapp'd upon' it one of those unnamed names 'Men constantly are disgusted with'. By avoiding saying something like, ' 'Tis pity she's a whore', Locke is already seduced into his nicely rhetorical final sentence, perhaps because he knew that saying something like ' 'Tis pity she's a whore' would not have saved him either. The brief step, or *pas*, of philosophy into rhetoric in this section introduces a veiled glimpse of the veiled delights of desire; Locke then moves quickly onto the remedies for what can be remedied, finishing his book on language, and gets on with the stern business 'Of Knowledge in General'.

Let me recapitulate briefly: rhetoric is not a local and corrigible abuse of language, a partial threat to Truth and Knowledge, as are the other imperfections and abuses. It involves, not so much a set of blunders or unfortunate inadequacies, nor yet a local dishonesty, as a completely different attitude towards language and its use, an incommensurability which is a generalized threat. Locke can be so brief and perfunctory in his treatment of rhetoric because his common ground with it is merely that of language. But he can be concerned by it and irritated with it because there is that common ground nevertheless. Having moved into the question of language in Book III of the *Essay* rather to his own surprise,[14] Locke inevitably confronts rhetoric somewhere. The rapidity and force with which the problem is discussed and dispatched, and the ambivalence of the condemnation, might be read as a symptom of a worry that rhetoric might turn out to be a big problem if it is *not* so dispatched. In this paper I want to suggest that it is indeed a big problem for Locke, in so far as it is coterminous with the problem of language in general. This argument implies that rhetoric escapes from the frontiers imposed on it in section 34 of chapter X of Book III, and permeates the whole of Book III, in so far (and that is not very far) as that is where Locke's discussion of language is located. As it can and will be argued that on Locke's own terms language as a problem cannot be confined within the frontiers of Book III, but invades the *Essay* as a whole, then rhetoric will expand to become a crucial problem in Locke's whole enterprise. I shall argue that rhetoric is in fact an undermining and eventually deconstructive force at work in the most basic elements of Locke's account of knowledge. As is the way with rhetoric, this argument seduces me and arouses my desire; this desire is ambivalent with respect to Locke, but I take comfort from the fact that, in part at least, it is his desire too – for in the 'epistle to the Reader', he encourages me by saying: 'If thou findest any thing wanting, I shall be glad, that what I have writ, gives thee any Desire, that I should have gone farther'.[15] Whether the object of this desire is the 'Delight' and 'Pleasure' Locke ascribes to the understanding's 'searches after truth', and whether such pleasure is indeed to be located in great part in 'the very pursuit', are questions I leave open. As I shall not have the time to support the possibly scandalous claim that rhetoric is basic to Locke's *Essay* as fully as it could be supported, I shall begin by specifying some things I think I shall *not* be doing, and by situating at least vaguely the position from which this text speaks.

First, I shall not be relying very much on Leibniz's comment in the *Nouveaux Essais sur l'Entendement Human* to the effect that Locke, in denouncing rhetoric, does so eloquently, and thus combats eloquence with its own arms,[16] nor on an extension of that point which would argue that the whole of the *Essay* (and philosophy in general) neces-sarily relies on rhetorical strategies to get its points across. Nor, for the extension of the argument about the importance of language to the whole *Essay*, shall I simply use the banal point that language *must* be important to the *Essay* as a whole in so far as it is, necessarily, written in language. I do not think that any of these arguments is negligible, but simply that in their apparent self-evidence they offer little purchase on the problems at hand: the particular rhetoric of the denunciation of rhetoric could always be explained as a momentary lapse on Locke's part, or as a controlled example of playfulness, in neither case affecting his general theses concerning language and knowledge. As for the general rhetoric of philosophy in this type of argument, it could be hived off from the rhetoric of persuasion by the use of oppositions such as that of rhetoric and dialectic, persuasion and conviction, figure and concept, and so on. The possible deconstruction of these oppositions cannot be presupposed, and will depend on the location of a force of rhetoric prior to the terms they deploy.

Finally, although I do not want to deny that I approach Locke's text from the side of literature, as it were, rather than from the side of philosophy, and am therefore predisposed to see philosophy as something like a literary genre, the literal as a secondary effect of the figural, the concept as 'done for' by writing,[17] this 'literary' approach is not made on the basis of comments such as that of Nidditch in the Foreword to his edition of the *Essay*, to the effect that the book 'has long been recognized as one of the great works of English literature of the seventeenth century' (p. vii). My concern is not with the institutional 'recognition' of the book as 'really' literary or not, with the question of, for example, whether it should be studied in either philosophy or literature departments, or both, and to what extent, and so on, but with the existence, or, better, the *insistence* of something like 'the literary' or 'the rhetorical' in the most 'philosophical' or 'conceptual' elements of Locke's text. The 'something like' in this formulation should not necessarily be taken to be a wishy-washy 'literary' or 'rhetorical' approximation, a second-best to definition and rigour. It is, rather, dictated by the type of rigour it also questions, and points to the complex space between, the *entre-deux* of the philosophical and the literary, the literal and the figural, which is the concern of this work.

This positioning of the analysis is neither an invitation to benign interdisciplinary dialogue between literature and philosophy, nor a simple dismissal of philosophy in favour of literature, in so far as philosophers have been aware of the figural in Locke. M.R. Ayers, for example, refers to Locke's 'terminology, if that is not too grand a term for what sometimes seems almost an affectedly imprecise and figurative way of expressing himself'.[18] But neither is it a simple invitation to dialogue, in so far as this recognition is seen by philosophers as an unfortunate obstacle to thought and precision, something to be deplored, as does Peter Alexander in a reference to 'Locke's well-known lack of clarity of expression'.[19] The attempt of philosophers to get at 'what Locke had in mind', either to dismiss whatever that was through a generalized teleological violence in the name of the Truth,[20] or to reconstitute the system of thought revealed, once the ambiguities are 'ironed out by reference to the context', as Ayers has it, commits them to a notion of reading of the most simplistic kind, and, more importantly, to a view of language as an ideally transparent vehicle of meaning which can claim no real privilege of sophistication over Locke's own view of language. Locke's brooding over the fact that '[his] meaning . . . is often mistaken' in that part of the 'Epistle' added for the second edition,[21] and Ayers's comment that, 'Whatever Locke's *substratum* is, if he wrote *compos mentis*, it cannot be an entity that is undifferentiated, or "other than" its properties, in fact',[22] share important presuppositions about how language works, failing to pose the question of what might be called, in Derridean fashion, the *necessary possibility* of meaning being 'mistaken', and the undecidability and ultimate irrelevance of whether Locke, or Ayers, or myself come to that, 'wrote *compos mentis*'.

A moment ago I suggested that the problem of rhetoric is 'coterminous with language in general'. I shall begin to approach that assertion through a consideration of general language. This is an attractive point of entry in that the doctrine of 'general ideas' and 'general words' has been recognized, at least since Berkeley's *Principles*, to be a difficult area of Locke's account of language, and also because the problem of general terms, and most acutely the 'names of mixed modes', on Locke's own terms, immediately inserts the problem of language into the heart of knowledge, and implies the necessity of a drift away from a notionally ideal propriety of terms on which any anti-rhetorical or anti-figural theory of language must depend. Just as Locke must ground his account of the origins of knowledge in the passive reception of discrete simple ideas by the mind, so he must attempt to ground his account of language in the dream of a language which would be a proper or literal nomenclature of those simple ideas. The attraction of this dream, and also its madness (and this madness at the very origin of Locke's theory already suggests that to wonder if Locke 'wrote *compos mentis*' might be to beg the questions both of writing and of madness), is well illustrated by Borges in his story, 'Funes the memorious':

> Locke, in the seventeenth century, postulated (and rejected) an impossible language in which each individual thing, each stone, each bird and each branch, would have its own name; Funes once projected an analogous language, but discarded it because it seemed too general to him, too ambiguous. In fact, Funes remembered not only every leaf of every tree of every wood, but also every one of the times he had perceived and imagined it. He decided to reduce each of his past days to some seventy thousand memories, which would then be defined by means of ciphers. He was dissuaded from this by two considerations: his awareness that his task was interminable, his awareness that it was useless. He thought that by the hour of his death he would not even have finished classifying all the memories of his childhood.[23]

Two vital, interrelated points are introduced here, beyond the immediate illustrative force of the passage: I shall have to be content to let
them work all but silently on what follows. Both involve problems of
temporality: the first asks questions about the time of a simple idea
(and for example about Locke's definition of the 'Instant' as *'that which
takes up the time of only one Idea* in our Minds'),[24] the second suggests on
the one hand an originary *delay* of language in its definitions and
classifications, and on the other an excessive *productivity* of language,
which would never be able to catch up with the business of renaming
and classifying all the memories provoked by the first activity of
naming and classification.

Even allowing Locke that his projection of a proper nomenclature is
not *already* 'too general', it is clear that, as Locke recognizes, such a
language (admitting for the moment that it is 'proper' to call such a
collection of names a 'language') is neither possible nor useful. The
argument for its impossibility is not strictly philosophical, in so far as
Locke ascribes it to a merely *de facto* limit in 'the power of Humane
capacity'.[25] The account of the uselessness of such a 'language' is more
interesting, and is subdivided into two parts. The first of these in fact
provides a more convincing philosophical reason for the *impossibility* of
this collection of proper names than did the argument designed to
demonstrate that impossibility. Men, it is argued, use language
(chiefly) to communicate their ideas. The use of a language of proper
names applying to a person's (own, proper) ideas would not achieve
the end of communication:

> This cannot be done by Names, applied to particular Things, whereof I
> alone having the *Ideas* in my mind, the Names of them would not be
> significant, or intelligible to another, who was not acquainted with all those
> very particular Things, which had fallen under my Notice.[26]

The second argument for the uselessness of such a view of language is
that it would not help much in the way of knowledge. For although
Locke grounds knowledge in simple ideas of sensation, he constantly
links it to generality,[27] and thereby to abstraction, for, as is well known,
it is through abstraction that ideas become general.[28] This process of
generalization is not, in the account of general ideas, given the type of
economic motivation it is given in the discussion of general terms and
general propositions, but is what 'properly' distinguishes men from
animals: animals do not, according to Locke, have the capacity for
abstraction and generalization – and as he infers this from the fact that
'they have no use of Words, or any other general Signs' this suggests, as
Berkeley was well aware,[29] that there is a more intimate connection
between abstraction and language in general than the ostensible link of

it to general language would allow for. (Incidentally, in a nicely ambiguous statement, Berkeley is able to suggest simultaneously that problems of generality are intimately bound up with language *and* that it is precisely language which has led Locke astray into his doctrine of abstraction and general *ideas*: 'if there had been no such thing as speech or *universal* signs there had never been any thought of abstraction'.[30] To show that Berkeley's and, through him, Hume's account of general terms do not solve the problems posed by Locke's position, but simply shift into problems inherent in a different notion of representation, lies outside the scope of this paper.)[31]

That abstraction is in fact coeval with *any* use of language (and this is why Funes found Locke's notion of a nomenclature still 'too general') becomes clear in Locke's genetic account of general words. For the apparently (and only apparently) simple proper names from which he sets out (the example is of a child using the words 'Nurse' and 'Mamma' as proper names for individuals, and I leave aside the problems raised by the possible incompatibility of the two examples) already presuppose the abstraction implicit in the ability to link the several temporal perceptions of Mother and Nurse under the same name. The 'normal' sense of a proper name is already highly abstracted with respect to the notional infinite propriety of a proper name for every occurrence of an *idea*. If it could be shown that the use of such abstracted proper names is all that ties together the various occurrences of the 'same idea', then a fair number of Locke's presuppositions would be unsettled.

But it could be argued that even such a demonstration would not be very worrying for a doctrine of propriety in so far as no one would take Borges's infinitely 'proper' language seriously (least of all Locke), and that the attenuated notion of propriety to a general idea in the mind (or, in Berkeley's revision, to a particular idea representative of a set of particulars) is perfectly defensible. All that would be needed in such a defence would be a certain directionality in the model of signification, posing, in the Lockean version, first things, then ideas of things, then words arbitrarily but consistently attached to those ideas (or, in the Berkeleyan version, first ideas, then words, or in the more 'common-sense' version, first things, then words). As long as the hierarchy implied in this type of listing is respected, the argument would go, then the notion of propriety, of the literal, is intelligible, and philosophy as a discourse can be protected against the aberrations of rhetoric. It is the desire to preserve the priorities of this type of model which can be read as determining Berkeley's shrinking back, at the end of the Introduction to the *Principles*, from the possibility of a generalized rhetoric

which his attack on Locke's doctrine of abstraction had led him to
envisage:[32] and he is right to shrink back, in so far as only these
priorities can preserve philosophy from what can *provisionally* be called
'the play of the signifier' which would, in Locke's terms, make monkeys
or parrots of us all and, more generally, ground the literal, and with it
philosophy, no longer in reassuringly simple ideas, but in a generalized and originary non-propriety of which the use of language claimed
by philosophy would be merely a local effect.

Now this type of reversal in Locke's model of language is precisely
what happens in the case of what we should more normally think of as
abstract terms, and specifically in the set of abstract terms which Locke
calls 'names of mixed modes'. In Locke's terminology, 'modes' are
'such complex *Ideas*, which however compounded, contain not in them
the supposition of subsisting by themselves', and are opposed to
'complex ideas of substances' which 'are such combinations of simple
Ideas, as are taken to represent distinct particular things subsisting by
themselves', and to 'relations', which are complex ideas and 'consist in
the consideration and comparing one *Idea* with another'.[33] Within the
category of modes, simple modes are made up of the 'same' idea
repeated (for instance, the idea of 'two' is a simple mode, made by
repeating the idea of a unity),[34] and mixed modes are made up of
'Combinations of simple *Ideas* of different kinds'.[35] Mixed modes and
their names immediately problematize Locke's valorized, directional
model of signification in so far as their 'originals' or referents are not
located outside the mind, which could begin by receiving the ideas of
them passively, but are made up by the mind actively. For it is at least
possible (and Locke thinks it more usual) that the idea of a mixed mode
such as 'hypocrisy' might first have been 'framed' without any 'pattern'
of events or behaviour being prior to that framing. The problems this
might provoke become clearer when Locke returns to the question of
the *names* of mixed modes. By an apparent clumsiness of a type very
common in the *Essay*, and not without its bearing on the questions at
hand, Locke begins his discussions of this naming in Book III by
repeating the discussion of the *Ideas* given in Book II; in the case of
mixed modes at least, this repetition is not merely an *aide-mémoire*, a
reminder of the doctrine of the idea to which the doctrine of the name
could be subsequently attached, for here the name is not *superadded* to
the idea, but is integral in the making of that idea. Locke has just
repeated the point that mixed modes do not suppose some real
existence of what they represent. He quickly reminds the reader that
this does not imply that the ideas making up a mixed mode are not, as
always, the simple units furnished by sensation and reflection, and
goes on to describe how mixed modes are 'made':

> Wherein the Mind does these three things: First, It chuses a certain Number [of ideas previously in the mind]. Secondly, It gives them connexion, and makes them into one *Idea*. Thirdly, It ties them together by a Name.[36]

This is Locke's attempt to maintain the purity of his general model of signification. But the third stage of the process, the naming, is clearly vital to the whole:

> For the connection between the loose parts of those complex *Ideas*, being made by the Mind, this union, which has no particular foundation in Nature, would cease again, were there not something that did, as it were, hold it together, and keep the parts from scattering. Though therefore it be the Mind that makes the Collection, 'tis the Name which is, as it were the Knot, that ties them fast together.[37]

This does not merely imply, as Locke recognizes, that 'now that Languages are made, and abound with words standing for such Combinations, *an unusual way of getting these complex* Ideas, *is by the explication of those terms that stand for them*,[38] although this recognition [39] does relegate the previous genetic account to the status of an anthropological fiction: rather it introduces language into the very process of knowledge, for given Locke's account of the temporality of ideas, it is clear that the length of time the bundle of ideas could be held together by the Mind without the securing knot of language is unthinkably small. And in so far as the only reason Locke can give for the naming (and thus the creation) of mixed modes is communicative and thereby *social*,[40] then what is introduced into the ideation of the individual knowing subject by the mixed mode is the disruptive alterity of the social.

This introduction of the social into thought is fundamentally ambivalent. In so far as the avowed priority of the name in this case seems to open up the use of mixed modes to the charge of psittacism, or monkeying about with words, on which Locke is elsewhere so prepared to pour scorn, then the temptation might be to minimize the importance of such terms and ideas. But given that questions of morality in general are questions concerning mixed modes, and given further that Locke declares that '*Morality is the proper Science, and Business of Mankind in general*',[41] then that temptation is evidently to be resisted. Further, in that Locke's discussion of mixed modes turns on examples necessarily involving *legislation*, it seems that the irruption into knowledge of language, the social and the moral necessarily involves a *scene of legislation* which is a heterogeneous element in an account of knowledge, and one not easily to be reduced. I wish to stress

this last point as a means of taking a certain distance from Paul de
Man's discussion of Locke in his essay 'The epistemology of metaphor',[42] which otherwise has a good deal in common with what I am
attempting to elaborate here: where de Man typically makes an intre-
pid move to the literary, listing the examples Locke gives and com-
menting, 'The full list of examples . . . sounds more like a Greek
tragedy than the enlightened moderation one tends to associate with
the author of *On Government*',[43] I should want to stress the importance
of the scene of legislation implied by the mixed mode, which is a scene
of laying down the law as, of and in the divided place where language
and thought and the social meet.

This importance of a scene of legislation is clearer still in Locke's
account of the complex ideas he calls 'relations'. Even in 'natural
relations' (for example, that holding between 'begetter' and 'begotten')
Locke says that 'Mankind have fitted their Notions and Words to the
use of common Life, and not to the truth and extent of things', and
goes on:

> It is very convenient, that by distinct Names, these Relations should be
> observed, and marked out in Mankind, there being occasion, both in Laws,
> and other Communications one with another, to mention and take notice of
> Men, under these Relations: From whence also arise the Obligations of
> several Duties amongst Men.[44]

It is precisely these 'moral relations' that link mixed modes to Rule and
Law and thus create 'Good' and 'Evil' out of the pleasure or pain we
can expect to result from the reward or punishment which follows our
observing or breaking the law.[45] Language is of vital importance in all
this, as by naming actions in terms of mixed modes and relations we
create 'the Mark of the value we set upon them'. The mixed mode is
the 'positive idea' of the action, the relation is what refers it to a rule or
a law: in the idea of 'stealing', for example, the relation is the element
which determines it as crime or sin. In fact, this normative element
called 'relation' must *already* be in the mixed mode to which Locke tries
to suggest that it is added, in so far as the mixed mode only prevents
itself from 'scattering' or dispersing because of the name 'stealing'
which ties it together, and 'stealing' is already the name of a crime. This
is no doubt why Locke returns for only two lines to the *names* of
relations, saying only, 'What has been said here of mixed modes, is
with very little difference applicable also to Relations'.[46]

Evidently, these problems could be extended to Locke's political
writings, in so far as the linguistic questions posed by mixed modes and
relations imply some account of the social. This would be the place to
examine, for example, the complicity between the priority of *propriety*,

in the *Essay* and that of *property* in the *Treatises*, the right to propriety of
the names of simple ideas (a propriety which can be asserted but not
defined) being homologous to the right to property (of his own body in
the first instance) asserted of the pre-social liberal individual. And it
would no doubt be possible to trace in Rousseau, for example, a similar
relation of complicity between the claim that property is *not* naturally
given and the claim that language is *not* originally proper but
figured.[47]

There is a certain euphoria in Locke's account of mixed modes, a
euphoria uniting the threats and promises generated by the new
priority of language at this point, a priority separating mixed modes
from the messy and disappointing concerns of complex ideas of
substances, which retreat into the unknowable. The attraction of
mixed modes is that as they are linguistic constructs with no 'pattern' in
reality, they may be totally circumscribed and known: in other words,
their real and nominal essences coincide. This allows Locke to claim,
for example, that '*Morality is capable of Demonstration*, as well as Mathe-
matics'.[48] Here the possibility of knowledge is in the primacy of the
word.

Mixed modes, then, seem to open up the possibility of a valorized
priority of language which disrupts to some extent the directionality of
Locke's basic model of signification. The special case of the mixed
mode would seem to incur the sort of denunciation Locke elsewhere
makes of such a priority of the word:

> Concerning Words also it is farther to be considered. *First,* That they being
> immediately the Signs of Mens *Ideas*; and, by that means, the Instruments
> whereby Men communicate their Conceptions, and express to one another
> those Thoughts and Imaginations, they have within their own Breasts, *there
> comes by constant use,* to be such *a Connextion between certain Sounds, and the*
> Ideas *they stand for,* that the Names heard, almost as readily excite certain
> *Ideas,* as if the Objects themselves, which are apt to produce them, did
> actually affect the Senses. . . . *Secondly,* That though the proper and imme-
> diate Signification of Words, are *Ideas* in the Mind of the Speaker; yet
> because by familiar use from our Cradles, we come to learn certain
> articulate Sounds very perfectly, and have them readily on our Tongues,
> and always at hand in our Memories; but yet are not always careful to
> examine, or settle their Significations perfectly, it *often* happens that *Men,*
> even when they would apply themselves to an attractive Consideration, do
> *set their Thoughts more on Words than Things.* Nay, because Words are many of
> them learn'd, before the *Ideas* are known for which they stand: Therefore
> some, not only Children, but Men, speak several Words, no otherwise than
> Parrots do, only because they have learn'd them, and have been accustomed
> to those sounds. But so far is there a constant connexion between the Sound

and the *Idea*; and a Designation, that the one stand for the other: without
which Application of them, they are nothing but so much insignificant
Noise.[49]

What happens then is this: in this type of psittacism, as in the 'proper'
use of mixed modes, language, which should be a secondary adjunct to
ideas, invented simply for the communication of those ideas which
could exist in their purity in a pre-social and pre-communicative
isolation, begins to come first. It is now the word which precedes the
idea and dominates thinking – the transparency to itself of personal
meditation among ideas becomes contaminated by its means of communication to others. The separation from the other which made
communication necessary (always already necessary, in so far as God
'designed Man for a sociable Creature', and 'furnished him also with
Language, which was to be the great Instrument, and common Tye of
Society')[50] here becomes a separation of the oneself from the other-in-
oneself: the thinking self becomes primarily a 'listening' self, 'alienated' from self-possession of thought because of this 'listening' to the
'sounds' of language. Locke's later mention of a second use of words
for recording one's own thoughts as a help to one's memory only
stresses this irruption of the other in the self. It remains to be shown
that this 'other-consciousness' which enters into the proper conception
and use of the mixed mode and haunts all language as the possibility of
its abuse (though this particular abuse does not fit easily into Locke's
list, but is rather the condition of possibility of all other abuses),
inhabits, from the start, self-consciousness and thereby, for the two go
together in Locke, consciousness itself.

Let us return first from the problematic heights of mixed modes,
retaining the suspicion they have introduced that language is bound
up with the possibility of knowledge in a more intimate way than Locke
would like, to the atomic units of those mixed modes, which are still, of
course, simple ideas of sensation and reflection. The attempt to
maintain propriety, and the secondary of language which propriety
implies, must ultimately depend on arguments conducted at this level.
Locke's account of why the aggregate of proper names for simple ideas
is impossible and useless omits a crucial reason for this impossibility
and uselessness. For if there *were* such a language, it would have to be a
language without propositions at all. If every proper name and every
idea were really discrete, isolated in its propriety or enclosed in its
property, no other name could be linked with it. The very attempt to
make such a link would presuppose the addition to the aggregate of
proper names of at least one more item, namely the copula, and such
an addition already breaks open propriety, immediately by introduc-

ing this heterogeneous particle into the aggregate, and secondly by presupposing the possibility of relations of identity and/or difference between the elements of that aggregate. Even if the role of the copula were purely negative, used only in propositions of the type 'A is not B', 'B is not C', and so on, then a minimal differential articulation is posited, and this is in fact the only way in which the supposed propriety of the terms could conceivably be maintained in the first place. And if the copula is used only to assert the self-identity of terms, in the form 'A is A' (and Locke recognizes that there are as many self-evident propositions of this type as there are simple ideas), then this is, on Locke's account, only a 'trifling' proposition, presupposed by the prior recognition of the idea: and it also, we might add, presupposes the type of temporal alterity suggested by Borges's fable, and it is only this alterity which allows for the repetition of the idea as the 'same' idea and the name as its name. More importantly, this recognition of the presupposition of the possibility of the copula among the names of simple ideas, although it is itself not a name (and given by Locke only the briefest of discussions in that briefest of chapters called 'On Particles'),[51] it already disrupts the ideal propriety of terms in the same movement with which it makes possible anything like an affirmation of that propriety.

These observations suggesting that Locke's positioning of language with respect to ideation cannot be simple and unproblematical can now be extended to the account of the acquisition of the basic units of all knowledge through sensation and reflection. It is clearly vital to Locke's account that sensation be the prior term, in so far as the mind must be provided with at least one idea of sensation before it has anything to reflect about. Reflection is defined as 'the *Perception of the Operations of our own Minds* within us, as it is employ'd about the *Ideas* it has got'.[52] Accordingly, the first idea of reflection is the idea of perception,[53] there having first been perception of an idea of sensation.

Now it can be argued, and has been argued by Douglas Greenlees,[54] on whom I draw for this preliminary point, that in so far as for Locke ideation entails consciousness of ideation, then any idea must be accompanied by the idea of 'idea': as Greenlees puts it, 'hence sensation, *from the beginning*, it follows, would have to be accompanied by the minimal reflective operation of the perception of having the sensory idea' – and he goes on to suggest that this means that the reflective idea of 'idea' is '*as old as* the idea of sensation'.[55] The formulations I have emphasized, 'from the beginning', and 'as old as' point nicely to the fact that there is no simple origin in Locke's account of origin. It is possible to radicalize this, and to argue that only the reflective idea (which is itself originally split in so far as it is also an idea of reflection) allows the sensory idea to exist as idea of sensation, and thereby gain any effect of propriety or identity. Clearly this implies a certain *marking* of the idea, a marking of it as different from other ideas, and this differential marking is a type of proto-language which is a condition of possibility for the proto-language of proper names of simple ideas, and can be assimilated to what Derrida calls '*archi-écriture*'.[56] This is another name for the split and never-present origin of ideas in Locke's theory, and suggests why it is unthinkable that any single or self-present idea could ever be present, or presented, to whatever august personage presides in what Locke preciously calls 'the mind's Presence-room'.[57] This split origin evidently disallows any simple notion of a *tabula rasa* or of a simple passivity of the mind. The mind is originally split *by* reflection, which becomes a condition of sensation. This split introduces something like 'activity' into the supposed first 'passivity' of the mind, and only this allows for the possibility of language, the use of which is thus grounded in a sort of primary 'abuse', in so far as it can never 'properly' name the non-proper *différance* which precedes and inhabits it. The split also suggests that the mind is always inhabited by alterity in so far as there are two agencies or instances at its beginning. Locke's secondary story about the usefulness of language in the self as a sort of *aide-mémoire*, which it will be remembered introduced the other into the self, can be read as a deferred figure of this originary alterity. There is always an other in the mind's presence-room.

This originary spacing is the space which allows for the necessary possibility of Locke's being 'misunderstood' (and for complaints that I have wilfully misunderstood him here, for example). It is also the space in which philosophy as a metalanguage tirelessly denouncing the 'abuse' of language called rhetoric, and rhetoric itself, are located. Locke depends on this originary drift from propriety for the possibility of doing what he does, which is thus a local activity within a generalized figurality. Locke needs the perfect cheat as the (feminine) matrix of his (virile) claims. Where Locke would like there to be a possible disjunction of the literal *or* figural, separated into their 'proper' places, there is only the literal *and* the figural, fighting over their common ground in a general rhetoric. There is no point in looking for agreement here, for the difference is original, and any supposed accord between the literal and the figural, and to that extent between the philosophical and the literary, is merely a secondary violence worked on this difference.

In the parallel reading of the political writing proposed a moment ago, the need for government as a supplementary instance to preserve (naturally achieved) property[58] would depend on a similar originary

shift, which Locke can only read as a sign that man is degenerate.[59]
The necessary possibility of violent misappropriation of others' property in Locke's otherwise benign state of nature dictates the formation
of society and government as an instrument of reappropriation, just as
the necessary possibility of the misappropriations of rhetoric dictates
philosophy's legislative reappropriations of words to ideas. A point of
entry into the common root of these problems might be provided by
§143 of the *First Treatise*, where Locke quotes Filmer (whom John
Dunn describes as having a 'strange, punning theory')[60] as saying: *'In
the dispersion of* Babel, *we must certainly find the Establishment of Royal
Power, throughout the Kingdom of the World'*, and, after a few general
comments, continues,

> If our A. has no better Foundation for his Monarchy than a supposition of
> what was done at the dispersion of *Babel*, the Monarchy he erects thereon,
> whose top is to reach to Heaven to unite Mankind, will serve only to divide
> and scatter them as that Tower did; and instead of establishing civil
> government and order in the World will produce nothing but confusion.[61]

If, then, we are among those who, in Locke's words, 'pretend *seriously*
to *search after*, or maintain *Truth*',[62] or at least pretend to pretend
seriously, then we might keep up the pretence rather than the pretension. This is still quite a *serious* pretence, and one of the things it
pretends seriously is that the pretension is not serious, *n'est pas sérieux*.
The divided unity of this serious pretence and frivolous pretension, of
the search which is also a maintenance, of the object of desire called
'Truth' which dissolves into, among other figures, both mother *and*
whore, is perhaps namable as a *'perfect cheat'*.

Notes

1. All references to Locke's *Essay* are to the edition by Peter H. Nidditch, Oxford 1975.
The numbers given refer to Book, chapter and section respectively. References to the
Epistle to the Reader are to the page number.
2. Locke, *Essay*, II, X, 1.
3. Ibid., III, X, 1.
4. Ibid., III, XI, 3.
5. Ibid., III, XI, 3.
6. Ibid., III, X, 34.
7. Ibid., III, XI, 1.
8. Ibid., III, XI, 1.
9. Ibid., III, X, 34.
10. Ibid., III, X, 34.
11. Ibid., III, X, 5.
12. Ibid., III, XI, 4.
13. Ibid., III, X, 34.
14. See the comments in Ibid., II, XXXIII, 19.
15. Ibid., p. 7.

16. G.F. Leibniz, *Nouveaux Essais sur l'Entendement Humain*, ed. Jacques Brunschwig, Paris 1966, p. 306.

17. Cf. Derrida's untranslatable comment somewhere in *Glas*, Paris 1974: 'Dès qu'il est saisi par l'écriture, le concept est cuit.'

18. M.R. Ayers, 'The Ideas of Power and Substance in Locke's Philosophy', in *Locke on Human Understanding: Selected Essays*, ed. I.C. Tipton, Oxford 1977, p. 85.

19. P. Alexander, 'Boyle and Locke on Primary and Secondary Qualities', in Tipton, ed., *Selected Essays*, p. 85.

20. I am thinking especially of Jonathan Bennet's *Locke, Berkeley, Hume: Central Themes*, Oxford 1971.

21. Locke, *Essay*, p. 11.

22. Ayers, 'The Ideas', p. 79.

23. Jorge Luis Borges, 'Funes el memorios', in his *Ficciones*, Buenos Aires 1956, p. 125. English translation by James E. Irby in *Labyrinths*, Harmondsworth 1970, p. 93.

24. Locke, *Essay*, III, XIV, 10.

25. Ibid., III, III, 2.

26. Ibid., III, III, 3.

27. See for example, Ibid., IV, V, 10 and IV, VI, 2.

28. Ibid., II, XI, 9.

29. G. Berkeley, *The Principles of Human Knowledge*, in *Principles, Dialogues and Correspondence*, ed. Colin Murray Turbayne, New York 1965, Introduction, §11.

30. Ibid., §18.

31. The argument is developed by E. Husserl in §29 of the second of his *Logical Investigations*, tr. J.N. Findlay, New York 1964.

32. Berkeley, *Principles*, Introduction, §20.

33. Locke, *Essay*, II, XII, 4, 6, 7.

34. Ibid., II, XIII, 9.

35. Ibid., II, XXII, 9.

36. Ibid., III, V, 4.

37. Ibid., III, V, 10.

38. Ibid., II, XXII, 3.

39. Repeated in Ibid., III, V, 15.

40. Ibid., III, V, 7.

41. Ibid., IV, XII, 11.

42. Paul de Man, 'The Epistemology of Metaphor', *Critical Inquiry*, 5, 1978–9.

43. Ibid., p. 21.

44. Locke, *Essay*, II, XXVII, 2.

45. Ibid., II, XXVIII, 5.

46. Ibid., III, V, 16.

47. The first of these claims is made especially in the *Discours sur l'Origine de l'Inégalité* and the second in the *Essai sur l'Origine des langues*.

48. Locke, *Essay*, III, XI, 16.

49. Ibid., III, II, 6–7. See in addition III, XI, 24.

50. Ibid., III, I. 1.

51. Ibid., III, IV.

52. Ibid, II, I, 4.

53. Ibid., II, IX, 1.

54. Douglas Greenlees, 'Locke's Idea of Idea', in Tipton, ed., *Selected Essays*.

55. Ibid., p. 44. My emphasis.

56. See for example *De la Grammatologie*, Paris 1967, and *Positions*, Paris 1972.

57. Locke, *Essay*, II, III, 1.

58. J. Locke, 'Second treatise on government', in *Two Treaties on Government*, London 1884, §94 and §124.

59. Ibid., §128.

60. John Dunn, *The Political Thought of John Locke*, Cambridge 1969, p. 75.

61. Locke, 'First treatise . . .' in *Two Treatises*, §143.

62. Locke, *Essay*, III, XI, 3.

7

Aberrations: de Man (and) the

Machine

Techne belongs to bringing-forth, to *poiesis*, it is something poetic.
Heidegger, *The Question Concerning Technology*

A letter of exhortation to a friend to encourage him to seek. And
he will reply: but what use will seeking be, nothing appears. And
reply to him: do not despair. And he would reply that he would be
happy to find some light. But that according to this religion even if
he were to believe in this way it would do him no good. And that
this being the case he may as well not seek. And at this point reply
to him: The Machine.

(Pascal, *Pensées*)

In the complete works of Blaise Pascal, the famous arithmetical
machine is the more-or-less absent referent of three texts, two of
which are by Pascal himself.[1] The first of these is a dedicatory letter
addressed to Chancellor Séguier, and apparently dominated by its
addressee in the form of the pronoun of respect, *vous*; the second is an
Avis (not quite an instruction booklet), destined to 'those who will have
the curiosity to see the said machine and make use of it', again
dominated by the addressee, but this time in the familiarity of the
pronoun *tu*, designating the *ami lecteur*; the third text is the *privilège* or
patent, granted and signed by the king, dominated this time by the
addressor, marked by the *nous* of royal prerogative and power.

For reasons to which I shall return, detailed description of the
machine is disappointingly sparse in these brief pages, and what
description is provided is of the most general kind. In its minimal
specification, the machine is intended to *perform* arithmetical operations in a mechanical manner, and to do so more quickly and
accurately than someone working with pen and paper or with
counters, the two alternative methods with which Pascal favourably
compares his machine (p. 189b). The attraction of the machine's

performance of its operations is thus that it is, simply enough, *performante*, a high performer when measured against rival methods according to the criterion of an input/output ratio. This high performance is, however, not just a result of speed and accuracy; the essence of the machine seems rather to lie in its capacity to stand in for and render unnecessary a certain number of the mental operations required of a human calculator: 'the most ignorant person finds in [the machine] as great an advantage as the most experienced; the instrument supplies [*supplée à*] the defect of ignorance or lack of habit, and, *by necessary movements*, it performs all alone, *without even the intention of the user*, all the abridgements possible to nature' (p. 189b, my emphasis). It will do all the 'borrowing' and 'carrying' that normally tire the human calculator's memory: 'it does of itself what he desires, without his even thinking about it' (p. 190a). Earlier, in the dedicatory letter, Pascal suggests that the machine he is presenting to the chancellor is capable of doing, 'by itself alone and without any work of the mind, the operations of all the parts of arithmetic' (p. 188a).

This *facility* promised by the machine is not simple or absolute or free, but enters into an economy with complexity, depth of thought and hard practical labour. In the dedicatory letter, Pascal presents with no small amount of pride and pathos (which go some way towards challenging the addressee's dominance over the text) a passably heroic account of his invention and realization of the machine. This *difficulty* in the production of *facility* is in fact figured in the machine itself, according to an opposition between its inside and its outside: pre-empting a possible objection that his machine is needlessly *composée* or complex, Pascal develops a nice economy which explains that such internal complexity is the necessary price to pay for external and operational simplicity – the simple and the easy are the effects of the difficult and the complex, the greater the one, the greater the other:

> in which you will be able to note a sort of paradox, namely that in order to make the movement of the operation the more simple, it was necessary that the machine be constructed of a more complex movement. (p. 190a)

In rudimentary form, Pascal's story of his machine appears to be a narrative of legitimation, and of legitimation by performativity, as Lyotard would say.[2] Here a generalizable facility is paid for, and paid off by, the quasi-heroic labour of the inventor, the genius. The performativity of the machine is ensured by its standing in for, as supplement or prosthesis, certain parts of the mind of its user: variously the memory, intention, expertise and mental labour in general. But if the machine can do this, it is because something of the mind of the inventor has gone into it, possibly at the expense of his health,[3] but certainly to the benefit of his name, his renown. Once the machine reaches its user, its mechanical supplementation of the mind is, in principle, *euphoric*; for once the heroism of invention has paid off any debt owed for facility, the machine goes on performing for free, and, in principle at least, for good (part of Pascal's long and long-suffering period of invention was concerned with ensuring the solidity and durability of the machine). This free performance continues after the death of its inventor, to which it is indifferent, and regardless of the death of any particular user; and this would appear to be part of the essence of machines in general, which are the death of inventors and users alike.

But if this indifference to death is conducive to euphoria, it is also troublesome for any such euphoria, and generates aberrations in the text. So far I have analysed the textual network of Pascal's machine in terms of description and performance, and neglected a whole pre-scriptive dimension. The smooth legitimation of technological advance is in fact constantly interrupted by a complex nexus of points for legislation, involving bodies and birth, orders, obligations and justice, legitimacy and falsification. In the terms of the dedicatory letter, Pascal may have 'conceived' the machine, but it owes its 'birth' to the chancellor's 'commands': those commands can be modalized as praise or guidance, 'seeing that in the young age in which I am, and with so little strength, I have dared to attempt a new road in a field bristling with thorns, and without a guide to open my path for me [*pour m'y frayer le chemin*]' (p. 188a). Recompense for Pascal's time and expense is not in fact adequately provided by the narrative of technical legitimation, and is only satisfactorily achieved, beyond the mere approbation of experts, in the judgement of the chancellor, as 'that same mouth which every day pronounces oracles on the throne of justice' (p. 188b).

This irruption, into a story of legitimation by performance, of quite different codes, can of course be linked to certain conventions and to a historically bound rhetoric of flattery: but we cannot dispose of the matter so simply; there is here a political and ethical tension that it would be foolish, as Paul de Man might have said, to 'historicize out of consciousness'. This tension can be read as the conflict between *legitimation* and *legitimacy*, and it is in fact as much in evidence in the *Avis* as in the dedicatory letter. Here, having disposed of the first possible objection to his machine (that it is unnecessarily complex), Pascal moves to a second possible cause of 'umbrage' to his addressee, and that is the existence of bad copies of his machine. These copies are described as 'little monsters', 'formless', 'useless abortions', 'little abor-tion[s]' (pp. 190a–191a). The 'illegitimacy' of such pseudomachines would, one might think, be sufficiently determined by the fact that they simply do not work, fail to perform, but Pascal analyses the question beyond this simple judgement (made within the discourse of legitimation by performativity) into a mythical romance about the marriage of theory and practice (*art*): monsters and abortions are the result of the presumption of the artisan to give birth *alone*, without the fecunding, prescriptive, intervention of theory. Whence the third text, the *privilège*, procured by the chancellor, signed by the king, which aims to prevent hasty condemnation by the public of 'true originals' it mistakes for bad copies, or hasty approbation of bad copies it mistakes for true originals: according to Pascal, the privilege 'stifles before birth all these illegitimate abortions which might be engendered somewhere other than in the legitimate and necessary marriage [*alliance*] of theory with art' (p. 191a). Here then is a concern with paternity and signatures, property and propriety, apparently quite foreign to the technical legitimation of the machine in terms of its performativity. The *privilège* duly forbids anyone to make any such machine without Pascal's instruction or permission, on the grounds of an aberrant logic that states simultaneously that the machine is both easy to counterfeit (and therefore in need of legal protection) and impossible to counterfeit in such a way that it will perform as it should (and therefore in need of legal protection). And this protection of the inventor's rights and signature quite consequently extends beyond the death of the inventor or signatory of the machine, and implicitly confirms that in an important sense the signatory is *already dead*: the *privilège* is also a tombstone.

How are we to read this impression of overkill in the second aspect of these texts? Simply this: that the prescriptive elements of the text are not *simply* extraneous to, or superfluous with respect to, an essentially performative legitimation, but that the apparently disruptive language of justice, legitimacy, paternity, and signatures is in fact called up precisely by the apparent indifference of the logic of performativity to any such concerns. For the logic of the supplementary machine is that it must be able to work independently of inventor or father, that it is necessarily cut from any origin in Pascal's intentions or mental labour, that it can be reproduced *ad infinitum* and respond promiscuously in the hands of anyone at all. The 'legitimate' machine has to have its legitimacy certified, signed and sealed, precisely because in its essence it exceeds legitimacy: the father lays claim to it precisely because it is essentially a bastard. And just as the machine can be said to function prosthetically, *supplying* defects of memory, intention and even intelligence, so it can be said to *dispossess* the user in general (including Pascal) of those same faculties.

Readers of Jacques Derrida will have recognized that the performing machine functions like the written text as described by Plato in the *Phaedrus*,[4] and gives rise to the same anxieties and prescriptive interventions: Pascal's myth of the marriage of 'theory' and 'art' is also the story of the *logos* reclaiming its own against the generalized threat of *techne*. And it will now come as no surprise that Pascal's 'disappointingly sparse' description of his machine is justified by the assertion that 'this doctrine [that of how to construct and use such a machine] is one of those that can only be taught *viva voce*' (p. 189a) – the voice as protection against the promiscuous availability of machine and written text alike.

'Pascal's machine', then, performs arithmetical operations, but also performs as text, staging scenes of performance, description, prescription, proscription, signature and so on. As supplement to the *logos*, it gives rise to facility only by opening up the possibility of uncontrollable mimetic doubling and degradation, and generates further apotropaic supplements to control and police that threat. The machine is thus both text and text-productive; conversely, the text is a machine and produces further machines. It follows that Pascal's machine is an 'allegory' of writing and/or reading, that writing and/or reading involve a complex of conflictual components or non-dialectizable 'moments' which simultaneously dispossess the 'subject' of writing/ reading and set up the drive to signature as a means of legislating for that 'subject' and its 'legitimacy' against such dispossession. The text as machine is thus both the life and the death, the life-death of anything like a subject, be that subject determined as 'author' or 'reader', 'inventor' or 'user'.

For this duplicity of the performance of the machine and the text clearly questions the pertinence of a number of the oppositions that have tended to dominate and confuse the questions of writing and reading. The recent enthusiasm for readers and reading in literary studies may have been beneficial in disrupting certain notions about the author, but has also brought with it at least as many regressive tendencies as it has afforded new insights. No sooner has the 'death of the author' been proclaimed, than all sorts of reassuring surrogate sovereign subjects appear on the side of reception and reading: empirical, existential, phenomenological, psychoanalytic, individual and collective, strong and weak, politically activist – just waiting to *respond*. To assert, for example, that 'the "primal scene" of literature is always an act of a reader rather than a myterious attribution of a text'[5] may well be no more helpful, and no less mysterious, than what it purports to attack, unless we are prepared to take the logic of 'primal scenes' and *Nachträglichkeit* a good deal more seriously than has usually

been the case in recent considerations of reading. It is the aim of the
present essay to clear some ground toward suggesting why, when Paul
de Man claims that 'the systematic avoidance of the problem of reading, of the interpretive or hermeneutic moment, is a general symptom
shared by all methods of literary analysis, whether they be structural or
thematic, formalist or referential, American or European, apolitical or
socially committed' (*Blindness and Insight*, p. 282), he is inviting anything but the return of the subject and the so-called act of reading. As
is so often the case, the work of Jacques Derrida might have served as
an early warning of the problems to come in this domain, although it
would evidently be facile to assert that we could have avoided all
manner of naiveties if only we had been able to *read* statements such as
those in 'Force and Signification' on 'the deferred reciprocity between
reading and writing',[6] or in 'Freud and the Scene of Writing on 'the
author who reads and the first reader who dictates':[7] facile because it
would presuppose the problem of reading that is here at issue.

But it might be no accident that the second of these two comments
from Derrida occurs in the immediate context of discussion of
machines, of the 'mystic writing pad', of *psyche* and *techne*, of life and
death: 'The subject of writing is a *system* of relationships between the
strata: of the Mystic Pad, of the psychical, of society, of the world.
Inside this scene, the punctual simplicity of the classical subject cannot
be found. In order to describe this structure, it is not enough to recall
that one always writes for someone; and the oppositions sender-
receiver, code-message, etc., remain extremely coarse instruments. We
would search the "public" in vain for the first reader, i.e. the first
author of the work. . . . The machine does not work all by itself, and
this means something else: a mechanism with no energy of its own.
The machine is dead. It is death. Not because we risk death playing
with machines, but because the origin of machines is the relation to
death.'[8] Writing, reading, machines and death: it would be hard to
find a more apposite and emotive cluster of terms with which to
approach Paul de Man. If de Man is dead (and they say he is), and if he
remains so alive (for one who knew him only as texts), then that life-
death is a question of writing, reading and machines as the economy of
life and death in life and death. The 'aberration' of Paul de Man's
death is also the aberration of a reading and writing machine, or
reading and writing as machine. And only the machine (and therefore
death) will allow us to avoid hasty assimilation of Paul de Man's work to
the long *théorie* of theories of reading.

Traditional literary studies habitually use the language of machines
in a negative way, deploring the mechanical and the technical as the
death of the values attached to life, form, inspiration and so on. At

best, a 'technical' use of concepts is accorded an uneasy neutrality, without ever being allowed to become the heart of the matter. Machines *repeat*, and repetition means danger – compulsion and death. No doubt even the most 'technicist' forms of structuralism never simply escape this type of values. Some of this can be found in de Man's writing: *Allegories of Reading* claims to use the word 'deconstruction' in a 'technical' sense (p. x), and refers to 'the techniques of structural analysis refined to near perfection' (p. 3). But elsewhere, as is also the case in Derrida,[9] this traditional system is disrupted: already in 'Semiology and Rhetoric' there are references to 'the programmed pattern of grammar', to 'semi-automatic grammatical patterns', to 'the impersonal precision of grammar' (p. 16), where the 'merely technical' or 'mechanical' sense is suspended; this will be increasingly the case as syntax is thought to be prior to semantics, grammar to reference, and so on. By the time de Man is discussing and to some extent adopting Rousseau's language of the machine in the context of the *Social Contract*, the mechanical is becoming dominant, and the final essay in the book explicitly charts a move from text-as-body to text-as-machine:

> The machine is like the grammar of the text when it is isolated from its rhetoric, the merely formal element without which no text can be generated. There can be no use of language which is not, within a certain perspective thus radically formal, i.e. mechanical, no matter how deeply this aspect may be concealed by aesthetic, formalistic delusions. . . . The text as body, with all its implications of substitutive tropes ultimately always retraceable to metaphor, is displaced by the text as machine and, in the process, it suffers the loss of the illusion of meaning. The deconstruction of the figural dimension is a process that takes place independently of any desire; as such it is not unconscious but mechanical, systematic in its performance but arbitrary in its principle, like a grammar. . . . Far from seeing language as an instrument in the service of a psychic energy, the possibility now arises that the entire construction of drives, substitutions, repressions and representations is the aberrant, metaphorical correlative of the absolute randomness of language, prior to any figuration or meaning. (pp. 294, 298, 299)

Other texts of the same period would confirm this displaced importance of the mechanical.

But if de Man's readings increasingly find machines in or as texts, what about those readings themselves? Here is a description by a reader of de Man of de Man reading:

> One listens to him as one witnesses a performance: one has the feeling beforehand that one knows what de Man will do, yet one is still awed by the

elegance, precision and economy of his performance; one has a reluctant but solid conviction that one could not duplicate it. De Man is thought to be highly original, yet, in a sense, he does exactly what we expect him to do.[10]

This description is, in part at least, that of the performance of a machine. De Man reads like a machine. But he also reads machines;[11] and in so far as his readings are texts, they are machines too: 'the punctual simplicity of the classical subject cannot be found'. Paul de Man is dead: what remains in the repeated (un)predictability of performance is the tensions we noted in Pascal, between high performer and a signature, between the supplementation of our inabilities and the suspicion of dispossession – de Man's death guarantees him the *privilège* of beng (in)imitable. The commonplace accusation that de Man's work is unduly 'aestheticizing', and even the aesthetic sense of performance evident in Godzich's description, is secondary to this mechanical dimension.

The performativity of de Man's readings, as well as this secondary notion of performance, inevitably points to the importance of the performative 'speech-act' in de Man's later writing.[12] It is this performative aspect of language that leads de Man to describe one aspect of textuality in terms of machines; and in so far as this machine-like performance is, in its disruption of cognition (in the guise of the referential dimension of descriptive or constative sentences), definitive of what de Man means by 'text', and thereby of what 'reading' might possibly mean, then it seems important to resist any temptation to read performance hastily in terms of the 'aesthetic', and to clarify its link to the machine.[13] And following the chain of terms we have already established, it would seem that our ability to read the sentence 'Paul de Man is dead', and *a fortiori* our ability to *mourn* his death, will depend on some such clarification.

There is a complication in the status of the machine-like performative that in fact depends on a principle of great generality that could no doubt be formalized: whenever one of a series of elements is also used transcendentally with respect to that series in order to totalize, dominate or explain it, aberration begins. As a preliminary example of this principle we might take Fredric Jameson's argument in favour of Marxism in *The Political Unconscious*: Marxism is one of a series of rival theories in the intellectual 'marketplace', but it is also the *best* of those theories because it is also the transcendental explanation and measure of the marketplace itself.[14] Or: Philosophy is one discipline among many, but it is the best of those disciplines because it can also explain and subsume the whole series of disciplines of which it is only one. Other examples would not be hard to find. This type of aberration seems to come from bogus reasoning and self-confirming claims. But now try this example: there are many sorts of language: constative, prescriptive, evaluative, interrogative, performative, etc. But just one of those elements also dominates the series. It is easy to imagine claims being made (and of course they always have been made) for one or other of the elements. Let us suppose that Austin's work amounts to saying that philosophy has always tended to assume that it is the constative that is dominant, but that in fact the performative deserves this privilege. Does such a claim give rise to the same sort of aberration as the previous examples? It seems clear that the answer is no, but perhaps less clear why that is the answer. I would suggest that *this* form of the question (which would have to be linked to Russell's set-theory paradox and Gödel's incompleteness theorem) leads us to de Man's own sense of 'aberration', or 'the impossibility of reading', and that the tension between the clarity of our no and the murkiness of its reasons is more a version of the problem than a mark of an inability to solve it. I would also suggest that the implication of de Man's work is that it is better to view this problem as an ethical rather than epistemological issue.

The generalized performance (as illocutionary force) that is the result of Austin's investigation has no more than a strategically privileged connection with the 'performative' from which he begins. Even if we decide that any speech-act is best discussed in terms of its 'felicity' or 'infelicity' rather than, say, its truth or falsehood, this 'second-level' felicity or infelicity is quite different from that affecting 'first-level' performatives. If a 'first-level' performative 'misfires' or is otherwise infelicitous, it is *not* in fact a performative, it fails to perform.[15] But this infelicitous act can be judged to be infelicitous only if there was nevertheless a performance of some kind. The non-performance of a performative (the failure to bring off the marriage between theory and art, for example) presupposes performance at this generalized level. 'First-level' performatives have only a heuristic privilege over constatives (for example) in this respect. Prior to any possibility of judgement as to felicity or infelicity, or prior even to any decision as to whether the 'act' in question might, at the 'lower' level, be considered a constative or a performative (for example), *there is* performance. Only this 'primary' performance can account for the possibility of distinctions between types of acts. The constative 'there is performance' presupposes and therefore cannot ground performance. It follows that this primary or archi-performance, of which there is no 'first' performance, cannot be spoken or written as such, and therefore cannot itself be performed, which would imply that it is another, and equally improper, name for what Derrida calls (among other things), *différance*, and what Lyotard in recent work calls *présentation*.

This derivation of the archi-performance cannot be repeated with other elements of the series: any attempt to derive an archi-constative or even an archi-prescriptive will presuppose performance. On the other hand, the fact that the archi-performance cannot be performed as such prevents it from falling into the simple aberration of earlier examples. But it brings its own sort of aberration, in so far as it would evidently be unreasonable to make it the basis for claims to truth or knowledge, for example. This would imply that the transcendence of the term 'performance' with respect to the series of which the 'performative' is one element cannot be simple or secure. And it further suggests that in so far as we are here workng with something prior to distinctions between types of acts, then our suspicion of the 'aesthetic' reading of de Man was justified.

This second type of aberration (one of de Man's favourite terms: it and its cognates occur at least fifty times in *Allegories of Reading*) is none the less intimately linked to de Man's new notion of the machine. Archi-performance *is* the machine, and is aberrant when approached in terms of secondary distinctions between different types of speech-acts. The disruption of those distinctions is disturbing, in so far as it looks like a celebration of blind force (of the machine), which can modulate into either the so-called rhetoric of authority[16] or into so-called aestheticism. This disturbance is unavoidably political and ethical, in a difficult sense,[17] and so it seems reasonable to approach it by means of de Man's reading of overtly ethical or political texts. An obvious place to look would be the reading of Rousseau's *Social Contract* offered in the chapter 'Promises' from *Allegories of Reading*, but as I have already had occasion to discuss this elsewhere,[18] I shall here return to Pascal and to a less well known essay by de Man, 'Pascal's Allegory of Persuasion'.

The first part of this essay is a difficult discussion of nominal and real definitions in Pascal's theory of language, and of the heterogeneous status of the zero in his number theory: in the second part of the essay, which is more approachable here, de Man, with all the elegance, precision and economy we have now come to expect, reads a number of the *Pensées* and reveals their 'rhetorical machine' as 'a fundamentally dialectical pattern of reasoning, in which oppositions are, if not reconciled, at least pursued towards a totalization that may be infinitely postponed, but that remains operative as the sole principle of intelligibility' (p. 20; see also esp. p. 13–19). Wondering whether any of the *Pensées* disrupt this pattern, de Man goes on to consider number

103 in the Lafuma classification, which reads as follows, in his own translation:

> It is just that what is just should be followed: it is necessary that what has the most power should be followed.
>
> Justice without power is impotent, power without justice is tyrannical.
>
> Justice without power is open to contradiction, because there are always wrongdoers. Power without justice stands accused. Justice and power must therefore be brought together, by making the just strong and the strong just.
>
> Justice is subject to dispute. Power is easily recognizable and without dispute. Thus it was impossible to give power to justice, because power has contradicted justice and said that it is unjust, and that it is itself just.
>
> And thus, not being able to make the just strong, one has made the strong just.

De Man wants to argue that whereas in his previous examples what was at stake was oppositions between two modes of cognition (or apparently contradictory constative sentences), here there is a disruption of that pattern because of the introduction of the performative dimension. Here is de Man's initial statement of the problem:

> The opposition is stated at the start in the contrast between 'il est juste' and 'il est necessaire', in which the first assertion depends on a propositional cognition, but the second on sheer quantitative power. . . . Propositional statements line up on the side of cognition, modal statements on the side of performance; they perform what they enunciate regardless of considerations of truth and falsehood.[19]

This analysis immediately calls to mind Godzich's characterization of de Man as machine: readers of *Allegories of Reading* both expect this type of distribution in terms of cognition and performance, and probably grudgingly admit that they would have had difficulty performing that distribution so powerfully and elegantly. It will be remembered, however, that the machine, in Pascal's description, works by 'necessary' movements, and so if we accept this mode of reading de Man's reading we are curiously already implicated, in the terms of the passage, on the side of necessity, power and indifference to truth and falsehood. Simply assenting to this reading is thus, in view of the passage read, a failure to read. It seems to follow that if we *are* to read this reading, we should ask the question, is it *juste*? This creates the problem of situating us, in de Man's terms, on the other side of the divide, on the aesthetically less attractive and technologically less powerful ground of cognition, and runs the risk of again failing to read. This seems to create a typically de Manian situation of aporia in which what his reading demonstrates is the impossibility of reading.

Luckily, things are not so simple. It seems plausible to argue, for example, that the statement 'il est nécessaire' depends on what de Man calls 'a propositional cognition' just as much, and just as little, as does 'il est juste'. 'Il est nécessaire' performs what it enunciates just as much, and just as little, as does 'il est juste': both are descriptives and can be the object of assent or disagreement. The contrast comes in the referents of these descriptives, that is, in the states of affairs indicated in 'what is just should be followed', and 'what has the most power should be followed'. The first of these states of affairs involves a prescription of the type: 'you should follow what is just' (*sollen*); the second a modal statement that is perhaps not clearly either descriptive *or* prescriptive, of the type 'you must follow what has the most power' (*müssen*). The tension of the passage stems not from a distribution in terms of cognition and performance, but from a split in words and concepts such as 'law' and 'right' in their reference to both obligation and necessity.

De Man's reading is not unaware of this additional complication, which suggests a certain originality of prescription (of the question of justice, precisely), when it goes on to suggest that the adjective *juste* can be linked both the cognitive value of *justesse* and to the juridical value of *justice* (cf. *Allegories of Reading*, p. 269); but this is rapidly reabsorbed into the familiar cognitive/performative distinction, for the importance of the juridical aspect for de Man is simply that it *weakens* cognitive claims and is the more vulnerable to usurpation by power.

Similarly, might here does not usurp 'the consistency of cognition', as de Man has it, but the quite different order of obligation, by playing on the descriptive/prescriptive undecidability of 'law' and on the sense of the verb *devoir*. The *coup de force* of force lies less in its claim to *epistemological* rightness, as de Man asserts, than in its claim to subsume the ethical under the epistemological. We might indeed accept that 'force . . . is pure performance' (p. 22), but, as our earlier derivation of archi-performance suggests, there is no particular reason to oppose this to cognition (constatation) rather than to prescription (for example). De Man is right to suggest that the conclusion of this *Pensée* discomforts reading, but the fact that he refers to this as a 'discomfort one *should* experience' (p. 22; my emphasis) shows the persistence of a prescriptive dimension that the analysis has not resolved. Pascal's text may well suggest that 'the tropological field of cognition is revealed to be dependent on an entity, might, that is heterogeneous with regard to this field', but if this is something of a scandal, that scandal is ethical rather than epistemological. The discomfort provoked by that scandal does not depend on some moral judgement delivered from a position exterior to the struggle of performance and cognition, but from the elusive *involvement* of the ethical in the heterogeneity of might with respect to cognition.

This is not to suggest that de Man is wrong or even unjust, with respect to Pascal or anyone else. At this level of the machine, such judgements would simply not be pertinent, and presuppose what is at issue. But just as Pascal's machine failed to function without generating its accompanying and aberrant scenes of prescription, so de Man's readings generate ethical preoccupations that they cannot dominate: they do this not through any lack of rigour, but because of their rigour. To suggest that de Man's work is somehow reprehensibly apolitical is therefore blindly superficial, as is the idea that taking a 'position' on ethical and political issues is, however necesssary, somehow sufficient to come to terms with the nature of the ethical and political. De Man's apparent 'neutrality' on such matters is no more and no less neutral than, for example, the question concerning technology. The unresolvable aporias revealed by de Man in terms of cognition and performance, the 'aberration' he regularly produces as reading machine, signal the unavoidability of attempting to resolve ethical and political questions either cognitively or performatively, and the equally unavoidable irreducibility of such questions to the terms of truth or performativity. 'Aberration' becomes a name for this type of situation, for the impossibility of constatives, performatives, prescriptives, and so on ever achieving purity or propriety, in the face of an unconditional demand that they nevertheless be separated and *respected* in their incommensurability.[20] The general milieu of this generalized aberration is what I previously called archi-performance. If the performative in the narrower sense is legitimated in terms of its performativity, the archi-performative is aberrant in its inaccessibility to any kind of legitimation. The blind performances of the archi-performance machine cannot be dominated by any language or by any notions of subjects, consciousness, life or death that might attempt to contain them. The belatedness of language with respect to these performances not only marks a failure of cognition to be able to account for its own production,[21] but also underlies the possibility of any sort of distinction between justice, truth, beauty, performativity, and so on, while simultaneously leaving perilously and necessarily ungrounded the obligation to respect some such distinctions.

In one of the *Pensées* de Man does not discuss, we find the following: 'The arithmetical machine produces effects that approach nearer to thought than anything animals do; but it does nothing that could make one say that it has will like animals' (Lafuma, p. 741). Let us read this as suggesting not at all some wonderful and mysterious quality of 'life', and clearly not of 'humanity', but rather as implying that nothing in the blind aberrant machine of archi-performance allows us the comfortable pathos of attributing any purpose or meaning to it: the machine has no will but generates what we call the will – before any specification as will to power, to truth, or to anything else, this 'will' strives for and against its blind 'origin' in the aberrant activity or passivity that opens the ethical. In this perspective, 'reading' as much as 'writing' becomes a matter of 'doing justice' to this aberration, in the sense neither of speaking the truth about it nor of judging it to be good or evil, beautiful or monstrous, but of working with it, respecting it, and letting it be.

'Death is a displaced name for a linguistic predicament,' wrote Paul de Man (*RR*, p. 81). 'Paul de Man', we might add, has become a displaced name for a set of machines and aberrations that are now as alive as ever. A signature, a tombstone, a text, a reading, a machine.

Notes

1. Blaise Pascal, *Oeuvres complètes*, ed. L. Lafuma, Paris: Seuil 1963, pp. 187–192. The slightly less accessible edition of Brunschvieg and Boutroux (Paris: Hachette 1908) gives some additional documentation and includes a letter from Belair to Huygens that provides fuller description of the machine itself (I: pp. 293-321).

2. See *La Condition postmoderne*, Paris: Minuit 1979; translated by Geoff Bennington and Brian Massumi as *The Postmodern Condition*, Minneapolis: University of Minnesota Press 1984, esp. Chapters 11 and 12.

3. See, for example, the remarks in Mme Perier's biography of Pascal, in the Brunschvieg and Boutroux edition, I: pp. 57–8.

4. As analysed by Derrida in 'La Pharmacie de Platon', in *La Dissemination*, Paris: Seuil 1972, pp. 71–197; translated by Barbara Johnson, Chicago: University of Chicago Press 1982. When I wrote this essay I did not know of Derrida's 'Psyché, Invention de l'autre', (in *Psyché. Inventions de l'autre*, Paris: Galilée 1987, pp. 11–61), which thematizes the question of invention, touches on de Man's text on Pascal, but, somewhat to my relief, does not discuss Pascal's arithmetic machine. *Ressentiment* pursues invention.

5. Bernard Sharratt, *Reading Relations: Structures of Literary Production. A Dialectical Text/Book*, Brighton: Harvester 1982, p. 31.

6. Jacques Derrida, 'Force et signification', in *L'Ecriture et la différence*, Paris: Seuil 1967; re-edited collection, 'Points' 1979, p. 23; translated by Alan Bass, Chicago: University of Chicago Press 1978, p. 11.

7. Derrida, *L'Ecriture et la différence*, p. 335; English trans., p. 227 (translation modified).

8. Ibid.

9. A reading machine would be needed to read all the machines in Derrida's work.

10. Wald Godzich, 'Caution! Reader at Work!' Introduction to *Blindness and Insight: Essays in the Rhetoric of Contemporary Criticism*, second edition, London: Methuen 1983, pp. xv–xvi.

11. See Godzich, p. xxvii: 'De Man's rhetorical inquiry consists in recognizing the finiteness of the text and in bringing out its rhetorical machine'; and Rodolphe Gasché, ' "Setzung" and "Übersetzung": Notes on Paul de Man', *Diacritics*, 11 (1981) pp. 36–57, 41–2: 'A rhetorical reading, then, sets out to explore the mechanics of grammar as well as of traditional rhetoric, the machinery that produces the effects of univocity and

totality'. Gasché further exploits the language of mechanics and machines (pp. 42, 43, 45, 51, 55).

12. Gasché's article provides a brilliant discussion of de Man's use of speech-act theory in general.

13. A full discussion of the relationship between aesthetics and the machine lies outside the scope of this essay: a starting point might be found in Lyotard's *Les Transformateurs Duchamp*, Paris: Galilée 1977.

14. Fredric Jameson, *The Political Unconscious: Narrative as a Socially Symbolic Act*, Ithaca, N.Y.: Cornell University Press 1981; see my discussion in Chapter 3 above.

15. Cf. Lyotard, *The Postmodern Condition*, p. 9.

16. This is the familiar charge brought by Frank Lentricchia in *After the New Criticism*, Chicago: University of Chicago Press 1980.

17. Cf. *AR*, p. 206: 'Allegories are always ethical'. The present essay might be read as an attempt to understand the paragraph in which the assertion appears.

18. See my 'Reading Allegory', *Oxford Literary Review*, 4 (1981); pp. 83–93, and for a more detailed discussion, my *Sententiousness and the Novel: Laying Down the Law in Eighteenth-Century French Fiction*, Cambridge: Cambridge University Press 1985.

19. P. 21: The printed text has 'model' rather than 'modal'.

20. This is also the problem and the demand of Lyotard's recent work: see *Au Juste*, Paris: Christian Bourgois 1979; and *Le Différend*, Paris: Minuit 1984. *Au Juste* is now available as *Just Gaming*, trans. Wald Godzich, Minneapolis: University of Minnesota Press 1985.

21. *AR*, p. 300: 'Any speech act produces an excess of cognition, but it can never hope to know the process of its own production (the only thing worth knowing).'

8

'Ces Petits *Différends*': Lyotard and

Horace

The 'Horace' in my title might well have been the Quintus Horatius Flaccus of *Ars Poetica* fame, and more specifically of *ut pictura poesis* fame. This would most obviously have provided access to a discussion of *Discours, figure*. For example, Lyotard refers to this statement, or to its presuppositions, in an analysis of the relationship of word and image in the doctrine of the Fathers of the Church:

> A pedagogy which finds its support in the ancient 'Ut pictura poesis' of Horace, of which Plutarch attributes the earliest formulation to Simonides. It is on condition that it speak 'clearly' that painting will be tolerated. This clarity must be taken literally: it is the transparency of signification in the linguistic term. . . . The figure thus strictly subjected to writing cannot create an illusion and its opacity cannot therefore capture and divert the movement of adoration. The function of the visible is [here] to signify the invisible. (p. 173)

The 'earliest formulation' referred to here returns later in *Discours, figure*, in a discussion of the rhetorical notion of figure:

> The tradition places the starting-point of rhetoric in the following words of Simonides of Ceos: 'Poetry is painting with words'. Painting, poetry and rhetoric are the places where there comes to the surface the figure which the Pythagorean-Platonic city has the pretension of breaking with. In truth, rhetoric and philosophy belong together to the universe of fragmentary discourses born of the breaking of the speech of *aletheia*. Nevertheless Platonism attributes to the figure the function of seducing, i.e. of separating the subject from itself and getting an ally within the enemy camp; this is evidently because the figure is the ruse of a force, namely desire. (p. 288 n6)

Complicated detours would have been necessary in such an account of 'Lyotard and Horace'; for example, the context of the 'ut picture poesis' statement in Horace himself suggests much less than is usually supposed a *general* analogy of poetry and painting (as arts of representation), and certainly does not imply the metaphorical equivalence suggested by Simonides (though some such equivalence *is* suggested in other parts of the *Ars Poetica*): here Horace is dealing, rather, with a particular analogy to do with conditions of reception, viewing and reading:

> Poetry is like painting. Some attracts you more if you stand near, some if you're further off. One picture likes a dark place, one will need to be seen in the light, because it's not afraid of the critic's sharp judgement. One gives pleasure once, one will please you if you look it over ten times. (ll. 361–5, trans. D.A. Russell)

This question of distance, of finding the right distance, would itself have to be referred to Lyotard's elaboration of the non-oppositional relationship of discourse and figure in the early parts of his book, around questions of depth, designation, perspective, deictics and so on, in the wake of Merleau-Ponty. Plotting the relationship of this essentially phenomenological account (which informs the first quotation from *Discours, figure*) with, on the one hand, a *semiology* of painting and discourse (as formulated most notably in this country by Norman Bryson, for example), and on the other with Lyotard's own attempt, in the second part of *Discours, figure* (and visibly so in the second quotation) to displace phenomenology via an appeal to a certain psychoanalysis, and later, to a 'libidinal economy' – plotting these relationships would be a redoubtable task which I shall not attempt here. But the idea that the function of the visible might be to signify or at any rate to allude to the invisible may yet provide a bridge between Lyotard's 'early' work, and that following his 'linguistic turn': for example, a 1981 text on the artist Daniel Buren is entitled 'Faire voir les invisibles, ou: contre le réalisme' [literally: 'make the invisibles seen, or: against realism'],[1] and this would of course be consonant with a number of recent formulations of the task of philosophy *and* art to 'présenter qu'il y a de l'imprésentable'.[2]

So not that Horace, though it might well have been. Nor even, in terms of the possible bridge linking early and late Lyotard, the Horatius from Book 2 of Livy's *History* or from Macaulay's famous and appalling poem from *The Lays of Ancient Rome*, who might defend such a bridge (defend its existence and/or prevent its being crossed). But the question of the bridge would inevitably, given the later Lyotard's insistent readings of Kant, and especially of the third *Critique*, have embroiled me in the 'bridge', which Kant attempts to throw over the 'abyss' between theoretical cognition of nature and practical laws of freedom,[3] a bridge the possibility of which Lyotard would want to interrogate between genres of discourse in general (see, for example, the 'Notice Kant 3' in *Le différend*, pp. 189–96). In a complex way I could scarcely unpack, it seems to me that both Kant *and* Lyotard are in some sense Horatius, defending both the possibility and impassibility of such a bridge: as Lyotard says in his analysis of the sublime, the 'passage' of the abyss becomes blocked in an agitation over the abyss (p. 240) – the bridge is neither crossed nor not crossed, defended, *défendu* in both senses. And I could scarcely have discussed this Horatius without looking at Heidegger's comment, in 'Building, dwelling, thinking', that 'the bridge does not just connect banks that are already there. The banks emerge as banks only as the bridge crosses the stream',[4] and at Derrida's analyses in *La Vérité en peinture* of the same passage in Kant, and notably the following statement:

> The bridge is not *an* analogy. The recourse to analogy, the concept and effect of analogy are or make *the bridge* itself – both in the [third] *Critique* and in all the powerful tradition to which it still belongs. The analogy of the abyss and the bridge over the abyss is an analogy which says that there must surely be an analogy between two absolutely heterogeneous worlds, a third term to cross the abyss, to heal over the gaping wound and think the gap. In a word, a *symbol*. The bridge is a symbol, passing from one bank to the other, and the symbol is a bridge.
>
> The Abyss calls for analogy – the active recourse of the whole *Critique* – but analogy plunges endlessly into the abyss as soon as a certain art is needed to describe analogically the play of analogy.[5]

But such an approach would scarcely be possible without some attempt to unravel the difficult issues of Lyotard's general relationship to Heidegger on the one hand and to Derrida on the other: this would also involve building and/or defending bridges, and I fear that the preliminary surveys are as yet not really complete.

Neither of these two possible Horaces or Horatii, then, but a third Roman Horatius, or rather *the* third Horatius, the one who survives and avenges his two brothers, killing all three Curiatii, thus deciding the war between Rome and Alba Longa, as first recounted in Book 1 of Livy's *History*. (David's famous painting of the three brothers' oath before the combat is, incidentally, the subject of an analysis by Bryson.[6]) The dispute between the two cities is the apparent result of border-raids by both sides, and the theft of cattle from each other. The dispute has not been settled by litigation, and the declaration of war by Rome answers the Alban leader's refusal to return the stolen goods. This failure of litigation does not of course automatically qualify the dispute as a *différend* in Lyotard's terms, and I shall return to this question in due course. There is any case a strong suggestion in Livy that the war is a result in the first instance, not of a simple matter of cattle-stealing, but of a renewal of Rome's conquering destiny by the new king, Tullus Hostilius: such a destiny has been promised to Rome at least since the death of its founder, Romulus, and Livy suggests that Tullus's 'one object was to find cause for renewed military adventure', [7] after the peaceful reign of Numa Pompilius, a man who had sought to give Rome an essentially religious unity, and who had, says Livy, 'a great reputation . . . for justice and piety' (p. 52). (This conjunction would immediately arouse Lyotard's suspicion, given that at least since *Instructions païennes* of 1977, he has been explicitly seeking for 'justice in impiety' (p. 11).)

But whatever cause is assigned to the war, its status is complicated by the fact that both cities come from a common mythical root, the Trojan refugees led by Aeneas: the Trojans had settled in Lavinium, Lavinians had settled Alba, and it was from Alba that Romulus and Remus set out to found Rome. Romulus's act of fratricide at the foundation of Rome is set by Livy in a quasi-causal chain of violence, involving usurpation, murder and rape (this rape of a Vestal Virgin, legendarily performed by the god Mars, leads to the birth of Romulus and Remus). Alba and Rome are successive products of this violent genealogy, and Livy says that 'war between them would be like father against son' (p. 57).

It is not Livy's account that interests me primarily, however, but that presented by Corneille's play *Horace* (1640). Pierre Corneille would also allow a number of trajectories or passages through Lyotard's work. In *Discours, figure*, for example, Lyotard juxtaposes a quotation from Corneille's earlier play *Le Cid* (1636) with one from e.e. cummings, to suggest that both texts are equally 'poetic' in their transgression of certain discursive rules. Lyotard goes on to suggest that this common 'poetic' quality implies a break (in Corneille as much as cummings) with the discourse of communication, but that the poetic function in the two cases is somewhat different:

> [The poetic function] today is critical; it used to be integrative, but even then, this integration of the collectivity in itself took place in a register different from that of the profane language of communication. It is individuals who communicate with each other, and the very category of communication can only become predominant in a society in which the crisis of institutions produces isolated groups of individuals who attempt to establish social links on a 'horizontal' contractual basis. The integrative function of poetic discourse presupposes, on the contrary, a coherent system of institutions culminating in a myth of origin, to which the poem, but also dance or the plastic arts or war, ceaselessly refer as their common meaning. (pp. 320–1)

And in the wake of this notion of an integrative poetic function, Corneille reappears in *Au juste* as Lyotard's example of 'classical' writing, defined in pragmatic terms as a set-up in which 'the author is able to write while simultaneously placing himself in the position of the reader' (p. 21.), as opposed to the modern writer who does not know for whom he or she writes, and who sends out books like bottles thrown into the sea, in search of their addressee.

But nowhere, I think, does Lyotard quote or discuss the statement from *Horace* which provides my title (although one other line from the play is quoted in *Le Différend*, and will reappear here in due course): Curiace, one of the three brothers who will be opposed to the Horatii, is recounting how the two armies were prevented from engaging in a full-scale final battle by a harangue from the Alban leader. The burden of this harangue is to do precisely with the common genealogy of Rome and Alba which I have pointed out in Livy:

> Souffrons que la raison élaire enfin nos âmes:
> Nous sommes vos voisins, nos filles sont vos femmes,
> Et l'hymen nous a joints par tant et tant de noeuds,
> Qu'il est peu de nos fils qui ne soient vos neveux;
> Nous ne sommes qu'un sang et qu'un peuple en deux villes:
> Pourquoi nous déchirer par des guerres civiles,
> Où la mort des vaincus affaiblit les vainqueurs,
> Et le plus beau triomphe est arrośe de pleurs?
> Nos ennemis communs attendent avec joie
> Qu'un des partis défait leur donne l'autre en proie,
> Lassé, demi-rompu, vainqueur, mais, pour tout fruit,
> Dénué d'un secours par lui-même détruit.
> Ils ont assez longtemps joui de nos divorces;
> Contre eux dorénavant joignons toutes nos forces,
> *Et noyons dans l'oubli ces petits différends*
> *Qui de si bons guerriers font de mauvais parents.*
> Que se l'ambition de commander aux autres
> Fait marcher aujourd'hui vos troupes et les nôtres,
> Pourvu au'à moins de sang nous voulions l'apaiser,
> Elle nous unira, loin de nous diviser.
>
> [At last let reason light our souls:
> We are your neighbours, our daughters are your wives,
> And hymen has joined us by so many bonds
> That few of your sons are not also your nephews;
> We are but one blood, one people in two cities,
> Why tear ourselves apart in civil wars
> In which the loser's death weakens the victor
> And the finest triumph is watered with tears?
> Our common enemies wait with joy

For one of the parties, defeated, to offer them the other as their prey –
Fatigued, half-broken, victorious: but for sole reward
Deprived of the help it has itself destroyed.
Long enough have they enjoyed our divorce;
Henceforth let us join against them our force,
And let us drown in oblivion these little différends
Which make such bad relatives of such good warriors.
If the ambition of commanding others
Today makes your troops march, and ours,
So long as we appease it with lesser spill of blood,
That ambition will unite far more than divide us.]

(ll. 287–306; my translation and emphasis)

And this leads to the proposal that the particular *différend* (never specified by Corneille) be settled by the combat of three champions from either side – which three champions are duly chosen as the Horatii and the Curiatii.

I have suggested that failure of litigation does not necessarily lead to *différend*, and in Lyotard's terms the particular *'petit différend'* involved here would seem not to deserve its name. In Lyotard's terms, a *différend* is 'a case of conflict between (at least) two parties that could not be resolved equitably for lack of a rule applicable to the two modes of argumentation' (*Le différend*, p. 9). Although, accepting Livy's account, the dispute in question here is to do with the very border-regions or *pagus* from which, in both *Instructions païennes* (pp. 42–3) and *Au juste* (pp. 74–5), Lyotard derives his notion of the 'pagan', and which returns in *Le Différend* itself as a privileged site (if not the *necessary* site) of *différends* (§218), it would seem that the issue in question here is essentially a litigation: if the dispute in question is to do with stolen cattle, then both sides use commensurable argumentation in requesting the return of their property. And if this be taken as a mere pretext for war, and something like the 'ambition of commanding others' referred to by the Alban leader be seen as the cause of the dispute, then we should still apparently be dealing with litigation rather than *différend*: acting out of imperial ambition, both sides are attempting to impose on the other a *name* (Rome, Alba) and therefore a *narrative* – the 'myth of origin' (and genealogy of heroes) recounted by Livy and referred to by Lyotard in the reference to Corneille just quoted from *Discours, figure*.[8] In so far as both sides are proposing sentences of the narrative genre, then the dispute is not a *différend* (and I wonder whether war could ever be a *différend* in Lyotard's terms: I suspect that in *Au juste* at least, a proportional analogy suggests that war is to terror as litigation is to *différend* – but the fact that the Alban leader describes this as 'civil war' might complicate the issue, especially in view of

Lyotard's image of a civil war of language against 'itself' (*Le différend*, §201; see too §§188, 190 and 231): this image being justified by the location of the *différend* as a general question of the relationship of genres).

This type of set-up, involving the imposition of name and narrative, which is, perhaps, that of imperialism in general, is not, in Livy's account, to be thought of as something Rome got into at a certain point of its history, but as something which constituted Rome from its very beginning: Romulus simply enclosed a certain area of ground and, following in this the standard practice of antiquity according to Livy, 'shark[ed] up a lot of homeless and destitute folk and pretend[ed] that they were "born of the earth" to be his progeny' (p. 42) – this would be, via the imposition of a name ('Romans'), the constitution of a *Volk* and a *Heim* from the *pagus* (see *Le différend*, §218). But Rome is not simply one example of this structure: it is *the* example – Lyotard analyses this set-up, in one of his oddest texts, *Le Mur du pacifique*, as a fundament-ally Roman set-up which has simply shifted its capital further and further west, at least as far as Washington and maybe to Los Angeles, where it meets the 'wall of the Pacific' and stops in this absolute west which can go no further without becoming the east. (This impossible line of separation between east and west gives its title to an essay by Lyotard on the Japanese-American painter Arakawa, 'Longitude 180° W or E'.)[9] (In *Le Différend* itself, Rome returns, again as more than just an example, in the chapter on names and referents, as a persistent and rather bizarre test case for the analysis of 'reality' (§§58, 59, 65, 66, 67, 68) – a little later we shall see why it might be possible to refer to Lyotard's whole philosophy as in some sense a philosophy of Rome, or a Roman philosophy.) In the case before us, however, Rome, which is born of the violent enclosure of a *pagus*, is attempting to annex another *Heim* or *Volk* in order to impose its own name and narrative on a rival name and narrative (that of the Albans). In *Le Différend*, this type of situation, in which the persistence of national worlds of names is seen to block movements of universalization of all sorts (including that of Socialist Internationalism) is analysed precisely *not* as a *différend*. A *différend* requires the attempt by one genre (be it cognitive, perform-ative, economic) to impose its hegemony on another genre (be it ethical or speculative), to enforce judgement of cases pertaining to one genre in terms of another. In the type of conflict we are examining, however, the genres in conflict are the same on both sides (narrative and nominative giving auto-nomination): the conflict is indeed a litigation, but an exacerbated type of litigation not easily to be dismissed – the point is that there is no tribunal which could settle the dispute *as* litigation: unless one posits a tribunal of world history, a hypothesis

Lyotard believes to be untenable (see §227). (And this possibility of an exacerbated litigation is matched by that of an exacerbated *différend*, in which no tribunal could even pretend to settle that *différend* as though it were a matter for litigation (see §160): Lyotard never really thematizes or classifies these situations in formal terms, but we shall see that this possible absence of the tribunal is not trivial, nor simply a contingent possibility.)

This exacerbation of litigation takes a curious turn in the case with which we are concerned: in so far as Rome and Alba belong to the same genealogy, then they essentially propose the same narrative of origins – if the Alban leader can claim that they are really one blood and one people, then in a sense they have the same name, or the difference between their two names is a sort of accident or catastrophe. This is why he can suggest that they share an essential identity, defined by their opposition to 'common enemies' – in so far as the outcome of the battle between them will be that one absorbs the other and re-establishes their nominal identity, then this will restore a unity accidentally broken: no need for a lot of blood to be spilt, and the blood that is spilt will be more that of blood-brotherhood than hatred, integrative rather than divisive. (The logic of his harangue is exactly that which informs the 'no enemies on the Left' argument around political differences, and which consistently identifies a 'real enemy' elsewhere in order to put an end to 'civil war' among natural allies. This masking of possible *différends* in the interests of establishing unity is of course suspect in Lyotard's terms.)

If Rome's battle against Alba is, as Livy suggests, that of son against father, then we could imagine an essentially Oedipal reading of the conflict, but also be at something of a loss to understand how the change of name came about. But in Corneille's presentation, Alba is not Rome's father but its mother, and this complicates any such analysis. In the opening scene of the play, Sabine, wife of the Horace who will emerge victorious in the name of Rome, but herself of Alban origin, makes this very clear: she readily accepts that Rome, in its infancy, can consolidate its power only by war, and welcomes the gods' promise that Rome will conquer the earth, beyond even the Latin region here in question; 'But', she adds, apostrophizing Rome,

> . . . respecte une ville à qui tu dois Romule.
> Ingrate, souviens-toi que du sang de ses rois
> Tu tiens ton nom, tes murs, et tes premières lois.
> Albe est ton origine; arrête, et considère
> Que tu portes le fer dans le sein de ta mère
>
> [. . . respect a city to whom you owe Romulus,

Ungrateful [*ingrate*: Rome is feminine], remember that from the blood of
its [i.e. Alban] Kings
You take your name, your walls, and your first laws.
Alba is your origin; stop and consider
That you are plunging your sword into your mother's breast].

(ll. 52–60)

This initial familial complication is relentlessly increased by the way
Corneille determines the relationship of the major characters. For
Sabine is not only an Alban become Roman through marriage to
Horace, she is also the sister of the three Curiatii that same Horace will
eventually kill. The play opens on the impossible situation this creates:
Sabine is caught in a double bind where she can only fear whatever
results from the confrontation, and produces elegantly balanced lines
such as 'Je crains notre victoire autant que notre perte' [I fear our
victory as much as our defeat] (l. 32), or 'Je ne suis point pour Albe, et
ne suis plus pour Rome' [I am not for Alba, and no longer for Rome]
(l. 88).

Sabine's dilemma is produced by a change of name: she was Alban,
but is now Roman; she was a Curiatius, now a Horace. Her appeal to
Rome to remember its origins in Alba doubles her own memory of her
own over-written origin: 'Albe, où j'ai commencé de respirer le
jour,/Albe, mon cher pays, et mon premier amour' [Alba, where I first
began to breathe the day/Alba, my dear country and my first love] (ll.
29–30). In Lyotardian terms, Sabine would be described as the referent of a sentence (or sequence of sentences) of the matrimonial genre,
which positions as its sender her Alban family (and specifically the
father of that family, as what determines its name) and as its addressee
her Roman family, and specifically Horace (who shares his name not
only with his two brothers, but also with his father). The meaning of
such a sentence is open to debate, of course, but part of that meaning is
that the referent of the sentence changes name and in principle
forgets that of the sender in favour of that of the addressee. Such at
least is the interpretation of Horace himself, and, more importantly, of
his sister Camille, who says that Sabine need only fear Horace's death,
and not that of her Alban brothers, for her attachment to her brothers
is cancelled by marriage; 'pour suivre un mari l'on quitte ses parents'
[to follow a husband one leaves one's relatives] (l. 886). This explication comes in the middle of a curious scene in which Sabine and
Camille are arguing about which of them is in the worse situation: for
Camille is not only Horace's sister, she is also to be married to one of
the three Curiatii. She is, as it were, the promised referent of a future
matrimonial sentence: or, perhaps, stranded between sender and
addressee, between Rome and Alba, between Horatii and Curiatii.

The judgement to be made of this situation can be agonistically debated: for example, Julie, a confidant figure, early in the play suggests quite plainly to Camille that it is possible to change one's lover (in the sense of fiancé), but not one's husband, and that Camille need only forget Curiace in favour of a perfectly acceptable match in Valère, a Roman (ll. 145–50). Camille, against such a view, suggests that on the contrary she is caught in an impossible suspension between departure and arrival: following the rules of the matrimonial genre, which we can now analyse further as involving a sentence which is a promise and the matrimonial sentence proper which fulfils that promise, she is pulled forward towards the second sentence (which the genre tends to propose as inevitable or natural), only to discover the truth of one of Lyotard's fundamental tenets, namely that necessity is only *that* a second sentence will arrive, but *what* sentence will arrive is a contingency (see *Le différend*, §40). In this sense, in so far as the most general sense of the *différend* is a situation which holds between sentences, on the occasion of the slightest 'enchaînement' or linking, in so far as incommensurable genres are always in conflict over the sentence which actually arrives, then Camille is 'in' the *différend* more radically than anyone, in the 'ontological' position of waiting for the event to come, for the 'Arrive-t-il?' (see *D*, §110): living respect for the event as intolerable anguish. (This would perhaps be the point at which to explore the essential differences between the type of reading sketched here and that offered from a dialectical-existential perspective by Serge Doubrovsky, to whose *Corneille ou la dialectique du héros* I am none the less indebted, as is any reader of Corneille today.)[10]

The relationship between Alba and Rome is, then, analogically one of genealogy (father and son for Livy, mother and daughter for Corneille), and really one of intermarriage, the 'exchange of women'. We might tentatively formulate the *différend* between the two cities as a product of the *différend* between this marital economy and this genealogical analogy, between a narrative of origins and an economy of exchange. But such a *différend* cannot simply be located *between* Rome and Alba: it must affect each from within. And in so far as the economy is essentially to do with the exchange of women by their fathers, then it is not surprising that women (and specifically Camille, caught in mid-exchange) should be, more than the male characters, the privileged witnesses to the *différend* staged by the play.

In Lyotard's terms, a *différend* is signalled by silence and/or sentiment, a frustration of language trying to phrase something in the absence of the means to do so (see *D*, §23). Sabine and Camille bear witness to that sentiment, in the impossibility in which they are placed of situating themselves as senders of possible sentences. Their language is therefore 'sentimental': Sabine at several points asking to die, in view of an obligation to choose where choice is impossible; Camille alternating between hope and despair. But if, as Lyotard also suggests, a *différend* is always a call to phrasing, to the search for an idiom in which to phrase the (as yet) unsayable or to present the (as yet) unpresentable, then Camille also provides an example to support this. The language with which she is provided to phrase her situation is the male language of family names and city-names: the language of the genealogical narrative. Horace and Curiace both produce sentences belonging to this language, finalized by the obligation to immortalize the city-name and through it the family name. Appealing to the operator of the 'belle mort', extensively analysed by Lyotard in the context of narrative legitimation in *Le Différend* ('Notice Platon', p. 40; §156), whereby the glorious death of the individual is sublated into the story of the name (and the pronoun 'we' (Horatii, Romans) who call ourselves, each other and the dead heroes by that name), both Horace and Curiace know how to behave. Virtue and glory consist in dying the 'belle mort' for the furthering of the name and the narrative.

Horace explains that in itself there is nothing very extraordinary about this; thousands have died in this way and thousands would want to (ll. 440–1). In the present situation, however, Horace will be fighting his brother-in-law to be, whom he loves; not just anybody, but 'un autre soi-même' (l. 444), and this makes the situation special: not at all regrettably, for Horace. If the law of the 'belle mort' prescribes a rigorous hierarchy of generic ends, and if it places the name of the state above that of the family and *a fortiori* of the individual, then the best (because most testing) situation will clearly be that in which the claims of the subordinated genres are the hardest to overcome. Horace wants to immortalize his own name, that of his family and that of the state: this is done by attempting to sacrifice the first two names to the last; paradoxically, this preserves the two sacrificed names all the better. ('It is true that our names can never die,' agrees Curiace (l. 453).) In so far as Rome *names* Horace as its champion (and it is essentially unimportant here that Rome names three Horaces: the other two never appear in the play, and have a functional importance only when an incomplete report of the combat suggests that they both died nobly (within the economy of the 'belle mort') whereas Horace fled ignobly; the other two Curiatii are even less important), he *becomes* Rome and must forget all else – the harder this is to achieve, the greater the virtue; in normal battle one does not know one's adversary as an individual name: knowing and loving Curiace, it is all the more heroic for Horace to be able to say to him, 'Alba has named you, I no longer know you' (l. 502). And in so far as Curiace is none the less another self for Horace, it follows that he no longer knows himself, *already* dying with the promise of his name's returning as immortal through the logic of the *belle mort*. The name thrives on the death of its bearer. Horace has to this extent *already* won his battle with Curiace, who says quite consistently, 'I do still know you, and that's what kills me' (l. 503). This does not in fact prevent Curiace from going to fight, and for both sides to insist on fighting even when the armies they represent want to stop the combat. The complexity here suggests that both Horace and Curiace want their own death, even in the attempt to kill each other.

Lyotard's analysis of the logic of the *belle mort* suggests that it stifles the *différend*: if the *différend* is indeed signalled by sentiment, then it is quite accurate for Horace to suggest that acceptance of the 'belle mort' prescribed by Rome for the preservation of its name 'Ought to stifle in us all other sentiments' (l. 494). But if the stifling of the *différend* in the constitution of identity under the name of *Volk* and *Heim* entails *différends* in the *pagus*, on the borders, then it is also no surprise that the *différend* suppressed by Horace should reappear with Camille, the character we have identified as being constitutively placed in that region. According to the imperial genre (name, narrative, *belle mort*), Camille is enjoined by Horace, before the combat, to receive the victor, whether it be himself or Curiace, in all his proven virtue: neither should be reproached with the other's death. Such behaviour is also recommended after the battle by her father (le vieil Horace), and demanded by Horace again when he returns in triumph. Against this genre, Camille reacts by a systematic and perfectly consequent repudiation of names. Already in Act I she has described Curiace as 'mon plus unique bien' ([my most *unique* good] – Doubrovsky stresses the importance of this: a Lyotardian transcription would suggest that this value of the unique would demand an *absolute* propriety in naming which family names do not respect),[11] and hastens, when Curiace arrives in the space between the Alban leader's harangue and the selection of the champions, to assume that this arrival means that he has fled the battle, refusing to fight under the name of Alba, and subordinating his *renommée*, his renown (almost, literally, his re-naming as the absolute representative of a collective name) to the particularity of his love for Camille – only to find that when chosen, Curiace, although admitting the attraction of obscurity over *renommée*, announces that 'Avant d'être à vous je suis à mon pays' [Before belonging to you I belong to my country] (l. 562), and that the names of the cities take precedence over relation-names such as 'brother-in-law' and 'sister' (referring to Horace and Sabine), and even that of 'fiancé'. Curiace is well aware of the threat to names posed by love (in the state of suspension before marriage, as we have seen for Camille), saying to Camille, 'Plus je suis votre amant, moins je suis Curiace' [the more I am your lover, the less am I Curiace] (l. 584). After Curiace's death, Camille violently denounces the violence of a paternal name which makes of her a Horace, forbidding even her grief for Curiace, and says, 'un véritable amour brave la main des Parques, /Et ne prend point de lois de ces cruels tryans/Qu'un astre injurieux nous donne pour parents' [A true love stands up to the hands of the fates, /And does not take its laws from those cruel tyrants/That an injurious star gives us as parents] (ll. 1197–8). (This would need to be placed against her earlier argument with Sabine, in which the impossibility of her position is stressed in terms of the importance of paternal recognition of the object of love, that recognition turning love as 'tyrant' into love as 'legitimate king' (l. 922).) Confronting the victorious and proud Horace, who is scandalized to find Curiace's 'name on [her] lips' (or, more literally, in her mouth), Camille denies her relationship as sister to Horace, and defines herself solely as a lover – and admonished by Horace in the name of Rome, she unleashes a famous imprecation (the first line of which is quoted by Lyotard as an example of a possible *enchaînement* onto the name of Rome in *Le différend*, §67):

> Rome, l'unique objet de mon ressentiment!
> Rome, à qui vient ton bras d'immoler mon amant!
> Rome, qui t'a vu naître, et que ton cœur adore!
> Rome, enfin, que je hais parce qu'elle t'honore!
>
> [Rome, sole object of my resentment!
> Rome, to whom your arm has just sacrificed my lover!
> Rome, which saw you born and which your heart adores!
> Rome, which I hate because she honours you!]

(ll. 1301–4)

And goes on to look forward to the destruction of Rome and the last Roman – the extinction of the name, at which she could 'die of pleasure' (l. 1318), in a sort of paroxysm of *jouissance* in anonymity which would be a generalized figure of the anonymity implied by her love for Curiace, as refusal of his name.

Horace kills her on the spot. This too is a sentimental sentence which attests to the *différend* in the attempt to suppress it: for this killing cannot be integrated into the blood-and-name economy of the *belle mort* which determined the main combat. Horace himself attempts to legitimate his act in terms of an erasure of names:

> Ne me dis point qu'elle est et mon sang et ma soeur.

Mon père ne peut plus l'avouer pour sa fille:
Qui maudit son pays renonce à sa famille;
Des noms si pleins d'amour ne lui sont plus permis;
De ses plus chers parents il fait ses ennemis;
Le sang même les arme en haine de son crime.
La plus prompte vengeance en est plus légitime;
Et ce souhait impie, encore qu'impuissant,
Est un monstre qu'il faut étouffer en naissant.

[Do not tell me that she is my blood and my sister.
My father can no longer recognize her as his daughter:
Whoever curses his country renounces his family;
Names so full of love are no longer allowed him;
He makes enemies of his dearest parents;
Blood itself arms them in hatred against his crime.
The speediest revenge is the most legitimate;
And this impious, though impotent wish [i.e. Camille's wish that Rome be destroyed]
Is a monster which must be stifled at birth.]

(ll. 1326–34)

And when Sabine, his wife, suggests he might kill her too, for her 'crimes' and 'miseries' are equal to Camille's, Horace again appeals to the name: 'Rends-toi digne du nom de ma chaste moitié' [literally: 'Make yourself worthy of the name of my chaste half'] (l. 1349), and prescribes the stifling of sentiment the right to which Sabine demands for herself. (Lyotard would no doubt find too 'anthropocentric' her description of the right to sentiment as 'human', as opposed to the 'inhumanity' or barbarity of Roman virtue.)

But the manifest sentimentality of Horace's killing of his sister cannot be so rapidly absorbed, and the whole of the last act of the play is taken up with the attempt to negotiate it. This act is the scene of judgement demanded by the *différend*. For Horace's action reveals the *différends* which, under the name of 'Rome', had in principle been controlled in an economy regulating the generic claims of love, individual renown, family ties and public duty. Camille is the sign of the possibility of the *différend* between all of these orders: by killing her (rather than simply ordering her silence as he does with Sabine), Horace spectacularizes the possibility of the *différend* in a way which might in principle fulfil Camille's curse and bring about the destruction of Rome. For as Valère, speaking to the king on behalf of 'all good people' (l. 1482) points out, the sentiment signalled by Camille is generalized, precisely because of the shared family ties of Rome and Alba – everyone has lost a relative in the war with Alba, and if Horace's triumph (in which, as I suggested, he momentarily *becomes* Rome) legitimates his suppressing of that sentiment, then 'Faisant triompher Rome, il se l'est asservie;/Il a sur nous un droit et de mort et de vie;/Et nos jours criminels ne pourront plus durer/Qu'autant qu'à sa clémence il plaira l'endurer' [In making Rome triumph, he has enslaved it to himself;/He has the right of life and death over us;/And our criminal existence can persist/Only so long as his clemency is pleased to endure it] (ll. 1507–10). If Horace is Rome and demands that the *différend* be suppressed, then he will in principle soon be the only Roman left, in so far as Rome is shot through with that *différend*: again the demands of the name will prescribe the death of its bearers, and Valère demands that Horace himself be executed to put an end to this possibility of terror.

But if the demands of the name prescribe in some sense the death of the bearer of the name, then it comes as no surprise that Horace himself wants to die too: precisely to preserve the honour of his name. His heroic action against the three Curiatii seemed to depend on a rigorous subordination of his own name and his family name to the name of Rome: but the very heroism of his action returns him to his own name and its immortality in glory – this can only be preserved by death, for the chance to live up to the reputation created by his act will hardly be guaranteed: Horace fears that he can hardly be a hero every day. Horace's father, however, is dissatisfied with both of these arguments, and suggests (1) that Horace was justified in killing Camille in that she had cursed Rome, and that in any case it was an impulsive action and as such not a crime; (2) that no one need fear his extending such action to the Romans in general in that this was in fact a family matter – Camille's curse, though a crime against Rome, was none the less essentially a slur on the name of her family, and had to be dealt with as such; (3) that the Romans would never tolerate the execution of the man to whom they owe their name:

> Romains, souffrirez-vous qu'on vous immole un homme
> Sans qui Rome aujourd'hui cesserait d'être Rome,
> Et qu'un Roman s'efforce à tacher le renom
> D'un guerrier à qui tous doivent un si beau nom?

> [Romans, will you tolerate the execution of a man
> Without whom Rome would today cease being Rome,
> And that a Roman try to stain the renown
> Of a warrior to whom all owe such a fine name?]

(ll. 1683–6)

(this argument is backed up by the idea that it would be impossible to find a suitable *place* for the execution: neither within the walls which only stand, nominally speaking, because of Horace, nor outside, on the scene of his action); (4) that he, the father, has lost three of his four children already that day, and maybe that's enough. Where Valère claims to speak for all good people, Horace *père* asserts that 'All of Rome has spoken through my mouth' (l. 1728).

This juridical dispute must be settled: unlike the litigation between Rome and Alba, which could not be presented to a tribunal, here there is a judge in the form of the king, Tullus, who has promised to provide justice (and implied that this is essentially what a king is for) (ll. 1476–80). Tullus rapidly determines what the issue is: Horace's suicidal urge is not considered, nor are the father's attempts to argue about impulsiveness and family questions. In terms of the law applicable to this case, Horace should die: no question about this. Horace's action is in this sense the object of a litigation – it has broken particular generic rules which can be reimposed. But here the position of the tribunal is complicated by the argument around the name of Rome. Without Horace, the tribunal would not exist because Rome would not exist – it would have become Alba. Although Horace's crime is 'great, enormous, inexcusable' (l. 1740), it was carried out by the same man, the same case, which has allowed there to be a tribunal, a king, and justice, under the name of Rome. 'Without [Horace] I would obey where now I give the law,/And I would be subject where I am King twice over [i.e. of both Rome and Alba]' (ll. 1745–6). There would be no law without the perpetrator of the case currently before the law. Tullus concludes that Horace's action places him above the law, and prescribes, from his position as distributor of the law, that that law be silent. Horace's being above the law places him before the law, as what makes the exercise of the law possible. The 'crime' can then, reasonably enough, be assimilated to the originary crime on which Rome was founded, namely the murder of Remus by Romulus: this originary (but already and now again repeated) violence must be dissimulated, as it is the condition of the name of Rome:

> que Rome dissimule
> Ce que dès sa naissance elle vit en Romule;
> Elle peut bien souffrir en son libérateur
> Ce qu'elle a bien souffert en son premier auteur.

> [let Rome dissimulate
> What at its birth it saw in Romulus.
> She can certainly tolerate in her liberator
> What she tolerated in her first author.]

(ll. 1755–8)

How to judge? Lyotard used to define as 'pagan' a situation in which
the obligation to judge went along with the absence of criteria according to which to judge. The critical judge, in Lyotard's transcription of
Kant, has no code of law or body of jurisprudence to determine the
judgement (see *L'Enthousiasme*, pp. 17–18). The law for the case must
be found, invented. But if the judge has no law at hand, it would seem
that the possibility of judging is given, in the name of Reason: our task
here (that of 'Judging Lyotard') puts us in the situation of having to
judge the case which thus prescribes judgement without grounding its
possibility: we therefore repeat the presupposition of a judgement in
the attempt to judge it. The name 'Rome' names an example (which
cannot be just an example) of this situation. Rome is instituted in
violence, out of the *pagus*, and this violence returns to question the
institution as it defends it. In a brilliant article called 'Lapsus Judicii',
Jean-Luc Nancy, wondering what happens when philosophy determines itself as essentially juridical, suggests that Rome (as opposed to
Athens) names this very situation. The question of the juridicalization
of philosophy is then, says Nancy, 'double and doubly heterogeneous':
'If philosophy is Greek, this is the *Latin* question of philosophy; if
Rome is the dissolution of philosophy, it is the *philosophical* question of
Rome.'[12] If, for Nancy, Kant is a repetition of that 'Roman' moment,
then Lyotard is another, displaced, repetition of Kant's repetition.

In Nancy's reading, the oddness of the juridical is that it must take
into account a sort of necessity of the accidental (in the form of the
case, the event): he goes on to elaborate this question in terms of an
essential fictional or fictioning activity of the law in its constitutively
impossible drive to predict the case, the accident, which cannot be
predicted as such. The law has an essential relation to the accidental.
And, more crucially, at some point the law must attempt to take *itself* as
a case and fictionalize its own institution or origin, stating the law of the
law (as case). In the case of *Horace*, the law cannot take his act as a case,
in that it precedes the possibility of the activity of law in general:
whether this be figured in terms of fratricide or not, it is clearly a
situation of violence, if only in that it falls outside the law as the very
possibility of its jurisdiction. In the paradoxical terms which Lyotard
finds in any attempt to derive or legitimate authority (see *Le différend*,
§203), the tribunal can only, as Nancy suggests, produce simultaneously a sentence or a judgement and the very institution of the law
which allows that judgement to be made. To do so it has to absolve the
violence which presides over that institution, and in so doing do
violence to the justice made possible by that violence: this is Tullus's
command to *forget* the founding fratricide and its repetition. This

violent secondary attempt to erase the primary violence can presumably be repeated indefinitely as Rome pursues its imperial adventure.

Can this be thought of in Lyotard's terms? For him, critical activity is
essentially an activity of judgement, respecting the case in its singularity, finding the appropriate rule always only after the event. This
peculiar temporality, much more than any periodizing hypothesis, is
in fact what constitutes the postmodern (which is anything but a
question of dating).[13] But what happens when the judgement that
judgement is what we must do is *itself* up for judgement? How do we
judge, for example, the judgement that philosophy is the discourse
that has as its stake the discovery of its rule (see *Le différend*, p. 12)? Or
the judgement that the 'object' of philosophy is a sentence, because a
sentence is indubitable (see *Le différend*, §94)? Lyotard would say, I
think, that these questions are *already* philosophy in search of its rule.
Nancy would argue that they imply that Lyotard cannot dissolve the
question of being into sentences, in so far as any sentence presupposes
this moment of pre-judgement, which Nancy, if I understand him
aright, calls Being. Lyotard retorts, in a note on Nancy's article
(*L'Enthousiasme*, p. 17n3), that this appeal to Being, along with its
corollary in the notion of fictionalizing, is to return to a problematic of
origins (and, eventually, subjects) which we are better without – and
this judgement of what is 'better' would argue from historico-political
names such as 'Rome' and, more urgently, 'Auschwitz': but can
perhaps do so only by prejudging judgement in the presentation of
particular cases which violently demand judgement before there is
time to judge. (The form of this problem seems to be linked to what
can appear to be a persistent equivocation in Lyotard's recent thought
between apparently transcendental claims and the use of historico-
political names in the refutation of rival claims. This situation, which
would demand new formulations of the relationship between philosophy and the historico-political, is perhaps programmed by the
location of a logic of presentation which holds for sentences in general
within a discourse which argues that there are no sentences in general,
but only particular sentences, now.)

This 'pre-', this 'before' (which would have to be read with Derrida's
notion of the trace, and its implication of an 'absolute past') is clearly
complex, to say the least. In their opening address to the 'Centre de
recherches philosophiques sur le politique' in Paris in 1980, Nancy
and Lacoue-Labarthe name this 'pre-', 'provisionally and over-
simplifyingly', *la mère*, 'the mother'[14] (Alba, then, in Corneille's terms:
Rome's mother). Lyotard explicitly disagrees with this nomination,
and proposes to think this 'pre-' analogically as *la mer*, the sea, the
milieu of the dispersion of the regimes and genres of discourse, the

place of attempted bridge-building and passages (*L'Enthousiasme*, p. 111). I do not know precisely the reason for Lyotard's objection: 'mother' can scarcely be criticized for being 'anthropocentric' in so far as it too can only be an analogical presentation – and is clearly neither simply empirical nor psychoanalytic in that we would have to presuppose the sense of this 'mother' in order to understand empirical and psychoanalytic notions of 'mother'. Is Lyotard, in the never-quite-instituted institution of philosophy as juridical and Roman, as refusal of the pre-eminence of the question of Being, in fact repeating the analogical violence of Rome towards its 'mother'? Is this a *différend* before the *différend* as described by Lyotard? Is this the possibility which allows for the exacerbated forms of litigation and *différend* which I chided Lyotard for not classifying and thematizing? Would this question, which I cannot presume to answer here, send us back to the first Horace's appearance in *Discours, figure*, to the postulation of the *figure-matrice* as the essentially invisible to be made visible, a sort of 'initial violence' of discourse and figure (p. 270), a sort of originary institution and transgression (institution as transgression, transgression as institution: this is, I think, exactly the sense of what Lyotard later calls, much more laconically, but perhaps more problematically, 'experimentation')? This moment is not a possible object of knowledge or judgement, but it is what, in *Discours, figure*, Lyotard calls the truth (see for example, p. 17). Truth before any tribunal or judgement, before the determination of genres and regimes, before even the indubitability of a sentence.

In *Horace*, this 'truth' is ultimately referred to the gods, and will be dealt with by the priests, the *pontifices*, the bridge-builders (l. 1773). Lyotard's effort, in its impiety, will have been to prevent the building of *that* bridge. The question left open here, in its enormity, would be whether Being (however named) can be respected by a *judex* who does not need to refer to a *pontifex* to absorb that initial violence; and if so, how.

Notes

1. J.-F. Lyotard, 'Faire voir les invisibles, ou contre le réalisme', in B. Buchloh, ed., *Daniel Buren: Les Couleurs, Sculptures; Les Formes, Peintures*, Paris: Central National d'art et de culture Georges Pompidou 1981, pp. 26–38.

2. This strictly speaking ungrammatical formulation appears, for example, in 'Réponse à la question: qu'est-ce que le postmoderne?' (*PE*, pp. 13–34, at p. 27): Régis Durant translates this as 'to present the fact that the unpresentable exists' (*PMC*, p. 78) – but the unpresentable is not a matter of fact and does not exist. The more literal translation: 'to present that there is (some) unpresentable' has its own disadvantages, however.

3. Kant, *The Critique of Judgement*, Introduction, §IX, trans. James Creed Meredith, Oxford: Oxford University Press 1928, pp. 36–7.

4. Heidegger, 'Building, dwelling, thinking', trans. Albert Hofstadter, in *Martin Heidegger: Basic Writings*, ed. D.F. Krell, London: Routledge & Kegan Paul 1977, pp. 323–9, at p. 330.

5. J. Derrida, *La Vérité en peinture*, Paris: Flammarion 1978, p. 43; *The Truth in Painting*, trans. Geoff Bennington and Ian McLeod, Chicago: University of Chicago Press 1987, p. 36.

6. Norman Bryson, 'David's *Oath of the Horatii* and the question of "influence" ', *French Studies* 37(4) (1983), pp. 404–25.

7. Livy, *The Early History of Rome*, trans. A. de Sélincourt, Harmondsworth: Penguin Books 1960, p. 57. Further references to Livy will be to this edition and will be given in the text.

8. In that analysis of the 'integrative function', the 'myth of origin' referred to could of course have been, for Corneille, only analogically the myth of the foundation of Rome. I shall be ignoring this obvious fact, which does, however, relate to difficult questions around Lyotard's notion of *genre*: clearly the way the sentences are linked together in Corneille's *Horace* would have to be described by Lyotard as obeying the rules of the tragic genre: but, equally clearly, crucial sub-sequences of sentences are *also* linked according to the rules of other genres, as I shall attempt to illustrate. It is not clear to me how to describe this multiple generic status of certain sentences or linkages which is clearly constitutive of much of what we call literature, and this question around the far from simple relationships between discursive genres and literary genres is perhaps, for me, the point of greatest difficulty in Lyotard's recent work.

9. J.-F. Lyotard, 'Longitude 180° W or E', in *Arakawa: Padiglione d'arte contemporanea*, Mailand: Edizione Nava Milano 1984.

10. Serge Doubrovsky, *Corneille ou la dialectique du héros*, Paris, Gallimard 1963. I cannot here attempt to specify the differences with Doubrouvsky's powerful reading of the play: perhaps the nexus of these differences is that whereas Doubrouvsky tends to treat characters as subjects, I try to treat them as supports for proper names.

11. Any such absolute propriety is of course illusory. See for example Derrida's discussion of Lévi-Strauss in *De la grammatologie*, Paris: Minuit 1967, p. 164: 'There was indeed a first violence in naming. Naming . . . such is the originary violence of language which consists in inscribing in a difference, in classifying, in suspending the absolute vocative' (*Of Grammatology*, trans. G.C. Spivak, Baltimore: Johns Hopkins University Press 1976, p. 112 (trans. mod.)).

12. Jean-Luc Nancy, 'Lapsus Judicii', in *L'Impératif catégorique*, Paris: Flammarion 1983, pp. 35–60, at p. 36. Lyotard's brief response to an earlier publication of Nancy's article can be found in *L'Enthousiasme: la critique Kantienne de l'histoire*, Paris: Galilée 1982, pp. 17–18n3, and Nancy's reply appears at the end of the version to which I refer.

13. 'Postmodern is not to be taken in a periodizing sense', (*Au juste*, p. 34).

14. P. Lacoue-Labarthe and J.-L. Nancy, 'Ouverture' in *Rejouer le politique*, ed., P. Lacoue-Labarthe and J.-L. Nancy, Paris: Galilée 1981, pp. 11–28, at p. 26.

9

The Rationality of Postmodern

Relativity

> The relativity and quantum revolution in language remains to be
> carried out.
>
> (Le Différend, p. 188)

The so-called 'debate' around 'postmodernism', 'postmodernity' and
'the postmodern' is probably most distinguished for its confusion.[1]
Clearly something is going on, but there is a perhaps unusual degree
of disagreement as to what it is, and even as to whether it is 'really'
going on, or somehow 'manufactured' by those who find their advantage in saying that it is. Perhaps the disagreement *is* all that is going on.
And if disagreement (or dissensus) be taken as a sign of the postmodern, then it would indeed seem reasonable not so much to look for
a 'true state of affairs' behind that disagreement as to take the
disagreement as the true state of affairs. In this sense, disagreement
about the meaning or existence of the postmodern would itself be the
postmodern, and we should have enforced at least the consensus that
there is a dissensus. And if a corollary of the conception of the
postmodern as disagreement is that the disagreement (which then
becomes a *différend* in Lyotard's sense) cannot be dominated and
resolved by one of the parties to the disagreement (and Derrida, for
one, has linked postmodernism to the end of a project of domination),[2] then it follows that it would be naive to attempt an 'overview' of
the so-called 'debate'. (A supplementary complication would arise
from the suspicion that most of the major items in the 'debate' are
nevertheless attempts at overviews.) The situation is complicated
further still by a recent tendency, in my own field at least, to conflate
postmodernism with 'so-called post-structuralism'. Some people try to
put some order into this by saying that post-structuralism is merely
part of a more pervasive postmodernism, but the general aim of such
conflation is to lump a lot of things together the better to get rid of
them without having to think very hard. A determined rationalist

might well see in this very situation the sort of unbridled relativism ('anything goes') s/he finds intolerable. I shall be suggesting that it is still possible to discuss these questions rationally but not rationalistically.

A slightly trivial and certainly naive illustration of some of the difficulties of this situation is provided by Charles Jencks's recent pamphlet, *What is Postmodernism?*[3] In the course of his remarks, Jencks suggests that the reaction of committed Modernists to postmodernism (a reaction he calls 'The Protestant Inquisition') is as 'paranoiac, reactionary and repressive as their Beaux-Arts persecutors were before them' (p. 14). On the one hand, Jencks rather welcomes this: 'I do believe that these characterisations have not done what they were supposed to do – stem the tide of Post-Modernism – but rather have helped to blow it up into a media event' (ibid.), and goes on: 'My nightmare is that suddenly the reactionaries will become nice and civil.' (Before moralistically condemning Jencks for what seems to be a complacent welcoming of 'media hype', we might pause to wonder what sort of 'event' today (and indeed what sort of event in general) would not be a 'media event', and to wonder also if this might also be a component of a 'postmodern condition'.) In any case, having apparently welcomed this violence of reaction and the consequent 'media event', Jencks goes on to deplore it too, because it has hidden what he calls 'the root causes of the movement'.

Jencks then proceeds to offer the reader the 'true story' of the movement called postmodernism. Despite the claims made on the pamphlet's cover-note about 'typical Post-Modern devices of exposition' (irony, parody, and so on), this story is academic and classical enough. Jencks in fact defines Post-Modernism in the most traditionally dialectical way imaginable, as 'the continuation of Modernism and its transcendence' (p. 7): cancellation and preservation in a nice Hegelian *Aufhebung*. In view of this, it perhaps comes as no surprise to find Jencks at the end of his text endorsing and appropriating Peter Fuller's call for 'the equivalent of a new spirituality based on an "imaginative, yet secular, response to nature herself"', seeking '"a shared symbolic order of the kind that a religion provides", but without the religion' (p. 48). Jencks explicitly sets this against the 'relativism' he suggests must inevitably result from Lyotard's arguments: but the result is that the 'disagreement' I was suggesting might be constitutive of the postmodern is here rapidly defused and absorbed into the pious projection of a horizon of consensus and even redemption, beyond current rows and media events. Nothing could be less postmodern than this type of schema of argument, and nothing could more invite deconstruction than the unquestioned value of 'nature herself', which is of a piece with the simple view of history I have described: let me quote from *The Truth in Painting* to illustrate this difficulty:

> If one were to consider the physis/tekhne opposition to be irreducible, if one were to accredit so hastily its translation as nature/art or nature/technique, one would easily commit oneself to thinking that art, being no longer nature, is history. The opposition nature/history would be the analogical relay of *physis/tekhne*. One can thus already say: as for history, we shall have to deal with the contradiction or the oscillation between two apparently incompatible motifs. They both come under one and the same logical formality: namely, that if the philosophy of art always has the greatest difficulty in dominating the history of art, a certain concept of the historicity of art, this is, paradoxically, because it too easily thinks of art as historical. What I am putting forward here obviously assumes the transformation of the concept of history, from one statement to the other.[4]

These problems with Jencks's conception show through most clearly in his attempt to re-describe as 'Late-Modern' (exaggerating 'properly' modernist tendencies) what other writers would call 'postmodern' (which Jencks wants to describe in the dialectical way I have mentioned). His main object of disagreement here is Jean-François Lyotard, whom he appears to be quite simply unable to read: I would suggest that this illiteracy is quite consistently programmed by Jencks's own simple historicizing and dialectical argument. Jencks is, for example, quite unable to make any coherent sense of the relationship between the three following propositions in Lyotard:

1. That the 'grand narratives' of legitimation are in decline, leading to a situation of generalized 'delegitimation'.
2. That a 'sensitivity to differences' and a 'war on totality' might be called for in this situation.
3. That, in a certain sense, the postmodern might be said to precede the modern.

I do not propose to dwell on Jencks's failure to distinguish in Lyotard between a *description* of a state of affairs as 'slackening' (of which the work of Charles Jencks might be taken as an example – Lyotard himself links Jencks's notion of the postmodern to an eclecticism attuned to the demands of capital),[5] and a *prescription* as to the appropriate (affirmative) way to think about that situation. The problems that arise from the third proposition I have isolated are more difficult and thereby more interesting. Jencks finds the idea of the postmodern somehow coming 'before' the modern 'amazing' and 'crazy' (irrational, then, although 'original') (ibid., pp. 39–42), and suggests that it leads Lyotard to 'confuse' postmodernism with 'the latest avant-gardism': he goes on to admit that 'it's embarrassing that Post-Modernism's first philosopher should be so fundamentally wrong', and to suggest rather condescendingly that because Lyotard is a philosopher and 'sociologist of knowledge', he is simply not sufficiently attuned to cultural differences to make sense of what is going on.

One of the reasons for Jencks's bemusement is that he takes the eminently rational view that the prefix 'post-' in 'postmodernism' must imply that the object it labels simply comes after modernism (although he would see this as a necessary but not sufficient qualification). This reasonable view is widespread, and the cause of a lot of trouble. Fredric Jameson, for example, in the longest of his contributions to the 'debate',[6] begins by saying of postmodernism that 'the case for its existence depends on the hypothesis of some radical break or *coupure*, generally traced back to the end of the 1950's or early 1960's'. This type of view, which is not entirely absent in Lyotard's own earlier writing on the subject (see, for example, the beginning of the Introduction to *The Postmodern Condition*, though the statement is complicated by a number of features of the text, and in particular modalized by the status assigned to what Lyotard describes as a 'working hypothesis') habitually makes a link between postmodernism and so-called 'post-industrial society', and tends to centre on the question of the reality of the referent of the term 'postmodernism'. Reading Jameson, I confess that I am unsure as to his conclusion on this point: on the one hand, he seems quite confidently able to identify certain features supposedly typical of postmodernism, such as superficiality, the 'waning of affect', loss of critical negativity, and so on; but on the other, he seems concerned to cast doubt on the 'radical break' supposed to be necessary to the establishment of that reality, to argue that postmodernism is a dialectical development of the culture of capitalism (a third stage following realism and modernism), just as post-industrial society would in his view be a third stage of the capitalist mode of production, rather than a radically new departure. I think it would not be difficult to show that this tension (which I imagine that Jameson, good Hegelian that he is, would have no difficulty in determining as itself a dialectical contradiction awaiting sublation) affects the very writing of Jameson's text: I am grateful to Rachel Bowlby for drawing my attention, on the one hand, to the abundance in Jameson's text of expressions of 'a whole new . . . ' something or other (as if he were trying to sell the latest product himself), of 'our now postmodern bodies', and so on; and on the other, to a persistent, awkward but determined use of terms such as 'authenticity' and 'realism'. As always in Jameson's work, there is a resolute and stirring promise of a breakthrough to a dialectical understanding yet to be achieved (though this always seems to involve regaining or recapturing something), in which we shall have produced (in this future perfect) 'a some as yet unimaginable new mode of representing' the postmodern, in spite of the postmodern's acknowledged challenge to representation, and in which 'we may again begin to grasp our positioning as individual and collective subjects'. What Jameson terms 'the political form of postmodernism, if there ever is any', 'will have as its vocation the invention and projection of a global cognitive mapping, on a social as well as a spatial scale' (p. 92).

So although Jameson appears to argue for the 'reality' of the postmodern, the discourse he uses to defend that reality is one which consistently ignores the questions that same 'reality' would put to that discourse's basic operators, which consistently aim, in however mediated a form, towards unification, totalization and universalization. Lyotard is, happily, philosopher enough to be suspicious of the sort of view, be it that of Jameson or Jencks, that would reduce what he is trying to think (provisionally and, I think he would agree, imprudently) under the name of the 'postmodern' to such terms. If Lyotard is right to insist on the temporal complexities of what he calls the *event* of presentation or even of presence, then we can be quite certain that standard sociologizing and historicizing accounts of what he is doing must be reductive at the very least. Our problem is and will be that what I would call journalism (with no pejorative intent), in its constitutive preoccupation to identify 'news' now, will almost necessarily reinforce that sort of reduction.

I should now like briefly to document Lyotard's arguments around these questions, not to administer a triumphant corrective, but to complicate, complexify, the issue if possible. First from *Au juste* (*Just Gaming*). Here Lyotard appends a footnote to a discussion of the question of the addressee of works of art, which question he thinks he can use as a principle of classification. In the body of the text, he works with a broad two-term distinction between 'classical' and 'modern'; and in the footnote wants to complicate the latter term:

> The modern addressee would be the 'people', an idea whose referent oscillates between the Romantics' Volk and the *fin-de-siècle* bourgeoisie. Romanticism would be modern, as would the project, even if it turns out to be impossible, of elaborating a taste, even a 'bad' one, that permits an evaluation of works. Postmodern (or pagan) would be the condition of the literatures and arts that have no assigned addressee and no regulating ideal, yet in which value is measured by the standard of experimentation. Or, to put it dramatically, which is measured by the distortion that is

inflicted on the materials, the forms and the structures of sensibility and thought. Postmodern is not to be taken in a periodizing sense. (p. 16)

This is still a difficult remark, because if the insistence on post-modernism's not being a concept of a 'period' is clear (and in the text itself Lyotard states categorically that 'the date is of no importance at all'), then its being placed against such a precisely historically defined notion of the modern is difficult. This complication is not immediately reduced by comments from the essay 'Answering the Question: What is Postmodernism?' First, Lyotard claims that the postmodern is 'undoubtedly part of the modern' (p. 79), and, in a sense, *prior* to the modern (this is what Jencks finds 'crazy'): 'A work can become modern only if it is first postmodern. Postmodernism thus understood is not modernism at its end but in the nascent state, and this state is constant' (ibid.). Although Jencks is sufficiently amazed to stop reading at this point, Lyotard suggests that this understanding is too 'mechanistic', and goes on to describe the postmodern as a particular modality of the modern: broadly speaking, an affirmative rather than a nostalgic modality. The nostalgic modality stresses a loss of reality and the powerlessness of the subject to comprehend the world: the affirmative modality stresses a power to conceive beyond the constraints of given reality or understanding or the given rules or theory of artistic activity. This affirmative, postmodern modality (which Lyotard is not dating as necessarily contemporary, in so far as Montaigne is thought to be postmodern in this sense) puts forward works which demand judgement, in the absence of any available criteria to ground such a judgement. The other, 'modern' modality puts forward works recognisable to a common 'taste' which would permit judgement to be made.

These descriptions obviously trouble any simple historicizing conception of the postmodern (i.e. *all* conceptions of the postmodern), and I shall stress that trouble by quoting what is the most important paragraph of Lyotard's essay:

The postmodern would be that which in the modern alleges the unpresentable in presentation itself, which refuses itself the consolation of good forms, the consensus of a taste which would allow nostalgia for the impossible to be felt in common; which inquires into new presentations, not in order to enjoy them, but the better to convey that there is the unpresentable. A postmodern artist and writer is in the situation of a philosopher: the text he writes, the work he accomplishes are not in principle governed by already-established rules, and they cannot be judged by means of a determining judgement, by application to the text or work of known categories. These rules or categories are what the work or the text is looking for. The artist and writer thus work without rules, and in order to establish the rules of what will have been done. Whence the fact that work and text have the properties of the event, whence too they come too late for their author or, what comes down to the same thing, their mise en oeuvre always beings too soon. Postmodern would have to be understood according to the paradox of the future (*post*) perfect (*modo*). (p. 81: tr. mod.)[7]

In this description, the postmodern would correspond neither to Jencks's 'Post-Modernism' (which Lyotard, as I have mentioned, would think of as a sort of eclecticism pandering to aesthetic confusion and in the service of Capital) nor to his 'Late-Modernism', but to an attempt to work with a particular question of temporality or historicity, and more specifically with a valorization of the event as a configuration which breaks simple linear temporality by opening the 'inside' of anything like 'modernity' to an 'outside' not (yet) nameable as such. (A similar type of argument can be found earlier, about literary modernity, in Paul de Man's essay 'Literary History and Literary Modernity.'[8]

Jameson, unlike Jencks, does acknowledge, in the Foreword to *The Postmodern Condition*, that Lyotard precisely does not 'posit a post-modernist stage radically different from the period of high modernism and involving a fundamental historical and cultural break with this last' (p. xvi: thus apparently contradicting the statement about break or *coupure* quoted above, but perhaps simply already preparing the argument that Lyotard is not, in fact, talking about the postmodern at all), and recognizes elsewhere that postmodernism involves a 'crisis of historicity'. But such a 'crisis' is located, as always, only in opposition to some lost authentic and good 'properly historical' possibility which is the absent plenitude which underlies all Jameson's thinking and lends his work its relentless pathos and rather tedious nostalgia. Similarly, Terry Eagleton, in an article which is in general hasty and keen to be as harsh on Lyotard as possible, does give the argument some 'qualified credence' at this point (the vital point: most of Eagleton's attacks on Lyotard are either unargued, or aimed at positions Lyotard does not in fact hold), for correctly locating in Modernism 'a revaluation of time itself:[9] and Eagleton links this to the same Walter Benjamin he had earlier castigated Lyotard for not taking seriously enough. But both Jameson and Eagleton rapidly draw back into more familiar notions of history in their anxiety to account for the postmodern in terms of their presupposition that whatever is going on now must be bad and alienated, and replaced as soon as possible in a perspective of redemption.

Jencks, Jameson and Eagleton are thus all keen to absorb events into continuities, genealogies and teleologies (Jameson's assertion that genealogy neatly escapes the problems of teleological history is never argued or put to the test). There is really little to choose between them in this respect. If they are able to think of an 'event', this must be thought of as a break and new start. Such a view is irremediably 'Modern' in inspiration,[10] and cannot begin to understand the temporal complexity Lyotard is attempting to address: it may well be that the very term 'postmodern' invites such a view so strongly that it self-destructs, that it cannot fail to be another 'modern' term – but it seems clear that attempts to periodize and classify so as to judge and expel or extol can only take place on the basis of a repression of the question of the event which Lyotard is attempting to elaborate.

Questioning in this way the essentially rationalist presuppositions which underlie the responses to Lyotard of Jencks, Jameson and Eagleton does not at all commit one to relativism and still less to irrationalism. Lyotard's purpose is not to attack rationality as such, but a particular rationalistic determination of reason. In the Kantian terms with which much of Lyotard's recent work is concerned, this involves a protest against the claims of the understanding to dominate the entire field of reason. In the realm of aesthetics, such a determination would involve a priority of the determinant over the reflexive judgement, in proceeding according to already determined rules: for Lyotard, the situation is not that the rules already exist, with the task of artist or architect (but also of politician and scientist, for he would wish to extend this situation to the areas of knowledge and politics too) being to produce 'cases' fitting these rules, but to 'experiment', to produce cases for which the rule must subsequently be discovered by the reflexive judgement. Whether or not the rationale or rationality of contemporary science really does conform to this schema (as *The Postmodern Condition* claims – and Lyotard's analogy between 'postmodern science' and the concern with justice which is the real guiding-thread of his book is certainly difficult, precisely because of its analogism, and would need patient analysis) is perhaps less important than the fact that nothing in this set-up would justify the charge of irrationalism, in so far as this activity of experimentation is, if not guided, then at least regulated by Ideas of Reason (such as Justice, to be sure, but also Architecture or Painting) resistant to determination by the understanding. If this entirely provisional insistence on the specificity of the Ideas of Reason[11] against the encroachments of the concept is enough to constitute relativism, then Lyotard evidently is a relativist: but if relativism be taken to imply that in the absence of conceptual determination everything is equivalent, and anything goes, then he clearly is not – if there is a meta-prescription implied in Lyotard's recent thinking, it would involve the obligation to judge precisely in the absence of determining criteria. Clearly this can be an uncomfortable ethical demand in the wake of our obsession with questions of epistemology and the critical panic which can ensue when epistemologies collapse. Talk of thinking (but also building, painting and politicking) in terms of 'tasks', 'honour' and 'dignity' can seem to involve an unappealing pathos. But it could quite easily be shown that pathos (in the rhetorical sense of aiming to produce an affect in the audience in the absence of rigorous argumentation) is more the quality of the work of Jencks, Jameson and Eagleton: this is the sign of the 'slackening' Lyotard deplores, rather than of the experimentation he advocates. By attempting, in their various ways, to exorcise the threat of 'relativism' they see in Lyotard, Jencks, Jameson and Eagleton all appeal to a superficial rationalism which rapidly does collapse into the pathetic. This does not indicate so much a triumph of relativism as the inadequacy of the opposition between rationalism and relativism (and still less irrationalism) to describe what is at stake in the 'postmodern'.

The same sort of point can be made about Derrida and deconstruction. Derrida suggests in his discussion of Tschumi that terms in post- are used 'as if yet again one wished to put order into a linear succession, to periodize, distinguish between the before and the after, limit the risks of reversibility or repetition, of transformation or permutation: progressist ideology' (this configuration would also mean, as Derrida has argued more recently,[12] that the 'new historicism', for instance, immediately denounces itself as old historicism in its very claim to be 'new' (the oldest claim there is)[13] – I suspect that the prefix 'post-' in terms such as 'postmodernism' and 'poststructuralism' can be worked with interestingly – non-journalistically – only if linked to Derrida's exploration of the postal system in *La Carte postale*.[14] Derrida's appeal to the word 'maintenant' in his analysis of Tschumi's project is an attempt to escape this type of temporal organization, and the tension of that 'maintenant' is directly comparable to what Lyotard means by the event. The term 'deconstruction' does not carry the immediately unfortunate periodizing connotations of the term 'postmodernism', although it is in some ways an unfortunate and misleading label (as Derrida himself has often said) for the work he and those inspired by him have done. Even accepting the label 'deconstruction', it would, for example, be quite inaccurate to suppose that this simply names something like a method or a technique or a theory or even a philosophy invented by Derrida in Paris at some ideally dateable moment in the 1960s. There are important and specifiable reasons why it is wrong to think of deconstruction as something Derrida or anyone else does or has done to a text or an argument or even a painting. Let me quote briefly from Derrida's short text, 'Letter to a Japanese Friend', which discusses, with a view to its translation into Japanese, the status of the term 'deconstruction':

> In spite of appearances, deconstruction is neither an analysis nor a critique. . . . It is not an analysis, in particular because the dismantling of a structure is not a regression towards the simple element, towards an indecomposable origin. . . . No more is it a critique, whether in a general or a Kantian sense. . . . I'll say the same thing for method. Deconstruction is not a method and cannot be transformed into a method.[15]

Our historicist and subjectivist or objectivist impulses are so ingrained that it is difficult to think this, but we have to try to understand that deconstruction is neither something done at a given date by an active and wilful or even heroic subject to a more or less resistant or complicit object, nor quite something that that object is shown to do to itself anyway, whether we like it or not. Here's Derrida again, in the same text:

> It is not enough to say that deconstruction cannot be reduced to some methodological instrumentality, to a set of rules and transposable procedures. It is not enough to say that each 'event' of deconstruction remains singular, or in any case as close as possible to something like an idiom or a signature. We should also make clear that deconstruction is not even an act or an operation. . . . Deconstruction takes place, it is an event which does not wait on the deliberation, consciousness or organisation of the subject, nor even of modernity. (p. 391 [5])

In *The Truth in Painting*, for example, Derrida does not more or less perversely deconstruct Kant's *Critique of Judgement*, but nor does Kant's *Critique of Judgement* deconstruct itself. The point is rather to locate in Kant's text elements which the overall argument has difficulty in containing satisfactorily and which have unsettling effects on that argument in its entirety: what Kant calls the parergon cannot adequately be described as either inside or outside the work of art, although without parerga the work of art would have no inside and outside. (*Mutatis mutandis*, this questioning of the frame – in the most general sense of the word – is also what interests Lyotard in the work of Daniel Buren, which is why Buren's 'installations' are difficult to locate as either inside or outside the institution of art: and one can be sure that if we were to try to frame Buren by deciding to call him a deconstructionist, he would respond by sticking his striped pieces of paper all over that frame too.)

If deconstruction is not, strictly speaking, a theory (given what Derrida calls the 'singularity' of its events: I suppose this is what gives some obscure motivation to Merquior's rather crass characterization of it as a 'dismal unscience'), then it cannot be taken to prescribe a practice. It is hard to imagine a painter scouring *The Truth in Painting* for instructions as to how to proceed. The two central essays, on Adami and Titus-Carmel, which can indeed be taken to express some admiration for the work discussed, hardly amount to a manifesto of what art should be up to now. But if deconstruction has effects on certain philosophical determinations of art, and if art has always been more or less complicit with its philosophical determination, never separable from busy discursive activities of all sorts, then of course deconstruction might give rise to artistic events of various types, to be invented. But in so far as deconstruction does not simply question the philosophical determination of the work of art from within, say, aesthetics, but questions the coherence of the systematic philosophical organization in which the domain of the 'aesthetic' is located, then just as Derrida is no longer, strictly speaking, writing philosophy, so deconstructive art criticism would no longer be, strictly speaking, art criticism, even if its object was work which appears to fail happily within the traditional determination of art. These consequences follow quite rigorously from the argument I quoted above from *The Truth in Painting*, where they are linked to the form of the question 'What is Art?' Whence the comments in the essay on Adami on the 'silliness' of discourse on painting in so far as it is compelled by a drive to philosophical or poetical 'mastery', and the effort made in that text to respond to Adami's work differently, answering the *trait* of Adami's line with a proliferation of words beginning in *tr*, producing a text which escapes our familiar sense of assessment, academic value and translation. The claim would be that something is happening in Adami's work: the academic response to that event is to bind it tight in the strictures of commentary and explication and historical location (including the strictures of the label 'deconstruction'). Derrida tries to let something happen in his text which is certainly not purely independent of Adami's event, but which bears a relationship to that event which is not simply servile and therefore masterful, not trying to sublate the sensuousness of paint into the truth of the concept. Despite appearances, this is not essentially different from what Lyotard is attempting to do when he writes about attempting to respect or bear witness to the event of presence given in painting, the 'that it happens' of the event which is what he is attempting to write in the 'post-' of the postmodern: such an event is 'prior' (and in this sense perhaps art is indeed 'a thing of the past') to the temporal organization of history as a narrative which Jencks has to presuppose.

According to the generalized sense of 'text' with which Derrida works, this type of approach also blurs the frame between work and commentary. Adami reads Derrida as much as Derrida reads Adami – no established criteria are going to decide which of these two 'texts' deserves priority in any sense. And Titus-Carmel's work is already as 'philosophical' as Derrida's discussion. There is no claim here that this situation is radically new or unprecedented: the most traditional philosophical views of art as mimesis, and its most academic practice, have always necessarily left uneasily open a sense of art as a dangerous event in which something happens to disturb the integrity of 'nature herself' (and not just 'respond' to her), somewhere resisting the grasp of concept and commentary, and through the insufficiency of attempted explanations of this event in terms of talent, inspiration or genius something of this deconstructive edge or 'point', as Derrida says, has always been at work. To this extent, art has always already been in excess of its concepts, already deconstructive, and deconstruction the motor or movement or element of art, whether in the relatively and historically variably unstable domain of painting or in the equally unstable domain of criticism, just as much as in philosophy. If there were ever to be a deconstructive movement in art, it would be a movement already dissolving its determination and resisting the restitution of its events to anything as stable as a nameable movement. Derrida again: '*Of Grammatology* places in question the unity of the 'word' and all the privileges with which it is in general credited, especially in its nominal form' (p. 392 [6–7]) – the messy and tense area left between determination and indeterminacy, where odd things happen, is where deconstruction is at work.

In this situation, where these several authors are clearly not all talking about the same thing, still less in agreement, it might however be possible to begin some tentative and entirely preliminary elaboration of the question of the event as it might possibly relate to architecture: I shall briefly consider the work of Venturi, Eisenman and Tshumi.

I take my cue here in the first instance from Venturi's *Complexity and Contradiction in Architecture*,[16] and specifically from chapter 9 of that book, 'The Inside and the Outside'. The question of the event appears explicitly here: arguing against the 'flowing space' of Modernism and the tendency to impose a continuity between inside and outside, Venturi argues that 'Since the inside is different from the outside, the wall – the point of change – becomes an architectural event' (p. 86). And in so far as most architecture is concerned at some point to build walls separating insides from outsdies, then it would appear simply enough that architecture is all about events.

In arguing for his complex and contradictory architecture, Venturi draws most of his cultural authority from sources in literary criticism, and notably in the tradition stemming from Eliot – and indeed, Venturi opens his Preface with quotations from Eliot about criticism and tradition. It seems to me that these references are inadequate to what Venturi is trying to think. It would not, I think, be difficult to trace the genealogy of his notions of complexity, contradiction, the 'difficult whole', and so on through this tradition. Mannerist and Baroque buildings are to Venturi what the English Metaphysical poets are to Eliot. In this tradition of literary thought, 'complexity' is valorized in so far as it is thought in terms of ambiguity, irony, balance: the 'difficulty' of the whole may well be partially an academic obscurity, and would exclude the potential populism of Venturi's 'is not Main Street almost all right?' (p. 104) and of *Learning from Las Vegas*.

To someone approaching architectural criticism from literary studies, these fundamental references in Venturi's work are a little surprising: the rather stuffy urbanity of Eliot's critical writing seems often to control rather than respect the more disruptive energies that might be detected in literary Modernism, and which would nowadays be approached through the work of Kristeva or Derrida rather than Eliot. In Derridean terms, this would lead to a wariness of the value of 'contradiction', because of its Hegelian ancestry – the determination of difference as contradiction invites the sublation of that contradiction into a totality (however 'difficult'),[17] and it would equally lead to suspicions about the notion of ambiguity: even extended to mean 'polysemia', ambiguity remains in the ambit of a notion of meaning as ideally unitary and recoverable – Derrida has detailed analyses questioning these values, especially in 'La Double Séance':

> If, then, there is no thematic unity or total meaning to be reappropriated beyond textual instances, in an imaginary, an intentionality or a lived experience, the text is no longer the expression of representation (happy or not) of some truth which would come to be diffracted or gathered in a polysemic literature. It is for this hermeneutic concept of polysemy that should be substituted that of dissemination.[18]

Dissemination disrupts the totality and any search for 'meaning', and to this extent is as uncomfortable for Venturi's book as for any other (but the constitutive vagueness of discursive terms in architectural criticism – does anybody, for example, really know what the word 'meaning' means when applied to architecture? – makes this problem both more urgent and, perhaps, more approachable here). But Venturi's book also invites closer reading with Derrida: in 1966, *Complexity and Contradiction* has its chapter entitled 'The Inside and the Outside';

in 1967, Derrida's *De la Grammatologie* has a chapter with the same title. Derrida is, of course, analysing the notion of the sign, especially as formulated by Saussure, whereas Venturi is analysing buildings. But the (inevitable) tendency of architecture to be discussed in terms of meaning should allow some cautious use of analogy between the analyses: and Derrida's appeal to initially spatial categories of inside and outside in what must, at least at first, seem like an analogical way (for what would it mean *literally* to suggest that signs have an 'inside' and an 'outside'?) suggests that the analogy does not only work in one direction.

Some care must be taken here to avoid hasty misunderstandings: at first sight, Derrida is suggesting that the opposition between inside and outside cannot be sustained, and duly follows his chapter with one affirming that the inside *is* the outside:[19] Venturi, on the other hand, is *attacking* the continuity between inside and outside he sees promoted by Modernism, with its 'emphasis on the oneness of interior and exterior space', and stressing that 'the inside is different from the outside' (p. 70). But the matter is more complicated than this apparent opposition would suggest: Venturi may indeed by arguing for separation as against any 'ultimate continuity of space' (p. 70), but the point of this is to move against the Modern dictum that 'the inside should be *expressed* on the outside' (ibid., my emphasis). And this presupposition that the outside expresses (or represents or signifies) an inside is of course also the object of Derrida's investigation. The whole classical notion of the sign as divided into signifier and signified rests on just such an inside/outside opposition, and on the presupposition that the outside somehow, more or less obliquely, reveals or manifests the inside. As Derrida shows, an underlying assumption here is that the inside, the signified, exists ideally prior to and independently of the outside: the outside is the accidental ('arbitrary') means of access to the inside, and should ideally not obstruct that access, should be transparent. The plate-glass 'walls' of the Modernist cube would appear to be analogous to such a transparency of the outside. On the other hand, in so far as there is an inside, then it must necessarily have an outside to define it as an inside: the border, even made of glass, must be at least as much a place of separation as a place of communication (this combination of separation and communication defining the notion of the limit as a place of articulation).[20] Even Modernist buildings must provide at least a *thermal* difference between inside and outside, as Venturi points out.

If one pursues the analogy a little further, then the modernist pretension (as analysed by Venturi – 'the truth of the matter' is not what is at stake here) to reduce the barrier between inside and outside to the diaphaneity of a sheet of glass would be an extension of the set-up diagnosed by Derrida as 'logocentrism', taking the need to 'express' the inside on the outside to the limiting case of reducing the outside to almost nothing. Or, in terms of Derrida's analysis of writing, such architecture would correspond to the Western investment in the excellence of so-called 'phonetic' writing, as opposed to the mysteries of hieroglyph and ideogram, which, as against the democratic access-ibility of phonetic script, protect an inside as a potential mystery, accessible only to the select few.[21] Paradoxes proliferate in this situa-tion: phonetic writing which apparently *reduces* the separation of inside and outside, might also be said to *enforce* it all the more – Derrida shows Saussure anxiously confirming writing in its exteriority to speech precisely by stressing the demands of the phonetic: if writing could only become that diaphanous means of access to interiority, then it could not be said to affect or penetrate that interiority at all, but to remain in its place outside.

A number of moves might be made in this situation, which is complexity itself. We might argue, for example, that one effect of Derrida's analysis is to demonstrate the impossibility of conceiving the inside prior to and independently of the outside. Only an outside defines an inside – in the analysis of the sign, this leads to the idea that in a sense there is no signified: a signified is no more than a signifier placed in a certain position by other signifiers. Look up a word in the dictionary to 'get at' its signified and you find more signifiers referring to ever more signifiers. What has always been thought of as the signified is no more than an effect (not quite an illusion) of the 'play of signifiers'.[22] Once this has been argued, it is difficult to retain the notion of signifier (and this marks Derrida's difference from doctrines of the 'materiality of the signifier', which is moreover a contradiction in terms):[23] 'signifier' can only imply 'what signifies a signified', and if there is really no signified to be signified, then there is really no signifier to signify it either (whence Derrida's introduction of the notion of the trace). The inside is the outside, but this rapidly leads to the conclusion that there is no outside either, but a generalized differential space organized into 'effects' (not quite illusions) of inside and outside. A radical 'flowing space' would not simply reduce the wall to a sheet of glass, but would show that the inside is merely a fold or invagination in a generalized 'outside'. The plate-glass window main-tains a separation all the more securely for promising its abolition – it might suggest a possible continuity and yet break your nose if you try to take that promise up, whereas nobody would walk into an honest wall.

Venturi, also suspicious of the expression of inside on outside, fights against the 'Saussurean' solution of reducing the outside the better to keep it outside (in our loose analogy, the 'transparent' walls of the Modern office-block keep the outside out all the more securely by displaying the power and mystery of the inside as power and mystery). Venturi's suggestion is that if the attempt to reduce the separation of inside and outside is an illusion, then better accept that separation and make something of it – Venturi likes the difference to be great and mysterious, and it is no accident that temples at Karnak and Edfu appear to illustrate the text at this point, or that he should refer to the 'partial mystery inherent in a sense of privacy' (p. 71) in this chapter.

It would be nice, but I think an oversimplification, to conclude that Venturi, faced with the failure of a certain Modernism's apparent denial of the inside/outside opposition, takes fright and moves regressively back to an insistence on their separation, whereas Derrida moves progressively on and demands that the opposition be deconstructed altogether. I would not deny the presence of 'regressive' moments in Venturi's text and 'progressive' ones in Derrida's. Such moments would encourage the placing of Venturi as the 'conservative' 'historicist' 'postmodernist' he undoubtedly partially is, and Derrida as the radical Modernist taking modernity to its ultimate conclusions. But it is just as easy to imagine a counter-argument whereby Venturi is the progressivist, arguing for a flexible and liveable negotiation of inside and outside, whereas Derrida's arguments lead him to the arcane mystery of an apparently hermetic script. The ease with which such characterizations can be constructed suggests that there is something wrong with them.

We can complicate this picture (and note that to do so we must jettison any simple notion of contradiction) so far as Venturi is concerned, by noting that his rejection of the Modernist argument for a continuity of inside and outside does not simply retreat into an affirmation of their radical separation. His use of the Egyptian temples does not in fact concentrate on any mystery eventually to be found at their centre, but on the graduated series of enclosures of enclosures. Such a set-up does not always imply a central mystery – Roland Barthes, for example, made persistent use of the formally identical model of the onion as an image of the text which was precisely made up of layers within layers but contained nothing at its centre: reading becoming the process of negotiating the layers rather than the triumphant arrival at any central 'core' of meaning.[24] Moreover, by advocating quite aggressively a different treatment of inside and outside surfaces of the wall, Venturi is splitting the line of limit or border in a way that might easily look to Derrida rather than Eliot for its language. And against his own declared location and valorization of 'contradiction' between inside and outside, Venturi also makes more subtle moves, leading to an idea of 'residual spaces' which cannot simply be accommodated into a rigidification of an inside/outside polarity:

> Residual space in between dominant spaces with varying degrees of open-ness can occur at the scale of the city and is a characteristic of the fora and other complexes of late Roman urban planning. Residual spaces are not unknown in our cities. I am thinking of the open spaces under our highways and the buffer spaces around them. Instead of acknowledging and exploiting these characteristic kinds of space we make them into parking lots or feeble patches of grass – no-man's lands between the scale of the region and the locality. (p. 80)

In this description, 'residual space' could not simply be described as either inside or outside: rather it would seem to be a pocket of outside within the inside, the 'no-man's land' of frontier and margin at the centre of the city's inside. (In Lyotard's terms, the zone of the pagus, from which he derives his notion of the 'pagan'.)[25] In spite of Venturi's insistence on 'the inside's being different from the outside', and his best or worst intentions in that direction, his own description of 'residual space' productively disrupts the very dichotomy he is trying to reinforce.[26] This disruption can be further illustrated in a quotation from Aldo van Eyck provided by Venturi, apparently wanting it to support his own arguments:

> Architecture should be conceived of as a configuration of intermediary places clearly defined. This does not imply continual transition or endless postponement with respect to place and occasion. On the contrary, it implies a break away from the contemporary concept (call it sickness) of spatial continuity and the tendency to erase every articulation between spaces, i.e. between outside and inside, between one space and another (between one reality and another). Instead the transition must be articu-lated by means of defined in-between places which induce simultaneous awareness of what is significant on either side. An in-between space in this sense provides the common ground where conflicting polarities can again become twin phenomena. (p. 82)

Despite the manifestly dialectical character of this description, it would not be difficult to take this notion of the 'in-between' (see Derrida's play on 'entre' and 'antre' in 'La Double séance')[27] and to see it, not as the ground of a dialectical mediation between contradictory or 'conflicting polarities', but as the generalizable 'medium' or milieu of the same (not the identical, as both Heidegger and Derrida insist)[28] in which differentiation takes place. In this type of reading, the in-between space would be something like the spatiality of space, the spacing of spaces, which cannot itself be simply defined as inside or outside, nor indeed as simply 'in' space at all. And, as the quotation from van Eyck suggests, architecture would then consist in the 'configuring' (differentiating) of space into spaces which are *always* intermediary. This reading would of course exercise a certain amount of violence on van Eyck's text, as it would lead to the idea that, in a sense, this *does* imply something of a 'continual transition or endless postponement' with respect to both place and occasion. We are very close to Derrida here, and specifically to his derivation of *différance*, differing and deferring.[29] This also takes up on the temporal aspect of what van Eyck says: for if we are to make any sense of architecture as to do with the event, then we must be talking about time as well as space. And to have a closer look at these possibilities, we shall have to leave Venturi and move to two architects who explicitly invoke the work of Derrida, namely Eisenman and Tschumi.

Paradoxically enough, the explicit invocation of Derrida in texts by and around Eisenman makes the discussion rather more difficult than in the case of Venturi. It may be that in some sense Eisenman is proposing a more or less rigorously 'deconstructive' architecture: this clearly does not imply that the discursive links of such an architecture with the work of Derrida are successfully negotiated. For example, in one of the essays in the *Fin d'Ou T Hou S* project, Jeffrey Kipnis picks up on the notion of in-betweenness I have just been discussing, and says the following: 'The betweenness reading, which Derrida calls "différance", is the always in flux space that constitutes the relations that are reading itself; scene of intrinsic subjectivity, it is the playground named Mind'.[30] Now whatever exactly 'intrinsic subjectivity' means here (or 'mind' for that matter), it is an odd way to talk about Derrida. Kipnis has earlier in his text introduced the notions of reading and subjectivity which inform the sentence I have just quoted: he says, for example, that 'Writing, in Derrida's formulation, is any and every organisation of form that stimulates an organised experience of reading' (p. 15), and that 'writing' in the generalized sense given to that word by Derrida, consists in 'subjectivity vested . . . forms caught up endlessly in referring to other forms . . . ' (ibid.). I really do not know where Kipnis has found the authority for these appeals to reading and to subjects, for there is no such appeal in Derrida. The inspiration is apparently much more Barthesian, for whom the proclaimed 'death of the author' (which would correspond closely enough to Eisenman's heralded absence as architect from his own programmed architecture) is all too rapidly paid for by the birth of the reader.[31] Derrida's 'writing' is, in fact, the death of the reader as much as the death of the author. In *Of Grammatology*, for instance, Derrida says that writing is other than the subject, in whatever sense one chooses to take those words.[32] And if 'experience' is invoked by Derrida around the argument that writing in his generalized sense is (among other things) the 'formation of form', this is an 'experience' which takes transcendental phenomenology to its limits before crossing through the notion of experience as derived and secondary to that of the trace. In passing, Derrida comments on the necessity of passing through these transcendental arguments, as otherwise the 'ultra-transcendental' text (which he is proposing) can all too easily look like the 'pre-critical' text, which I fear Kipnis has provided.[33] (The same error that Derrida's philosophy is somehow a form of subjectivism is also perpetrated in the presentation of the recent interview in the review *Domus*.)[34]

Eisenman's own presentations are also quite obscure and uneven. In the Romeo and Juliet material,[35] for example, the attempt to disrupt the value of presence by opposing it to void and by redefining absence, is potentially confusing: and that re-definition of absence as 'either the trace of a previous presence' (in which case it 'contains memory'), or else as 'the trace of a possible presence' (in which case it 'contains immanence') could be shown to fall short of the Derridean account of the trace on which it is clearly attempting to draw: this account is essentially that of a phenomenology such as is traversed by Derrida in *Of Grammatology* and *Speech and Phenomena*. By thinking in terms of memory and past or future presences, Eisenman is still within the metaphysical and essentially linear account of time which Derrida has so patiently undermined. It is also noticeable that Eisenman is still thinking in a fundamentally dialectical way, both in this account of absence and the temporality of the site, and in the three 'structural relationships' he takes from the story of Romeo and Juliet (the dialectic of division, union, and then union-and-division of the lovers in the tomb). Derrida's own discussion of Romeo and Juliet (which there is no reason to assume that Eisenman would or should have known)[36] disrupts this simplicity with a non-dialectical complexity, in which 'division' inhabits union as a non-accidental 'accident', and division inhabits identity in, for example, the simultaneous unity and division of Romeo and his name. It may well be, of course, that Eisenman's project in some sense *shows* this, even if his discourse does not quite *describe* it. But as the logic of Eisenman's work is that it is difficult if not impossible to perform a neat separation of building and discourse, this unevenness cannot be ignored.

Whatever the value of Eisenman's descriptions, and whatever the doubts that might be levelled at his particular appeal to the notion of self-similarity, which could lead to closure as much as to opening if too quickly interpreted in terms of the *mise-en-abyme*, (and Eisenman's idea of the architectural object becoming 'internalized', 'self-definitive', 'true to its own logic', proposing 'an intrinsic value system' suggests that he is no stranger to that over-hasty interpretation)[37] it is clear that his is an attempt to think time in the space of architecture, beyond the obvious and simple sense of the time of a building's building or existence. If it is true that this is an attempt at an architecture of the event, then it clearly cannot simply mean that the building of a building is an event, nor that it provides a space in which events may take place.

It is precisely this concern which Derrida explicitly finds at work in Tschumi's Villette project (see p. 3 for the point just made). I asked before if anyone really knew what it meant to talk of meaning in architecture: even if no one really does, the fact would remain, according to Derrida, that in general the meaning of architecture is that it should have meaning (Derrida presents this as the basic postulation underlying four invariables traversing the history of the concept of architecture (p. 8).) The meaning of architecture cannot itself be architectural, and to this extent architecture is governed from principles outside itself (p. 9). Derrida's complex argument is designed to suggest that Tschumi's project disrupts this configuration. It is clear that this is again a question of the deconstruction of an inside/outside polarity, if not quite in the sense I was trying to sketch out apropos of Venturi. It is emphatically not a question, in Derrida's reading of Tschumi, of simply refusing the outside, the 'extrinsic' meanings imposed on architecture, in favour of some notional internal purity or propriety of architecture, as we might still suspect to be the case with Eisenman. Just as Venturi's apparent desire to mark a strong separation of inside and outside led to a complication of the structure of the limit separating inside and outside, so Tschumi's project both includes the outside (it does not refuse external demands of utility, and so on), and opens the inside to its other (photography, cinema, and so on). Tschumi's architecture would thus by definition not be *proper* architecture, and it would be unreasonable, as in the case of Eisenman, simply to separate the building 'itself' from texts, drawings and so on, which accompany it as more and less than 'projects'. In this case, it is Tschumi's fortune to be able to include a text by Derrida in his intertext.

In Derrida's reading, Tschumi's effort is to 'maintain the dis-jointed as such', to 'give dissociation its due, but to put it to work as such in the space of a gathering' (the gathering that is the fundamental motif of Heidegger's 'Building, Dwelling, Thinking'). The logic here is precisely that which governs Derrida's general thinking on inside and outside (and thereby his thought in general, in so far as separating inside and outside is the act of separation itself, the analysis, critique, conceptualizing which defines philosophy): the 'points' on Tschumi's grid gather their own separation, hold together and apart both togetherness and apartness, 'associate and dissociate both association and dissociation', in a tension which refuses the dialectical solutions proposed by Eisenman, and which could not give rise to the suspicion of closure invited by Eisenman's appeal to 'self-similarity' (pp. 13–5: I would want to argue that such an 'economy of dissociation' is identical to that briefly proposed under the sign of 'dissensus' by Lyotard at the end of *The Postmodern Condition*, against Habermas – Derrida here talks of 'a socius of dissociation' (p. 14).) This tension cannot be thought in simply spatial terms, nor in terms of a temporality itself thought of as *external* to space (it is not simply a question of providing a space in which temporal events might occur). But the spacing of Tschumi's grid (which is not just its space, as we suggested above in relation to Venturi and Van Eyck) is an attempt to work at the root of space and time – each of Tschumi's differentiated cubes is caught in the play of all the others: none is simply a self-present and self-sufficient unity. Effects of inside and outside are certainly produced here, but they are neither the simple separations recommended by Venturi, nor simply the flowing space he is concerned to attack. Tschumi's points interrupt the flow as much as they allow for it, and are themselves as divisible as they are punctual. The 'maintenant' stressed by Derrida, the now and the maintaining, is a maintenance not of presence but of spacing and interruption, of what he calls 'the relation with the other as such' (p. 16.).

The relation with the other as such (the 'as such' is important, marking that what is at stake here is respect for the *alterity* of the other, not an attempt to reduce that alterity to familiarity), which defines some of Derrida's most 'technical' thinking, [38] and which marks that thinking as profoundly ethical, is still all to do with insides and outsides, walls and events. Our 'deconstruction' of the wall in Venturi is not an attempt to deny the force or urgency of his insistence that the outside is different from the inside, but to modulate its mildly exasperated common sense into something like Tschumi's 'folies', where the difference of outside and inside is, as it were, already inside anyway. The 'promise' or invitation to the Other located by Derrida in Tschumi's project is not at all simply an invitation (addressed to 'the public') to come into the warm, nor to become a community (again). The ethico-political importance of this would quickly be made clear in a comparison of the Villette project and *Learning from Las Vegas*, where the socius in dissociation is apparently to be abandoned to the virtues of the strip. Dissociation, which is an absolute condition of the political, rather than the unfortunate failure of community it is often taken to be, need not accept its traditional (even dialectical) negative marking: as the active and necessarily unpredictable negotiation of walls between insides and outsides rather than their intolerant institution or illusory abolition, dissociation proceeds as an aleatory series of events. What will happen at La Villette remains: to be seen.

Notes

1. This is the full text of an essay parts of which have been used elsewhere: as a lecture to the Architectural Association School of Architecture in February 1987; as a paper at the Architectural Association's conference on 'The Relative and the Rational', in May 1987; and as a paper at the Tate Gallery International Symposium on deconstruction, May 1988. The later part of the essay appeared in a slightly earlier and edited version, under the title 'Complexity without Contradiction in Architecture', in *AA Files*, 15 (1988), 15–18.

2. Jacques Derrida, interview with Eva Meyer, 'Architecture ove il desiderio può abitare', in *Domus*, 681 (1986), 17–24.

3. Charles Jencks, *What is Post-Modernism?*, London: Academy Editions/New York: St. Martin's Press 1986. References will be given in the text.

4. Jacques Derrida, *La Vérité en peinture*, Paris: Flammarion 1978, p. 25; tr. *The Truth in Painting*, Chicago: University of Chicago Press 1988, p. 21.

5. Jean-François Lyotard, 'Réponse à la question: qu'est-ce que le postmoderne?', in *Le Postmoderne expliqué aux enfants*, Paris: Galilée 1986, pp. 13–34 (p. 22); tr. Régis Durand as 'Answering the Question: What is Postmodernism?', in *The Postmodern Condition*, Minneapolis: University of Minnesota Press/Manchester University Press, 1984, pp. 71–82 (p. 76).

6. Fredric Jameson, 'Postmodernism or the Cultural Logic of Capitalism', *New Left Review*, 146 (1984).

7. For some further explication of this paradox, see my paper 'Towards a Criticism of the Future', Chapter 12 below.

8. Paul de Man, 'Literary History and Literary Modernity', in *Blindness and Insight: Essays in the Rhetoric of Contemporary Criticism*, second edition, London: Methuen 1983, pp. 142–165.

9. Terry Eagleton, 'Capitalism, Modernism and Postmodernism', in *Against the Grain: Essays 1975–1985*, London: Verso 1986, pp. 131–47 (p. 139).

10. Cf. Lyotard, 'Note sur les sens de "post-" ', in *Le Postmoderne expliqué aux enfants*, pp. 119–26 (120–1): this is a rewritten version of the 'Defining the Postmodern', in Lisa Appignanesi, ed., *Postmodernism*, (ICA Documents 4 and 5) (1986), pp. 6–7 (reprinted London: Free Association Books 1989: pp. 7–10).

11. I say 'provisional' because, since *Au juste* at least, Lyotard points out a problem in attempting to think 'multiplicity', 'divergence', 'dissensus', etc., according to the Kantian description of the Idea. Cf. my *Lyotard: Writing the Event*, Manchester: Manchester University Press 1988, p. 160.

12. In 'Some Statements and Truisms about Neo-logisms, Newisms, Postisms, and Other Small Seismisms, in D Carroll, ed., The State of Theory, University of Columbia Press, 1989.

13. See again de Man, pp. 144 and 161.

14. See my 'Postal Politics and the Institution of the Nation', Chapter 13 below.

15. 'Lettre à un ami japonais', in *Psyché. Inventions de l'autre*, Paris: Galilée 1987, pp. 387–93 (p. 390); tr. in Wood and Bernasconi, eds, *Derrida and Différance*, Warwick: Parousia Press 1985, pp. 1–8 [pp. 4–5]: page references will be given in the text (I have modified the translations a little here and there).

16. Robert Venturi, *Complexity and Contradiction in Architecture*, New York: Museum of Modern Art 1977. Page references will be included in the text.

17. This implies that contradiction, despite appearances, in fact works towards homogenization, whereas a thought of difference, despite its apparent modesty, respects heterogeneity.

18. Jacques Derrida, *La Dissémination*, Paris: Seuil 1972, p. 294.

19. Jacques Derrida, *De la grammatologie*, Paris: Minuit 1967. In fact, in a notorious gesture, Derrida crosses through the copula in this chapter-title, to stress a movement of excess with respect to traditional ontology, and to block potential confusion with the Hegelian 'speculative proposition'.

20. See, for example, *De la grammatologie*, Chapter 3, Section III, but this logic of the limit pervades all of Derrida's thinking.

21. See especially the analyses in 'Scribble (pouvoir/écrire)', preface to William Warburton, *Essai sur les hiéroglyphes* (Paris: Aubier 1979).

22. On this sense of the word 'effect', which cannot be reduced to the couple cause/effect any more than to the couple truth/illusion, see especially Derrida's *Positions*, Paris: Minuit 1972, p. 90.

23. Simply because the identity of the signifier is secured despite its potentially very disparate material repetitions, and must therefore essentially involve ideality. It is odd that Derrida has been so widely misread on this point, given the clarity of his statements: see for example *De la grammatologie*, pp. 20, 45, 138–9.

24. See, for example, Barthes's own reflection on his use of this type of image, in *Roland Barthes*, Paris: Seuil 1975, pp. 54–5. Compare with the empty centre of Jewish tabernacle or temple, at least in the description given by Hegel's *Spirit of Christianity* (see Derrida's commentary in *Glas*, Paris: Galilée 1974, p. 60a; tr. John P. Leavey Jr. and Richard Rand University of Nebraska Press 1986, pp. 49a–50a).

25. See Jean-François Lyotard, *Instruction païennes*, Paris: Galilée 1977, pp. 42–3; *Au Juste*, Paris: Bourgois 1979, pp. 74–5, *Le Différend*, §218.

26. This is also true of Venturi's remarks about 'open poché'.

27. *La Dissémination*, pp. 240–1.

28. See especially Derrida's essay 'La Pharmacie de Platon', and Heidegger's *Identity and Difference* and 'Building Dwelling, Thinking'. This difficult theme of the non-identical same-in-*différance* is vital to an understanding of Derrida's thinking.

29. See especially Derrida's essay 'La Différance' (in *Marges – de la philosophie*, Paris: Minuit 1972, pp. 1–29).

30. Jeffrey Kipnis, 'Architecture Unbound: Consequences of the Recent Work of Peter Eisenman', in Peter Eisenman, *Fin d'Ou T Hous*, AA Folio V (1985), pp. 12–23 (p. 16). I should like to thank Jeffrey Kipnis for his very gracious acceptance of these criticisms since the appearance of the first version of this paper.

31. Roland Barthes, 'La Mort de l'auteur', in *Le Bruissement de la langue*, Paris: Seuil 1984, pp. 61–7 (p. 67). The final sentence of Barthes's article makes it clear that he is simply proposing a reversal of the traditional model which forgets the reader in favour of the author. (This point has been made very forcibly by Peggy Kamuf in her recent *Signature Pieces*, Cornell University Press 1988.) The stress on the addressee in general has been persuasively argued by Vincent Descombes to be characteristic of structuralism, and to limit its claims to break with a 'philosophy of the subject': see *Le Même et l'autre: quarante-cinq ans de philosophie française (1933–1978)* Paris: Minuit 1979, especially pp. 114 and 123–4.

32. 'Le constituant et le disloquant à la fois, l'écriture est autre que le sujet, en quelque sens qu'on l'entende', *De la grammatologie*, p. 100.

33. Cf. *De la grammatologie*, p. 90. It should be made clear that there are degrees of the

pre-critical, or possibly a stage of the pre- pre-critical. For example, Kipnis's text is of a quality not to be confused with that of recent descriptions of deconstruction as a 'style' or a 'world-view'.

34. *Domus* interview presentation.

35. Peter Eisenman, *Moving Arrows, Eros and Other Errors*, AA Box 3 (1986).

36. Jacques Derrida, 'L'Aphorisme à contretemps', in *Psyché: Inventions de l'autre*, Paris: Galilée 1987, pp. 519–33; tr. Nicholas Royle, in Derek Attridge, ed., *Acts of Literature*, London: Routledge 1992, pp. 414–33.

37. Derrida, 'Point de folie . . .', p. 9: 'In reinstituting architecture in what should have been singularly proper to it, it is above all not a matter of reconstituting a simplicity of architecture, a simply architectural architecture, by a purist or integrist obsession. It is no longer a matter of saving the proper in the virginal immanence of its economy and of returning it to its inalienable presence, finally non-representative, non-mimetic and referring only to itself. This autonomy of architecture, which would claim in this way to reconcile a formalism and a semanticism in their extremes, would do no more than accomplish the metaphysics it was claiming to deconstruct.' Much of the Eisenman material I have seen would appear vulnerable to these remarks.

38. See, for example, the elucidation of the 'trace' in *De la grammatologie*, pp. 68–9.

10

Spirit's Spirit Spirits Spirit

> . . . a certain point in my reading, at a moment which is no doubt
> for me that of the greatest hesitation and the gravest perplexity.
>
> (*De l'esprit*)

De l'esprit seems to me one of Derrida's oddest, most enigmatic books.[1]
Maybe this is partly because of my having had a hand in translating it –
that odd mix of quoting and ghosting, using and mentioning, signing
and effacing one's signature, which means I find *The Truth in Painting*
an odd book too. *De l'esprit* is odd, at least in the first instance, not
because of the sort of thing that has made people find works such as
Signéponge or *Glas* (or even *The Truth in Painting*) odd – no 'hectic word
play' here[2] – nor *simply* because of the relative absence of that sort of
thing ('hectic word play' and the like having been so much exaggerated
and misunderstood by the commentators, be they sympathetic or
hostile) and we're certainly not unused to quite sober expository texts
from Derrida, even – or even especially – recently. The oddness of the
book can't be explained in that way, and indeed many of its moments
and emphases will seem curiously familiar in spite of the oddness:
most obviously, perhaps, and still managing to scandalize some people,
the insistence, in addressing the biggest questions imaginable, on
apparently tiny textual detail, in quotation-marks, for example,
around the word 'spirit'.

It could be, of course, that the oddness is to do with this being
Derrida's longest published commentary to date on Heidegger. The
hypothesis would then be that because he is at least arguably closer to
Heidegger than to any other thinker, close enough, perhaps, to
understand him as no one else has, in some ways his double or his
ghost, *right up against him*, Derrida necessarily goes a little odd, or
odder than usual, when writing about Heidegger, that in this circum-
stance of intimate and violent doubling, which sets apart the scene of
Derrida's writing about Heidegger from the scene of his writing about

196

anybody else, something indeterminate or indetermining happens, or might always happen, and suddenly it's unclear what's going on exactly. What exactly is Derrida saying or signing in *De l'esprit*? What is he taking on in his own name, on his own account, what is he making his own? Where does commentary on Heidegger stop and assertion by Derrida begin?

What is going on exactly in *De l'esprit*? One of the oddities of the essay, compared to many others by Derrida, is perhaps that so much is going on so clearly. Even a cursory reading of the book will reveal that Derrida is trying to show at least the following things:

1. That 'spirit' is a persistent theme or motif in Heidegger from first to last, and that this seems to have been systematically overlooked or repressed by both supporters and opponents of Heidegger;
2. That this is not just a neutral addition to the knowledge we may have or think we have of what Heidegger's persistent themes are: whatever relation the theme or motif of spirit holds to other, more familiar or recognized themes or motifs, it cannot be that of simple addition to a list, but must disrupt the formation of that list;
3. That if it seems undeniable that this theme of spirit is not unconnected with the question of Heidegger's Nazism, then we must be careful not simply to assume that a 'spiritualistic' Nazism is better than a biologistic one, but careful too not to denounce it quickly as, say, a *cause* of that Nazism, in so far as Heidegger in fact shares this theme or motif with thinkers such as Husserl or Valéry, who could not be suspected of Nazi sympathies, and in fact shares it with humanism in general;
4. That this theme or motif of *Geist* seems to be in some sense more powerful than the theme or motif of the *question* in Heidegger, and seems to name what Derrida calls 'the unquestioned possibility of the question', and even the very resource of deconstruction.

On the basis of this very partial list, it seems that it is harder to organize an account of *De l'esprit* than of most other works of Derrida's. We might hazard the hypothesis that the 'usual' structure of a Derrida essay (or at least one on a 'philosophical' text) involves the location, alongside the reading of the text most obviously and actively encouraged by the text itself[3] (that 'reading' – for every text necessarily proposes at least one reading of itself – habitually relying on presuppositions or positions which invoke or rely upon some part at least of that complex configuration that Derrida calls the 'metaphysics of presence'), the location alongside that, then, of apparently incompatible elements which can be shown to infiltrate, undermine, outflank, etc. that 'first' reading, which can then be shown to have always

depended surreptitiously on those other elements which it none
the less also systematically subordinates, denounces, marginalizes
or attempts to exclude. By being thus both primary and secondary,
both central and marginal, both crucial and trivial, these elements
on which Derrida concentrates come to occupy the position it's
increasingly fashionable, following Gasché (who is, however, following
Derrida himself in this) to call 'quasi-transcendental', where the
excluded, marginalized or secondarized element is now seen to be
simultaneously the condition of possibility *and* impossibility of
the system set up in the first, obvious and 'official' reading. The
quasi-transcendental thus becomes what the text says without saying,
thinks without thinking, signs without signing. And one of the most
disconcerting features of the quasi-transcendental that these
infuriating formulations attempt to capture is that it seems to defy
any simple assignation: the logic of supplementarity is stated or
signed neither simply by Rousseau nor simply by Derrida (who found
it all in Rousseau, who he is certainly not making look stupid the better
to look intelligent himself, as Gillian Rose mistakenly thought:[4] my
impression is rather that Derrida makes almost all the authors he reads
look frighteningly clever, uncannily clever) – and this difficulty
of assigning (and therefore dating) doctrine or belief obviously
explains why deconstruction disrupts any simple history of philosophy
or ideas, which would need to know, for example, *when* the logic
of supplementarity was thought or invented (in the mid-eighteenth
century by Rousseau, or the late twentieth by Derrida – it makes quite a
difference in the history of ideas), but cannot know any such thing, for
supplementarity exceeds and precedes dating, as its condition of
(im)possibility, precisely.

Now there is of course something of this in *De l'esprit*. For example,
when he is summarizing in Chapter 2 the four threads of his 'open
questions' around Heidegger, Derrida picks up Heidegger's claim that
'the essence of technology is not technological', and sketches a reading
that would show how this 'obvious' reading is undermined by an
originary 'contamination' by *tekhné* of all thought and language, and
therefore of any essence whatsoever, including that of *tekhné* itself –
and this would go along with a suggestion of Gasché's about one of the
ways of understanding the difference between Heidegger and Derrida, the former still thinking essences (in however complicated a way),
the latter thinking the quasi-transcendental as the complex unity of
possibility and impossibility I've just outlined.

Our problem, however, and the feeling of oddness, appear to come
from the difficulty involved in transferring this familiar – if far from
easy or straightforward – configuration to the way that Derrida deals

with the theme or motif of 'spirit' itself. Here the set-up appears different, and to echo or ghost the set-up found, not in the reading of Rousseau, for example, but in that of Lacan in 'Le facteur de la vérité', or Foucault in 'Cogito et Histoire de la folie'. Here the operation seems all but reversed: instead of reading, against obviously or clearly asserted metaphysical themes, an undermining force elsewhere, Derrida reads, against apparently non- or anti-metaphysical themes or motifs (in Lacan, for example, the stress on the signifier, on the split subject, on the alienation of the subject in the discourse of the Other, and so on), other textual details which confirm an attachment to the metaphysics that the more obvious claims or emphases apparently denied. At first sight at least, it *looks* (as indeed, *mutatis mutandis*, it looks as though that's what he's doing in two earlier Heidegger readings, 'Les fins de l'homme' and 'Ousia et grammé'), it looks as though this is the sort of thing Derrida is doing in *De l'esprit*,[5] showing how Heidegger's claimed 'Destruktion' of the history of metaphysics (and in this book Derrida consistently translates this as 'deconstruction', ghosting again, as though 'deconstruction' were no more than the translation of the German term, but each time insistently providing the German word in parentheses immediately afterwards, perhaps to that extent not quite assuming or signing the value of 'deconstruction' in these contexts, or precisely not quite asserting its identity with the 'deconstruction' he, Derrida, practises or at least names in other contexts, and does seem to sign, to assume as his own, in spite of frequent reservations about the word and its fortunes) how that *Destruktion* in fact stops short of deconstructing the value of *Geist*, which would then haunt the apparently non-metaphysical text with the spectre of a metaphysical residue insufficiently processed in Heidegger's thinking, this metaphysical residue making it all too easy for Heidegger to make a disastrous misreading of Nazism, and leading him later to some of his sillier remarks about, for example, the primacy or priority or excellence of the German language in philosophy.

One of the reasons why this type of reverse set-up is trickier to deal with than the first is that it looks very much like the set-up of *critique* which Derrida has many times insisted deconstruction is not. Where the readings of, say, Plato, Rousseau, Kant, Hegel or Saussure are, in general, and quite obviously – despite the misconceptions of early commentators – celebratory and affirmative of their objects, revelling in the complex resources bequeathed to the reader in these texts (and this would appear to be even more the case in the readings of Mallarmé, Blanchot, Ponge or Celan, which would perhaps have to form a third category in this tentative, provisional and no more than heuristic typology) the second set-up seems, at least at various points, to say, in a way that is unusual in Derrida's writing more generally. 'That's wrong'. Lacan says that the letter is indivisible, and he's wrong; Foucault that Descartes's *Meditations* are in some fundamental sense complicit with the internment of the mad, and he's wrong; Searle that the notion that concepts must have sharp boundaries is a logical positivist idea, and he's wrong.

Can we say the same for *De l'esprit*? One of the features of the more 'critical' readings seems to be a quite confident assigning of signatures: this type of reading needs to be able to assign with confidence the assertion that's wrong to the person who is wrong. In the Rousseau-type readings, this does not seem to be quite so clearly the case — obviously such readings rely on a corpus of texts attributed to Rousseau or whoever it might be, but they play out, via explicit questions as to what constitutes a corpus or an *oeuvre* (in the *Grammatologie* and 'La Pharmacie de Platon', for example), a complex middle-voiced strictly unattributable set of propositions which in the end are signed neither simply by Derrida, nor simply by Rousseau. There are signs of this need for assignment in *De l'esprit*: for example, in the early overview of the argument presented in Chapter 1, Derrida says, 'Heidegger notes that Trakl always took care to avoid . . . the word *geistig*. And, visibly, Heidegger approves him in this, he thinks the same' (p. 12); and this assertion is repeated in Chapter 5: in the *Rektoratsrede*, Heidegger stresses the word *geistig*, 'the word which twenty years later will be opposed to *geistlich*. The latter would no longer have anything Platonico-metaphysical or Christian-metaphysical about it, whereas *geistig*, Heidegger will say then, *in his own name and not in a commentary on Trakl*, remains caught in the metaphysico-Platonic-Christian oppositions of the below and the beyond, of the low and the high, of the sensible and the intelligible' (p. 56). Still in chapter 5, Derrida is describing the definition of spirit given in the *Rektoratsrede*, and says this:

> At the centre of the *Address*, for the first time to my knowledge · · · · , Heidegger offers a definition of spirit. It is certainly presented in the form of a definition: S is P. And without any possible doubt, Heidegger takes it up for his own [*la prend à son compte*]. He is no longer mentioning the discourse of the other. No longer speaking of spirit as in Descartes, Hegel, or later Schelling or Hölderlin . . . (p. 58)

These confident assignments are complicated by at least two passages elsewhere in the book. The first of these comes at the end of Chapter 4, which has been plotting the later vicissitudes of the term *Geist* in *Sein und Zeit*, after Heidegger's early warning not to use the term, to avoid it: Heidegger comes back to *Geist* in quotation-marks, 'does not take it up as his own' (*prendre à son compte* again, and this in spite of the remark, a couple of pages earlier, that in these late usages from *Sein und Zeit* Heidegger 'finally takes up [*prend enfin à son compte*] the word "spirit" as his own, but *twice in quotation marks*; (p. 49), quoting being a way of taking up without taking up, but of course the presence or absence of quotation-marks would be a very crude criterion in general of what it means to sign or take up as one's own).[6] This inspires a 'provisional' use, 'for convenience', of the use/mention distinction as a way of describing this situation. First, says Derrida, Heidegger *uses* the word spirit, but in a negative way, in fact rather mentioning it as a word whose use should be avoided; then he *really* uses it 'on his own account' (*à son compte*, again), but in quotation-marks, thus signalling a sort of quotation or borrowing from the discourse of the other. But it is none the less this second 'use' which is also a 'mention' (and this quite complicated use (or mention) of the use/mention distinction describes quite accurately, it would seem, the sort of complicated imbrication of signatures that I was suggesting marked out Derrida's own 'standard', paleonymic reading practice, on Rousseau, Plato, etc., with the play of crossings-through and quotation-marks that this implies, as indeed it is rapidly described once more at the end of *De l'esprit* (p. 177) – this second use-mention, then, which is here presented as the first stage of 'the slow work of reappropriation which will merge, as I should like to demonstrate, with a re-Germanization' (p. 44) the story of which Derrida goes on to tell in the body of the book.

Let me not rehearse that story, but follow a little more this *à son compte*, this 'on one's own account' or 'for one's own' that we've encountered so frequently in these pages. What happens when we finally reach the moment, '25 years later', in the text on Trakl, when Heidegger approves Trakl for avoiding *geistig* and preferring *geistlich*? Chapter 9 by now, and it looks at first as though these confident decisions as to signature, as to whose account is to be credited or debited around the use or mention of the word 'spirit' – it looks as though they have to stop:

> In this *Gespräch*, there will be no deciding [this translates *on ne décidera pas*, which could also, perhaps more plausibly, taken as 'we *will* not decide'] whether the thinker speaks in his name or in correspondence with Trakl. In the face of such statements [i.e. statements saying, for example, 'Spirit is flame'], there will be no deciding [or: we will not decide] whether visible or invisible quotation marks, or even some still more subtle marks, must suspend the assigning of a *simple* responsibility. In order to decide, a long meditation would be necessary, before such an assigning, as to what Heidegger says at the beginning about double speech and doubly addressed speech – *Gespräch* and *Zwiesprache* – between thinker and poet. It

would be necessary to meditate on the difference but also the reciprocity (*Wechselbezug*) between the *Erörterung* (the situation, the thought of the site, *Ort*) and the *Erläuterung* (the elucidating reading, the 'explication') of a *Gedicht*, the difference between *Gedicht* and *Dichtungen*, etc.

But now, suddenly, something cutting through this apparently endless complication of signing and quoting, using and mentioning, asserting and reporting:

> Just as I cannot translate these words without lengthy formalities, so for lack of time I will have to restrict myself to this gross affirmation which I think is hardly contestable: statements like those I have just cited and translated by *spirit in-flames* are obviously statements *of* Heidegger. Not his own, productions of the subject Martin Heidegger, but statements to which he subscribes apparently without the slightest reluctance. . . . It would be completely irrelevant to reduce these statements in ontological form to 'commentaries'. Nothing is more foreign to Heidegger than commentary in its ordinary sense . . . (pp. 134–5)

So here, in a context where the uncertainty and indirection appears to be at its height, where the distribution of uses and mentions appears the hardest of all, where we are suspending even the decision as to the suspension of responsibility, where we apparently cannot even decide that the question 'who signs?' is undecidable, Derrida still does not, apparently, hesitate to assign this assertion that spirit is flame to Heidegger, not as something he invents, of course, but as something to which he nevertheless subscribes, to which he puts his name. This is immediately qualified further, however: of course, says Derrida, such statements of Heidegger's are inspired or induced by lines in Trakl, though of course the lines Heidegger quotes are determined by what he is saying himself – this coming and going being the very structure of the *Gespräch*. But, says Derrida first, he'll try at least '*up to a certain point and provisionally*' to sort out of this intermeshing what belongs to Heidegger, what comes down to, or back to, Heidegger (*ce qui revient à Heidegger*, perhaps what returns to haunt him), but then adds immediately that that's really *not* the question . . . (I'm afraid I have to modify the translation at this point as it is not strictly accurate; this is another reason why books one has translated seem odd and return to haunt the translator):

> Given this, the question that counts is not that of finding out who says 'spirit-in-flames' – they both say it in their fashion – but to recognise what Heidegger says *of spirit* in order to *situate* such an utterance, both to explain it and to lead it back to its place – if it has a place, and one that is absolutely its own. (p. 136)

It's clearly vital for Derrida to be able to make some assignment of responsibility to Heidegger – if not in a naive way by assuming that Heidegger is in any straightforward or traditional sense the *author* of what he says, but in the sense (which is the only deconstructive sense that can be made of authorship) that he subscribes, underwrites, appends a signature to, certain propositions. The story *De l'esprit* tells is one where an initial gesture of avoidance of spirit slowly becomes an appropriation, the initial ghosting of the word through the use of scare-quotes returning to haunt Heidegger at or until the end.

I said at the beginning that this looks more like the sort of structure that informs Derrida's more 'critical' readings of such authors as Foucault and Lacan. There, elements are identified which, in spite of more or less aggressive claims to the contrary by these authors, are taken by Derrida to show a residual unthought attachment to metaphysics which in fact contaminates the whole of their thought. Is this where we are left with '*Geist*' in Heidegger? This is perhaps the most obvious way to read the book – Heidegger failed in his own 'deconstruction' of metaphysics at least to the extent that he failed to deconstruct this value of *Geist*. This is, at any rate, how *De l'esprit* is read by Lyotard in his little book on *Heidegger et 'les juifs'*. He summarizes the book quite convincingly thus:

> Jacques Derrida has devoted the resources of the most scrupulous deconstruction to picking out the fate of *Geist*, *geistig*, and *geistlich* in Heidegger's text, both philosophical and political. The demonstration here is blinding, that the action of the rector is nothing but the knowing in act of the thinker, but that it has however to give itself the supplement of spirit to find its effective place and address. . . . Spirit, a region withdrawn from deconstructive anamnesia, a blind white zone which authorises a politics that the existential-ontological thinking only permitted.[7]

This allows Lyotard to suggest that whatever the excellence of Derrida's work in this respect, it amounts simply to a dutiful and filial continuation where Heidegger left off, seeing that Heidegger himself failed to deconstruct far enough (leaving this value of spirit unquestioned), and kindly doing the job for him. Lyotard can then say that that's all very well, but that the real 'fault' of Heidegger's (i.e. his silence after the war on the death camps) can in no way be explained along these deconstructive lines. This question, which Lyotard links to an account of 'the jews' as a sort of primarily repressed event in Western culture, cannot according to him be addressed by deconstruction at all, which is thus more generally condemned (as it was in *Economie libidinale* in 1974, and, implicitly at least, at Cerisy in 1980),[8] for being pious and nihilistic.

I cannot here reconstruct Lyotard's arguments with due care. Essentially, he wants to make a radical distinction between the still 'Greek' Heidegger (still thinking Being) and a 'Jewish' thinking (thinking the Law) which Heidegger, and by extension Derrida, are unable to think, despite all appearances of an apparently 'Jewish' attentiveness to forgetting, avoiding, complications of origin, and so on.

But after the passages from *De l'esprit* I've just quoted, Derrida moves on (and Lyotard does not mention this at all) to the idea that something for Heidegger *precedes* the question that elsewhere in his work appeared to be the highest dignity of thought. One of the greatest oddities of *De l'esprit* is that this apparently vital point is made largely in a huge, excessive, footnote, and the oddity is increased by the fact that the book explicitly states that the footnotes were all added *after* the delivery of the text at a conference in 1987, even though it was apparently at an *earlier* conference at Essex that the material for that crucial footnote was brought to Derrida's attention, and the note is re-marked as being of unusual importance for a note by being the object of a dedication. One of the things that this footnote imagines is a 'perverse' reading of Heidegger that acted literally on all of Heidegger's recommendations about crossings-through, avoidance of terms, and so on; one might wonder how perverse it is to imagine *De l'esprit* without this footnote, as heard by its first addressees. That something in Heidegger which precedes the question (of Being) is not quite the Law in Lyotard's sense, but something like a *promise*, which Derrida would certainly want to say precedes Law as much as it precedes Being. Further still, and again Lyotard is silent on this, Derrida locates a 'foreclosure' (a word Lyotard also uses in his description of his hypothesized primary repression of 'the Jews' in western thought) in Heidegger's brutal triangulation of the question of the language of Spirit around the Greek, German and Latin languages, and asks: 'Does [this triangle] not remain open from its origin and by its very structure onto what the Greek and Latin *had* to translate by *pneuma* and *spiritus*, that is, the Hebrew *ruah*?' (p. 165).

The point here is that if Heidegger is pushing the *geistliche* in Trakl towards what *ought to be* a point of contact with the very Judaic tradition that Lyotard is claiming Heidegger (and by extension Derrida) just can't think, then on the one hand, Heidegger's text would be opening to deconstruction *all* his own earlier thinking (or unthinking) about *Geist*, but on the other, simultaneously, foreclosing any access to that 'other' tradition by the violent historical delimitation of Greek, Latin and German as the arena in which the matter is to be decided. But allowing that opening (which is of course quite different from the sort of radical difference Lyotard has always been pursuing), the textual resources for which are thus to be found in Heidegger, through the curious imagined dialogue that ends the book, in which Derrida ghosts, quotes 'mentions', uses and abuses the discourse of all the supposed interlocutors, at the crossroads at which the location of the archi-originary is no longer an ontological or transcendental search – allowing that opening shifts and troubles anything like the opposition I sketched between two sorts of texts by Derrida, who is here *affirming* a reinscribed *Geist* as *Geist's* ghost, as return of the same as other, repetition as alterity doubling again, here as everywhere else, as both the 'theme' of deconstructive writing and its 'style', its uses already used as mentions, writing *always* also its own ghost. And this is, then, what deconstruction will always have been saying on its own account, on its own behalf, in its own name, this is deconstruction's very signature: SPIRIT'S SPIRIT SPIRITS SPIRIT: spirit's spirit (or ghost ghosts or) spirit (the 'official' metaphysical value of) spirit (and therefore also the metaphysical value of ghost) which was thus always already also its own altering repetition, its own ghost, another name, therefore, for the necessarily odd, duplicitous, haunting and, of necessity, endlessly resourceful resource of deconstruction itself, its other.

Notes

1. This is a very slightly revised and extended version of a talk given at a Warwick conference. I have made no attempt to minimize the oral and informal character of the piece. Most of the footnotes were in the original talk.

2. Nor, strictly speaking, in *Signéponge* or *Glas* either, but the reader will know what I mean.

3. And not just the reading, as de Man mistakenly thought in his early essay on the *Grammatology*, that happens to have been dominant in a tradition of deluded commentary, nor, as Barbara Johnson mistakenly thought in her essay on Derrida and Lacan, a sort of second-class student's 'standard reading' that the master can or could then correct.

4. In *Dialectic of Nihilism*, Oxford: Blackwell 1984. I have attempted to refute Rose's reading of Derrida in 'L'Arroseur arrosé(e)', Chapter 5 above.

5. Despite the fact that the book was, I think, quite widely seen in France as an attempt to *defend* Heidegger at all costs, just as Derrida's writings on de Man were widely seen in the United States as attempts to defend de Man, or even to whitewash the whole 'affair': surely Derrida is more uncompromisingly, thoughtfully, critical in both cases than almost anyone else.

6. A very Derridean paradox is at work here, namely that signing something as one's own, as one's very own, as incomparably idiomatic, would involve putting one's name to something incomprehensible and unrecognizable, to oneself as much as to others. This necessary incomprehensibility of what one most genuinely signs (the rest being in some sense quotation) is what links the figure of the writer to that of the legislator, who, in so far as he really legislates, necessarily proposes a law that is incomprehensible not only to its prospective subjects, but also to the legislator himself. I have had two attempts at analysing this structure with reference to Rousseau, in *Sententiousness and the Novel*,

Cambridge: Cambridge University Press, 1985; and in *Dudding: des noms de Rousseau*, Paris: Galilée 1991.

7. Jean-François Lyotard, *Heidegger et 'les juifs'*, Paris: Galilée 1988, p. 119.

8. Cf. *Economie libidinale*, Paris: Minuit 1974, p. 305; 'Discussions ou: phraser "après Auschwitz" ', in P. Lacoue-Labarthe and J.-L. Nancy, eds, *Les Fins de l'homme: à partir du travail de Jacques Derrida*, Paris: Galilée 1981, pp. 283–310 (p. 284).

11

Mosaic Fragment: If Derrida Were an

Egyptian . . .

To Onias High Priest, greeting. A document has come to light which shows that the Spartans and the Jews are kinsmen descended alike from Abraham. (Bernal, 1987, p. 110)

It was also at about this time that Hekataios of Abdera set out his view that the traditions of the Egyptian expulsion of the Hyksos, the Israelite Exodus and that of the Danaos' landing in Argos were three parallel versions of the same story. (Bernal, 1987, p. 109)

Has then the master-hand indeed traced such a vague or ambiguous script in the stone that so many different readings of it are possible? (Freud 14, p. 258)

Jewgreek is greekjew: but greekjew is Egyptian.

Hieroglyphs and pyramids, Thoth and Isis, colossi and the Sphinx: Egypt repeatedly returns to haunt Derrida's writing. From the two (or three) great Plato readings to the two great Hegel readings, via discussions of Freud and Warburton,[1] Egyptian motifs regularly appear at important moments in the texts. What is the place of 'Egypt' in deconstruction? Is there any sense in insisting on Derrida, greekjew or jewgreek, as North African, analogically 'Egyptian'?

Consider this example. If one says 'Moses did not exist', this may mean various things. It may mean: the Israelites did not have a *single* leader when they withdrew from Egypt – or: their leader was not called Moses – or: there cannot have been anyone who accomplished all that the Bible relates of Moses – or: etc, etc.

It is only by hearsay that you will get to know about psychoanalysis . . . Let us assume for a moment that you were attending a lecture not on psychiatry but on history, and that the lecturer was telling you of the life and military deeds of Alexander the Great. What grounds would you have for believing in the truth of what he

reported? At first glance the position would seem to be even more
unfavourable than in the case of psychoanalysis . . . but
nevertheless I cannot think you would leave the lecture-room in
doubts of the reality of Alexander the Great. . . . The outcome of
your examination would undoubtedly be reassuring in the case of
Alexander, but would probably be different where figures such as
Moses or Nimrod were concerned. (Freud 1, pp. 42–3)

– We may say, following Russell: the name 'Moses' can be defined by
means of various descriptions. For example, as 'the man who led the
Israelites through the wilderness', 'the man who lived at that time and place
and was then called "Moses" ', 'the man who as a child was taken out of
the Nile by Pharaoh's daughter' and so on. And according as we assume
one definition or another the proposition 'Moses did not exist' acquires a
different sense, and so does every other proposition about Moses. – And if
we are told 'N did not exist', we do ask: 'What do you mean? Do you want to
say . . . or . . . etc.? (Wittgenstein, §79).

Given the manifest impossibility of considering Derrida's work to be
straightforwardly 'philosophical', and the no less manifest impossibility of locating it philosophically as some 'regional' discourse (perhaps within the human sciences), how are we to place his writing, once
the rather silly temptation to write it off as literature has been resisted?
I recall two now traditional ways of viewing Derrida's work: the one as
Hegelian in spite of itself, the other as anti-Hegelian. The second has
noticed Derrida's 'definition' of deconstruction in *Positions*, as the

a little later, Egyptian hieroglyphy will provide the example of what resists
the movement of the dialectic, history, logos (*M* p. 96; cf. *GL*, p. 352a).

systematic interruption of the Hegelian *Aufhebung* (*POS*, 55), and talks
easily of deconstruction not liking, criticizing or attacking such things
as totalization and absolute knowledge. This seems to leave Derrida in
the position of sifting through the dustbins of metaphysics for
remainders and leftovers discarded by the tradition or not assimilable
by its digestive system. Whence the fact that Derrida does not 'do'
philosophy, but 'reads' it – there being no better occupation for a
philosopher once the 'closure of metaphysics' has been named. The
other description suggests that as philosophy has always in fact pro-
ceeded by appropriating what was previously marginal or external to it
(and Derrida himself opens *Margins* with a description of philosophy
behaving in precisely such a manner (*M*, p. I), then deconstruction is
still a totalizing philosophy blind to its own Hegelianism, still a metaphysics, a particularly perverse strategy aiming to legitimate an essentially traditional continuation of a discipline which should nowadays be
doing something quite different. Apparently contesting Hegelianism,
deconstruction has in fact found a way of playing an interminable
game with it, which it is desperately important not to seem to have won,

at risk of having to accept the end of any 'foundationalist' philosophy, and therefore the uselessness of such erudite questioning of it. In spite of its apparent modernism or even post-modernism, deconstruction would on this view be an essentially conservative ruse the better to legitimate an antiquarian attachment to the history of philosophy. The point to be made against deconstruction would not be that one should

> It seemed to me that I had been transported into a country far away from this country, into an age remote from this age, that I stood in ancient Egypt and that I was listening to the speech of some highpriest of that land addressed to the youthful Moses.

simply 'turn the page' of philosophy (cf. *ED*, pp. 421–2), but that it is possible to get on philosophically without suffocating in the library of the Western tradition: it is possible, on this view, to get through one's mourning for metaphysics and get on with some philosophy, instead of trying all ways ('demi-deuil' and the rest) to justify what is essentially a melancholic attachment to dead problems and ambitions.[2]

Naturally enough, the case with which these alternative views can be constructed suggests that there is something wrong here. After the fashion of the Kantian antinomies, it is easy to see apparently convincing arguments on both sides of the question, and to formulate something like the 'interests of reason' in the conflict. My purpose here is to maintain something of a Kantian rather than a Hegelian flavour to the way of formulating such problems, but to attempt to escape such antinomies, not of course by choosing one alternative over the other, nor by taking the Kantian route of sharpening up the distinction between phenomena and things in themselves, but by recasting the antinomy in terms of Jew and Greek, and by suggesting a non-dialetical way out through the suggestion that Derrida is neither Jew nor Greek, but 'Egyptian', in a non-biographical sense to be explored.

> From that moment – how can I say it – I felt as displaced in a Jewish community, closed unto itself, as I would in the other (which they used to call 'the Catholics'). The suffering eased in France. At nineteen I naively believed that anti-Semitism had disappeared, at least where I was living then. But, during my adolescence, and that was the real tragedy, it was there for everyone else (because there was everyone else, which was perhaps just as much a determining factor; you see, we give in to a certain kind of facility or curiosity by selecting this sequence of events; why involve me in that side of things?). A paradoxical effect, perhaps, of this bludgeoning was the desire to be integrated into the non-Jewish community, a fascinated but painful and distrustful desire, one with a nervous vigilance, a painstaking attitude to discern signs of racism in its most discreet formations or in its loudest denials. Symmetrically, oftentimes, I felt an impatient distance with regard to various Jewish communities, when I have the impression that they close in upon themselves, when they pose

themselves as such. From all of which comes a feeling of non-belonging that
I have doubtless transposed . . . (Bernasconi and Wood, 1985, p. 75).

Recent work on Derrida suggests, if only through the considerable
explanatory power of a term such as 'quasi-transcendental',[3] the
interest of elaborating a Kantian-critical filiation for deconstruction. It
seems important to maintain the importance of such a filiation, despite
the relatively small place Kant occupies in Derrida's published work, if
only to complicate the almost automatic tendency to place Derrida in a
supposedly phenomenological or hermeneutical 'tradition' usually
associated with Hegel, Husserl and Heidegger (cf. Kearney, 1984,
p. 109). One fruitful way of approaching Derrida's evident interest in

> For we are indeed dealing here with the imagination, that is the agency in
> which are blurred or cancelled all the Kantian oppositions regularly criticized
> by Hegel. We are here in that zone – let's mark it with the title 'Critique of
> Judgement' – where the debate with Kant looks most like an explication and
> least like a break. But it is also for convenience that we here oppose
> development to displacement. We should also have to reconsider this
> couple of concepts. (*M*, pp. 90–1)

> [The *pharmakon*] is, rather, the anterior milieu in which differenciation in
> general is produced . . . this milieu is *analogous* to that which later, after and
> according to the philosophical decision, will be reserved to the
> transcendental imagination . . . the element of the *pharmakon* is the site of
> combat between philosophy and its other. Element *in itself*, if one can still
> say that, *undecidable*. (*D*, pp. 144, 158)

> Occupying the *middle* [milieu] in the succession of the types of writing, the
> hieroglyph, as we shall see, is also the elementary milieu, the medium and
> general form of all writing. (*SCR*, p. 23)

the relation between Kant and Hegel is that suggested In *Glas*, where
the Kantian position, at least as Hegel construes it, is consistently linked
with that of the Jew. It is hard not to want to pursue the possibilities of
an at least analogical relation in which Hegel is the Greek to Kant's Jew,
and therefore to Derrida himself, and to extend that analogy to the
perhaps more vexed question of Derrida's relationship with Levinas
the Jew (against whom Derrida has said he never feels he has any
objections (*A*, p. 64)) and Heidegger the Greek (without whose work
Derrida has said none of his own thinking would have been possible
(*POS*, p. 74)). It is not hard to construct an essentially 'Jewish' Derrida,
not only on the basis of a vaguely 'talmudic' feel to his interminable
commentaries and glosses,[4] but in a more fundamental way, to do with
a sense that Derrida's is, for example, a thinking of a law which is
given, which *il y a*, pre-ontologically, not for understanding so much as
for negotiation, with no *telos* of comprehension or absolution. There is

some comfort in a scenario which would attempt to appropriate Derrida for a Jewish thought opposed to (or at least not assimilable by) a supposed tyranny of the Greek *logos*, a thinking of the Law not to be absorbed by a thinking of Being, a thinking of justice which would not be (subordinate to) a thinking of truth, an archi-original passivity or passibility which precedes and undermines all claims to mastery, etc.

Hegel places the Jew under the sign of a cutting: cut from mother nature after the flood (*GL*, p. 52aff), breaking from and opposing the life of community and love with Abraham, self-condemned to wandering in the desert away from any fixed domicile, marking this cut with the sign of circumcision (*GL*, 58aff), the better to remain bound to the cut itself, subjected as a finite being to the cut-off infinite of a jealous God. The attempt to secure his own finite mastery leaves the Jew in the grip of mastery by an infinite he can never understand, plunged in finitude, in matter. The Jew is alienated, in touch not with a transcendent truth but with a quasi-transcendence which can only take the (formless) form of a command and of a law one cannot understand – which cannot therefore be rational – but which is suffered, without mediation, in its letter rather than its spirit (*GL*, 72–5a). Kant, structurally speaking, occupies the place of the Jew in Hegel (*GL*, 47a).

> *And it seemed to me that I heard the voice of that Egyptian highpriest raised in a tone of like haughtiness and like pride. I heard his words and their meaning was revealed to me.*

Kant's autonomy, for example, the obedience to the 'ought' of the moral law, merely interiorizes the absolute heteronomy of the Jewish God, and is therefore no autonomy at all, but, on Kant's own terms, pathological (*GL*, pp. 80–1). Just like the Jews, Kant remains caught in the oppositional thinking of the understanding, stuck between a formalism of the law and an empiricism of events. By claiming to fix the boundaries of what a finite subjectivity can know, Kant prevents all knowledge of the infinite to which he thus remains enslaved.

Imagine first, then, that Derrida is Kant: but not so much the Kant of the Enlightenment, as Hegel's Kant (or Hölderlin's Kant, 'The

> But when I make a statement about Moses, – am I always ready to say: By 'Moses' I understand the man who did what the Bible relates of Moses, or at any rate a good deal of it. But how much? Have I decided how much must be proved false for me to give up my proposition as false? Has the name 'Moses' got a fixed and unequivocal use for me in all possible cases? – Is it not the case that I have, so to speak, a whole series of props in readiness, and am ready to lean on one if another should be taken from under me and vice versa? (Wittgenstein, §79)

Moses of our nation')[5] – yet not quite Hegel's Kant, but a Hegel's Kant whose YHWE is Hegel. Here then is Derrida, Jewish, condemned to the interminable elaboration of a law always in retreat and mystery, jealous of its truth that we can never know, but whose traces we can follow, at best, never arriving at a present perception or an experience (*GL*, pp. 299–300a). By following the tracks of what should be *another* Hegel (another reading of metaphysics), a Hegel who says something other than what Hegel says, Derrida, himself become Hegel's shadow or double, has made Hegel his doubly mysterious God, hiding all the better for pretending to appear in the light. In spite of all of Hegel's efforts to overcome the cut, Derrida will have insisted on cutting him from himself, cutting himself from him, and therefore stays, fascinated, in the effort to show that Hegel is the fascinated one, still attached to the very thing (the cut) from which he tried to cut himself. Show that Hegel never really escaped from Judaism by making him your YHWE. Striving for finite mastery of the letter of philosophy, enslave yourself to the infinite you admit you cannot understand. Whence deconstruction's vertigo, fascination and repulsion, nomadic wandering in the desert, failure to announce any truth or promise any knowledge.

> The city and the desert, which are neither countries nor landscapes nor gardens, lay siege to Jabès's poetry and ensure for his cries a literally infinite echo. City and desert at once, that is Cairo from which comes Jabès, who as we know, also had his departure from Egypt. The dwelling built by the poet with his 'daggers stolen from the angel' is a light tent made of words in the desert where the nomadic Jew is struck by infinity and letter. Broken by the broken Law. Divided in himself – (the Greek language would no doubt tell us a great deal about the strange relationship of the law, of wandering and non self-identity, about the common root – *nemein* – of sharing, of nomia and of nomadism). (*ED*, p. 105)

> Unfortunately, I do not feel inspired by any sort of hope which would permit me to presume that my work of deconstruction has a prophetic function. But I concede that the style of my questioning as an exodus and dissemination in the desert might produce certain prophetic resonances. It is possible to see deconstruction as being produced in a space where the prophets are not far away. But the prophetic resonances of my questioning reside at the level of a certain rhetorical discourse which is also shared by several other contemporary thinkers. The fact that I declare it 'unfortunate' that I do not personally feel inspired may be a signal that deep down I still hope. It means that I am in fact still looking for something. So perhaps it is no mere accident of rhetoric that the search itself, the search without hope for hope, assumes a certain prophetic *allure*. Perhaps my search is a twentieth century brand of prophecy? But it is difficult for me to believe it. (Kearney, 1984, p. 119)

Hegel's Kant, Hegel's Moses: proposing to the Jews in Egypt an unintelligible liberation in a rhetoric so abstract and forced, a writing so artificial and full of tricks, that it is like a foreign language (*GL*, p. 67a) – a writing analogous to the tabernacle, mere construction of bands, empty inside, signifier without signified, nothing at its centre (*GL*, p. 68a).

And yet what could be more Greek than the Derrida of 'Violence and Metaphysics', defending Heidegger against Levinas, insisting on the absolute necessity of speaking alterity in the language of the Greek *logos*, claiming thereby that if Jewish thought is other than Greek thought, it can none the less not be absolutely external to it, but folded back in via the non-dialectical figure of invagination, non-identical same which is not different from *différance*, but the *milieu* of history in general. Derrida cannot be Hegel's Kant, nor Hegel's Moses, if all his thought is concerned to show the incoherence of any absolutized cut or separation: so far, for example, from attempting to salvage absolute difference from Hegel's description, Derrida agrees with Hegel to the extent that *différance* must be thought of as the name for the impossibility of difference ever being absolute or pure (cf. *ED*, p. 227n1).

And in fact the comfort of a 'Jewish' reading can hardly fail to be disturbed by Derrida's relation in general to Heidegger, still apparently too Greek for such thinking – and we can suggest quite confidently that any attempt to make Derrida *essentially* a Jewish thinker will always end up finding that he is somehow not Jewish enough, still too Greek (but the problem is that the attempt to find Derrida 'essentially' Jewish is already a Greek gesture: the Jewish reading is a Greek reading). Whence the disturbance caused by some of his comments on the recent Heidegger and de Man 'affairs'.[6] We need to look for something 'before' the opposition of Greek and Jew: but we need to beware any tendency to call that 'before' '*mythos*' or 'sophistry', for example, for, as Derrida shows in 'La pharmacie de Platon', 'mythos' is itself a philosophical concept, determined only from the point of view of *logos*, and 'sophistry' too is a Platonic concept, marking as much as inseparability as a rupture:

> Can we set off in search of another guarding, once the pharmaceutical 'system' constrains not only, in one and the same hold, the scene of the *Phaedrus*, the scene of the *Republic* and the scene of the *Sophist*, Platonic dialects, logic and mythology, but also, it appears, certain non-Greek structures of mythology? And if it is not certain that there is any such thing as non-Greek 'mythologies', for the opposition *mythos/logos* only ever has its authority *after* Plato, to what general and unnamable necessity are we referred? In other words, what does Platonism as repetition signify? (*D*, 194)

In proposing 'Egypt' as one name of that 'unnamable necessity', we are not naming any thing, any place or any date. If the question 'what is . . . ?' is dated (*SCH*, pp. 30–1), and dated as 'later' than 'Egypt', we cannot ask 'what is Egypt?'[7]

> Once again I am prepared to find myself blamed for having presented my
> reconstruction . . . with too great and unjustified certainty. I shall not feel
> very severely hit by this criticism, since it finds an echo in my own
> judgement. I know myself that my structure has its weak spots, but it has its
> strong points too. On the whole my predominant impression is that it is worth
> while to pursue the work in the direction it has taken. (Freud 13, p. 281)

Jewgreek is neither Greek nor Jew, nor greekjew as mix or *Aufhebung*. I
call the non-teleological becoming Greek of the Jew, or the non-
originary having been-Jew of the Greek, 'Egypt': always left, never left,
that 'veille du platonisme' which Derrida mysteriously suggests might
also be the 'lendemain du hegelianisme' (*D*, pp. 122–3).

> *Why will you Jews not accept our culture, our religion and our language?*
> *You are a tribe of nomad herdsmen; we are a mighty people. You have no*
> *cities nor no wealth: our cities are hives of humanity and our galleys, trireme*
> *and quadrireme, laden with all manner merchandise furrow the waters of the*
> *known globe. You have but emerged from primitive conditions: we have a*
> *literature, a priesthood, and agelong history and a polity.*

> While I consider it essential to think through this copulative synthesis of
> Greek and Jew, I consider my own thought, paradoxically, as neither Greek
> nor Jewish. I often feel that the questions I attempt to formulate on the
> outskirts of the Greek philosophical tradition have as their 'other' the model
> of the Jew, that is, the Jew-as-other. And yet the paradox is that I have
> never actually invoked the Jewish tradition in any 'rooted' or direct manner.
> Though I was born a Jew, I do not work or think within a living Jewish
> tradition. So that if there is a Judaic dimension to my thinking which may
> from time to time have spoken in or through me, this has never assumed the
> form of an explicit fidelity or debt to that culture. In short, the ultimate site
> (*lieu*) of my questioning discourse would be neither Hellenic nor Hebraic if
> such were possible. It would be a non-site beyond both the Jewish influence
> of my youth and the Greek philosophical heritage which I received during my
> academic education in the French universities. (Kearney, 1984, p. 107)

The subaltern and supplementary god of writing and supplementarity
is an Egyptian god (*D* pp. 96–107). Thot supplies and supplants,
repeats and contests the sun-god, Rê or Amon or Osiris. Thot is the
ungraspable god of death, of calculation, of ruse, of history, of the
plurality of languages, of the game, with no fixed character or place, a
principle of mobility and (therefore) of subversion in the pantheon of
the gods, a mediator who merely simulates mediation, unreliably, with
no eschatological resolution as the horizon of his manoeuvres.

> Jewish consciousness is unhappy consciousness and *The Book of*
> *Questions* is its poem; inscribed in the margin of the phenomenology of spirit
> along with which the Jew wants to go only a little way, without eschatological
> provision, so as not to limit his desert, close his book and scar over his cry.
> (*ED*, p. 104)

It is true that I interrogate the idea of an *eschaton* or *telos* in the absolute formulations of classical philosophy. But that does not mean I dismiss all forms of Messianic or prophetic eschatology. I think all genuine questioning is summoned by a certain type of eschatology, though it is impossible to define this eschatology in philosophical terms. (Kearney, 1984, p. 119)

Freud, hesitant and a little embarrassed, wants to suggest that Moses was perhaps an Egyptian. First of all, the name 'Moses' looks like an

There is a well-known comic anecdote according to which an intelligent Jewish boy was asked who the mother of Moses was. He replied without hesitation: 'The Princess.' 'No', he was told, 'she only took him out of the water.' 'That's what *she* says', he replied, and so proved that he had found the correct interpretation of the myth. (Freud 1, p. 195)

Egyptian name, a suffix meaning a child, usually attached to the name of the god who gave the child. Among Freud's examples are 'Amen-mose' and 'Thoth-mose' (Freud 13, pp. 244-5), and later he suggests 'Tuthmosis' may have been the name (Freud 13, p. 301). One of the reasons for Freud's hesitation is the fear of being 'classed with the school men and Talmudists who delight in exhibiting their ingenuity without regard to how remote from reality their thesis may be' (Freud 13, p. 254). And how are we to reconcile the rigid monotheism of Mosaic religion with the distressing plurality and confusion of the Egyptian gods, all identified with each other (thus Amen and Rê, gods

You pray to a local and obscure idol: our temples, majestic and mysterious, are the abodes of Isis and Osiris, or Horus and Ammon Ra. Yours serfdom, awe and humbleness: ours thunder and the seas. Israel is weak and few are her children: Egypt is an host and terrible are her arms. Vagrants and daylabourers are you called: the world trembles at our name.

of Thebes and Heliopolis) in a mass from which only Osiris emerges, himself sun-god for Derrida, god of death for Freud? (Freud 13, p. 256).

Osiris, killed in a plot with the participation of Thoth – who later changes sides, supports Osiris – and whose wife, Isis, finds all the pieces of his dismembered body except the penis (*D*, p. 102; *TA*, pp. 43–57). Isis is the veiled goddess, Nature, the figure of the enigma for Hegel, who goes with a mysterious inscription, and a sun: 'the fruit of my flesh is Helios' (*GL* p. 357a), and is, too, in Kant's pamphlet against the mystagogues, the figure of their relation with the wisdom they claim to sense but cannot show (*TA*, p. 44ff). Elsewhere, Kant says that the inscription on the temple of Isis ('I am all that is, has been and will be, and no mortal has lifted my veil', quoted by Hegel as symbol of the enigma, as the being-enigma of the enigma (*GL*, p. 357a)) is

perhaps the most sublime (*EC*, p. 73). But there is a risk of emascula-
tion, of a castration of reason by the mystagogues, partisans of the veil
that can above all not be lifted.

> God of the sun: god of death. The sun is death, however, insofar as looking
> directly at it brings mortal blindness: cf. especially *D*, pp. 93–4, 192; *M*,
> p. 289. Life as the economy of death begins in the turning away from this
> blinding presence.
>
>> But it is precisely the *sight* of the chieftain that is dangerous and
>> unbearable for primitive people, just as later that of the Godhead is
>> for mortals. Even Moses had to act as an intermediary between his
>> people and Jehovah, since the people could not support the sight
>> of God; and when he returned from the presence of God his face
>> shone . . . (Freud 12, p. 158).
>
> Exodus, XXXIV, 30: 'And when Aaron and all the children of Israel saw
> Moses, behold, the skin of his face shone; and they were afraid to come
> nigh him'. A different interpretation of this passage has Moses not shining,
> but wearing a bull's mask, with horns,[8] whence the iconographical tradition
> of the horned Moses, as in Michelangelo's statue.
>
>> He spoke on the law of evidence . . . of Roman justice as
>> contrasted with the earlier Mosaic code, the *lex talionis*. And he
>> cited the Moses of Michelangelo in the Vatican . . .
>>   He said of it: *that stony effigy in frozen music, horned and
>> terrible, of the human form divine, that eternal symbol of wisdom
>> and prophecy which if aught that the imagination or the hand of
>> sculptor has wrought in marble of soultransfigured and
>> soultransfiguring deserves to live, deserves to live.* (Joyce, 1960,
>> pp. 140–1)
>
> Frozen music. Schönberg in 1933: 'My Moses is like Michelangelo's, if only
> in appearance. He is not at all human' (Wörner, 1963, p. 42).

We know the story. There was a monotheistic religion among the
Egyptians, under Akhenaten, a religion of the sun or the sun-god,
based in On, 'Heliopolis, city of the sun, to which Plato made a trip,
perhaps (*D*, pp. 96–7n12)), and in emulation of which the priests of
Hermopolis, city of the secret, of Hermes (who is not other than
Thoth), invented a cosmogony in which Thoth played the leading part
(cf. *D*, pp. 102–3n26 for the possible relations with the Greek *logos*, and
the *Sophia* of the Alexandrian Jews). The religion of Aten, new sun-
god, persecutes that of Amun, old sun-god in the polytheistic pantheon, and forbids any representation of the god other than that of the
sun. Moses preserved the cult by leaving Egypt on Akhenaten's death
and the persecution of his religion, having made his followers adopt
the Egyptian custom of circumcision. Circumcision, Freud says later,
'has repeatedly been of help to us , like, as it were, a key-fossil' (Freud

'the conclusion of my study, which was directed to the single aim of introducing the figure of an Egyptian Moses into the nexus of Jewish history.' (Freud 13, 293) Like a circumcisor's knife. 'If all poets are Jews, they, the poets, are all circumcised or circumcisors,' (*SCH*, p. 100)

13, p. 279. Later, the religion of YHWE is founded by *another* Moses, and picks up the Egyptian part of the story, including circumcision.

> The text however, as we possess it today, will tell us enough about its own vicissitudes. Two mutually opposed treatments have left their traces on it. On the one hand it has been subjected to revisions which have falsified it in the sense of their secret aims, have mutilated and amplified it and have even changed it into its reverse; on the other hand a solicitous piety has presided over it and has sought to preserve everything as it was, no matter whether it was consistent or contradicted itself. Thus almost everywhere noticeable gaps, disturbing repetitions and obvious contradictions have come about – indications which reveal things to us which it was not intended to communicate. In its implications the distortion of a text resembles a murder: the difficulty is not in perpetrating the deed, but in getting rid of its traces . . . I am aware that a method of exposition such as this is no less inexpedient than it is unartistic. I myself deplore it unreservedly. Why have I not avoided it? The answer to that is not hard for me to find, but it is not easy to confess. I found myself unable to wipe out the traces of the history of the work's origin, which was in any case unusual . . . I determined to give it up; but it tormented me like an unlaid ghost. (Freud 13, 283, 349)

Cut circumcision from its Egyptian origins – which will return to haunt us – by claiming that YHWE had already introduced it with Abraham. But this is a 'clumsy invention' says Freud, for then a Jew transported into Egypt would have had to recognize all Egyptians as his brothers in the covenant, and it is precisely this that was to be avoided (Freud 13, p. 285).

> In the *Timaeus*, the old Egyptian priest taught Solon that they, the Greeks, resort to myth only because they have no writing to preserve the memory of the city through its recurrent catastrophes. But the Egyptians have guarded that memory in the hypomnemic form denounced in the *Phaedrus* (CH, pp. 283–4). 'The people who had come from Egypt had brought writing and the desire to write history along with them; but it was to be a long time before historical writing realized that it was pledged to unswerving truthfulness. To begin with it had no scruples about shaping its narratives according to the needs and purposes of the moment, as though it had not yet recognized the concept of falsification. As a result of these circumstances a discrepancy was to grow up between the written record and the oral transmission of the same material – *tradition*. What had been omitted or changed in the historical record might very well have been preserved intact in tradition. Tradition was a supplement but at the same time a contradiction to historical writing. (Freud 13, pp. 310–11)

YHWE, volcano-god: 'an uncanny, bloodthirsty demon who went about by night and shunned the light of day' (Freud 13, p. 273). 'Coarse, narrow-minded . . . violent and bloodthirsty' (Freud 13, pp. 290).

Moses, murdered by 'his' people, the fate of all legislators. Biblical style from Freud, explaining the inexplicable (cf. *PRE*, p. 116): 'There came a time when people began to regret the murder of Moses and to seek to forget it' (Freud 13, 288–9). Strange link: in regretting one cannot forget, in trying to forget one never stops remembering. Killing keeps alive the better. Incorporation according to Abraham and Torok, who also treat the organism as a hieroglyphic text, part of what Derrida calls a 'general hieroglyphics' (*F*, pp. 38–9; 58–9).

> A suspicion even arises that the Israelites of that earliest period – that is to say, the scribes of Moses – may have had some share in the invention of the first alphabet. [Note: If they were subject to the prohibition against pictures they would even have had a motive for abandoning the hieroglyphic picture-writing while adapting its written characters to expressing a new language] (Freud 13, p. 283).

Jean-Jacques Rousseau, trying to theorize the most Greek of Greek

> The only reason for doubting that [Plato's] *Republic* was based on Egypt is the fact that he does not say so in the text. This omission, however, has an ancient explanation. As his earliest commentator, Krantor, wrote within a few generations of Plato:
>
>> Plato's contemporaries mocked him, saying that he was not the inventor of his republic, but that he had copied Egyptian institutions. He attached so much importance to the mockers that he attributed to the Egyptians the story of the Athenians and the Atlantines to make them say that the Athenians had really lived under this regime at a certain moment in the past.
>
> . . . Thus, for Plato, if one wanted to return to the ancient Athenian institutions, one had to turn to Egypt. In this way he resembled Isokrates, who both called for a Panhellenic combination of Athens and Sparta and extolled the Egyptian constitution that was a purer version of the Lakedaimonian one. *The deeper they went towards the true Hellenic roots of Greece, the closer they came to Egypt.* One reason for this was that both Isokrates and Plato maintained that the great lawgivers and philosophers like Lykourgos, Solon and Pythagoras had all brought back Egyptian knowledge. (Bernal, 1987, pp. 106–8)

states as absolute autonomy, ends up reduced to bringing in a legislator to make his state whole and repair its necessarily flawed sovereignty. The law was to be generated by the purely immanent reflection of the general will upon itself: but this can never quite be achieved. The citizen was to give himself the law (and thus, in Hegelian terms, become properly human: cf. *GL*, p. 40a). Enter the legislator, essentially a foreigner (for if the law did not come from elsewhere, then it could indeed be generated autonomously, but the legislator is made necessary only by the failure of any such generation). As the legislator is a necessary moment of the foundation of any state whatsoever, and as this must therefore be true of *the first state* too, then the legislator is in essence not so much an empirical foreigner as a figure of absolute exteriority: the state constitutes its 'inside' only by bringing into its centre this element of an absolute outside, which it will never quite manage to absorb – this (empty) central exteriority is the (place of the) law. The legislator speaks a language incomprehensible to those for whom he legislates: only his law will make the people capable of

> Moses is said to have been 'slow of speech': he must have suffered from an inhibition or disorder of speech. Consequently, in his supposed dealings with Pharaoh, he needed the support of Aaron, who is called his brother. This again may be a historical truth and would make a welcome contribution to presenting a lively picture of the great man. But it may also have another and more important significance. It may recall slightly distorted, the fact that Moses spoke another language . . . (Freud 13, p. 272)

understanding his law. In the absence of understanding, the legislator must act violently, illegally, to get the law accepted: he pretends it was given by God. In the absence of understanding, the people cannot

> What must be received to make free choice possible cannot have been chosen, except after the event. In the beginning was violence. (Levinas, 1968, p. 82)

know that this is the legislator and not a charlatan – what indubitable signs could there be of a real legislator? 'The great soul of the Legislator is the true miracle which must prove his mission' (*Social Contract*, Book II, Chapter VII). But Rousseau knows very well that there are no indubitable signs, that nothing can prove a miracle to be a miracle, that in the moment of his coming, the legislator always might be a charlatan, and may well now know himself which he is. Rousseau offers a second criterion which can no longer help the people faced

> Discussing religious doctrine in the *Lettres écrites de la montagne*, Rousseau argues as follows, in a way which is strictly applicable to the situation of the legislator: God has distinguished his envoys with a number of signs which make them recognizable for what they are to all; these signs are 1) the nature of the doctrine they profess – this is the surest sign, but accessible to very few people (and has been ruled out in the case of the legislator in advance – we have seen that the people cannot understand the law when it is given); 2) the character of the envoy himself: 'This is the sign which strikes above all good and righteous people who see truth everywhere they see justice, and hear the voice of God only in the mouth of virtue. This characteristic still has its truth, but it is not impossible for it to mislead, and there is nothing prodigious about an impostor tricking good people, nor about a good man tricking himself, led on by the ardour of a saintly zeal that he takes for inspiration'; 3) The production of miracles. But miracles cannot be essential, for a) until we know all the laws of nature, we cannot be certain that a given phenomenon breaks them miraculously; b) even if there are real

miracles, it is impossible to distinguish them with certainty from false or
merely apparent miracles: 'When Aaron cast his rod before Pharaoh it was

> Aaron: In Moses' hand a rigid rod: this, the law.
> In my own hand the most supple of serpents: discretion
> *Klugheit*; prudence'. (*Moses and Aaron*, Act 1, Scene 4;
> Wörner, 1963, p. 141)

changed into a snake, the magicians cast their rods too and they were
changed into snakes. It does not matter whether this change was real in
both cases, as Scripture says, or whether only Aaron's miracle was real and
the magician's trick [*prestige*] was merely apparent, as some Theologians
claim; this appearance was exactly the same . . . Now men can only judge
miracles through their senses, and if the sensation is the same, the real
difference, which they cannot perceive, is nothing to them. Thus the sign,
qua sign, proves no more on one side than on the other, and in this the
Prophet has no advantage over the magician. . . . When Moses changed
water to blood, the Magicians changed water to blood; when Moses
produced frogs, the Magicians produced frogs. They failed with the third
plague; but let us stay with the first two which God himself had made proof
of divine power. The Magicians also produced that proof.

As for the third plague that they were unable to imitate, it is hard to see
what made it so difficult, to the point of marking *that the finger of God was
there*. Why could they who could produce an animal not produce an insect,
and how could they not produce lice, having produced frogs? . . . The same
Moses, instructed by all these experiences, orders that if a false Prophet
comes to announce other Gods, that is a false doctrine, and if this false
prophet authorises what he says by predictions or successful wonders, one
must not listen to him but put him to death. So true signs can be used to
support a false doctrine; a sign in itself proves nothing. (Rousseau III,
pp. 745–6)

with a possible legislator: after the event (for this is an event), we can
know from the longevity of the legislator's institution whether or not
he was a real legislator or only a charlatan:

> Any man can engrave tablets of stone, or buy an oracle, or feign a secret
> commerce with some divinity, or train a bird to speak in his ear, or find
> other crude means of tricking the people. He who knows only that much
> might even gather by chance a troop of lunatics, but he will never found an
> empire, and his extravagant work will soon perish with him. Vain wonders
> [*prestiges*] form a transient bond, but only wisdom makes it durable. Judaic
> law which still subsists, the law of the son of Ismael which for ten centuries
> has ruled half the world, still today announce the great men who dictated
> them; and while proud philosophy or blind partisan spirit sees in them only
> happy impostors, the true politician admires in their institutions that great
> and powerful genius which presides over durable institutions.
>
> We must not conclude from all this with Warburton that politics and
> religion have for us a common object . . . (Rousseau III, p. 384)

(This is of course the same Warburton whose writing on hieroglyphs
and dream-interpretation is the subject of Derrida's 'Scribble', and an

extended discussion in 'Freud et la scène de l'ériture': Freud introduces Warburton in connection with the second of two popular
methods of dream-interpretation he is rejecting before presenting his
own sample analysis – the first of these methods, that of 'symbolic'
interpretation, is illustrated by Freud (Derrida does not mention this)
with the example of Joseph interpreting Pharaoh's dream (Freud 4,
p. 170): it is of course the success of Joseph's interpretation which
leads eventually to the prosperous establishment of the Jews in Egypt
prior to their oppression, and liberation by Moses.)

> In opening remarks to Rousseau's *Considérations sur le gouvernement de
> Pologne* (III, 956–7) Moses is the first named of three figures described by
> Rousseau as the three principal legislators of the ancient world (the other
> two being Lycurgus and Numa Pompilius). In a fragment which Rousseau's
> editors entitle 'Des Juifs', Moses appears dominant: 'The Jews give us this
>
>> The Jews in the wilderness and on the mountaintop said: *It is meet to be
>> here. Let us build an altar to Jehovah.* The Roman, like the Englishman
>> who follows in his footsteps, brought to every new shore on which he
>> sets his foot (on our shore he never set it) only his cloacal obsession. He
>> gazed about him in his toga and said: *It is meet to be here. Let us
>> construct a water-closet.* [. . .]
>>
>> Moses, Moses, king of the jews,
>> Wiped his arse in the Daily News
>> (Joyce, 1960, pp. 132, 443)
>
> astonishing spectacle: the laws of Solon, Numa, Lycurgus are dead, those
> of Moses which are much older live on still. Athens, Sparta and Rome have
> perished and have left no more children on the earth. Sion destroyed has
> not lost its children; they are preserved, they multiply, they spread
> throughout the world and always recognize each other, they mix with all
> peoples and never become part of them; they no longer have leaders and
> are still a people, they have no land and yet are still citizens.' (Rousseau III,
> p. 499) But this is further complicated in another very ambivalent fragment,
> which reads as follows in its entirety:
> 'What are you doing among us, O Hebrew, I see you here with pleasure;
> but how can you find pleasure here, you who despised us so strongly, why
> did you not remain among your people.
> You are mistaken I come among my own. I have lived alone on earth,
> among a numerous people I was alone. Lycurgus, Solon and Numa are my
> brothers. I have come to rejoin my family. I have come at last to taste the
> sweetness of conversing with my kind, of speaking and being heard. It is
> among you illustrious souls, that I have come at last to enjoy myself [*jouir de
> moi*].
> You have changed greatly in tone, in feelings and ideas . . . '. [crossed out
> words in the manuscript suggest a 'dialogue des morts' scenario for this
> dialogue with the 'Hebrew', presumably Moses, arriving no doubt in the
> Underworld].
> Hegel: in its letter, Mosaic law looks very like the laws of Solon and
> Lycurgus – but its spirit is different: or rather, it has no spirit (*GL*, p. 74a).

But we know from elsewhere in Rousseau that the duration of a political institution is not in fact indubitable proof of its quality (just as any sign of the genuineness of the legislator is necessarily open to the possibility of counterfeiting, so a durable state may always be a mere

> The rabbis whose words you quote are charlatans. (Jabès, quoted *ED*, p. 112)

simulacrum of a good one). Legislator and charlatan thus remain radically undecidable: it is in fact perfectly in the logic of Rousseau's argument to say that Moses might still (have) turn(ed) out to be a charlatan after all. Hegel: the Jew cannot become a citizen, cannot have true State laws (*GL*, p. 72aff); Hegel again: Thoth is reputed to be the first legislator (*M*, p. 117).

This situation is generalizable: not only can the logic of the legislator

> The philosopher is not an artificer in the field or reason, but himself the lawgiver of human reason. (Kant, *Critique of Pure Reason*, A839; B867)

> The legislator is a writer. (*D*, p. 129)

be extended to that of Jean-Jacques Rousseau,[9] but to writing and thinking in general. Any event of thought, in so far as it is an event and not simply a programmed repetition, involves this undecidability and temporal *après-coup*, and the incidence of absolute exteriority I have here described with the help of Rousseau's political thinking.[10] A traditional description would no doubt call this event something like 'inspiration', or communication from the muse, and link it to poetry. But nothing in the description we have given can justify any such simple regionalization. For Derrida, this is philosophy:

> With this distinction between the empirical and the essential, a limit is blurred, that of the philosophical as such, the philosophical distinction. Philosophy then finds itself, *finds itself again [se trouve, se retrouve]* in the *parages* of the poetic, or even of literature. It finds itself again for the indecision of this limit is perhaps what most provokes it to thought. It finds itself again, it does not necessarily lose itself as is thought by those who, in their tranquil credulity, believe they know where this limit passes and hold themselves on it fearfully, ingenuously (though not innocently), devoid of what one must call *philosophical experience*: a certain questioning crossing of limits, insecurity as to the frontier of the philosophical field – and especially the *experience of language*, always as poetic or literary as philosophical . . . (*SCH*, p. 80)

Transfer this set-up to the domain of academic discipline, and it is no surprise that Martin Bernal, for example, arguing against what he sees as the systematic repression of the Afroasiatic and more especially Egyptian roots of Ancient Greece, finds himself in the situation of the legislator, coming from outside and potentially condemned to expulsion. Fundamentally new approaches tend to come from outside, says Bernal, acutely aware that this privilege brings with its the equally fundamental uncertainty as to whether the outsider isn't just a 'crank'. Academics, says Bernal, academically nervous of his own 'amateur' status, quite typically accept that their discipline was founded by amateurs (as it necessarily must have been, insofar as what counts as a 'professional' in this sense can be determined only after that foundation, which is constitutively illegitimate), but reject any new input from the amateurish outside, just as Moses, once accepted as legislator, orders the putting to death of any new aspirant arrivals. Founders of discourse, as Foucault would call them (imprudently making of them a modern phenomenon, but giving Freud as a major example), are always as Moses, or Thoth, *before* Pharaoh. Israel in Egypt, Egypt in Israel. 'It is honour enough to the Jewish people that they could preserve such a tradition and produce men who gave it a voice – even though the initiative to it came from outside, from a great foreigner. . . . Unluckily an author's creative power does not always obey his will: the work proceeds as it can, and often presents itself to the author as something independent and even alien' (Freud 13, pp. 292; 350).

> And yet [Freud] was also Moses, giving the law of psychoanalysis, restraining his wrath in the face of the unbelievers who attacked him from all spheres of the Gentile academic society to which he so desperately desired to belong. (Handelman, 1982, p. 133)

> In the centre, Moses, the Jew, dispossessed of his identity, barred, castrated, become Egyptian again, oscillating between the all-power of the legislator and the fault or parapraxis of a man who lets drop the tables of the law . . . If one turns the pages of *Moses* . . . , one can read between the lines the epic of a legendary city whose Nile is called Danube and whose Egyptian hero is a Moravian Jew. (Roudinesco, 1986, I, pp. 88, 100)

> We are certainly getting ahead; if I am Moses, then you are Joshua and will take possession of the promised land of psychiatry, which I shall only be able to glimpse from afar . . . (Freud to Jung, 17 January 1909)

Freud too, naturally, is Moses, Mosaic, capital M, from Moses: small m, from Greek *mousa*, Muse.

> To my critical sense this book, which takes its start from the man Moses, appears like a dancer balancing on the tip of one toe. If I could not find support in an analytic interpretation of the exposure myth and could not pass from there to Sellin's suspicion about the end of Moses, the whole thing would have had to remain unwritten. In any case, let us now take the plunge. (Freud 13, p. 299)

As pirouette, the dance of the hieroglyph cannot fully be played out inside. Not only because of the 'real space, or the stage', not only because of the point which pierces the book's page or image, but above all because of a certain lateral displacement: turning incessantly on its point, the hieroglyph, the sign, the cipher leaves its here, as though mocking, always here in passing from here to there, from one here to another, inscribing in the *stigmé* of its here the *other* point towards which it continuously moves, the other pirouette which, in each volt, in the flight of each tissue, instantaneously remarks itself. Each pirouette is, then, in its turning, only the mark of another pirouette, entirely other and the same. (*D*, pp. 271–2)

But, ladies and gentlemen, had the youthful Moses listened to and accepted that view of life, had he bowed his head and bowed his will and bowed his spirit before that arrogant admonition he would never have brought the chosen people out of their house of bondage nor followed the pillar of cloud by day. He would never have spoken with the Eternal amid lightnings on Sinai's mountaintop nor ever have come down with the light of inspiration shining in his countenance and bearing in his arms the tables of the law, graven in the language of the outlaw.

Suppose I give this explanation: 'I take "Moses" to mean the man, if there was such a man, who led the Israelites out of Egypt, whatever he was called then and whatever he may or may not have done besides.' – But similar doubts to those about 'Moses' are possible about the words of this explanation (what are you calling 'Egypt', whom the 'Israelites' etc.?).
   The sign-post is in order – if, under normal circumstances, it fulfils its purpose. (Wittgenstein, §87)

That is oratory, the professor said, uncontradicted.

Notes

References in the text are to the following:

Martin, Bernal *Black Athena: the Afroasiatic Roots of Classical Civilisation*, London: Free Association Books 1987.

Robert Bernasconi and David Wood, eds, *Derrida and Différance*, Warwick: Parousia Press 1985.

Derrida, Jacques,

   (A) *Altérités* (with Pierre-Jean Labarrière), Paris: Osiris 1986.

   (*CH*) 'Chora', in *Poïkilia: études offertes a Jean-Pierre Vernant*, Paris: EHESS 1987.

   (*CP*) *La carte postale de Socrate à Freud et au-delà*, Paris: Aubier-Flammarion 1980.

   (*D*) *La Dissémination*, Paris: Seuil 1972.

   (*EC*) 'Economimesis', in *Mimesis des articulations*, Paris: Aubier-Flammarion 1975.

   (*ED*) *L'Ecriture et la différence*, Paris: Seuil 1967.

   (*EP*) *Eperons: les styles de Nietzsche*, Paris: Flammarion 1978.

(*F*) 'Fors: les mots anglés de Nicolas Abraham et Maria Torok'. Foreword to Nicolas Abraham and Maria Torok, *Cryptonomie: le verbier de l'homme aux loups*, Paris: Aubier-Flammarion 1976.

(*GL*) *Glas*, Paris: Galilée 1974.

(*GR*) *De la grammatologie*, Paris: Minuit 1967.

(*M*) *Marges de la philosophie*, Paris: Minuit 1972.

(*POS*) *Positions*, Paris: Minuit 1972.

(*PRE*) 'Préjugés: devant la loi', in Lyotard et al., *La Faculté de juger*, Paris: Minuit 1985.

(*PS*) *Psyché: inventions de l'autre*, Paris: Galilée 1987.

(*SCH*) *Schibboleth: pour Paul Celan*, Paris: Galilée 1986.

(*SCR*) 'Scribble'. *Préface à l'Essai sur les hiéroglyphes de Warburton*, Paris: Aubier-Flammarion 1978.

(*TA*) *D'un ton apocalyptique adopté naguère en philosophie*, Paris: Galilée 1983.

(*UG*) *Ulysse gramophone*, Paris: Galilée 1987.

(*VEP*) *La Vérité en peinture*, Paris: Flammarion 1978.

(*VP*) *La Voix et le phénomène*, Paris: PUF 1967.

Sigmund Freud *The Pelican Freud Library*, vols 1, 4, 12, 13, 14.

The Freud-Jung Correspondence, London: Picador, 1979.

Susan Handelman, 'Reb Derrida's Scripture', in *The Slayers of Moses*, Albany: State University of New York Press 1982.

James Joyce, *Ulysses*, Harmondsworth: Penguin 1960.

Richard Kearney, *Dialogues with Contemporary Continental Thinkers*, Manchester: Manchester University Press 1984.

Emmanuel Levinas, *Quatre lectures talmudiques*, Paris: Minuit 1968.

Elisabeth Roudinesco, *La Bataille de cent ans: histoire de la psychanalyse en France*, Vol. 2, Paris: Seuil 1986.

Jean-Jacques Rousseau, *Oeuvres complètes*, ed. Gagnebin and Raymond, 4 vols to date, Paris: Gallimard, 1959 –.

Ludwig Wittgenstein, *Philosophical Investigations*, Oxford: Blackwell 1953.

Karl Wörner, *Schönberg's 'Moses and Aaron'*, London: Faber 1963.

1. Referring to 'La Pharmacie de Platon', *D*, pp. 17–197; the opening of 'La Double Séance', ibid., pp. 201–318; *CH*; 'Le puits et la pyramide', *M*, pp. 81–127; the left-hand column of *Glas*; 'Freud et la scène de l'écriture', *ED*, pp. 293–340; 'Scribble (pouvoir-écrire)', introduction to Patrick Tort, ed. William Warburton, *Essai sur les hiéroglyphes*, Paris: Aubier-Flammarion 1977, pp. 7–43.

2. This view is to be found in whole or in part in quite disparate places: see, for example, Vincent Descombes, *Le Même et l'autre: quarante-cinq ans de philosophie française (1933–1978)*, Paris: Minuit 1979; and *Grammaire d'objets en tous genres*, Paris: Minuit 1983; Jean-François Lyotard, *Economie libidinale*, Paris: Minuit 1974, pp. 12 and 305; some of this attitude to deconstruction is still in evidence in Lyotard's *Heidegger et 'les juifs'* Paris: Galilée 1988, pp. 119, 122–3.

3. The term is most consistently and fruitfully exploited by Gasché, and although Derrida had used the term intermittently before the publication of Gasché's book, he appears to have used it more regularly since. See, for example, *CP*, p. 430; *GL*, p. 227a; *PS*, pp. 220, 593, 641–2; *UG*, pp. 116, 141; cf. the use of 'similitranscendental' in *GL*, p. 340a. Cf. my discussion of this and other terms in Gasché in 'Deconstruction and the Philosophers (The Very Idea)', Chapter 1 above.

4. See, for example, Susan Handelman, *The Slayers of Moses: the Emergence of Rabbinic*

Interpretation in Modern Literary Theory, Albany: State University of New York Press 1982. Despite the considerable interest of Handelman's book, her readings of Derrida, which have him 'gleefully proclaiming a new liberation', and generally advocating 'freeplay', are seriously insufficient.

5. I am grateful to Diane Morgan for drawing this reference to my attention.

6. This aspect of the problem is brought out most clearly by Lyotard, in *Heidegger et 'les 'les juifs'*, Paris: Galilée 1988, especially pp. 119ff, and, for the supposed 'missing' of the essential character of Jewish thinking by Heidegger, 'Le temps aujourd'hui', in *L'Inhumain*, Paris: Galilée 1988, pp. 69–88 (p. 88); ['Time today', translated by Geoffrey Bennington and Rachel Bowlby, *Oxford Literary Review*, 11 (1989), 3–20].

7. Add Egypt to the list of 'things' evading the question 'What is . . . ?' in Derrida: see, for example, *D*, pp. 169, 203, 253; *EP*, pp. 57, 92; *GL*, p. 47a; *GR*, pp. 31, 110; *SCH*, p. 30; *UG*, p. 122; *VEP*, p. 24; *VP*, p. 26.

8. Cf. J.R. Porter, *Moses and Monarchy: a Study in the Biblical tradition of Moses*, Oxford: Blackwell 1963, p. 20.

9. For a more detailed account of the legislator in Rousseau, see my *Sententiousness and the Novel: Laying Down the Law in Eighteenth-century French Fiction*, Cambridge: Cambridge University Press 1985, pp. 166–71. For the generalization of this argument, see my *Dudding: des noms de Rousseau*, Paris: Galilée 1991.

10. In some work in progress, I try to derive a similar description from Kant's political writings, in preparation for an analogical transfer of this structure to Kant's philosophy as a whole. On this reading, exorbitant absolute exteriority just is Reason.

PART III

Openings

12

Towards a Criticism of the Future

Discussing Saussure in *Of Grammatology*, Derrida suggests that, in the former's doctrine, the relation of *parole* to *langue* is one of a fundamental passivity.

> but in a sense of passivity that all intramundane metaphors could only betray. This passivity is also the relationship to a past, to an always-already-there that no reactivation of the origin could fully master and awaken to presence. This impossibility of absolutely reanimating the manifest evidence of an orginary presence therefore sends us back to an absolute past. This is what has authorised us to call *trace* what does not allow itself to be resumed in the simplicity of a present.[1]

This insistence on a past which was never present is, I take it, one of the more familiar, if still enigmatic, aspects of Derrida's work. The passage I am quoting continues by taking into account a possible objection:

> Now it could indeed have been objected that in the indecomposable synthesis of temporalisation, protention is as indispensable as retention. And their two dimensions are not added to each other but imply each other in strange fashion. What is anticipated in protention disjoins the present from its identity to itself no less than what is retained in the trace. [The force of this possible objection is then recognized, and partially neutralized.] Certainly. But giving the privilege to anticipation would run the risk of erasing the irreducibility of the always-already-there and the fundamental passivity called time. Further, if the trace refers to an absolute past, then it obliges us to think a past which can no longer be understood in the form of modified presence, as a past-present. And as past has always signified past-present, the absolute past which is retained in the trace no longer rigorously deserves the name 'past'. Another name to place under erasure, [and now an apparently new concession to the objection dealt with above] all the more so as the strange movement of the trace announces as much as it recalls: *différance* defers. With the same precaution and under the same erasure, one can say that its passivity is also its relation to the 'future'. [And now the

229

> generalizing moment familiar from other deconstructive arguments.] The
> concepts of *present, past* and *future*, everything which in the concepts of time
> and history presupposes their classical self-evidence (i.e. the metaphysical
> concept of time in general) cannot adequately describe the structure of the
> trace. [Final caveat] And to deconstruct the simplicity of the present does
> not only come down to taking account of horizons of potential presence . . .
> (p. 97 [66–7; tr. mod.])

Derrida's complicated stress in this passage on the 'absolute past' is no
doubt necessary: there is an obviousness about the link of writing to
the future (one writes when the absence of the addressee makes
speaking impracticable, but in view of a future presence of that
addressee) which would tend to block recognition of the radicality of
the trace. But the concession to the argument around protention
seems to encourage *some* investigation of 'writing the future', while
discouraging at least one temptation of how to do so: and that is quite
simply the temptation of prediction, which precisely involves positing
'horizons of potential presence'. Or perhaps, paradoxically, it encourages the prediction that a criticism of the future will not be able to
follow the advocates of reception theory, which is also to do with such
horizons. So perhaps, for Derrida, writing the future is just a waste of
time? Although I shall not here attempt to follow Derrida's discussion
of the future through his writing, it is clear that the passage I have
quoted is not (for good reasons) his last word: from the stress on the
necessary possibility of writing-as-death in *Speech and Phenomena*,
through the necessary possibility of a letter's not arriving at its destination in the disagreement with Lacan, via analysis of 'An Apocalyptic
Tone Recently Adopted in Philosophy', to the very recent discussion of
the question of dates in relation to the poetry of Paul Celan,[2] Derrida
has in fact constantly been writing (about) the future, *without making any
predictions*. What I shall be attempting to do here is no more than an
elaboration of that structure.

So although I shall talk about the future of writing in a sense, and of
the future of criticism in a sense, this will not be a prediction, and still
less an exercise in futurology: for whereas a prediction is a statement
(sometimes a narrative) which happens before the referent or reference it positions, all my references will be of the past, without being
historical in any simple or strict way.

The first of these references will be Kant's *Prolegomena to any Future
Metaphysics that will be able to come forward as Science*,[3] which condenses
many of our problems in its very title. The *pro*-in 'prolegomena'
already anticipates the future appearance of the word 'future' later in
the title, and its referent – the metaphysics yet to come which will
relegate these prolegomena to the past. This aggressive double future

in the title is taken up and complicated in the work's preface, itself a sort of prolegomenon to these prolegomena. (I shall not here repeat Derrida's analysis of the preface in *La Dissémination*.) The Preface in fact repeats with respect to the body of the text of the *Prolegomena* the gesture of that text as a whole with respect to the Metaphysics to come. The *Prolegomena* do not, and cannot, expound such a metaphysics for, Kant says, 'there is, as yet, no such thing as metaphysics' (p. 2): the prolegomena, in the future projected for them by the preface, will themselves project only the future discovery of such a metaphysics.

This already complex relation to the future (of preface to text, of text to metaphysics) is written by Kant against a different kind of relation to the future: and this polemical relation is presented in terms of the addressee of the text. (And clearly writing the future has to do with the question of the addressee, even if, as I have suggested, reception aesthetics are in principle unable to deal with that question.) The first paragraph of the preface states clearly enough to whom the body of the text will *not* be addressed:

> These *Prolegomena* are not for the use of pupils but of future teachers, and even the latter should not expect that they will be serviceable for the systematic exposition of a ready-made science, but merely for the discovery of the science itself. (p. 1)

But the second paragraph adds a further exclusion to this (and points up the complex relation of Preface to future: the Preface is, perhaps like all prefaces, still addressed to readers who will be excluded from the body of the text): and this further exclusion is clearly vital:

> There are scholars for whom the history of philosophy (both ancient and modern) is philosophy itself; for these the present *Prolegomena* are not written. They must wait till those who endeavour to draw from the fountain of reason itself have completed their work; it will then be the turn of such scholars to inform the world of what has been done. Unfortunately, nothing can be said which, in their opinion, has not been said before, and truly the same prophecy applies to all future time; for since the human reason has for many centuries speculated upon innumerable objects in various ways, it is hardly to be expected that we should not be able to discover analogies for every new idea among the old sayings of past ages. (p. 1)

So, Kant will be writing for those (the future teachers) for whom there will be metaphysics, as against those for whom there has been or will (always) have been metaphysics: writing for what I venture to call the future proper as against the future perfect, at least in so far as the future perfect has always already been contained in the past. This type of attitude is, along with the tendency to appeal to 'common sense', a persistent object of Kant's sarcasm in this rather bad-tempered text – for example, noting (in the 'Preamble' to the *Prolegomena*, which follows the Preface, and continues to look forward) that a hint of the division of judgements into analytic and synthetic is to be found in Locke's *Essay Concerning Human Understanding*, Kant remarks:

> Such universal and yet determinate principles are not easily learned from other men who have only had them obscurely in their minds. One must hit on them first by one's own reflection; then one finds them elsewhere, where one could not possibly have found them at first because the authors themselves did not know that such an idea lay at the basis of their observations. Men who never think independently have nevertheless the acuteness to discover everything, after it has been once shown them, in what was said long since, though no one could ever see it there before. (p. 18)

Those who identify philosophy with the history of philosophy can happily foresee the future as a necessary repetition of the past: future perfect because *perfectum*, complete already, and therefore not future at all.

Against this gesture, according to which everything that will be said will already have been said, Kant will stress the future. And yet his scorn for the future perfect does not lead him to the notion that what I have called the future proper is radically open or unpredictable, still less to the notion (to which all I shall say will have been an approach, and which I imagine, as I write for *this* future, will be, or will have been, quoted more than once in this book) that, again in Derrida's *Grammatology*:

> The future can only be anticipated in the form of absolute danger. It is what breaks absolutely with constituted normality and can therefore only announce or *present* itself in the form of monstrosity. For this world to come and for what in it will have shaken the values of sign, speech and writing, for what here guides our future perfect, there is as yet no exergue. (p. 14 [5: tr. mod.])

Or, perhaps, no prolegomenon. It will be necessary to stress again that this is not a prediction on Derrida's part, despite the possible air of assurance over the future perfect, whereas Kant, *apparently* opening the future against what will have been, the future perfect, allows himself none the less at least *one* explicit prediction, which is again tied to the question of the addressee:

> Nevertheless, I venture to predict that the independent reader of these *Prolegomena* will not only doubt his previous science, but ultimately be fully

persuaded that it cannot exist unless the demands here stated on which its possibility depends be satisfied; and, as this has never been done, that there is, as yet, no such thing as metaphysics. But as it can never cease to be in demand – since the interests of human reason in general are intimately interwoven with it – he must confess that a radical reform, or rather a rebirth of the science according to a new plan, is unavoidable, however much men may struggle against it for a while. (pp. 2–3)

Kant's prediction of a rebirth, a new start, his desire, as he puts it early in the Preface, to pose the question of the possibility of metaphysics, 'disregarding all that has been done' (p. 1), can be linked to a temporal and historical configuration known as 'the Enlightenment', and to a certain transcendental optimism (or what Lyotard has called a 'Grand Narrative')[4] of progress. But the apparent simplicity of this positioning of the future is troubled and troubling. (The term 'rebirth' is already ambivalent.) For the resolute demand to disregard all that has been done excludes at least one thing that has been done, namely Kant's own *Critique of Pure Reason*, to which the *Prolegomena* is both a sequel and, ambiguously, an introduction and a defence. To condense the problem a little brutally, we can say that *precisely* because, in Kant's view, the *Critique* is so new, so utterly cut from the past, so difficult of access to the recuperative future perfect of historians of philosophy, Kant fears that it will have no future at all because it will be simply unreadable (as indeed it necessarily would be if it were *absolutely* new). Some of this anxiety (which is less a psychological state than a property of the structure of writing itself in the irreducible relation to the future which I shall have been attempting to sketch out) can be read in the 'Appendix' to the *Prolegomena*, where Kant writes:

I feel obliged to the learned public even for the silence with which it for a long time honoured my *Critique*, for this proves at least a postponement of judgement and some supposition that, in a work leaving all beaten tracks and striking out on a new path, in which one cannot at once perhaps so easily find one's way, something may perchance lie from which an important but at present dead branch of human knowledge may derive new life and productiveness. (p. 119)

But it is again in the Preface that the problem is formulated in its most acute form:

If in a new science that is wholly isolated and unique in its kind we started with the prejudice that we can judge of things by means of would-be knowledge previously acquired, even though this is precisely what has first to be called in question; then we should only fancy we saw everywhere what we had already known, because the expressions have a similar sound. Yet

everything would appear utterly metamorphosed, senseless, and unintelligible, because we should have as a foundation our own thoughts, made by
long habit a second nature, instead of the author's. However, the longwind-
edness of the work, so far as it depends on the science itself and not on the
exposition, its consequent unavoidable dryness, and its scholastic precision
are qualities which can only benefit the science, though they may discredit
the book. . . . I flatter myself that I might have made my own exposition
popular, if my object had been merely to sketch out a plan and leave its
completion to others, instead of having my heart in the welfare of the
science to which I devoted myself so long; in truth, it required no little
constancy, and even self-denial, to postpone the sweets of an immediate
success to the prospect of a slower, but more lasting reputation. (pp. 7–8)

This pathos, and the tension it introduces between a disinterested
'scientific' pursuit of truth in general, and a concern for 'reputation'
(which, following a familiar economic schema of deferral, is made in
principle the more secure by temporary renunciation) – a 'reputation'
by which what Kant called the 'independent' reader will be tied to a
recognition of the singularity of a signature, and therefore, in the
future, to an event in the past which is in principle to be forgotten –
this pathos and tension are not accidental intrusions into 'the Enlightenment's' relation to the future. This could be illustrated by a bizarre
text from the French *Encyclopédie*, perhaps the paradigm project of the
Enlightenment: in the article from the *Encyclopédie* called 'Encyclopédie', Diderot interrupts an exposition of the nature and pretensions
of the Encyclopedic project with the following projection:

We saw that the *Encyclopédie* could only be the undertaking of a philosophical century; that that century had arrived; that renown, bearing to immortality the names of those who carried out that undertaking would perhaps
not disdain to take charge of our own, and we felt revived by this idea, so
consoling and sweet, that people would talk about us too, when we were no
longer; by this murmur so voluptuous, which made us hear in the mouths
of some of our contemporaries what would be said of us by the men for
whose instruction and happiness we were sacrificing ourselves, and whom
we esteemed and loved, although they did not yet exist. We felt growing in
us that seed of emulation which envies death the best part of ourselves and
steals from the void the only moments of our existence which really flatter
us. Indeed, man shows himself to his contemporaries as he is, a bizarre
compound of sublime qualities and shameful weaknesses. But the weaknesses follow the mortal remains into the tomb and disappear with them;
the same earth covers them; all that remains are the qualities made eternal
in the monuments he has raised to himself, or that he owes to public
veneration and gratitude; honours which the sense of his own merit allows
him to enjoy in anticipation; an enjoyment [*jouissance*] as pure, as strong, as
real as any other enjoyment, and in which the only thing that can be

imaginary is the basis on which one's pretensions are founded. Ours are deposited in this work; posterity will judge them.[5]

But it is in Rousseau, who stands in an ambivalent (but thereby, I would argue, in some sense exemplary) relation to the philosophers of the *Encyclopédie* and to the Enlightenment in general, that I shall follow a little of this logic of writing and the future. Again for the sake of economy of presentation, I shall look at Rosseau's late *Dialogues*, otherwise known as 'Rousseau juge de Jean-Jacques', and more specifically the curious appendage of appendix to that text, the 'Histoire du précédent écrit', which recounts Rousseau's tragic or pathetic efforts to ensure the transmission of his manuscript to the future, in the face of what he is convinced is a universal plot devoted to preventing any such transmission.[6] These extremely unstable texts, which constraints of time will force me to treat with some violence, work in 'pre-', in 'pro-', and in 'post-'; the pre- of prediction, the pro- of providence, the post- of posterity. The question is whether posterity will ever know the truth about Jean-Jacques Rousseau, and whether Providence can be trusted to help in the delivery of the texts which will reveal that truth. In a first moment there is an aggressive confidence that this transmission will indeed take place and the truth come to light:

> Whatever they can do, his books transmitted to posterity will show that their Author was not as people are endeavouring to depict him, and his regulated simple uniform life, the same for so many years, will never agree with the terrible character they want to give him. This shady plot formed in such a deep secret, developed with such great precautions and followed with such zeal, will have the same fate as all the works of men's passions which are passing and perishable like them. A time will come in which the century in which J.J. lived will be held in the same horror as that century shows for him . . . [7]

But this confidence, expressed by the character in the dialogues called 'Rousseau', is soon undermined by the character called 'The Frenchman', who points out that there can be no grounds for assuming that truth always comes to light, in so far as there would be no way of knowing that a given 'fact' was in fact a lie if the alternative 'truth' happened to remain covered over. And any confidence placed in the survival of Rousseau's books simply fails to take into account the necessary possibility that they be more or less systematically disfigured and falsified, as they have been already.

Kant's scientific project allowed an apparently residual concern with name and reputation to emerge: in Rousseau, such a concern is primary, and the key to his so-called paranoia towards the end of his life. I should point out that Rousseau is one of relatively few French eighteenth-century authors systematically to sign his published work (though not, as Burt notes, his autobiographical texts, which were all published posthumously): this signature, of which Rousseau is proud, is supposed to signal an authenticity confirmed by the motto Rousseau adopted: *Vitam impendere vero*. The problems and paradoxes involved are condensed around Rousseau's attempt to take a distance from falsified versions of his texts, from the attribution to him of texts he did not in fact write: to do so he produces an aberrant document[8] warning the public to have no faith in the legitimacy of texts bearing his signature, but has of course to sign that document in order to give its disavowal legitimacy. And further, as the *Dialogues* suggest, Rousseau's enemies were able to publish this document as proof not that texts had been falsified, but that Rousseau admitted the pernicious nature of his earlier writing and so wanted to deny 'paternity' of it. (I suspect that the link between this structure and Rousseau's abandoning of his children to the foundlings' hospital is less trivial than it might appear.) Having once signed a work, Rousseau is caught in the necessary possibility that work and signature be disfigured, and further signatures only exacerbate that possibility. (This structure also generates a perpetual necessity to write *more*, lest Rousseau be seen to have signed his silence as consent, as is the case with his famous reply to D'Alembert's article on Geneva in the *Encylopédie*.)

But what of the text in which the knowledge of such possible or inevitable falsification is displayed? In so far as that falsification (which is simply another name for reading) affects the whole corpus of Rousseau's work, then it affects the *Dialogues* too, which are part of that corpus, whether Rousseau likes it or not. Rousseau's text is not blind to the implications of this, and poses the problem clearly enough in a sort of preface entitled, 'On the subject and form of this text':

> What will become of this text? What use will I be able to make of it? I do not know, and this uncertainty has greatly increased the discouragement which has not left me while working on it. Those who have me at their disposal knew about it as soon as it was started, and I see in my situation no possible means of preventing it from falling into their hands sooner or later. Thus, following the natural course of events, all the trouble I have taken is a pure waste of time [*à pure perte*]. I do not know what course of action heaven will suggest to me, but I shall hope to the end that it will not abandon the just cause. Whatever the hands into which it causes these sheets to fall, it is enough for me if among those who will read them there is still the heart of a man, and I will never despise the human race enough to find in this idea no cause for confidence and hope. (p. 666)

A note appended to this passage refers the reader to the 'Histoire du précédent écrit', which follows the text of the *Dialogues* proper, for confirmation of the inevitability of the text's falling into the hands of Rousseau's enemies. This 'Histoire' explicitly addresses the two sorts of relation to the future we saw in Kant's *Prolegomena*: Rousseau writes that the 'Histoire' will tell 'what was [my text's] destination, and what has been its destiny' (p. 977): destination as projection to the future, destiny as the inevitable folding back of the future perfect. Or vice versa. I shall suggest that the drama and pathos involved in these texts are not to be read as symptoms of Rousseau's character or pathology, but as extreme indications of the structure of writing in general in its irreducible relation to the future, to both destination and destiny.

It will now come as no surprise that in Rousseau's case, too, these questions are focused on the problem of the text's addressee or *destinataire*, and made the more acute by the conviction that *destinataires* are *themselves* destined, addressed, sent by an agency which might always be Providence, but might always also be the author or authors of the plot against Jean-Jacques Rousseau. In an attempt to short-circuit this problem, Rousseau decides to address his text to the presumed good sender or addressor of those addressees, by placing a copy of his manuscript on the altar of Notre-Dame:[9] at 2 o'clock in the afternoon of Saturday, 24 February 1776, Rousseau, postman for his own text, finds that they way to the altar is blocked by an iron grille he had never noticed before, and the delivery cannot be made. After a momentary doubt that perhaps Providence is *itself* part of the plot against him, Rousseau realizes that even if he had succeeded in placing his manuscript on the altar it would none the less have fallen into his enemies' hands, and so it is Providence itself that he has to thank for blocking his way. This structure determines Rousseau's remaining efforts to ensure the arrival of his text, via Providence, to Posterity: he hears that his old friend Condillac has just returned to Paris, and sees in this event 'a direction from Providence' – but Condillac's cool reception of Rousseau's manuscript soon undermines any such conviction, and in a movement programmed by the structure I am attempting to elucidate, Rousseau shifts catastrophically from the conviction that Condillac was the best possible addressee of his text to the certainty that he was the worst. A young English admirer calls unexpectedly on Rousseau, and again, 'like all unhappy people who believe they see in everything that happens to them [*dans tout ce qui leur arrive*] a deliberate direction of fate [*une expresse direction du sort*]' he again see Providence at work, only to switch again to the opposite conviction as soon as the man has left: the certainty that the man was *sent* or *destined* remains, but the sender is no longer identified as Providence, but as the plot.

(I should point out, incidentally, that both Condillac and the Englishman, Boothby, carried out Rousseau's instructions scrupulously, and ensured the transmission to posterity which allows us to read these texts today: this fact, far from simply suggesting that Rousseau's fears were groundless, allows the continuation, in the so-called 'act' of reading, of the very falsification and disfigurement he feared.)

Rousseau's final active attempt to counteract disfigurement is to distribute at random in the street a circular letter addressed 'To all Frenchmen who still love justice and truth', only to find that scarcely anyone will accept that position of addressee: again, the text of this letter predicts its own fate or destiny (which I am suggesting is destiny itself), by recognizing in a *post*script that the present state of the plot will prevent any interest being taken in the letter, which will (or so Rousseau 'dares to predict' (p. 991)) none the less one day seem more interesting, when the plot has been dissipated, partially by this very letter . . . which is thus strictly unreadable, or writes an impossible future by assigning a place to its addressee which it is impossible to occupy.

The failure of these various attempts leads to a state of resignation, an acceptance of destiny as the inevitable frustration of determinate destination:

> To multiply incessantly copies of [my text] so as to place them here and there in the hands of people who approach me would be uselessly to exceed my strength, and I cannot reasonably hope that of all these copies thus dispersed a single one would arrive whole at its destination. (p. 987)

This is destiny itself, the trace of the future in all writing, the life and death of the author:

> This destiny of my papers, which I see as inevitable, no longer alarms me. Whatever men may do, Heaven will in turn accomplish its work. I do not know the time, the means or the species of this work. What I know is that the supreme arbiter is powerful and just, that my soul is innocent and that I have not deserved my fate. That is enough for me. Henceforth to give in to my destiny, no longer stubbornly to fight against it, to let my persecutors deal with their prey as they wish, to remain their plaything without any resistance for the rest of my old and sad days, to abandon to them even the honour of my name and my reputation in the future, if it please Heaven that they should have these at their disposal, no longer to be affected by whatever arrives; this is my last resolution. Let men henceforth do whatever they like, after I have done what I ought, they may well torment my life, they will not prevent me from dying in peace. (p. 989)

The structure I have been attempting to pick out, of writing the future as the destiny of indeterminate or disfigured destination (Derrida's *destinerrance*), has consistently been marked by a negative pathos, at best by a sort of stoical resignation. It would seem that in Rousseau at least this pathos is the result of a drive to determine the addressor of this destiny as persecutory, and to postulate a possible good counter-addressor as God. My claim in this paper will have been simple: such a determination of an addressor of this 'destiny' is arbitrary, as is the drive to separate 'good' and 'bad' versions of it, and thereby to maintain any simple distinction between destination and destiny. If such determinations are resisted, writing can be seen as an affirmation of that imbrication of destination and destiny rather than a regret. Such an affirmative version of writing the future is none other than what Jean-François Lyotard calls the postmodern.[10] Future imperfect.

Notes

1. Jacques Derrida, *De la grammatologie*, Paris: Minuit 1967, p. 97; *Of Grammatology*, trans. Gayatrti Chakravorty Spivak, Baltimore and London: The Johns Hopkins University Press 1976 p. 66. Subsequent references to these editions will be included in the text. Here and in other quotations from *De la grammatologie*, I have modified the published translation a little.

2. *La Voix et le phénomène*, Paris: PUF 1967; 'Le Facteur de la vérité, in *La Carte postale de Socrate à Freud et au-delà*, Paris: Aubier-Flammarion 1980; *D'un ton apocalyptique adopté naguère en philosophie*, Paris: Galilée 1983; *Schibboleth: pour Paul Celan* Paris: Galilée 1986.

3. Immanuel Kant, *Prolegomena to any Future Metaphysics that will be able to come forward as Science*, trans. Paul Carus, revised by James W. Ellington, Indianapolis: Hackett Publishing Company 1977: page references will henceforth be given in the text.

4. Jean-François Lyotard, *La Condition postmoderne*, Paris: Minuit 1979. In subsequent work Lyotard has attenuated the importance previously accorded to narrative: see *La Différend*, Paris: Minuit 1983.

5. My translation. This passage is also partially quoted in James Creech's reading of Diderot's article: ' "Chasing after advances": Diderot's article "Encyclopedia" ', *Yale French Studies*, no. 63 (1982), pp. 183–97.

6. These texts have been the object of a much more detailed reading by Ellen Burt: 'Rousseau the Scribe', *Studies in Romanticism*, vol. 18, no. 4 (1979), pp. 629–67. I cannot here attempt to do justice to Burt's careful argument, nor specify the limits to my agreement with it.

7. Jean-Jacques Rousseau, *Oeuvres complètes*, ed. Marcel Raymond and Bernard Gagnebin, 4 vols to date, Paris: Gallimard 1959–), I, 956. Subsequent page references to Rousseau are to this volume and will be given in the text. All translations from Rousseau are my own.

8. ibid., pp. 1186–7.

9. Rousseau explicitly addresses his text to Providence, but in the hope that it will reach the king: I cannot go into this complication here.

10. I shall attempt to support this assertion elsewhere: but only some such understanding of the 'postmodern' (rather than arguments about periodizations and alleged 'breaks') can help to avoid the rather crass terms of much of the 'debate' reputedly going on around it.

13

Postal Politics and the Institution of

the Nation

Approaches

It is tempting to try to approach the question of nation directly, by aiming for its centre or its origin. And there is almost immediate satisfaction to be had in so doing; for we undoubtedly find narration at the centre of nation: stories of national origins, myths of founding fathers, genealogies of heroes. At the origin of the nation, we find a story of the nation's origin.

Which should be enough to inspire suspicion; our own drive to find the centre and the origin has created its own myth of the origin – namely that at the origin is the myth.[1] In this story, narration comes too easy, too soon; investigating the nation is here complicit with the nation's own story. The problem is no doubt a result of the pretension to reach the centre directly, whereas such access is in general illusory: the approach to the nation implies borders, policing, suspicion, and crossing (or refusal of entry) – try to enter a country at the centre (by flying in, say), and the border is still there to be crossed, the frontier shifted from periphery to centre.

But the need to approach the nation via its edges immediately complicates the problem, in so far as it implies a difference, not merely between centre and circumference, but between inside and outside. The frontier does not merely close the nation in on itself, but also, immediately, opens it to an outside, to other nations. Frontiers are articulations, boundaries are, constitutively, crossed or transgressed. This formal point has been made clearly by Edgar Morin:

> The frontier is both an opening and a closing. It is at the frontier that there takes place the distinction from and liaison with the environment. All frontiers, including the membrane of living beings, including the frontier of nations, are, at the same time as they are barriers, places of communication and exchange. They are the place of dissociation and association, of separation and articulation.[2]

At the centre, the nation narrates itself as *the* nation: at the borders, it must recognize that there are other nations on which it cannot but depend. It follows that the 'origin' of the nation is never simple, but dependent on a differentiation of nations which has always already begun. The story of (the institution of) the nation will be irremediably complicated by this situation.

'Method'

This type of formulation of the problem, with its insistence on margins as against centres, on difference as a prior condition of identity, can quickly be labelled 'post-structuralist' in its inspiration. The label 'post-structuralist' (which is not itself a post-structuralist label) cannot, however, be simply applied from a methodological or theoretical 'outside' to designate a particular way of approaching a predefined question (in this case, that of 'nation and narration'): for the question of 'post-structuralism' *itself* immediately involves questions of nationality (French, American, English, German . . .), but also general questions of *institution* which cannot be separated from those involved in the problem of the nation. More especially, the name 'post-structuralism' immediately raises temporal or historical questions which will further complicate the spatial complications of frontiers sketched out above.

In more than one way, the name 'post-structuralism' is improper: it is an English name for an essentially (apparently, originally) French movement; it designates as 'literary theory' a complex set of work in philosophy, psychoanalysis, literary studies, and so forth; the thinkers grouped together under this name are in fact more or less violently opposed to each other. With the exception of Lyotard (and I shall return to this exception) none of these thinkers has, to my knowledge, laid claim to (or even used with reference to their own work) a name beginning with 'post-'. It is no doubt necessary to investigate the naiveties and misunderstandings induced by the use of the term 'post-structuralism', to write the history and sociology of this phantom movement or institution.[3] The institutionalization of 'post-structuralism' (which begins at least as early as the invention of the name) is a complex enough phenomenon to be worth this type of study: and as it seems that this English name for a French movement has itself been recently reimported into France,[4] then that complexity would immediately engage with the questions of nationality (notably via the question of translation) which are the concern of this volume.

However necessary and difficult such an analysis, and whatever refinement it showed, it would encounter, sooner or later, a necessary and troubling limit. Any socio-historico-institutional analysis of post-structuralism (or the postmodern) would rely on an understanding of the prefix 'post-' as designating 'what comes after', 'what supersedes', possibly even 'what sublates'. A first, parodically 'post-structuralist' observation would reply that, from the point of view of what is still, mistakenly, called 'the materiality of the signifier', the 'post-' is 'pre-': it is a prefix, and thus comes before and not after. The post is at the beginning, and precedes, in a certain linear order of the signifier, the name (structuralism, the modern) with respect to which it is thought to come after. This type of observation is not just a joke, however, and the (serious) claim that the post comes first, at the beginning, at 'the origin', does not imply that the truth is to be found in that so-called 'materiality of the signifier'. Take for example a slightly perplexing tension to be found between Lyotard's *The Postmodern Condition* proper, and the essay 'Answering the question: what is postmodernism?', printed as an appendix in the English translation of the book.[5] On the one hand, *The Postmodern Condition* tends to give the impression that the postmodern does indeed come after, in the order of history, and this conforms to the presuppositions of the type of analysis just mentioned. According to this obvious and apparently unproblematical schema, we enter the post-modern condition as we enter so-called postindustrial society, after a modern condition and an industrial society. This move from modern to postmodern seems to go along with a certain view of technical and technological 'progress', notably in the domain of computer technology. But on the other hand, if we are to take seriously the critique of 'grand narratives' which is the philosophical core of Lyotard's book, then it is difficult to accept this type of representation, which Lyotard has himself subsequently described as being itself 'modern'.[6] If the postmodern involves the decline or the loss of credibility of grand narratives, it is difficult to describe it in terms of a grand narrative of technology. And in the 'Answering the question . . .' essay, it becomes clear that the post-modern is no longer to be thought of in terms of such narratives, nor in terms of some break that would simply *separate* the modern and the postmodern. 'A work can become modern only if it is first postmodern. Postmodernism thus understood is not modernism as its end, but in the nascent state, and this state is constant' (p. 79). The post does indeed come first, then, and Lyotard goes on to elaborate this strange logic in terms of a temporal paradox of the future perfect.[7]

Can the same be said of post-structuralism? Apparently so, if we follow Robert Young's analysis,[8] which plays elegantly on the temporal sense of 'post' ('what comes after'), and its spatial sense ('what is placed behind'), and concludes that post-structuralism, coming after structuralism, none the less comes *behind* it, and therefore, in a bizarre sense, *before* it. Robert Young quite rightly invokes Freud's *Nachträglichkeit* to describe this situation.

History begins to lose its grip at this point: or rather history (which suffers from an inability to answer the question 'When?' asked of a text, or from an inevitable tendency to believe that there could be a *simple* answer to this question) only maintains its grip by a violent reduction of this scandalous instability of the prefix 'post-', which raises philosophical questions in excess of history. On the other hand, it cannot be denied that there are indeed historical and socio-institutional *effects* of post-structuralism, and these have to be addressed: this is a *political* question, and it is via the effects of the post-that it can best be approached. It is no accident that most of the adverse reactions of post-structuralism have been dictated by political concerns, and it may well be that the political question put to philosophy always demands simplicity, and that the philosophical answer to that question always insists on complexity. To the extent that the present essay is more on the side of the philosophical, then it too will stress complexity, in part by suggesting that the 'method' of the enquiry cannot here be separated from its 'object' (post-structuralism as an institutional phenomenon can itself only be understood in terms of postal politics). But in so far as this 'complexity' might only be another name for 'the political', then maybe a certain simplicity will emerge after all to satisfy current demands: and as such demands increasingly invoke certain values (clarity, communication, dialogue, rationality) which are those of the Enlightenment,[9] it is to authors of the Enlightenment that I shall turn for some help in elaborating the complex of spatial and temporal problems raised so far.

Postal Politics

In order to approach these questions of politics, institutional effects, of nation and narration, I shall insist on another network, or translation, of 'post'. I have already suggested that the prefix 'post-' disturbs history, and even that in some sense it comes 'before' history. What now of the post as postal network? Eugène Vaillé's, monumental *Histoire générale des postes françaises*[10] provides the following definition on page 1:

> [The post] can be defined as a regulated and usually governmental institution, which ensures, in conditions established in advance, both for the duration and price of transport and for its regularity, the transmission of

the thought of the sender as he has transcribed it himself on a material support. (p. 1)

Just before this definition, Vaillé states that 'the post has the essential advantage of carrying out the transport of the very support which bears the thought of the sender as he has formulated it himself, which is a guarantee of absolute authenticity' (ibid.). This does not prevent him, two pages later, from 'making the transportation of thought a postal affair without waiting for the appearance of the material support which will receive the writing' (p. 3). This comes down to privileging the messenger or the postman, the transport over the support, and this 'extended' definition allows Vaillé to deduce the existence of the post at the dawn of civilization: 'As an institution indispensable to social life, the post, whose utility is manifest from the beginning of civilisation, must have appeared along with the constitution of that life' (p. 18). In his effort to locate and define his object, Vaillé all but makes communication *in general* a postal affair: and thereby postal affairs a precondition of history – it is perhaps significant that the first part of Vaillé's book is entitled 'The post before history'.[11]

What, then, of postal politics? A starting point can be found in a short text by Montesquieu, entitled *Of Politics*, which probably dates from 1725, and which is the only remaining fragment of a lost *Treatise on Duty*.[12] This text contains a strange and obscure statement, made all the more strange and obscure by being isolated in the text by blanks which cut it off from its immediate context. In its disturbing simplicity, this sentence reads simply: 'It is the invention of the post which has produced politics' (p. 174). We should immediately note the catastrophic reversal which this sentence operates on a reflection by Vaillé, for whom 'no doubt political necessities were behind the creation of the post'. For Vaillé, the post is *posterior* with respect to politics, its servant or follower; for Montesquieu it comes before, in an absolute anteriority which is our whole problem.

Montesquieu's statement is a little intimidating because of its aphoristic or gnomic aspect: this impression is not diminished by the discovery of two almost identical sentences in the collection entitled *Mes pensées*,[13] and therefore in a more explicitly gnomic context (assuming that it is possible to speak so simply of 'context' for this type of sentence). These two sentences are to be found under the rubric 'Politics' (third sub-section in the eighth main section of the collection, 'Political education and political economy'). This sub-section contains other sentences which do not immediately appear very 'political', and one might wonder what brought Montesquieu's first editors to place them here, were it not for the fact that the text explicitly entitled *Of Politics* also contains such sentences, on chance, on the unforeseeable and overdetermined nature of effects – for example, in *Mes pensées*, 'There are few facts in the world which do not depend on so many circumstances that it would take the eternity of the world for them to happen a second time' (no. 1,763), and the following, in *Of Politics*: 'Most effects come about in such singular ways, or depend on causes so imperceptible and so distant, that one can scarcely foresee them' (p. 172). I cannot here attempt to establish the links, which I believe to be tight,[14] between this type of reflection and the sentence on the post, and its two displaced repetitions in *Mes pensées*: 'The invention of the post produced politics: we do not politick with the Mogol' (no. 1,760), and 'Politics, as it is today, comes from the invention of the post' (no. 1,761).

We do not politick with the Mogol, first because he does not belong to the same network as us, but also, perhaps, because he does not belong to any network, because he practises a politics which is other than postal, and thus other than 'politics as it is today', which is supposed to come from the invention of the post. These two sentences thus, unlike the version in *Of Politics*, give a glimpse of, on the one hand, the possibility of a Mogolian politics, and on the other of a politics anterior to that of today: in both cases, of a non-postal politics. Montesquieu does not say whether all non-postal politics would be necessarily Mogolian (and therefore despotic), although this is clearly enough the essential question: it would be no exaggeration to claim that this is the whole problem of the Enlightenment, and the whole problem of politics.[15]

The argument of this strange essay *Of Politics* is that politics, 'as it is today', suffers from being too complicated, too refined, too secretive, too full of detours, too postal. But Montesquieu's examples are far from being clear and univocal. I shall quote what is perhaps the simplest of them:

It is said that M. de Louvois, wanting to organise an expedition in Flanders, sent a packet to the intendant, forbidding him to open it before receiving orders to do so. It was a matter of organising the march of troups dispersed on all sides, and the packet contained orders for all the people subordinate to the intendant in the execution of this project, so that the intendant would only have to sign, and so that the messengers would not reveal the secret. This is pitiful. Did not this packet, which remained for two weeks in foreign hands, expose its secret? What purpose did it serve except that of exciting curiosity? What is more, could the secretaries of the minister not be unfaithful as much as those of the intendant? Was the two-hour period needed to write these orders enough to reveal the secret of an expedition?

It is often more petty to show off useless precautions than not to take enough. (p. 174)

We could say that in this description politics primarily involves secrecy. But as the secret is that of an 'expedition' (the word has a strong postal connotation in French), and as it must be sent, *expédié*, committed to the postal network, there is the risk that the secret be lost or disseminated: even though it remains sealed during its time in this network, the packet or letter opens none the less, becoming an open letter or a postcard (as Derrida would say),[16] while it waits for the signature or counter-signature of the addressee, here the intendant. The letter, the aim of which was to order or subordinate a dispersion, runs the risk of being itself dispersed. This brings with it a proliferation of letters or *expéditions* which all aim to avoid the dispersion of the first letter, to keep the secret of that expedition: alongside the sealed packet, there must be an order which states openly that the packet must not be opened (this order could be written on the outside of the packet), and later there must be a second order authorizing the opening of the packet which contains the real orders. . . . Too many *expéditions*, too much politics, too much post, too much secret: which, because of this very excess, opens and is lost. Montesquieu thinks it better to do things more directly. As he says a little earlier in this same essay: 'a simple and natural conduct can just as easily lead to the aims of government as a more devious one' (p. 173).

There follow two examples designed to illustrate the excesses of the political behaviour of the Cardinal de Richelieu:

I have often heard praised the action of the Cardinal de Richelieu who, wanting to pay over 2 millions in Germany, had a German come to Paris, sent the 2 millions to one of his men, with an order to give them, without a receipt, to a man with no name, of such-and-such dress and appearance. How is it that people don't see in this a ridiculous affectation? What was more simple than sending good *lettres de change*, without loading onto this German such a large sum, which could expose him infinitely; or, if he wanted to give the money in Paris, why did he not give it himself?

This minister, who used to buy comedies so as to pass as a good poet, and who used to try to swindle all sorts of merit, was always tormenting himself to find ways of getting new esteem.

Here is another show of bravado!

A man in whom he had confidence having remained in his office while he went out to accompany someone, the Cardinal remembered that he could have read some important papers that were on his table. He immediately wrote a letter which he gave him to take to the governor of the Bastille, which letter gave the governor orders to hold him for a month, at the end of which time the secret would expire: which was done, and, after a month, the prisoner was released with a large reward. Pure bluster, prepared and set up at leisure, and even without much judgement. Firstly, one does not receive several people in an office where there are papers of such importance. Prudent people write such letters in code. Finally, there were a thousand less showy ways of repairing this gross error. But he wanted to make a noise and be a great minister, at whatever price. (p. 174)

I cannot here comment on these examples as fully as they deserve: there would be much to say about the nameless and yet infinitely exposed German, and about what could be called the Bellerophon effect (or Hamlet effect) of the second example, from which it might be possible to deduce that the post always in some sense desires the death of the postman.[17] But if Montesquieu seems to be attacking a 'political' effect which depends on too much post, it is not clear that the remedy implies a simple quantitative reduction of postal complications. Writing *lettres de change*, and especially letters in code, surely complicates the network rather than simplifying it. What Montesquieu reproaches politics with is apparently not so much the post as such, as the fact of wanting to achieve, by postal means, effects on a secondary addressee, the public, by means of 'making a noise':[18] politics cannot want absolute secrecy, but the open, expiring secret constituted by a letter in the post. The secret is never absolutely secret, but announces itself as secret, and this can be the sign of the skill of a 'great minister'. (No doubt this schema remains valid for the analysis of a number of recent political events in Britain, around the Secret Services or so-called 'official secrets'. It will be remembered for example, that one episode of the British 'Westland affair' of 1986 turned on the interpretation of the words 'secret and confidential' written on the outside of a letter, on whether these words referred to the *content* of the letter, or to its very *existence*. The fact that the ensuing 'noise' was taken to be the sign of an *incompetent* minister simply confirms Montesquieu's point.)

Montesquieu's analysis is not simple. On the one hand, he appears to recommend a reduction of postal effects, a political simplicity which would have to do with a certain postal directness. But the remedies proposed appear to increase these same effects in the very effort made to avoid them. It is not hard to imagine that such a structure would produce paradoxes according to which an absolute reduction of postal politics would give rise to an absolute increase of postal political effects: 'In our own time we have seen another minister who never had a single paper on this desk and who never read any. If he had succeeded in his principal projects, he would have been looked upon as an intelligence who governed a state as would the spirits' (p. 174). And this paradox will allow us to read the final two sentences of

Montesquieu's text: 'There is nothing so easy for a man in certain positions as to astonish people by a great project: there is something false in this. It is not the means which should be brilliant, but the ends. True politics consists in getting there by obscure routes' (p. 175).

True politics is not then simply the absence of the post, but a postal network which would itself be secret, distributing the mail in the dark without exhibiting its expeditions and letters *en souffrance*, an underground network keeping the secret secret. The logic implied here also governs the *writing* of Montesquieu's text, which is thus also '(An example) of politics': at the outset, Montesquieu declares that 'it is useless to attack politics directly',[19] and that 'it is better to take a circuitous route' (p. 172) – the structure of the argument thus repeats the structure of its object.

Autonomy

The post wants the letter to arrive at its destination, at what Montesquieu calls its 'brilliant end': this end is the death of the postman and the end of the post. As postal network, all politics wants politics to end. The arrival of the letter should erase its delivery. The end of politics is the end of politics. All of this would have to be inscribed more generally in a notion of *nature* as a postal network, in which, as Montesquieu says in a near-contemporary text, 'toutes les créatures . . . s'entretiennent par une correspondance qu'on ne saurait assez admirer'.[20] For a whole Enlightenment, what is admirable in this natural correspondence is that it is ruled by inflexible and necessary laws: the end of politics would be to be absorbed into a *simulacrum* of this natural and necessary network. Through a slippage in the sense of the word 'law', positive laws are assimilated to the laws of nature, via the notion of 'natural law'. This type of schema rules, for example, the first book of Montesquieu's *De l'esprit des lois*, and also famous readings of Montesquieu by Auguste Comte and Louis Althusser. Kant too works within the same structure, which he complicates, certainly, but maintains.[21]

If such a simulacrum were to be achieved, then there would be no question of nation and narration, but only of nature and no narration. This can be shown by a brief consideration of Rousseau's political thought, which never, to my knowledge, makes the kind of direct appeal to the post made by Montesquieu, but which none the less presents a more rigorous and less anecdotal account of the same structure. Rousseau's aim, as formulated in *Emile*, is indeed to provide a model according to which the state would attain the necessary functioning of the Newtonian universe:

If the laws of nations could have, like those of nature, an inflexibility that no human force could ever overcome, then dependency on men would become again dependency on things, in the Republic all the advantages of the natural state would be linked with those of the civil state, to the liberty which maintains man exempt from vice would be joined the morality which raises him to virtue.[22]

In the *Social Contract*, the doctrine of the general will is designed to achieve this: in the light of the reading of Montesquieu, it seems possible to describe the general will as the sending of a letter (a circular letter) by the citizen as member of the sovereign to that 'same' citizen as subject. The citizen does not pre-exist the sending of this letter, but is created by it: 'sovereign' and 'subject' are Rousseau's names for the sender and addressee of the legislative letter, and 'citizen' the name which implies that the structure of the law allows the identity of sender and addressee to be asserted.[23] Given this postulated identity, Rousseau can claim that 'the Sovereign, by the simple fact that it *is*, is always what it *should be*', and that 'the general will is always right'.[24] The citizen sends himself the law, and in this sending names himself as citizen: this structure is that of autonomy in general, and implies a concomitant autonomination.

From the 'post-structuralist' perspective assumed earlier, we can see that this theory presupposes that letters arrive at their destination. If this were so, then the desire of politics to end the post would have been achieved, and there would be no need of politics at all – if the legislative letter always reached its destination (always in fact being returned to the sender), then there would be no need for it to be sent, for it would have always already arrived. The fact that this is not the case is sufficiently proved by the existence of Rousseau's theories, which presuppose that politics has come adrift from the natural network and can only attempt to reproduce it in the form of a radical fiction.[25] The immediate implication is that politics is a name for the necessary possibility of the failure of autonomy to close into the circuit which names the citizen as citizen, and that the designation 'citizen' is always inhabited by an element of impropriety. This impropriety is both the condition of possibility of politics and the reason why autonomy can never be achieved: this margin, which can be called 'freedom', is also the ground of differentiation which allows for the fact that 'citizens' are always in fact bearers of so-called 'proper names', and are not just isomorphic points. Rousseau also recognizes this in so far as he cannot let the law remain in its pure generality, but formulates the need for a government or executive power to allow its particular applications: the government being something like a central sorting office, 'an intermediary body established between the subjects and the

Sovereign for their mutual correspondence'.[26] But more importantly for our concerns here, this necessary failure of autonomy also denies the absolute closure of the circuit of the general will in the form of the absolutely autonomous state. If the doctrine of the general will were not troubled by the necessary possibility of the letter's not arriving, then the state would be absolute and have no relation to any outside: it could not strictly speaking be a *nation*, and it would have no history, and thus no narration.[27] In order to have a name, a boundary and a history to be told at the centre, the state must be constitutively imperfect. The closure of the state becomes the frontier of the nation, and, as we have seen, the frontier implies that there is more than one nation.

We have to go further, and say that this complication is not an *accident* which befalls the state in its ideal purity, but that it is originary: just as, for Derrida, the possibility that the letter not arrive or that the performative misfire is not an empirical but a *necessary* possibility,[28] so national differentiation does not come along to trouble the state *after* its perfect constitution, but precedes the fiction of such a constitution as its condition of possibility. Rousseau also recognizes this, implicitly in the *Social Contract*, more clearly in, for example, the *Project for a Constitution for Corsica*. This text has, for us, the considerable advantage of recognizing national difference in its very title, while none the less maintaining a proximity to the theoretic rigour of the *Social Contract* itself. Corsica had in fact been named within the *Social Contract* as the only country in Europe still capable of legislation,[29] and the text of the *Project* duly lays down demands of autonomy and self-sufficiency:

> With whatever aim the Corsican nation wants to organise itself politically [*se policer*] the first thing it must do is to give itself all the consistency it can have. Whoever depends on another and does not have his resources within himself cannot be free. Alliances, treaties, the faith of men – all this can tie the weak to the strong and never ties the strong to the weak. So leave negotiations to the powers and count only on yourselves. . . .
>
> Here, then, are the principles which in my view should serve as a base for their legislation: make of their people and their country as much as is possible; cultivate and assemble their own forces, rely on them alone, and think of foreign powers as little as if none existed. (pp. 903–4)

The 'as if' in the final recommendation marks an awareness of fiction in the notion of autonomy: and, earlier, the text has in fact recognized that Corsica is practically at the mercy of foreign powers and would be the more so were it to prosper. There is here at work an insidious logic which de Man has analysed in a different fragment of Rousseau's political writing, and which can be found taken to an extreme in the

Marquis de Sade: briefly, in Rousseau, autonomy is defined in part by independence from other nations – but this independence implies that the other nations in turn become dependent on, and jealous of, the 'autonomous' nation, whose autonomy is thus measured in terms of the other it is supposed to ignore. In Rousseau, this means, ideally, as in his recommendations to the Corsicans, that other nations in fact be forgotten in what we can now see to be a vain attempt to achieve the closure of autonomy and self-sufficiency: in Sade, the same logical process leads to the conclusion that the only consistent *internal* policy is one which encourages depravity, corruption and permanent insurrection.[30] These two conclusions are, clearly enough, dialectical opposites, and the possibility of such a dialectic depends on some recognition of a relation with an outside, repressed in Rousseau, invasive and pervasive in Sade.

Some progress beyond this dialectic can be made, typically, via Kant, who takes the crucial step of recognizing that these problems do not simply befall the autonomous state but constitute its possibility and its limit: implicitly in his *Perpetual Peace*,[31] where we find the following:

> Even if people were not compelled by internal dissent to submit to the coercion of public laws, war would produce the same effect from outside . . . each people would find itself confronted by another neighbouring people pressing in upon it, thus forcing it to form itself internally into a *state* in order to encounter the other as an armed *power* (p. 112)

and explicitly in the seventh proposition of the *Idea for a Universal History with a Cosmopolitan Purpose*:

> The problem of establishing a perfect civil constitution is subordinate to the problem of a law-governed *external relationship* with other states, and cannot be solved unless the latter is also solved. What is the use of working for a law-governed civil constitution among individual men, i.e. of planning a *commonwealth*? The same unsociability which forced men to do so gives rise in turn to a situation whereby each commonwealth in its external relations (i.e. as a state in relation to other states), is in a position of unrestricted freedom. Each must accordingly expect from any other precisely the same evils which formerly oppressed individual men and forced them into a law-governed civil state. (p. 47)

The state of nature is a state of war, or of the necessary risk of war,[32] and, again, this is constitutive and not accidental: and if it is difficult for us to accept the transcendental optimism of Kant's teleological view of nature progressing towards a perpetual peace, then that state of war is permanent, and susceptible only of degrees of more or less, never of final solution.

Nation is, then, always opened to its others: or rather, it is constituted only in that opening, which is, in principle, violent. The status of
the individual nation and, within it, of the individual citizen, is derived
from that primary 'global' violence by a process analogous to the
'morphogenesis' of catastrophe theory.[33] Faced with this situation, the
nation resorts to narration of one sort or another, and proceeds by the
sort of *Nachträglichkeit* constitutive of institutions in general, and which
we saw above to be operative in the very name of post-structuralism.
The social contract is one such narrative, projecting, aporetically, an
impossible moment of foundation and legitimation: another narrative
is that of the legislator, the giver of laws, the founder of the state. In
Rousseau, the legislator comes from outside and leaves again:[34] in the
time of his coming, it is impossible to decide as to his legitimacy – in
view of quite traditional paradoxes of authority, the final establishment of that legitimacy can only be projected into an indefinite
future.[35] The radically performative laying down of the law by the
legislator must create the very context according to which that law
could be judged to be just: the founding moment, the *pre-*, is always
already inhabited by the *post-*. In the absence of final criteria for such a
judgement, the nation narrates the founding moment and produces
effects of legitimacy through repetition. These two narratives (that of
the contract and that of the legislator) are not independent: the
essential postal possibilities we have recognized in the mechanism of
the general will open it to the coming of the legislator – and, more
importantly, will prepare the state in question to extend its demand for
autonomy by playing the legislator to all other nations. The doctrine of
the social contract is essentially intolerant of national differences, and
will attempt to absorb them in the creation of an autonomous 'humanity', for example. The American and French declarations duly formulate a confusion between the names of their respective nations and
postulated universal 'rights of man', on the basis of which they have felt
able to play the legislator the world over.[36]
     The idea of the nation is inseparable from its narration: that
narration attempts, interminably, to constitute identity against difference, inside against outside, and in the assumed superiority of inside
over outside, prepares against invasion and for 'enlightened' colonial-
ism. In this structure, the legislator is never far away. In Rousseau's
doctrine, the legislator is always, undecidably, also a charlatan: and no
doubt that insistence of the charlatan is becoming increasingly visible
in international politics today. The arrival of the legislator is proof
enough that the law to be laid down will never achieve its desired
identity with the laws of nature, and that politics will never reach its
goal (which is always that of wresting a realm of necessity from a realm

of freedom), and to this extent is probably not simply to be deplored. But it should no doubt still be a source of amusement: legislators in general cannot fail to lay down the law and cannot fail to be laughable as they do so – this is no less true of the 'legislators' of institutions such as 'post-structuralism' than of any others, with the difference that the law they lay down allows some understanding of the necessary imperfection of legislation in general, and undercuts the faith in origins and ends which narration perpetuates. It also allows us to understand 'post-structuralism' more as a *movement* and less as an *institution*, while enabling an understanding of the effects of institution which necessarily ensue. And whether the law be formulated as *différence* or *différend*, it is also a law of the inter-nation (though not as international law), with which to negotiate a survival.[37]

Notes

1. 'We know the scene: there are men gathered round, and someone telling them a story. . . . They were not gathered before the story, it is the telling that gathers them. . . . It is the story of their origin. . . . We know this scene well. More than one story-teller has told it to us, having gathered us into learned fraternities, destined to find out what were our origins . . . . These stories have been called *myths*. . . . We also know, henceforth that this scene is itself mythical': Jean-Luc Nancy, *La Communauté désoeuvrée*, Paris: Galilée 1986, pp. 109–13. See too Lyotard's analyses of the narratives of the Cashinahua Indians: *La Condition postmoderne: rapport sur le savoir*, Paris: Minuit 1979, pp. 38–43 (tr. *The Postmodern Condition*, Manchester: Manchester University press 1984, pp. 18–23); *Au Juste*, Paris: Bourgois 1979, pp. 63–6 (tr. *Just Gaming* , Manchester: Manchester University Press 1986, pp. 32–3); *Le Différend*, Paris: Minuit 1983, pp. 219–23; *Le Postmoderne expliqué aux enfants*, Paris: Galilée 1986, pp. 56–9 and 73–5: and, for a brilliant analysis of Freud's version of the story, Mikkel Borch-Jakobsen, *Le Sujet freudien*, Paris: Aubier-Flammarion 1982, especially pp. 159–292.

2. Edgar Morin, *La Méthode*, vol. 1, *La Nature de la nature*, Paris: Seuil 1977; reprinted collection 'Points', 1981, pp. 203–4: the structure is also that of the 'hinge' (*la brisure*) described by Derrida in *De la grammatologie*, Paris: Minuit 1967, pp. 96–108 (tr. *Of Grammatology*, Baltimore and London: Johns Hopkins University Press 1976, pp. 65–73).

3. I am not aware of any serious attempt to do this: a precondition of such an attempt would be the recognition that it could not, by definition, constitute a critique (and *a fortiori* not a refutation) of the work labelled 'post-structuralist'. An earlier condensed version of the analysis of the 'post-' offered here appeared in French as 'Post', in D. Kelley and I. Llasera, eds, *Cross-references: Modern French Theory and the Practice of Criticism*, London: Society for French Studies, 1986, pp. 65–73.

4. Historically speaking, the word might have been used in French first: the earliest usage I am aware of in either language is in Jean-Joseph Goux's *Freud, Marx: Economie et symbolique*, Paris: Seuil 1973, p. 47, where the word already appears in quotation marks. The Anglo-American use of the term seems to have become common after about 1979, and seems from its earliest uses to have commonly appeared in the form 'so-called post-structuralism'. This situation has been analysed by Robert Young in an unpublished paper called 'The improper name'. The reimportation into French seems to begin with Vincent Descombes's *Grammaire d'objets en tous genres*, Paris: Minuit 1983 (tr. *Objects of All Sorts: A Philosophical Grammar*, Oxford: Blackwell 1986), is massively implicit in Jacques Bouveresse, *Rationalité et cynisme*, Paris: Minuit 1985, and, under the name 'the thought

of '68', in Luc Ferry and Alain Renaut, *La Pensée '68: Essai sur l'anti-humanisme contempor-ain*, Paris: Gaillimard 1985: the simplistic nature of this last book has been sufficiently demonstrated by Jean-François Lyotard and Jacob Rogozinski, 'La Police de la pensée, *L'Autre Journal*, 1 (1986), pp. 27–34.

5. Lyotard, *La Condition postmoderne*; 'Réponse à la question: Qu'est-ce le post-moderne?', *Critique*, 419 (1982), pp. 357–67 (reprinted in Lyotard, *Le Postmoderne expliqué*, pp. 13–34). The implicit reference of this title is of course to Kant's famous article of 1784, 'Beantwortung der Frage: Was ist Aufklärung?' (tr. 'An answer to the question: "What is Enlightenment?" ', in *Kant's Political Writings*, ed. Hans Reiss, Cam-bridge: Cambridge University Press, 1970, pp. 54–60).

6. 'Defining the postmodern', in *Postmodernism*, ICA Documents 4 and 5, London: Institute of Contemporary Arts 1986, p. 6. A slightly reworked version of these initially improvised remarks appears in French as 'Note sur les sens de "post-" ' in Lyotard, *Le Postmoderne expliqué*, pp. 119–26 (pp. 120–1).

7. '*Postmodern* would have to be understood according to the paradox of the future (*post*) perfect (*modo*)', Lyotard, 'Réponse', p. 33 (*The Postmodern Condition*, p. 81, tr. mod.). The various possible readings of the expression 'future perfect' are the object of work in progress.

8. Robert Young, 'Poststructuralism: the end of theory', *Oxford Literary Review*, vol. 5, nos 1–2 (1982), pp. 3–25, p. 4.

9. This (apparent?) shift from Marxist to Enlightenment demands seems to stem from Habermas's notorious Adorno prize speech of 1980: 'Modernity – an incomplete project', in *The Anti-Aesthetic: Essays on Postmodern Culture*, ed. Hal Foster, Port Townsend, Washington: Bay Press 1983 (reprinted as *Postmodern Culture*, London: Pluto Press 1985), pp. 3–15; *The Postmodern Condition* and the 'Answering the Question' essay are of course partially written against Habermas. The importance of what is at stake can be judged from the large amount of discussion this 'confrontation' has already received: see, most interestingly, Philippe Lacoue-Labarthe, 'Où en étions-nous?' in J. Derrida, V. Descombes *et al.*, *La Faculté de juger*, Paris: Minuit 1985, pp. 165–93 (reprinted in Lacoue-Labarthe's *L'Imitation des modernes (Typographies II)*, Paris: Galilée 1986, pp. 257–85) (tr. 'Talks', *Diacritics*, vol. 14, no. 3 (1984), 24–37); Richard Rorty, 'Habermas and Lyotard on postmodernity', *Praxis International*, vol. 4, no. 1 (1984), pp. 32–44 (and the subsequent discussion between Lyotard and Rorty at the 1984 Johns Hopkins 'Case of the Humanities' conference, printed in French in *Critique*, no. 456 (1985), pp. 559–84); Peter Dews, 'From poststructuralism to postmodernism', in *Post-modernism*, pp. 12–16; see, too, various articles in *New German Critique*, no. 33 (1984). In the ICA volume, Lyotard suggests, in response to Terry Eagleton, that 'We must recognize that Marxism is one of the versions of the Enlightenment' (p. 12): it would be interesting to test this statement against the eighteenth-century nostalgia of Eagleton's *The Function of Criticism*, London: Verso 1984, itself of course heavily influenced by a particular account of Habermas – Eagleton's own discussion of the postmodern ('Capita-lism, modernism and postmodernism', *New Left Review*, no. 152 (1985), pp. 60–73, reprinted in *Against the Grain* (London: Verso 1986), pp. 131–47) does not address the question, although it is very critical of Lyotard.

10. Eugène Vaillé, *Histoire générale des postes françaises*, 6 vols, Paris: PUF 1947–53).

11. The full title of this part of Vaillé's book is 'La poste avant l'histoire et la poste gallo-romaine': a less tendentious translation of the first part of this title would be, 'The post in prehistory', which would still make the point well enough. Given the inevitable regressions of Vaillé's attempts to define his object, it is clear that from our perspective his project is inconsistent – if the post precedes history, it cannot be an object of history.

12. Montesquieu, 'De la politique', in *Oeuvres complètes*, ed. Daniel Oster, Paris: Seuil 1964, pp. 172–5. All references to Montesquieu will be to this edition and will be included in the text. All translations from Montesquieu are my own.

13. *Oeuvres complètes*, pp. 853–1082: the collection consists of 2,204 numbered frag-ments taken from Montesquieu's notebooks and organized into thematic groups by a late nineteenth-century editor.

14. The immediate reference in Montesquieu would be to the final two books of *De l'esprit des lois*, which contain a notoriously long historical discussion of feudal law and the birth of the French monarchy, the structural role of which in Montesquieu's work as a whole has baffled the commentators. The tension can be immediately pointed out and linked to the problem at hand, by placing the title of Book 30 ('*Theory* of Feudal Laws . . .' (my emphasis)) against its first sentence, which claims, against the generality promised by the word 'theory', that its object is 'un événement arrivé une fois dans le monde, et qui n'arrivera peut-être jamais' (literally and mysteriously, 'an event happened once in the world and which will perhaps never happen') (p. 755): this 'event' is inseparable from the invasion of Gaul by the Franks, and engages Montesquieu in a polemic with Boulainvilliers and Dubos which is too complicated to summarize here, though it is precisely to do with telling a story which would ground the identity of the French nation. The problematic nature of the founding 'event' might be linked to Derrida's remarks on the 'singular event' of the institution of psychoanalysis (*La Carte postale de Socrate à Freud et au-delà* Paris: Aubier-Flammarion 1980, p. 7; see too p. 17 on 'une seule fois') – the present essay could be situated as an approach to the question of the event in recent French thought.

15. Montesquieu's *Lettres persanes* dramatizes this problem, but can do so only by having already drawn the figure of the Oriental 'despot', Usbek, into the postal network which gives the novel its existence, and simultaneously into the progress of 'enlightenment'. A despotic system of government is in principle, apparently non-postal: the despot's will has *immediate* force of law. But this concentration of all power in the despot is simultaneously, according to the *De l'esprit des lois*, the possibility of absolute delegation of that power: 'It is a result of the nature of despotic power that the single man who exercises it have it exercised similarly by a single man. . . . It is thus simpler that [the despot] abandon that power to a vizir who will, first of all, have the same power as he' (II, 5, p. 536); 'In the despotic government, power passes entirely into the hands of him to whom it is given. The vizir is the despot himself; and each individual officer is the vizir' (V, 16, p. 553). The despotic model is thus both absolutely postal and absolutely non-postal, and this is why it is the object of such fascination and loathing for Enlightenment thinkers. This structure also accounts for the inherent capacity of utopias to undergo catastrophic reversals into dystopias.

16. See *La Carte postale*, passim: the analysis offered here presupposes recognition of the force of Derrida's arguments against Lacan ('Le Facteur de la vérité', ibid., pp. 441–524 (partial tr. 'The purveyor of truth', *Yale French Studies*, no. 52 (1975), pp. 31–114).

17. On the story of Bellerophon, see Derrida's note in *De la grammatologie*, pp. 379–80 (tr. p. 349n.1), and especially the comment, 'In an endless chain of representations, desire carries death through the detour of writing' (tr. mod.): Bellerophon does not in fact die as a result of the message he carries, and his death is not reported in the *Iliad* at all. Hamlet does not die in this way either, though in his case the postal effect does work, on Rosencrantz and Guildenstern. Following the fate of the messenger would soon return us, beyond *Hamlet*, to *Oedipus Rex*; but also, via the Greek ἄγγελος (messenger) to a community of angels, which could again be shown, in the thought of both Rousseau and Kant, to be a purely postal polis returning to a pure absence of post.

18. 'Noise' here can be understood in a quasi-cybernetic sense; what Montesquieu condemns in Richelieu's politics is its interference with the clarity of the message – at the second level (the public as meta-addressee) this 'noise' is converted into information, according to a logic laid out by Michel Serres in 'The origin of language', *Oxford Literary Review*, vol. 5, nos 1–2, pp. 113–24 (p. 118–19).

19. In their opening text to the collective volume *Rejouer le politique*, Paris: Galilée 1981, Lacoue-Labarthe and Nancy radicalize this 'uselessness' of attacking politics directly into an impossibility (p. 23): this guarantees, beyond any slogan, that writing on the political is itself necessarily political. Thomas Pynchon's *The Crying of Lot 49* might be read as an allegory of all the issues raised here.

20. 'Essai touchant les lois naturelles et la distinction du juste et de l'injuste', *Oeuvres complètes*, pp. 175–81 (p. 175). Literally, 'All creatures support each other by a

correspondence it is impossible to admire enough'; but the French verb 's'entretenir' also has the sense of 'to have a conversation', 'to talk about'.

21. The complication in Kant stems from his explicit insistence on the originality of the ethical (and thereby political) with respect to the natural world as a mechanism: in the immediate context of the discussion here, see his *Perpetual Peace: a Philosophical Sketch* (1795–6), in *Kant's Political Writings*, pp. 93–130, and especially pp. 122–5, where the distinction between the 'political moralist' and the ' moral politician' depends on the fact that the former views questions of right in merely 'technical' or 'mechanical' terms, whereas the latter sees them as properly moral questions. More succinctly, the argument suggests that were the simulacrum of laws of nature to be achieved, there would be no freedom, and hence the concept of 'right' would be empty (ibid., p. 117). That this simulacrum would not be incompatible with despotism can be seen by grafting in another quotation from *De l'esprit des lois*: 'In despotic states the nature of government demands extreme obedience; and the will of the Prince, once known, must have its effect as infallibly as a ball thrown against another must have its effect' (III, 10, p. 539: Hume, billiard-balls, oughts and is's are not far away). But Kant none the less maintains the structure in all his moral philosophy, via the operator of *analogy*: one of the formulations of the categorical imperative demands that I act as if the maxim of my action were to be a 'universal law of nature'. The 'as if' in this formulation raises complicated questions of what Kant calls the 'type': see Lyotard, *Le Différend*, Paris: Minuit 1984, pp. 181–3.

22. Jean-Jacques Rousseau, *Emile*, in *Oeuvres complètes*, ed. Bernard Gagnebin and Marcel Raymond, 4 vols appeared to date, Paris: Gallimard, 1959–, vol. 4, p. 311. All references to Rousseau are to this edition, and all translations are my own. What follows on the *Social Contract* is largely a summary of the more detailed argument presented in my *Sententiousness and the Novel: Laying Down the Law in Eighteenth-Century France*, Cambridge: Cambridge University Press 1985, pp. 159–71.

23. 'The words "subject" and "sovereign" are identical correlations brought together in the single word "citizen": *Oeuvres complètes*, vol. 3, p. 427.

24. *Oeuvres complètes*, vol. 3, pp. 363 and 373.

25. This fiction can be called 'radical' simply because it is at the root of the political: it thereby leads us back to the question of narration and myth from which we began.

26. *Oeuvres complètes*, vol. 3, p. 396.

27. The time of the sovereign is that of a succession of pure presents. The intermediary body of government attempts to deliver the post which would allow that time to exist, but in so doing takes time, breaks open the time of the sovereign, and gives rise to history and the possibility of the nation's narrating to itself what it should have been. For a useful derivation of the aporias of the idea of absolute autonomy or immanence, see Nancy, *La Communauté désoeuvrée*, pp. 16–19.

28. This much misunderstood distinction is made most clearly by Derrida in 'Limited Inc.', *Glyph*, 2 (1977), pp. 162–254.

29. *Oeuvres complètes*, vol. 3, p. 391: 'There is still in Europe a country capable of legislation; the Island of Corsica. The valour and constancy with which this brave people managed to recover and defend its liberty would merit that some wise man teach them how to conserve it. I have some premonition that one day this little island will astonish Europe'.

30. For a fuller analysis of the structure in Rousseau, see Paul de Man, *Allegories of Reading: Figural Language in Rousseau, Nietzsche, Rilke, and Proust* New Haven and London: Yale University Press 1979, pp. 254–7: and for a summary of Sade's arguments, see *Sententiousness and the Novel*, pp. 198–9.

31. For a slightly different use of Kant's essay in a similar context, and an appeal to Rousseau's *Considérations sur le gouvernement de Pologne* rather than the text on Corsica, see Victor Goldschmidt, 'Individu et communauté chez Rousseau', in Bénichou, Cassirer *et al.*, *Pensée de Rousseau*, Paris: Seuil 1984, pp. 147–61: it is worth pointing out that the volume in which Goldschmidt's text appears is presented (by Todorov) as in opposition to the whole 'post-structuralist' movement.

32. See Kant, *Perpetual Peace*, p. 98: 'Man (or an individual people) in a mere state of nature robs me of any . . . security and injures me by virtue of this very state in which he

coexists with me. He may not have injured me actively (*facto*), but he does injure me by the very lawlessness of his state (*statu iniusto*)', and §54 of the selections from the *Metaphysics of Morals* translated in the same volume (p. 165). Rousseau's insistence that the state of nature is *in fact* a state of peace would not trouble this argument at the level of right.

33. See Lyotard's presentation of this aspect of René Thom's thought, *La Condition postmoderne*, p. 96 (tr. p. 59), this 'analogy' must be treated with care, lest it return us to a new desired simulacrum based on a post-Newtonian account of 'nature': this problem haunts *The Postmodern Condition*'s appeal to 'postmodern science' as something of a model for a postmodern justice.

34. Rousseau tells some good stories about this essential feature of the legislator, and especially of Lycurgus, forced to resign all position of power put up with hostility and eventually leave Sparta in order to enforce his legislation. Moses too is an object of admiration for Rousseau, essentially because of the durability of his legislation: it is not easy to see how the principles of Mosaic law could be reconciled with an ideal of autonomy, but a detour via Freud would rapidly confirm the importance of all the problems raised here. The incorporation of the essentially foreign legislator into the founding narration of an institution is pervasive, and returns, notably around the figure of Derrida, in accounts of post-structuralism: Frank Lentricchia's *After the New Criticism*, Chicago: University of Chicago Press 1980 is a particularly blatant example.

35. For a succinct formulation of these paradoxes, see Lyotard, *Le Différend*, §203.

36. This tension is analysed by Lyotard with respect to the French declaration of 1789 in *Le Différend*, pp. 209–13, and, with a different emphasis on the question of the *signature* (which would be an important focus for any attempt to analyse the figure of the legislator), by Derrida in the first part of *Otobiographies: l'enseignement de Nietzsche et la politique du nom propre*, Paris: Galilée 1984.

37. This survival is discussed by Nancy in *La Communauté désoeuvrée* around a notion of 'community' conceived of *against* or *beyond* the themes of autonomy and narration I have been concerned to question.

14

The Frontier:

Between Kant and Hegel

This paper is really no more than a series of fragments and summaries of analysis and commentary which form part of some work in progress, linked to a three-year seminar I have been running at Sussex under the aegis of the *Collège international de philosophie*. One of the reasons for proposing the general title 'frontiers' for the seminar was a vague sense of a need to keep things open, and according to what is only an apparent paradox – and which in fact is perhaps really all I shall be arguing – frontiers, far from simply enclosing and encircling and limiting, seemed to promise opening, and a certain *lack of definition* that seems potentially productive. Keeping the theme of the seminar open and vague was important to me not just because it was desirable for it to be able to accommodate the interests of D.Phil. students working on a broad range of topics, but because three years seemed a luxuriously long time in which to work, and a time I was anxious not to circumscribe too limitatively. Attempting to 'thematize' frontiers (though we might already suspect that there is something about frontiers that will evade thematization) seemed a good way to prevent, or postpone, any *particular* frontier from enclosing the work before it got started. Working *on* 'the frontier (in general) promised the possibility of not having to work within any particular frontier. Frontiers may limit and enclose, but *the* frontier, whatever sense we might be able to give to that general singular, seemed rather to open. Naturally enough, one of the things I hoped to be able to think about was why this enabling situation might be so.

Frontiers is in itself a vague enough term: I didn't want to predetermine its relationship with a cluster of other terms in the same semantic field or region or territory – being on the frontier for three years also seemed to involve thinking about being at the border, on the edge, at the limit, in the margin, on the boundary, on the barrier or the barricade or maybe even sitting on the fence: and perhaps especially about being in the no-man's land (or on the frontier, border, edge,

limit margin, boundary, barrier, barricade or fence) *between* these
various non-synonymous concepts or *terms*. One, perhaps parodically
philosophical way (deconstruction being in part describable as parodically philosophical) of going about dealing with this situation would
involve, precisely, attempting to fix the meaning or 'grammar' (in
Wittgenstein's sense) of these various terms as carefully and precisely
as possible. And it does of course, as should go without saying, seem
important to get as clear as possible about concepts and their differences. But in this case, at least, that 'getting as clear as possible' marks
less a straightforward and honest 'Enlightenment'-style ambition towards a clarity and illumination which could ideally (though perhaps
not empirically) be achieved, than the sense that such an effort would
quite rapidly come up against its *own* limit (or frontier, or boundary, or
barrier, etc.), in that any attempt to fix such concepts or terms would
involve drawing frontiers or boundaries or edges between them, and
would thus seem to presuppose what is at issue in thinking about
frontiers, boundaries and edges. It would no doubt be nice to fix the
frontiers of the concept of the frontier, but hard to see how this could
be done without somehow assuming that we know in advance what
frontiers are, and therefore slipping into dogmatism in the very effort
to avoid it. It seems to me that this dogmatism is the dogmatism of
Enlightenment itself. The concept or term 'frontier' seems to share
with terms or concepts such as 'difference' the feature (which can't be
simply a *conceptual* feature) of saying something about what it is to be a
term or concept at all: and this seems to give it an ambiguous privilege
which I follow Derrida and Rodolphe Gasché in terming 'quasi-
transcendental', in the awareness that *that* term names a problem to be
further explored. And of course the term 'term', which I've been using
to avoid or inflect what may already seem too philosophical in the term
'concept', cannot escape this complication: the term 'term' means a
boundary, border or frontier of territory (a term can be a stone or post,
carved with the image of Jupiter terminus, god of boundaries). It
seems unsurprising, then, to find that the sort of philosophy which
demands rigorous fixing of concepts (and I don't imagine for a
moment that any thinking can be *simply* indifferent to such a demand)
should resort almost inevitably to an analogical language of territory
and frontier when it attempts to conceptualize that conceptual fixing,
that assigning of terms to its terms. Frege most famously goes in for
this,[1] and Wittgenstein equally famously contests this necessity, typically enough by pursuing Frege's analogy or 'picture' (which Frege has
said 'may be used only with caution', and to which he himself could not
accord conceptual status – Frege's passage is, on its own terms, a non-
conceptual description of what a concept is or must be, but it's hard to

see how he could give an account of the conceptuality of concepts without stepping outside strict conceptuality, over the frontier of the concept in general, in order to do so).[2]

I'm not going to go into these texts in detail here. We would find in them a complex association of frontiers and boundary-lines with signposts and pointing across those frontiers, which would lead us quite rapidly on to Heidegger (the first two examples of signs given in §17 of *Being and Time* are of signposts and boundary-stones), and then to Lyotard and Derrida and their difficult disagreement over the status of deictic terms in Husserl.

More surprisingly, perhaps, we should have to take account of arguments in Derrida's 'Afterword' to *Limited Inc.*, around the status of conceptual boundaries, which we have just seen Wittgenstein suggest need not be rigid or precise. Searle accuses Derrida of hanging on to the Fregean assumption (which Searle rather sarcastically associates with logical positivism) of a need for rigid distinctions, and Derrida retorts, surprisingly no doubt for many of his readers, that he does indeed think that concepts must have sharp boundaries.

But any attempt to address the general question of *conceptual* boundaries or frontiers, to which we have been led almost immediately by the specific question of the concept of the frontier, would almost inevitably lead quite rapidly to Kant. Kant's philosophy in general is of course all about drawing frontiers and establishing the legality of territories. In the introduction to the third *Critique*, for example, there is a famous use of the spatial analogy in the distinction between conceptual fields, territories and realms.[3] There is, too, the passage from the end of the transcendental analytic on leaving the well-charted island of the understanding for the stormy seas of Reason.[4]

There is much at stake in this language of boundaries, mapping and possession of territory. We should need to follow it not only in Kant, but in Lyotard's recent readings of Kant (and notably perhaps, in *Le différend*, his extension of Kant's island analogy to that of the archipelago of discursive genres: there's the suspicion of a residual naturalism here which may be troublesome). Hegel's critique of Kant, for example, is crucially concerned to undermine the legitimacy of this boundary-language, seeing it as the culprit for the diremption in Kant between understanding and Reason and eventually between the concept and the law. Both in the *Phenomenology* and in the *Greater Logic*, there are powerful arguments against this Kantian set-up. We might hazard a guess that in so far as the philosophy loosely entitled 'post-structuralism' or maybe 'postmodernism' might usefully be thought of as a non-Hegelian questioning of Kantian frontiers (and I suspect that the term 'quasi-transcendental' gestures in this direction), then working with the quasi-concept of the frontier might help our understanding of what this involves.

This *general* problem of conceptual boundaries (or frontiers, or edges, or limits) may seem, in classical fashion, to be preliminary to any investigation at all of our problem. It looks as though we ought to clarify the conceptual frontiers of the concept of frontier before we try to clarify problems with 'real' frontiers. I want to resist that implication, and at least postpone that clarification. I suggest this partly for 'pragmatic' reasons, but partly in the spirit of the deconstructive argument against the possibility of absolutely justifiable starting-points. According to the *Grammatology*, and implicitly throughout Derrida's work, we must start 'somewhere where we are, in a text already . . .', and move on following our noses to see where we might be going. This also implies that it is in principle impossible for the sorts of question I have been raising to be settled as a simple methodological preliminary to the real business at hand. Wittgenstein says at the beginning of the 'Lecture on Ethics' that the problem resides in the fact that 'The listener is unable to see both the road he is being led to take and the goal to which it leads' (in this case – but in fact in general – this is as true of the speaker as of the listener): here that necessary contingency (I take it that deconstruction is in part describable as a philosophy of the 'necessity of contingency', though it would require almost infinite care to separate a deconstructive reading of that expression from a Hegelian reading)[5] pushes me to return rather more literally to Wittgenstein's and Kant's language of spaces and areas with or without frontiers – in other words, to a language of *territory*. The preliminary claim is that it is impossible to clarify the conceptual status of the frontier without working through its political status: or, to put it in a slightly more sloganizing form, that there is an irreducible conceptual politics of the frontier. The guiding hypothesis of what I'm trying to do, so far as 'Kant' and the 'Enlightenment' are concerned, is that there is at the very least an uneasy relationship between the desire to establish sharp *conceptual* frontiers on the one hand, and on the other, to abolish *political* frontiers through cosmopolitanism, and, as far as Hegel is concerned, that the negotiation of these problems, though immeasurably more sophisticated, founders on a point that it is difficult not to describe as dogmatic.

The more general, 'deconstructive' point of this is probably less to attempt to do 'political philosophy' than to argue for an essential complication of any frontier between regions called the 'political' and the 'philosophical': and this complication ought to be sufficient to prevent any falling into trivial readings of sloganizing propositions such as 'everything is political', or 'philosophy is the politics of truth', and so on. It ought also to complicate what is to my mind the entirely unsatisfactory formulation, in the programme of this conference ('A very, very new idea of Enlightenment . . . ' Utrecht, December 1991), of 'post-structuralist' thought as to do with 'those who insist on the fact that thought should rather concentrate on the contingent poetical and rhetorical dimensions' of texts (I do not accept this formulation *at all*, though I regret that in what follows there will be no time to dwell on the properly textual complexity of Kant and Hegel), and operate something like a pre-emptive cross-border strike at the supposedly alternative position, 'which systematically reconstructs the universal conditions of the possibility of an intersubjectively valid argumentation'.

The suspicion that guides this 'political' approach to the frontier is that political philosophy has tended to begin with an attempt to deduce, found or describe *the* polis, to circumscribe it, draw a frontier around it to separate it from, say, an anterior and exterior 'state of nature'. Once these questions have been more or less successfully negotiated – but I'll be trying to suggest, obliquely, that they never can be – the question arises of the relationship between the state in question (in its generic singularity – we might wonder naively, or empirically, what '*the* State', the habitual object of political philosophy, can possibly be) and other states the existence of which suddenly becomes obvious.

Marx says that exchange begins 'accidentally' at the frontiers of 'natural communities'. Is the frontier of a natural community a natural frontier? A working hypothesis I'd like to suggest (it's quite a commonplace one) is that there are no natural frontiers: but an apparently paradoxical (and perhaps less commonplace) corollary of this quite banal hypothesis would seem to be that all frontiers are natural. For if all frontiers are non-natural inscriptions, then in some sense all frontiers are frontiers of nature, marking off nature, drawn against a nature on the other side. This situation seems to go with many traditional descriptions of the formation of the *polis* out of a so-called state of nature. By means thought of in a variety of ways, politics emerges from nature, possibly naturally, but comes into its own by drawing a frontier against the nature from which it has come. It may be, as in Aristotle, that the *polis* is thought to be itself in some sense natural, or maybe what is most natural, but this does not seem to alter the fundamental set-up.

This can be seen in Kant quite clearly: for Kant, it is nature (herself) which pushes man out of the 'state of nature' into political organization, as part of its teleological purpose of promoting the highest possible development of man's faculties. Kant disrupts any arcadian reading of the state of nature by stressing that this development involves a measure of strife.

But we should be as careful of jumping at too rapid a reading of nature's desire for discord as at too arcadian a reading. For Kant, nature does not want discord in any absolute sense:

> Man wishes to live comfortably and pleasantly, but nature intends that he should abandon idleness and inactive self-sufficiency and plunge instead into labour and hardships, so that he may by his own adroitness find means of liberating himself from them in turn. The natural impulses which make this possible, the sources of the very unsociableness and continual resistance which cause so many evils, at the same time encourage man towards new exertions of his powers and thus seem to indicate of a wise creator – not, as it might seem, the hand of a malicious spirit who had meddled in the creator's glorious work or spoiled it out of envy.[6]

This means that nature must be thought of as *already* violent, and therefore, I suspect, no longer quite nature at all (you'll have guessed that, if it's true, the argument about frontiers being of nature but not natural would entail the claim that *nature* is not natural). It is not so much that nature *wishes* violence, as Kant has just said, but that nature *is* already and essentially violent.

It's important to be clear about the status of this discord or 'violence'. It may be, says Kant, that the state of nature is *in fact* peaceful, or *in fact* violent. But because nothing is to *stop* it being violent, *it is therefore violent*, even if, empirically, it is in fact absolutely peaceful (there's already a valuable hint in this reasoning about the asymmetrical status of the terms in oppositions such as peacefulness and violence or peace and war: potential violence is already violence, which is why the only peace worth its name would be perpetual peace). This transcendental argument is put most clearly in the 'Perpetual Peace' essay: 'A state of peace among men living together is not the same as the state of nature, which is rather a state of war. For even if it does not involve active hostilities, it involves a constant threat of war breaking out.'[7]

I think it is possible to show in fact that nature here is never a thinkable state at all, but a name for the suspended crossing of its own frontier. The fiction of a 'state of nature' in philosophers as diverse as Hobbes, Spinoza, Montesquieu, Rousseau and Kant seems to be such that it is *not* in fact a state at all, but a frontier always already crossed. My hypothesis is that this reasonably constant fictional basis for political philosophy is in fact a retrospective projection (if I can say that) of a supposedly *secondary* state of nature, which is that which *returns* at the *frontier* of the *polis*. Although only Aristotle appears fully aware of this complication – in that in the *Politics* he tells a story about how the *polis* comes about as a result of a process of association which begins with the unsustainability of the state of nature for an isolated individual, but then claims a natural *priority* for the *polis* even though it comes *last* in the order of the narrative he tells – my suggestion is that this reversal is generalizable, and that the implication of this is that the nature with which to start political stories is not the unfindable nature which supposedly preceded the formation of political groupings, but the nature which *returns* at the frontiers between political groupings once they are formed. The frontier is *haunted* by nature, and therefore violence. The frontier just is where nature returns – but nature just is what returns at the frontier, already a ghost.

We seemed, then, to have crossed the frontier from nature to right and politics by founding the State, but *that* frontier returns when the 'literal' question of the *state's* frontiers is raised. The frontier surrounding the lawfully constituted *polis* in its generic singularity and autonomy, the frontier which marked the separation from the state of nature (even if that separation is naturally inspired, even if, as I have suggested, that frontier is more natural than nature), this frontier immediately also marks the return of nature or the return to nature, in the relation between states, as soon as its outer edge is taken into account.

This situation causes some trouble – and it is worth saying immediately that the reason for focusing on Kant in the discussion of this problem is that he seems to face that difficulty rather more explicitly than most. This problem posed by the return of nature at the frontier seems intractable, and it seems to me that its foreclosure in political thought is a generalized foreclosure (indeed a foreclosure that defines political thought at least in its traditional form), which must in principle have left traces that we ought to be able to locate. It is to be expected that these traces will not only have to do with the question of the frontier as a *theme* for political thinking, but will themselves repeat that question by drawing frontiers of various sorts within the texts we are reading.

If it is true that political thought builds its *polis out of* nature (with the ambiguity that that implies – nature as the material from which the *polis* is built, and nature as the state left behind through the building of the *polis: à partir de* nature) only to find nature returning to haunt it at its frontier, then it is reasonable to suppose that *this* nature, the one that *returns* in an apparently *secondary* position, is in fact the *real* or primary problem. This parodically Aristotelian reversal (in Aristotle's deduction what came last in the natural process was really first) implies, with Aristotle, that the *really* first natural thing is not the *apparently* first natural thing (i.e. individuals unable to subsist in nature without forming associations), but also suggests, against Aristotle, that no more is it the *apparently* last natural thing turning out to be *really* the first (the State as the *telos* and therefore the *nature* of the natural progress of associations and associations of associations), but the stage *just beyond* the last stage, the stage *after the last*, which ought, then, to turn out to be also the stage *before the first*. Aristotle claims that the State, which comes last in the story he tells about associations, is really first: I am suggesting that what is *really* first must be the quasi-natural state of nature *between* states. Before the state, which is before the individual, are relations between states, which do not yet exist. These formulations are paradoxical enough to undermine terms such as 'first' and 'last', and what temporality they involve we can at present only guess at. Our whole problem henceforth will be to make some sense of this difficult idea, and of its apparent *necessity*.

The general sense, in tune with a broadly 'Enlightenment' reading, is, I imagine, that Kant solves these problems by projecting an Idea of Perpetual Peace as the teleological principle whereby this returning nature and violence can be overcome. Once mankind has abandoned the supposedly primary state of nature and formed lawful groupings, the frontier clashes of these groups spread them out across the surface of the earth, until its spherical form (which seems to have an almost transcendental status in Kant's argument here, which itself bears some investigation in the light of the first Antinomy of the Transcendental Dialectic) forces them to meet up again and form frontiers: the argument is that the inevitable and intolerable violence of those frontiers must be overcome by the attempted realization of perpetual peace. This straightforward view of Kant certainly seems encouraged by the 'Universal History from a Cosmopolitan Point of View', which, despite many complexities in the argument which I cannot go into here, ends up projecting a happy cosmopolitan state beyond current violence, and it looks as though that cosmopolitan state is the promise of the removal of frontiers to allow everyone to be, precisely, a 'citizen of the world', and to that extent the promise of the overcoming of nature as violence, the final realization of the political as something like the community of free rational beings which guides the ethical writings. And this would support Kant's claim that there can be no incompatibility of morality and politics. It is quite easy to show that this end of politics would be the end of politics (Kant's cosmopolitan situation is one which he explicitly imagines would maintain itself *automatically*:[8] the perpetual peace which would accompany that existence would be *by definition* undisturbable, otherwise it would not be perpetual, and therefore not really peace).[9] The suspicion that this has a broader implication for philosophy as a whole is one I'll just indicate by referring to Heidegger's suggestion in *Kant and the problem of metaphysics* that the three questions around which Kant claims 'all the interests of my reason combine' (in the 'Canon of Pure Reason' near the end of the *First Critique*), viz. 'What can I know?', 'What ought I to do?' and 'What may I hope?' (A805; B833), that these questions define man not as a natural being but as, precisely, a 'citizen of the world', that they define the object of philosophy '*in weltbürgerlicher Absicht*' and to that extent define the field of true philosophy (§36).

My suggestion is that, in spite of its title, the 'Perpetual peace' essay of 1796 seriously complicates this set-up, and, by extension, the whole organization of Kant's philosophy. In it, Kant is acutely aware that the perspective of perpetual peace can always be a perspective of death (the text opens on a slightly uneasy joke about an inn called the 'Perpetual Peace' which has a sign depicting a graveyard, and the image returns several times in the course of the essay). This is a more complex text than I suspect has been recognized, and I won't have time to do it justice here. But through a variety of apparently contradictory arguments, according to which a frontierless world state is presented as (1) desirable but impracticable, as (2) a contradiction in terms, and as (3) undesirable but perhaps all too possible in the form of a 'soulless despotism' which would necessarily revert to anarchy and the sort of natural violence we started from, Kant in fact, against all his explicit statements, draws back from the very notion of cosmopolitan perpetual peace, even as a regulative Idea, and formulates instead an ideal in terms of a federation of states in which frontiers are very definitely preserved in what he calls a 'healthy rivalry', and are still associated with the dispersive force of nature, now seen 'wisely' to separate the nations through linguistic and religious differences. Perpetual peace turns out to be possible only as the perpetual postponement of its own perpetuity.

This means that Hegel is no doubt right when he says that Kant's conception of perpetual peace remains 'infected with contingency' (*Philosophy of Right*, §333, remark). What Hegel means is that Kant has failed to secure any *necessity* for his desired progress towards perpetual peace, and this is because in the sort of confederation of states that is Kant's mitigated aim, there is nothing to prevent any *one* state unilaterally breaking the terms of the agreement and committing an act of violence on the others. To the extent that Kant maintains frontiers, and we have seen that he decides he must to prevent the worse violence that would result from any attempt at their straightforward abolition, then he maintains contingency. The frontier just is the place of contingency, where states touch on one another, the place, as we have seen, where natural violence, or nature as violence, returns to haunt the political organization that was in principle set up to escape from precisely that natural violence, or at least the 'original' of which this is the ghost. And this situation appears to be precisely that seen by Hegel, for whom contingency, and violence, is precisely the domain of nature, and the passage through it a necessary part of spirit's coming to knowledge of itself, in philosophy, as absolute.

Hegel also, of course, builds into his description of the state the necessity that there be this violence on the frontier. He insists throughout his work, from the early 'German Constitution' text to the late *Philosophy of Right*, via the *Natural Law* essay, that states must defend themselves actually (and not just declare their intention to do so) if they are to be worthy of being considered as states. Whereas in Kant, in his explicit arguments at least, war and peace were asymmetrical concepts in so far as peace was only worth its name if it was perpetual peace (any other notion of peace in fact being already warfare simply as threat of war), in Hegel peace is only worth its name if it is *not* perpetual peace, in other words, only if it is already troubled by the promise of war as actual defence of the state on its frontier. Hegel makes an eloquent point in the *Natural Law* essay about the healthy ethical aspects of war which prevents the state stagnating and rotting, and is pleased enough with it to quote it again in the *Philosophy of Right* (§324). This does not, however, mean that Hegel is in any straightforward sense recommending war as such, or implying that a permanent state of warfare among states is a desirable state of affairs. This is not simplistic warmongering. But any possibility of peace is never a prospect of *perpetual* peace, as that would imply the quiescent death of the restless negativity of Spirit and a return to the mere *an sich* of matter. We seem to reach something remarkably like the result of our reading of Kant, i.e. peace as a sort of rhythmic oscillation of war-and-peace.

The problem this poses for Hegel is none other than that of contingency in general, which we have said *is* the problem of the frontier. States, which are the ethical totality in Hegel (or rather, 'the' State is the ethical totality: the whole problem being, of course, that Hegel recognizes that states are constitutively and originarily plural, so there is necessarily more than one ethical totality) – states are only states to the extent that they are perpetually not quite established as frontiered units, but perpetually defending themselves by paradoxically exposing the values of civil society to destruction along frontiers which have never quite formed but which can never quite be abolished, and which are none the less the measure of the State's statehood.

It is precisely here that we must pause and draw a frontier in Hegel's text, in spite of Hegel. In so far as the frontier is the place of contingency (and Hegel does nothing to deny this, except of course in general to affirm the dialectical identity of the contingent and the necessary, but that is just what is in question here), then Hegel is committed to its sublation. We have seen that that sublation cannot take the form of an immediate cosmopolitanism, for reasons that are not essentially different from those that Kant comes to see, almost in spite of himself. Hegel can, of course, allow himself to entertain contingency to a much greater extent than almost any other philosopher, and this is no doubt the reason for the immense power of the speculative dialectic, but he must none the less demonstrate its *necessity* by sublation *into* necessity. At the end of the *International Right* section of the *Philosophy of Right*, Hegel happily and almost complacently recognizes that with the frontier clashes between states (which is, remember, the only sense we can give to the identity of states, their not-yet and already-no-longer identity as self-dissolution) we have reached what he calls 'the highest point of external contingency' (but contingency could scarcely be other than external for Hegel).

Here is §340, ending and summarizing the whole section on International Right and preparing the transition to the section on Universal History: first the recognition of the apparently almost uncontrollable degree of contingency we have reached at this point:

> In their relations among themselves, because they are determined as *particular*, there is to be found [*fällt*: there befalls, precipitates out, linked of course to the case (*fall*), but also to *Zufälligkeit*, contingency] the most mobile play of the inner particularity of passions, interests, talents and virtues, violence, injustice and vice, of external contingency *in the greatest dimensions of its appearance* [my emphasis] – a play in which the ethical totality itself, the independence of the state, is exposed to contingency.

But we know of course that this cannot be so in reality, i.e. in the life of the Spirit, and that this has always already limited the degree of possible contingency, making possible the apparent recklessness and high drama of Hegel's descriptions. If we didn't know Hegel better, we might feel that things would get stuck here, in a situation which is directly comparable to the one we ended up with in Kant, and which, if this were really the end of the *Philosophy of Right*, would retrospectively remove the justification for Hegel's complaint about the contingency remaining in Kant's version of perpetual peace – and indeed have much greater retrospective effects than that. So the second part of the paragraph starts reeling it back in:

> The principles of the spirits of peoples [*Volksgeister*] are essentially limited [*beschränkte*, enclosed by a frontier, precisely] by the particularity in which

they have their objective reality and their self-consciousness as *existing* individuals, and their destinies and actions in their relations one with another are the phenomenal manifestation of the dialectic of these spirits as finite, out of which dialectic *universal* spirit, the *World-Spirit*, as unlimited [*unbeschränkt*, frontierless] is brought forth [or 'brings itself forth', *sich hervorbringt*] and it is it which exercises on them [i.e. on the finite particularities that the various states are] its Right – and its Right is the highest of all – in world-history as world-tribunal [*in der Weltgeschichte, als dem Weltgerichte*]. (§340)

This world-tribunal must clearly be situated on a level different from that of the states themselves – everything we have seen shows that it cannot be thought of as a sort of United Nations Organization or cosmopolitan agency. From the point of view of world-spirit, the apparently contingent and violent play of the particular interests and passions of the various states (which we have consistently been able to link to the notion of a state of nature as it returns to haunt the *polis* at its frontier) is indeed seen to be on the side of nature, as it were, in so far as nature in Hegel is the necessary self-alienation of Spirit as part of the hetero-tautological movement of its own return to itself as absolute knowledge through philosophy. World history cannot be left to the apparent blind necessity/contingency of warfare dictated by particular passions:

> Universal history is, furthermore, not the simple judgement of *force*, i.e. the abstract and irrational necessity of a blind fate [*eines blinden Schicksals*], but, as it is in and for itself *Reason*, and as the being-for-itself in spirit is a knowledge, it is, from the *concept* of its liberty alone, the necessary development of the *moments* of reason, and with it its self-consciousness and its liberty – the interpretation and *actualisation of universal spirit*. (§342)

But this moment in the *Philosophy of Right*, which is the moment of transition to history 'itself' (the final section of the book being essentially a summary of the *Philosophy of History*), is dogmatic and non-dialectical. Hegel accurately describes, more explicitly and more precisely than does Kant, exactly the sort of violent quasi-natural dispersion of states that we have suggested just is (inter-) national politics. But he attempts to resolve that situation by a violent temporal re-serialization of what is a violently plural spatial dispersion. The dialectic does violence to violence in the attempt to sublate it, in contingently attempting to determine contingency as necessity. It can in fact be shown that the whole of the *Philosophy of History* remains 'infected' by *this* contingency, by this violence done to violence, by this contingent dealing with contingency. This problem has very little to do with any supposedly 'contingent poetical and rhetorical dimension' which is supposed to be the domain of post-structuralism.

The frontier is indeed contingency. But does not a reading of Kant and Hegel such as that I have sketched out transform that contingency into a necessary contingency, to be affirmed? If, as goes without saying, the state of nature is indeed a state of intolerable violence, and if, as Kant shows rather in spite of himself, and as Hegel says clearly, cosmopolitan perpetual peace would return first of all to the worst despotism and then to a new state of nature, do we not have to affirm the political as the space (which is doubtless not a territory, still less a realm, and perhaps not even a field, according to the classification from the Introduction to the third *Critique*, but in fact the space of the frontier itself, the spacing of the frontier) as the space of this 'contingency' which will never sublate into any necessity other than that of its contingency? From this point of view, we shall say that the concept of 'frontier' cannot be a concept like another concept (which will imply that in fact there is never a concept like another, to the extent that the concept of 'concept' must presuppose an understanding of the frontier), but that the work of this quasi-concept of the frontier in the texts of Kant and Hegel *inscribes a frontier* in their textual system, so that whereas the concept of dog does not bark and the concept of sugar is not sweet, the 'concept' of frontier *is a frontier*, and cannot to that extent remain the concept that it is.

If we can show on the basis of these texts that frontiers can never be absolutely established (which would come down to having only an inside, absolute immanence) nor entirely abolished (which would come to the same thing) nor even speculatively sublated, then we should have to re-read all the 'literal' and 'metaphorical' (but this opposition is no longer strictly pertinent here) frontiers in Kant and Hegel (for example) as the figure of a non-figurable absolute alterity that any enlightenment of any sort necessarily presupposes, and which provides as much the conditions of *impossibility* of, for example 'an intersubjectively valid argumentation' as its conditions of possibility (these conditions, as always in deconstruction, in fact being the same conditions, this sameness defining the quasi-transcendental). There is no 'debate' to be had here, in so far as deconstruction affirms this quasi-transcendental, and any Habermasian position must presuppose it. I hope and trust, to that extent, that we shall not *reach* agreement. Let not the end of our discussion be the end of discussion.

Notes

1. 'The concept must have a sharp boundary. If we represent concepts in extension by areas on a plane, this is admittedly a picture that may be used only with caution, but here it can do us good service. To a concept without sharp boundary there would correspond an area that had not a sharp boundary-line all round, but in places just vaguely faded away into the background. This would not really be an area at all; and likewise a concept that is not sharply defined is wrongly termed a concept. Such quasi-conceptual constructions cannot be recognized as concepts by logic; it is impossible to lay down precise laws for them. The law of excluded middle is really just another form of the requirement that the concept should have a sharp boundary. Any object that you choose to take either falls under the concept or does not fall under it; tertium non datur, e.g. would the sentence 'any square root of 9 is odd' have a comprehensible sense at all if square root of 9 were not a concept with a sharp boundary? Has the question 'Are we still Christians?' really got a sense, if it is indeterminate whom the predicate 'Christian' can truly be ascribed to, and who must be refused it?' (*Grundgesetze der Arithmetik*, Vol. 2, 56: *Translations from the Philosophical Writings of Gottlob Frege*, ed. Black and Geach, third edition (Oxford: Blackwell 1980), p. 139).

2. One might say that the concept 'game' is a concept with blurred edges – 'But is a blurred concept a concept at all?' – Is an indistinct photograph a picture of a person at all? Is it even always an advantage to replace an indistinct picture by a sharp one? Isn't the indistinct one often exactly what we need?'

Frege compares a concept to an area and says that an area with vague boundaries cannot be called an area at all. This presumably means that we cannot do anything with it. [You'll remember that Frege actually complains about an impossibility of laying down the law for it, which may not be quite the same as saying that we cannot do anything with it: this inaccuracy in Wittgenstein seems far from trivial] – But is it senseless to say: 'Stand roughly there'? Suppose that I were standing with someone in a city square and said that. As I say it I do not draw any kind of boundary, but perhaps point with my hand – as if I were indicating a particular spot. (*Philosophical Investigations* §71)

Or again, a little earlier:

I can give the concept 'number' rigid limits in this way, that is, use the word 'number' for a rigidly limited concept, but I can also use it so that the extension of the concept is not closed by a frontier. And this is how we do use the word 'game'. For how is the concept of a game bounded? What still counts as a game and what no longer does? Can you give a boundary? No. You can draw one; for none has so far been drawn. (But that never troubled you before when you used the word 'game'.)

'But then the use of the word is unregulated, the "game" we play with it is unregulated'. – It is not everywhere circumscribed by rules; but no more are there any rules for how high one throws the ball in tennis, or how hard; yet tennis is a game for all that and has rules too. (§68)

And finally, for now:

If I tell someone 'Stand roughly here' – may not this explanation work perfectly? And cannot every other one fail too?

But isn't it an inexact explanation? – Yes; why shouldn't we call it 'inexact'? Only let us understand what 'inexact' means. For it does not mean 'unusable'. And let us consider what we call an 'exact' explanation in contrast with this one. Perhaps something like drawing a chalk line round an area? Here it strikes us at once that the line has breadth. So a colour-edge would be more exact. But has this exactness still got a function here: isn't the engine idling? And remember too that we have not yet defined what is to count as overstepping this exact boundary; how, with what instruments, it is to be established. And so on.' (§88)

3. 'Concepts, so far as they are referred to objects apart from the question of whether knowledge of them is possible or not, have their field [*feld*], which is determined simply by the relation in which their Object stands to our faculty of cognition in general. – The part of this field in which knowledge is possible for us, is a territory (*territorium*) for these concepts and the requisite cognitive faculty. The part of the territory over which they exercise legislative authority is the realm (*ditio*) of these concepts, and their appropriate cognitive faculty. Empirical concepts have, therefore, their territory, doubtless, in nature as the complex of all sensible objects, but they have no realm (only a dwelling-place, *domicilium*), for, although they are formed according to law, they are not themselves legislative, but the rules founded on them are empirical, and consequently contingent' (Kant, *The Critique of Judgement*, tr. James Creed Meredith, Oxford: Clarendon 1928, p. 12).

4. 'We have now not merely explored the territory of pure understanding, and carefully surveyed every part of it, but have also measured its extent, and assigned to everything in it its rightful place. This domain is an island, enclosed by nature itself within unalterable limits [presumably it is because it is "enclosed by nature" that Kant uses the example of an island, i.e. a territory with a so-called natural boundary]. It is the land of truth – enchanting name! – surrounded by a wide and stormy ocean, the native home of illusion, where many a fog bank and many a swiftly melting iceberg give the deceptive appearance of farther shores, deluding the adventurous seafarer ever anew with empty hopes, and engaging him in enterprises which he can never abandon and yet is unable to carry to completion. Before we venture on this sea, to explore it in all directions and to obtain assurance whether there be any ground for such hopes, it will be well to begin by casting a glance upon the map of the land which we are about to leave, and to enquire, first, whether we cannot in any case be satisfied with what it contains – are not, indeed, under compulsion to be satisfied, inasmuch as there may be no other territory upon which we can settle; and, secondly, by what title we possess even this domain, and can consider ourselves as secured against all opposing claims' (Kant, *The Critique of Pure Reason*, tr. Norman Kemp Smith, London: Macmillan 1929, p. 257 [A235–6: B294–5]).

5. This is the task of a sub-sequence from the seminar.

6. 'Idea for a Universal History with a Cosmopolitan Purpose', in *Kant's Political Writings*, ed. H. Reiss, tr. B. Nisbet, Cambridge: Cambridge University Press 1970, p. 45.

7. *Kant's Political Writings*, p. 98.

8. Ibid., p. 48.

9. This 'the end of x is the end of x' formulation seems to me to be broadly applicable, at least to 'Enlightenment' thought and its offshoots. It seems clear, for example, that on a Habermasian view of communication, its end is its end. This (suppressed) mortal effect of teleological thinking is presumably the opening (or the closing) whereby appeals to the excellence of communication and rational argumentation can so easily become intolerant and exclusionary. Again, the confrontation of this type of analysis of Enlightenment with Hegel's version of it in the *Phenomenology* is part of work in progress.

15

Index

The listener is unable to see both the road he is being led to take
and the goal to which it leads.
Wittgenstein, 'Lecture on Ethics'

This is what I have to say.
What I have to say is – this.

Indexes are an important, if rather disreputable means of access to a
book. How many of us make a preliminary – and often final – judgement of a book on the basis of what is or is not in its index, or on the
basis of a short passage or two that its index points out?

So it came as something of a surprise to me to discover that Gérard
Genette's *Seuils*, a sort of poetics of approaches to books (titles, prefaces, acknowledgements, dedications, cover-notes, etc.), does not
include a chapter on indexes. I was unable to discover this by consulting the index, although the work does have one, a little unusually for a
French publication of this kind. This index is itself presided over or
approached (assuming one approached indexes from the top) by the
following preliminary note:

> With the usual load of errors and omissions [I can confirm that there are
> several incorrect entries], this index refers to actual occurrences of authors'
> names and their implicit occurrences through mention of a title. A little
> more useful would have been an index of titles (sometimes several per
> work), with an indication of names (same remark) and dates (same again),
> but I am told that such an index would have been longer than the book.
> Such as it is, as with most indexes, its real function is to avoid the shaming
> remark: *'no index'*.

What is an index? Henry B. Wheatley's path-breaking book of that title
(1879) opens with a confident definition: 'An index is an indicator or

274

pointer out of the position of required information, such as the finger-post on a high road, or the index finger of the human hand' (p. 7). One hundred years later, Borko and Bernier's *Indexing Concepts and Methods* wants to say that the road is already an index with respect to the places it links, and that the road-sign is an index to that index; and if this extension of the definition allows them to assert confidently that 'social interaction, as we know it today, would be impossible without indexes', it no doubt also permits the suspicions we may have of the definition they subsequently quote from the American National Standards Insti-tute, according to which an indexing system is 'the set of prescribed procedures (manual and/or machine) for organizing the contents of records of knowledge for the purposes of retrieval and dissemination.'

Roads, road-signs, pointing fingers and prescription: let these be an index of the problems awaiting us.

Some preliminary propositions:

☞ A book that could be exhaustively indexed would already be its own index.
☞ All indexes are constitutively imperfect.
☞ There is no absolutely indexless book.
☞ Indexes are the *end* of what they index.
☞ No index can index itself.

Indexes are not usually thought of as integral parts of the books they index. In order to index at all, they must be separable from what they index. Only this allows us to make any sense of Genette's possibility that the index be longer than the book – this would be a meaningless idea if the index were really and inseparably part of the book. An index may usually be bound into the volume it indexes, but need not be, just as the catalogue of a library usually stands on the shelves of the library it catalogues, but can also stand on the shelves of other libraries, in whose catalogues it appears as one book among others. And just as a catalogue would not usually include any entry to itself, so an index would not normally have an entry for itself, nor would each of its entries normally end with a reference to the page on which that entry occurs. There is no need to put up a signpost pointing to the place where you are.[1] One of the Latin senses of the word 'index' is catalogue, as in the *Index Librorum Prohibitorum*.

This position of relative exteriority means that often enough indexes are not compiled by the author of the (rest of the) book, and are not generally thought to be part of what the author's signature subscribes to or is answerable for (although Wheatley does quote 'the great Spanish bibliographer Antonio', himself quoting a 'once cele-brated Spaniard' to the effect 'that the index of a book should be made

by the author, even if the book itself were written by someone else'
(p. 191). Works of French philosophy, such as Derrida's *La Vérité en
peinture*, often do not contain an index, but translators of such works
are sometimes invited to compile one.

There are traditionally two sorts of indexes, derived, I imagine,
from the Scholastic distinction between nominal and real definitions,
and although neither Wheatley nor Borko and Bernier recommend
such a division, it is not difficult to see why it might be made: an *index
nominorum* essentially records the places where names or their obvious
substitutes (unambiguous pronouns, definite descriptions such as 'the
author of *Waverley*', 'the Stagirite', 'the left-hander from Liverpool',
etc.) appear in the text, and it is something a computer can compile
quite easily, with a little help in the case of the substitutes. An *index rerum*
does not record the occurrence of words at all, but of sentences dealing
with, referring to or otherwise discussing certain 'things' or concepts
or themes. Particular words in the text can be a useful guide in compiling
such an index, but an *index rerum* will typically not record every
occurrence of the word that figures at the beginning of a given entry,
and may well refer to pages where that word does not appear at all. It
will certainly not contain an entry for every word that appears in the
text, whereas an *index nominorum* can reasonably be expected to contain
an entry for every proper name that appears in the text. A computer
has trouble with an *index rerum*. An index is not a concordance.

Lyotard's *Discours, figure* and *Le différend* are fairly unusual among
works of French philosophy in that they contain indexes. Each has
both an *index nominorum* and an *index rerum*. In the first of these, one of
the names to appear, between those of Lyotard, Corinne and Lyotard-
May, Andrée, is that of Lyotard, J-F. Even though Lyotard, J-F. wrote
every page of *Discours, figure*, the entry here does not just read 'passim',
because the name in question does not appear on every page. Nor does
it include an entry to the cover of the book and the title-page, where
the proper name it is indexing does however appear, because these
occurrences are already in principle part of the larger index formed by
the catalogue, allowing whole works to be distinguished from each
other by means of their title. This is also why it is possible for the index
of names in *Le différend* not to include the name of Lyotard, J-F. at all.

All six of the references to Lyotard, J-F. are to footnotes in the text.
One of these footnotes suggests how the discussion of fantasy being
developed in the text could be applied to the theatre, and ends with a
list of references to work in this field. The last reference here is to an
article by J-F. Lyotard, who appears in the list with no marks to
distinguish him from the other authors cited or to link his name with
that of the book's signatory (p. 345n). One other of the six entries

refers to an article co-authored by Lyotard with Dominique Avron (who also has an entry in the index referring to this same note) (p. 89n). Of the remaining four entries, one seems mysteriously to be referring to a piece by Bruno Lemenuel, and one has to have read or seen that piece to know that Lyotard is again its co-author (p. 373n). This absence of the proper name to which the index might be referring is also the case in one of the other entries, where the footnote refers to an article without giving an author's name, and one infers from an introductory 'Que le lecteur me permette de renvoyer à . . . ' that Lyotard is its author (which the index entry then apparently confirms) (p. 355n). Neither of the two remaining entries yields a proper name either, but in both cases the pronoun 'je', which we refer without difficulty to the proper name on the title page, and the 'subject of enunciation', or more accurately the signatory, of the book as a whole.

This name in the *index nominorum*, then, does not quite obey the rules we thought we could detect by stating that such an index referred to occurrences of words in the text. It is not simply that in the case of the author of the book we include in the index occurrences of the word 'je' (or 'nous', or 'on', or 'l'auteur de ces lignes', etc.), for there are many such occurrences in the course of the text which are not indexed and which one would not expect to see indexed. The principle seems to be that the *index nominorum*, which we have suggested does not really form part of the book it indexes, refers from its position more or less outside the book to references the book *itself* makes to outside the book: the author's own name appears in it to the extent that the book refers to other work by him not in the same volume, or not in the same unit of writing (in the case of a collection of essays, for example). And when the pronoun 'je' or its surrogates appear, they count as replacing the author's proper name, and are therefore indexed, only when referring to the author as author of *other* work, and not the present book as a whole. But the fact that these pronominal substitutes can occur in this way only in the case of the name of the author suggests a claim over those external texts which can pull them into the field dominated by the signature and no longer simply the proper name of the author.

On this hypothesis, the *index rerum* would be different, referring from outside the book to pages within the book where certain questions or concepts or objects are discussed. Whether the book then refers outside itself to other texts on these matters would presumably be a question for the *index nominorum* again. Compiling an *index rerum* involves weighty philosophical decisions. It suggests as a basic principle that the compiler is able to distinguish between a purely verbal occurrence of a word, and a thematically or conceptually significant occurrence. It also assumes that the compiler is able to recognize the presence of a concept or theme in the absence of its name. The compiler of the index for the English translation of *La Vérité en peinture* soon realized that something about that book made it virtually impossible to compile a satisfactory *index rerum*, and wondered why. There was no obvious sense in which the book did not need such an index (it does not index itself), but a suspicion that Derrida's work defied indexing according to the traditional rules. Quite apart from the fact that Derrida explicitly and exhaustively casts doubt on the coherence of notions such as theme, concept or meaning, is it always possible to distinguish in Derrida's writing between merely verbal occurrences of words and conceptually significant occurrences, or to give a name to a theme being treated but not named in certain pages of his work? The temptation is strong just to write 'passim' after an entry such as 'writing' or 'text', for example – but 'passim' is the least useful reference an index can provide, and would seem here to duplicate the sort of error or misunderstanding that would be involved in writing 'passim' after the author's name in the *index nominorum*.

It might be worth consulting *Discours, figure* to try to find out more about indexes, and what better way than by using the index it provides? In the 'Index des concepts et des termes allemands' of Lyotard's book (this conjunction giving quite some food for thought) there is no entry for 'index'. This may seem surprising, not because the book contains indexes (we've already seen that indexes do not refer to themselves – though it seems reasonable for the existence of an index to be indexed in the table of contents, somewhere between the index proper and the catalogue), but because the term appears in the title of the first main section of the book ('Dialectique, index, forme', first part of 'Signification et désignation', immediately following an introductory section), and the term 'index' appears several times in the text. But scanning the index for cognate terms, we do find an entry for 'indicateur'. This 'indicateur' (in French the word means a variety of things ranging from a police informer to a signpost to a railway timetable) provides no page-references proper, but refers the reader back to the entry 'déictique'. This sort of intra-indexical reference need not surprise us or be taken as transgressing the rule that indexes don't refer to themselves, so long as the term referred to elsewhere in the index provides page-references to the text (in Borko and Bernier, the longest entry in the index ('prepared by Charles L. Bernier, Past President of the American Society of Indexers, in accordance with the recommendations of that society') is the entry for the term 'index', which entry consists exclusively of cross-references to other entries in the index) – and the entry for 'déictique' duly does so – first to the very opening pages I have just referred to, in which the term 'index' occurs, then to pages dealing with Benveniste's theory of deictics, then to Husserl (these references also of course appear in the index of names). But after these references there is a surprise: the final reference in the entry reads: 'exemples de [déictiques], tous les termes de l'Index en tant que tels' ('examples of deictics, all the terms in the Index as such', where the 'as such' qualifies the terms).

If all the terms in Lyotard's index, or in an index in general, are deictics (or indexicals, as I believe they are called in analytic philosophy), then this would seem to be because they point out or indicate, as *indicateurs* ('indicators' being indeed the technical indexer's term for such references, as Borko and Bernier point out, as opposed to cross-references of the sort we have just seen) the places in the volume to consult for discussion of the concept concerned. The term 'deictic' is itself no exception to this, in its first entries at any rate, pointing us to those pages of *Discours, figure* which discuss deictics. But this final reference is not an indicator of this type, giving no page-numbers, nor is it a cross-reference referring to other entries which do give page-numbers, but refers to all the terms of the index *en tant que tels*, as such, in so far as they are terms in an index, in so far as indexing, indicating, pointing out is what they do. We would not understand in what sense the terms exemplified deixis unless we understood what a deictic was: so this index-entry clearly has a privilege over all the others. Of all the terms in the index, 'deictic' is in some sense the *most* deictic, it says what it does as it does it, it accumulates or capitalizes in itself the being-deictic of all the other entries by promising to tell, if we refer to the pages it indicates, what a deictic, and therefore an index-entry 'en tant que tel' is. We were using Lyotard's index to try to find out about indexes, but we need to refer to certain pages in the text to discover what we are up to in so doing – except that this final reference is not to elsewhere in the text at all, but tells us to stay just were we are, 'you are here', where deixis and indexing are exemplified. So if the whole entry to 'déictique' seemed to capitalize the being-deictic of the deictics that index-entries are, then this final reference in that entry ought to capitalize that capitalization itself, showing or indicating itself as deixis or indicating itself. By pointing to all the terms in the index as such, at the as such of index entries, this one is really pointing to itself as what points, as *the* example of an indicator, the most indexical index in the index. But this is precisely the one entry that no longer indexes at all, as it is neither an indicator nor a cross-reference – we've seen that an index is only an index to the extent that it points outside itself and not to itself, which this entry seems to do. Unless we have to imagine that the entry which best tells us something about pointing outside can only do so by pointing at itself pointing. Truth itself presenting its own self-presentation, *index sui*. And if we consult the entry for deictics in the index of *Le différend*, which has no entry for 'index' either, then we find that the final reference, after the section numbers where deixis is most explicitly a theme in the book, is a reference to another term in the index, which happens to be the term 'sui-référence', self-reference.

If the concentration of self-reference happens here around the term 'deictic', which, according to the pages of *Discours, figure* we have now located with the help of the index, implies a pointing out or designating which always involves a specific negativity generated by the distance between the pointer and what is pointed to, then we seem to have a paradox whereby the term or type of term which allows language the ability to point outside itself (for we are talking about nothing less then the problem of reference here), cannot help pointing *to* itself, or else the term that points to itself and seems to run the risk of enclosing us in the index and never allow us out is precisely the term that points out(side), or at least points out the pointing out(side) of deictics in general, here demonstrated by all the terms in the index as such, except the term that says so. One item in the list of indexed or indexical terms has grown to monstrous proportions, bigger than the set of which it is a member. We might link this to a suspicion that this mysterious final non-reference of the final entry for 'déictique' is something like the *word* 'Index' which *entitles* the Index in which all the terms, including the term 'deictic' appear. This title, 'Index', is not itself an index on the same level as are the terms gathered under its title, though it is something like an index, as we have said, when it appears on the contents-page. But to see that, and to make the link with the last reference of the entry for 'déictique', we have to allow that reference somehow to point to that title, and the title to point to the entry, in a way that still looks like the deixis to which this was supposed to be an exception. ('Index' in Latin also means 'A title'.) And maybe this is not so unlike the problem we encountered with the entry to 'Lyotard, J-F' in the *index nominorum*, or at least with those references where the proper name did not explicitly appear: just as the 'je' in the text could only communicate with the 'Lyotard' in the index via the position of the author's proper name on the title page or the cover, in a position which seems similar to that occupied by the word 'Index' entitling the Index, exposing its external surface to a greater index (the contents page).

This turning of the inside out, the way in which apparent self-reference seems to implicate the exposure of a title or a cover, the outer limits of a frame or an enclosure, reminds me of the cover of one of my dictionaries, which bears a reproduction of part of one of the pages within the dictionary – the page which happens to contain the entry for the word 'dictionary', which entry is circled in red, in imitation of the way an enthusiastic but inconsiderate user might highlight a particularly important entry. This has the obvious advantage to the publisher that anyone in the bookshop who sees the dictionary but does not know what the word means can consult the dictionary to find out, without yet having to know how to open and consult a dictionary. The word 'dictionary', even when it appears in or on a dictionary, is not of course a dictionary, in the way that Lyotard's index implied that the word 'deictic', in an index at least, was a deictic. But the word 'dictionary' in a dictionary could be a deictic, even though at first sight it doesn't look as though a dictionary is really an index. Maybe we can find out more about all this by consulting the dictionary, which we now know how to use. One of the things that we might discover from the entry reproduced on the cover is the etymology of the word 'dictionary' (and the etymology of the word 'etymology', which it gives as the Greek words *etumos* and *logos*, meaning 'true' and 'word' (or suchlike)): the word 'dictionary' comes from the Latin *dictio*, the action of saying. 'Index', on the other hand, comes from the Latin 'index', meaning an indicator, a discoverer, an informer, a catalogue or list, an inscription, the title of a book: the index finger is so called because it is the one used for pointing to or out. But I know from watching a video of Michel Serres in the Musée d'Orsay talking about dictionaries that the true etymology of this Latin etymology of 'dictionary' is the Greek verb *deiknumi*, I show, I indicate, I point out. In which case the 'true meaning' of 'dictionary' begins to look very close to that of 'index' after all.

We've never really managed to get out of the index, then, away from the indicator, the pointing finger. There was a slogan in May '68 which said, 'Quand le doigt montre la lune, l'imbécile regarde le doigt' ('When the finger points to the moon, the imbecile looks at the finger'). In his demonstration of the vacuity of imagining that language or language-acquisition can satisfactorily be thought of in terms of a fundamental ostensive definition, Wittgenstein shows, among other things, that this supposed primal scene (pointing finger, index, *deiknumi*, accompanied by the name of what's pointed to – 'this is an index', 'this is a dictionary', and so on) can never reduce a necessary uncertainty as to what exactly is being pointed out (this a result of the irreducible exteriority of what's pointed to with respect to the pointer, as also stressed by Lyotard), and goes on to detect a slightly different problem, no longer to do with what is pointed at, but with the gesture of pointing itself – why assume that it is self-evident that one should look in the direction going from wrist to finger-tip rather than the reverse?[2] 'This is the moon', says the pointer, and Wittgenstein's imbecile looks at the person pointing: or, for there is no *a priori* reason to assume that the imbecile knows that pointing is pointing in any direction at all, he just looks at the finger. (Heidegger half envisages this possibility in §17 of *Being and Time*, where his exemplary sign is not a signpost (though that is in fact the first example he gives), but a red arrow apparently fitted to cars at the time, in lieu of what we would now call indicators, precisely, to allow the driver to point out the way he is going to turn. No point looking for something pointed out here, nor simply staring at the arrow itself – the point is to get out of the way before the car runs you down: Heidegger's example has an imperative element which his own analysis does not take up. The root of Wittgenstein's point is that no indicator can simultaneously indicate and indicate that indicating is what it's doing. If pointing out is how we are supposed to learn language, how do we learn the language of pointing out? (*Philosophical Investigations*, §§9, 38) – it's as though we learned how to use signposts because the first one we saw had a signpost marked 'signpost' pointing at it. The question whether Wittgenstein's notion of rules, which he *also* describes as signposts (§85), solves this problem, would take us down another road, and involve using this whole question of pointing, showing or indicating to cast some doubt on the supposed radicality of the break between the Wittgenstein of the *Tractatus* and the Wittgenstein of the *Investigations*, with a detour via *On Certainty*, where the moon has a part to play (in fact there's a whole planetary and even galactic drama underlying everything I'm trying to say here, running from earth to moon, to Mars, to the sun, to the starry sky above my head).[3] 'This is the moon': I look firmly at the finger. Trying to save the situation, the disconcerted pedagogue corrects himself, saying, 'No, sorry, this is a pointing finger'. 'What is?' I ask. 'This', he says, pointing at it with the index finger of his other hand. 'And what's *that*?' I ask, staring at the second finger. The finger is soon pointing at me, and I can hardly avoid looking at it now, in the sort of curious foreshortening of perspective that reduces the finger to a directionless blob in those posters of Kitchener or Uncle Sam picking me out for service. At which point the feeling of imbecility becomes an uncomprehending sense of obligation, doom and destiny.

Staring at the last part of Lyotard's index entry for the term 'deictic', which is the one place in the index not doing what it should be doing, though it seems as though it ought to be the most indexical part of the index, I feel just such an imbecility descend. Finger pointing at itself pointing. Self-reference: but the terms that are pointed out as pointing to themselves are the terms that point out of the system at something else. They are precisely what should save us from being trapped in the dictionary and its system of intra-linguistic signification. For, if we finally turn to the pages of *Discours, figure* indicated by the index-entry, we find that deictics are precisely *not* like most words in the language in that they really have no meaning in the system of *langue* in Saussure's sense, as we can verify by looking in the dictionary. Most words in the language are given an effect of semantic content by being defined in terms of other words on the same level in the system – according to Saussure's 'differences without positive terms' definition, each term gains its identity and value by definition in terms of other terms, according to what Saussure calls the associative and syntagmatic axes, and Jakobson the operations of selection and combination. In most cases, it is possible to give a more or less approximative substitute term, or to unpack semantic subsets which will define a whale, for example, as an aquatic mammal or a hut as a small wooden house. But if selection and combination can account exhaustively for all the features of language at the phonematic level, this attempted extension into the semantic level runs into trouble, says Lyotard, with deictics, because deictics have no meaning outside their actualization in particular acts of discourse or *parole*. The same cannot really be said for other words, because the dictionary is able to give more or less exhaustive lists of the potential meanings which can be actualized for them in any given act of *parole*, whereas for deictics all the dictionary can give is a *grammatical* definition in terms of function, not a list of possible meanings. It seems clear enough that Lyotard is right to say that the lexical definition of 'whale' as 'aquatic mammal' is of a different order to the grammatical definition of 'I' as 'first person pronoun'. In other words, deictics seem to defy the distinction between *langue* and *parole*, at least as Saussure describes that distinction: the system of language should prescribe the meanings possible in the acts of *parole* but in the case of deictics that meaning only happens at all in the instant of utterance. For the Lyotard of *Discours, figure* at least,[4] deictics have the privilege of allowing the 'flat', horizontal negativity of the language-system to communicate with, and be disturbed, by, the 'deep' vertical negativity of space (thought of here in phenomenological terms as the sensory, and essentially visual space around the 'origin-point' of the body in the world). This 'origin point' is defined in terms of the deictics 'I-now-here' which get their meaning each time differently in each act of discourse. From that point, the object of the discourse is designated at a distance by further deictics: 'Indiquer, c'est tendre l'index vers un lieu' ('To indicate is to stretch out the index finger towards a place' (p. 37)). There is something irreducibly non-linguistic (at least in the sense of a system of *langue*) here, and deictics are the trace in language of that alterity. (It might be worth pointing out that it does not seem that defiance of lexical definition in a dictionary is a sufficient criterion for the identification of a deictic – lots of non-deictic terms (particles, syncategoremes in general) only get a grammatical definition, and proper names seem to defy both lexical *and* grammatical definition.[5] It is also not clear how the various very different deictics would be distinguished in this description, nor why they should all (including 'now', 'yesterday', and so on) be given a description which is essentially *spatial*.) Whence a critique, in these early pages of *Discours, figure*, of Hegel's description of sense-certainty at the beginning of the *Phenom-enology*: Lyotard reads Hegel as demanding that the spatial depth of the sensory field as marked by deictics should be sublated into the language of the concept via an assimilation, which Lyotard argues against, of the two types of negativity. Here Lyotard opposes to dialectics what he calls a diadeictics:

> Diadeictics is not a dialectic in Hegel's sense, precisely in that the former presupposes the empty gap, the depth separating shower and shown, and even if this gap is referred onto the table of what is shown, it will there be open to a possible index, in a distance which language can never signify without remainder.[6]

And if we turn now to what is said of deictics in *Le différend*, we find that although the phenomenological perspective is dropped, deictics retain a not dissimilar role as designators functioning only in terms of the 'now' of the event of each sentence, replaceable by the appropriate proper names (including dates, measures, place-names, etc.), but distinct in their operation from signification as such. Deictics operate as designators, not signifiers, and now not even bodily presence in a sensory field precedes them, in so far as 'I' is a deictic among others and is no more foundational or secure than any other.

Which leads me to think that Lyotard ought, even with *Le différend*, to maintain his criticisms of Derrida's reading of Husserl's account of the deictic 'I'.[7] It is in fact quite difficult at first to see how the two types of reading can even communicate. It will be remembered that Derrida takes Husserl's recognition of the status of the deictic 'I' (as an 'essentially occasional expression') to undermine the search for a purity of expression untouched by, precisely, indication. Even in the intimacy of interior monologue where indication and indexes should not be necessary, such 'occasional' expressions defy replacement by 'objective' expressions.

Derrida's deduction, at two different moments in *La voix et le phénomène*, claims that the statement 'I am' implies my death: the presence of the present of the I/here/now implies an ideality of the present generated by the possibility of its formal repetition as present in my empirical absence, and therefore also after my death. Knowing the presence of the present means knowing my transience with respect to it. The argument is similar in 'Cogito et histoire de la folie',[8] where it is suggested that the transcendental status of the thinking subject is only deduced on the basis of the necessary possibility of the death of the empirical subject, which death can then, from the transcendental vantage point attained only thus, be relegated, *après coup*, to the status of an empirical accident. This supposed empirical accident then becomes, in a manoeuvre constant in Derrida's thinking, the quasi-transcendental of the transcendental itself, and is as such no longer strictly empirical or transcendental at all – which is also why conditions of possibility in Derrida are always also conditions of impossibility. The trick of transcendental philosophy in this case can reasonably be formulated as an undercover operation performed on the deictic 'I' in its transformation into the so-called philosophical 'I', which no longer functions strictly as a deictic at all, but as a sort of bogus proper name of the transcendental subject.

The second moment of Derrida's deduction is based on the general possibility, recognized by Husserl, of the absence of the object of intuition in the functioning of discourse. A proposition must be able to be understood in the absence of its object. Now Derrida says that if this is true in general, it must also be true of the object of the pronoun 'I' – what I say must be at least minimally understandable not only in the absence of what I say I see, for example, but in the absence of me seeing. In so far as it is legitimate to say that a proposition bespeaks the absence of its object (and it *is* legitimate if we accept the logic of the 'necessary possibility', which functions throughout Derrida's work to disrupt all oppositions of the type essence/accident or law/case, etc., and is perhaps the major challenge to any attempt to formalize deconstruction or to write its operations in a symbolic logic) then it is legitimate to say that it also bespeaks the absence of the speaking subject, and a quick way of saying that absence in its most radical possibility is to refer to it as death. When I say 'I am', then, I say 'I am dead'.

Lyotard's polite objection to this in a long footnote in *Discours, figure* runs as follows: the point about deictics in general is that they cannot be understood in terms of the flat negativity of the system of language, which they traverse towards an exteriority ruled by the incompatible 'deep' negativity of perceptual space. The disagreement with meta-physics, as represented for Lyotard here by Hegel's *Phenomenology*, is that it attempts to bring that second negativity into the domain of the first, under the domination of the first, and therefore think deictics along the same lines as other elements in the language-system – which cannot legitimately be done. In Husserl's terminology, this is a general attempt to rescue the exteriority implied by indication to the supposed interiority of expression, or the ideality of meaning. Derrida, at least in the second part of the deduction I have just recalled, treats the deictic 'I' as though it were assimilable to any element of the language system (it must be able to function in the absence of its object like any other sign) – but treating the 'I' as ideally assimilable to other words is just what Lyotard wants to criticize Husserl for, and so Derrida must apparently be going wrong if he does the same thing. This criticism would go along with the more general suspicion that Derrida enfolds everything in his notion of text, and Lyotard's refusal, much later in his book, to assimilate what he calls 'difference itself' to what Derrida calls the trace.[9]

This is not an easy argument to untangle. Let me recall that Lyotard detects a complication in Saussure (from whom he takes the notion of language-system as at least initially satisfactory for terms *other than* deictics – and we have already suggested some reservations about this view in terms of other sorts of non-lexical items): everything Saussure says tends towards the description of that system in terms of value calculated in the differential way since become so familiar. Why then does he persist in using the traditional (metaphysical) terminology of signifier and signified, when the notion of value should disallow anything as metaphysical as a signified? Precisely (and this works as an oblique confirmation of Lyotard's general argument) because in describing language Saussure is taking it as the *object* of his discourse, and therefore, as all discourse does with its object, setting it at the distance constitutive of reference, the distance betrayed, within the flatness of the system, by deictics, and therefore spontaneously thematizing it in terms of the negativity of depth: just as a perceived object presents one aspect but constitutively hides others (Merleau-Ponty's cube that cannot show all six sides at once), so *langue*, when taken as the object of discourse by a linguist, tends to show up as revealing one side (signifiers) and therefore, it is assumed, hiding another (signified). Saussure constantly confuses his correct description of *langue* as a system of values with a description of *langue* as a system of signs, whereas the real signs are the referents of language, at least in so far as those referents are objects of sensory perception offering a manifest side and therefore hiding another side. Lyotard can preserve his two initial types of negativity – which he *then* wants to complicate by demonstrating that deep negativity really is at work in language, first of all via designation, as revealed within the system by those unaccountable deictics – only by purifying Saussure's description of the wrong sort of infiltration by the other negativity in the form of signs, for if language really were a system of signs rather than values, then on Lyotard's account of what a sign is, it would be no different from other worldly objects, and therefore invulnerable to any attempted subversion by the deep negativity Lyotard wants to play against the flatness of the system. Having thus shown to his satisfaction that deictics don't fit into the system, Lyotard is understandably unhappy to find Derrida apparently treating the deictic term 'I' as though it were any old term in the system in *langue*.

Lyotard's argument is attractive in that it seems to reintroduce the question of reference into a tradition of thinking which, as everyone knows, is supposed to go wrong by forgetting or bracketing out the referent. It is no accident that the long footnote which takes its distance from Derrida should appear at the end of a section of *Discours, figure* which discusses a text scarcely known in France at the time, by a certain Gottlob Frege, entitled 'Über Sinn und Bedeutung', and which was made available to Lyotard as a duplicated hand-out of the German text (there being no French translation) from a course of Paul Ricoeur's.[10] We're back with the moon here, and don't want to be caught stupidly looking at the finger (even though we now know that there is an irreducible moment of stupidity in the need to look first at the finger to see where it might point). Lyotard makes a great deal of Frege's astronomical analogy whereby *Bedeutung* is likened to the real moon up there, *Sinn* to the real (rather than virtual) and therefore still objective image of the moon in the telescope, and the subjective idea or representation of the moon to the retinal image in the eye of the observer.[11] There can be several expressions having a different sense but the same reference, just as there can be several different real images in several different observatories all observing the one same moon. Lyotard likes this analogy because it is optical (his whole account of 'deep' negativity depending on an account of visual space – which is why, incidentally, painting is so important in Lyotard's thought), and annexes the essential elements of Frege's description to his own, ending this footnote by denying that his arguments about designation commit him to a 'metaphysics of presence', as he fears Derrida may fear, and making quite a large 'lunar' claim:

> Frege distinguishes the moon (*Bedeutung*) looked at through the lens of an astronomical telescope, and its image (*Sinn*) situated in the optical system of that telescope. The comparison makes it clear that the moon is not more objective than the image, that the image is not less objective than the moon, and that the only pertinent difference resides in that one is in the (optical, and analogically linguistic) system and the other outside it. With Frege's

moon and Benveniste's deictic, thought withdraws from the Platonic sun of
presence. The *Einseitigkeit* of the designatum renders illusory any
Erfüllung.[12]

We should probably not worry too much here about this language of
images, which might end up looking a little like the much-maligned
early Wittgenstein. But are Frege's astronomers looking at the finger
or the moon here? They certainly *can* look at fingers if they decide to,
because of Frege's dictum about the reference of an 'indirect' sentence
being its customary sense. In Lyotard's exploitation of the astronomical analogy, this comes out a little oddly as an observer in observatory
1 expressing something said about the object in observatory 2 – which
breaks the visual analogy by smuggling into it the notion of expression
which the analogy is supposed to be clarifying: in the terms of that
analogy, it would presumably have to be that some sort of relaying
device transmitted to observatory 1 the real image of the moon in the
telescope of observatory 2. In this case what is being looked at is not the
moon but the *image* of the moon, and what observatory 1 is inspecting
is not the moon but observatory 2's image of the moon. I imagine a
confused astronomer in observatory 1 asking a colleague what exactly
they're looking at here, and the colleague pointing at the image on the
screen and saying, 'This'.

The *Einseitigkeit* Lyotard is stressing is not quite yet the insistence on
the event which will dominate *Le différend*, but one of perspective, no
doubt based on a radicalization of Husserl's *Abschattungen*. What is
Einseitig, one-off, is apparently the *Sinn*, not the *Bedeutung* – though
complications for the analogy (Frege of course would say it's *only* an
analogy)[13] start when we remember that it's possible to look at the
moon directly without a telescope (for example when someone points
to it and says 'Look at that'), whereas according to Frege's analysis it is
impossible to get a *Bedeutung* without going via a *Sinn*. *Le différend* does
not get tangled up in the same optical analogy: here there's a much
more late-Wittgenstein explanation: if the bewildered astronomer fails
to grasp the sense of the deictic 'this' (and *a fortiori* the reference), then
his colleague can spell it out for him by providing names: 'it's a relayed
image of the view of the moon from observatory 2 at 0300 hours on
such and such a date'. It's not so much that the deictic 'this' is a
pronoun, but that the names (places and dates) are pro-deictics (or
quasi-deictics, as Lyotard puts it), allowing designation beyond the
confines of the sentence in which they appear, or, in the phenomenological language of *Discours, figure*, beyond the speaker's 'origin point'.
We might imagine an explanation here whereby names are used to
avoid misunderstanding, just as Wittgenstein says that descriptions are

given when names might lead to misunderstanding.[14] So just as a 'What's this?' elicits an answer clarifying the reference of 'this' in terms of a 'world' no longer dependent on the 'universe' of the sentence preceding the question, but defined as a network of names, a 'who am I?' will elicit a proper name in reply, and thus ruin the foundational privilege of the deduction it interrupts, in that the proper name must already have been given in advance of the deduction which ought for Descartes to precede it.[15] Derrida undermined that privilege by appealing to a necessary ideality of the sense of the 'I' which immediately fissured the event of its pronunciation and therefore its certainty by revealing its basis in a possibility of mechanical repetition which is quite indifferent to whether I am or think at all: Lyotard undermines the same privilege by stressing the evanescence of the 'I', and then showing that the ability to synthesize its two occurrences as designating the same 'subject' presupposes a proper name which must have been received in a contingency and passivity prior to the supposedly founding moment of the *cogito*. Derrida's deduction is apparently all about repeatability of sentences, Lyotard's all about their singularity.

I wonder, though, whether this apparent incompatibility is only apparent. Derrida's argument goes something like: 'any singular sentence must necessarily be repeatable, quotable, etc. *as* the same sentence – but these repetitions of the same sentence cannot be *identical* with the "first" sentence (otherwise they would not be repetitions, but still the first sentence), so the first sentence already implies the necessary possibility of its own alteration, simulation, untruth, etc., in its apparently singular or one-off occurrence – the very thing which makes a sentence identifiable as the sentence it is (its repeatability as the same, for there is no sameness without repetition) immediately splits that sentence with the necessary possibility of its ghostly doubling.' Lyotard is claiming something like: 'The philosophical attempt to reduce the singularity of sentences to a type of which they are tokens, or a proposition they are supposed to express, overlooks the fact that each time a sentence is singular – including the sentence which claims that two or more other sentences are tokens of the same type or express the same proposition.' Lyotard's reproach to Derrida in *Discours, figure* would be something like, 'by stressing repeatability you pull singularity into the domain of the concept, which is exactly what philosophy has always done', to which Derrida might reply something like, 'but you will be unable to account either for the singularity you want to respect or the fact that philosophy has been able to go wrong about this unless you presuppose something like my iterability, which you do whenever you say that what looks like the same thing in "I think" and "I am" is not in fact the same.'

I notice that in *Writing the Event*, trying to communicate Lyotard's insistence on the singular event of a sentence, I wrote that 'A sentence is always *a* sentence, *this* sentence'. I can now quote that sentence, which makes the 'this' it contains enigmatic, and seems to attenuate the eventhood it is trying to stress, in a way that Derrida's notion of iterability seems to explain. I can at any rate hardly have meant that sentence very literally: I imagine no one reading the book would imagine that I was claiming, in saying that 'A sentence is always *a* sentence, *this* sentence', that all sentences really were in any sense *that* sentence. The claim is obviously the reverse of that, namely that any sentence is always only the singular sentence it is in its event. In the sentence I wrote, the stressed deictic 'this' in fact, in accordance with Hegel's analysis of sense-certainty at the beginning of the *Phenomenology*,[16] signifies a general 'this-ness' rather than indicating the event of the sentence it apparently indicates, but only hopes it can somehow enact or simulate because of course that event has already been missed by the time the deictic tries to catch it. Just like the final entry under 'déictique' in Lyotard's index, which seemed to be simultaneously the least and the most deictic term of all, the sentence which attempts to state the this-ness or singularity of all sentences ought to be the most singular but ends up being the most general. But compared with other deictics, 'this' appears to have possibilities which are not available in the canonical triad of I/here/now supposed to define the origin point in phenomenology. For example, if I had written 'Every sentence is always a sentence *now*', then the mild air of paradox could easily be removed by appealing to Lyotard's own difficult analysis in *Le Différend* of the distinction between 'now' and 'the now', where the *Einseitigkeit* is ensured by the argument that each sentence happens in the event of an absolute 'now' 'before' the temporal syntheses that distribute events in a time then thought on the basis of '*the* now'. A similar analysis could be made of the deictic 'here'. But this cannot quite be done for 'this', which is not only indeterminate as to temporal and spatial reference, but also brings with it a supplementary complication that the other deictics do not display.

'This' might indeed be taken as the canonical deictic, rather than 'I' or 'here' or 'now', in that it would accompany the pointing finger in Wittgenstein's refutation of the view of language built from ostensive definition. 'This' can refer to itself as word or utterance or token or event, whereas 'I', 'here' and 'now' can only refer to the agent of the saying, and the place and time in which what is said is said. 'This' always might mean just this, itself, its own self. At which point the finger *can* point to itself pointing, which seems to lead us to absolute imbecility, or absolute knowledge. Absolute deixis would then be no deixis at all, just as absolute knowledge is knowledge of nothing determinate. And this ('this') is really the problem I suggested earlier may haunt both early and late Wittgenstein as a sort of unthematizable residue, which the elegant self-destruction of the end of the *Tractatus* may handle more satisfactorily than the endless divagation of the *Investigations*, through the ineffable notion of *showing*, though one way of reading the *Investigations* is as showing, precisely, that that supposedly ineffable moment is in fact present all the time in the most usual practices of language. 'This' as appearing in expressions such as 'This is simply what I do' (§217) when justifications and explanations run out, I shall examine elsewhere in its complicated relationship with the 'this' in the ostensive view of language Wittgenstein is concerned to criticize. But 'this' appears in less obvious and explicit ways too, in §144, for example, which ends with '(Indian Mathematicians: "Look at this")'. More enigmatically, in §16, Wittgenstein is arguing that the colour samples in one of his elementary language games may as well be reckoned among the instruments of the language, even though they are not words, because there is no essential difference between their role and the role that words themselves can play, if one gives someone a sample of language by saying, for example, 'Pronounce the word "the"'. The paragraph ends with a sentence enclosed in two pairs of brackets (sentences enclosed in brackets are a common way of ending paragraphs throughout the *Investigations*, but this use of doubled brackets is rare in the first half of the book, though more common later),[17] which reads '((Remark on the reflexive pronoun "*this* sentence"))'.[18] There are a number of ways of reading this: it might, for example, be suggesting that the paragraph in which it is the last sentence can or might be read as a remark on the reflexive pronoun '*this* sentence', in which case there is an implicit deictic apart from the one in quotation marks: 'That was a remark on the reflexive pronoun "*this* sentence". This seems a little implausible. The sentence might also be a sort of reminder or incitement to author or reader to supply, on the basis of that paragraph – which would then be thought of as providing the means so to do – just such a remark. ('I've now provided the rules for writing that sort of remark, go ahead and do so here': finger points, now I can go on, now I can't go on, I must go on, I'll go on.) Or it might be simply marking the place where such a remark might pertinently be made, without implying that the means to formulate such a remark are already given. In which case the fact that the remark itself does not appear, but only an index marking where it should have been, might signal a particular difficulty in formulating any such remark intelligibly ('This would be the place to put a remark on the reflexive pronoun "*this* sentence", if I'd managed to write one').

But then again, the sentence might itself just *be* a remark on the reflexive pronoun '*this* sentence'. In this last case, the fuller form would involve a doubling of the deictic 'this', and give 'This remark is a remark on the reflexive pronoun "*this* sentence", or 'This sentence is a remark on the reflexive pronoun "*this* sentence"'. But as the words enclosed in quotation-marks are not in fact a reflexive pronoun, it might be safer to avoid this dubious grammatical description and say rather, '((This sentence is a remark on "*this* sentence"))'. Or perhaps, if we do really want it to be about a reflexive pronoun, '(("This is a remark on "*this*"))'. But as this 'this' in quotation-marks already signals by those marks that 'this' is being reflected or remarked upon, then we might reduce it further, to simply '(("*this*"))'. Here it doesn't look as though the italics are doing any work any more, so we might decide they can go. '(("This"))', then. But the quotation-marks are no longer really necessary now, either, as there is nothing left for the 'this' to remark but itself: so, '((This))'. This '((this))' would be something like a pure deictic or index, in all its imbecility.

This imbecilic 'this' precedes the starting-point of phenomenology, whether it be the Hegelian version that Lyotard wants to resist or the Merleau-Pontian version he thinks can help in that resistance. This 'this' is not the 'this' of sense-certainty, though no doubt *that* 'this' would not be possible without it. Hegel gets going only because the this immediately and apparently without difficulty (being already *the* This, and not 'this'), splits into subject (or consciousness) and object, and into here and now, this this and that this. But it seems as though in the Wittgensteinian version this does not happen: *there is* this this ('showing') before any question of consciousness or certainty or objects or knowledge. Maybe we're getting closer here to what has happened in Lyotard's thinking between *Discours, figure* and *Le différend*: in the former, the deictic turned against Hegel in the reading of the passage on sense-certainty is essentially the 'here' of spatial location, still rooted in a corporeal sensorium, already a subject. In *Le différend*, what I am here calling 'this' is not really part of the analysis of deictics proper at all, but, before that analysis, something like the event of presentation which a sentence is. In that case, what I'm calling 'this' is what Lyotard calls 'that', not in a deictic sense at all, but in a grammatical usage: 'that there is a sentence' preceding all questions as to what the sentence is or even what a sentence is. In that case, presentation shows up as a trace in sentences no longer in deixis, but in a grammatical particle. This 'that' would still escape lexical definition in a dictionary, and this seems to confirm our earlier suspicion about the apparent specificity accorded deictics in *Discours, figure*. But then the argument with Derrida loses its apparent force, because in insisting on the effects of iterability of the I, Derrida was not necessarily treating it just like a lexical item in a system of *langue*, once we recognize that there is more in play here than an opposition between deictics and all the rest. By arguing on the basis of an essential iterability of the deictic 'I', Derrida is less assimilating an indexical item to a lexical item, than infiltrating lexical items in general with indexicals – which is in fact the general drift of his demonstration that Husserl cannot purify expression of indication. But if lexical items are thereby indexed, then it would follow that far from reinforcing too unitary a view of *langue* in Saussure's sense, as Lyotard suspects in the footnote from *Discours, figure*, Derrida is opening any such system, and in fact any transcendental realm whatsoever, to the contingency, eventhood and 'mere probability' attendant on Husserl's notion of the index. Or if Lyotard's suspicion was that Derrida's analysis would be unable to account for a Fregean reference, but enclosed us in the operations of sense, it now appears that that Fregean opposition would be deconstructed not on the basis of sense, as has often been assumed, but of reference. *Différance* just is the movement of reference, and sense is not then the route to the reference, but already the movement of reference 'itself', of the *renvoi*, already lunar.[19] To the (limited) extent that Frege's analysis of *oratio obliqua* captures this entanglement of sense and reference, then we can say that Derrida makes all discourse oblique in a certain sense (or a certain reference), which would again appear to be confirmed by his claim that language does not answer to any rigorous distinction between its reality and its representation. But this *also* means that, in so far as iterability entails non-identity, each event really is singular, as Lyotard's later thought would wish, but singular only through the iterability that can also always allow its singularity to be reduced, as philosophy has always done, to the status of exemplification of an ideality, or a case subsumable by a rule. To that extent what I'm calling 'this' is singular only in so far as it also gathers itself (binds itself to itself, as Derrida would say in another context) through an always incomplete self-reference (whereby 'this' is always also a reference to itself as deictic) which is a condition of its reference to any other 'this', just as we have to look, however briefly, at the pointing finger to know where it is pointing our gaze. 'This' seems a reasonable 'name' for this because of its constitutive undecidability between auto- and hetero-reference. The pointing finger, which we first thought could point at anything except itself, cannot *but* point to itself if it is to point elsewhere, and this seems to prescribe a moment of imbecility as a part of any claim to intelligence. In Wittgenstein, this shows up in the eccentric or recalcitrant pupil figures who people his examples, and in

Lyotard and Derrida as a sort of radical passivity of thought before the event.

Saussure argues, against traditional conventionalism, that we receive the system of *langue* like the law. Our relation to its is primarily one of subjection, rather than one of contractual agreement. I imagine too that there is a similar force in Wittgenstein's saying that he follows the rule *blindly*.[20] In both cases there is a suspicion of difficulty in explaining how that law never seems to be absolutely binding – which is another way of asking how questions of ethics and politics are possible (for they are only possible to the extent that the law is *not* absolutely binding), and suspecting that Wittgenstein's remarks about banging one's head against the limit of language are necessarily too absolutist in character. And I imagine the scene of the law as precisely one involving staring and imbecility: the legislator moves an index finger away from the near horizontality of indication, through a 90° rotation not, as Lyotard wanted in *Discours, figure*, from the lateral space of the linguistic system to the deep space of the world, but into that sort of absolute verticality which designates something beyond even the moon.

This is what I had to say.

Notes

1. The paradox of knowing whether the catalogue of all catalogues not including entries to themselves should include an entry to itself is not far from the problems indicated for us.

2. See *Philosophical Investigations*, §185. In the *Philosophical Grammar*, §52, Wittgenstein makes it a matter of 'human nature' to understand pointing as going from wrist to finger-tip rather than vice versa, but this naturalism disappears in his later work.

3. The reading of Wittgenstein along these lines is the object of work in progress.

4. For a fuller exposition, see my *Lyotard: Writing the Event*, Manchester: Manchester University Press 1988, pp. 56–66.

5. Lyotard's logic here goes as follows: Saussure defines language as system S; but a set of indubitably linguistic elements D cannot be included in S; therefore 1) Saussure is wrong to define language as S, and 2) D reveals the essential truth of that error. But there are other indubitably linguistic elements which are part of neither S or D, so Lyotard's second claim appears vulnerable.

6. *Discours, figure*, p. 41.

7. *Discours, figure*, 115–6n18; cf. *Writing the Event*, p. 64. For a brief discussion of Lyotard's more general criticisms of Derrida, see 'Spirit's Spirit Spirits Spirit', Chapter 10 above.

8. In *L'Ecriture et la différence*, Paris: Seuil 1967, tr. Alan Bass as *Writing and Difference*, Chicago: University of Chicago Press 1978.

9. *Discours, figure*, p. 328; cf. *Writing the Event*, pp. 101–2.

10. See *Discours, figure*, p. 105n1.

11. 'The following analogy will perhaps clarify these relationships. Somebody observes the moon through a telescope. I compare the moon itself to the meaning [*Bedeutung*]; it is the object of the observation, mediated by the real image projected by the object glass in the interior of the telescope, and by the retinal image of the observer. The former I compare to the sense, the latter is like the idea or experience [*Vorstellung oder Anschauung*]. The optical image in the telescope is indeed one sided and dependent upon the standpoint of observation; but it is still objective, inasmuch as it can be used by several observers. At any rate it could be arranged for several to use it simultaneously. But each one would have his own retinal image', Gottlob Frege, 'Über Sinn und Bedeutung', in I. Angelelli, ed., *Kleine Schriften* (Hildesheim: Georg Olms 1967), pp. 143–62 (p. 146); tr. Max Black as 'On Sense and Meaning', in P. Geach and M. Black, eds, *Translations from the Philosophical Writings of Gottlob Frege*, 3rd edition (Oxford: Blackwell 1980), pp. 56–78. In work in progress I try to show how Frege's celebrated distinction is fundamentally incoherent.

12. *Discours, figure*, p. 116n.

13. The classical philosophical response to criticism of illustrations or analogies or examples is to write off the difficulties to the 'only' in the expression 'only an analogy'.

14. *Philosophical Investigations*, §79.

15. Cf. *Writing the Event*, p. 123.

16. G.W.F. Hegel, *Phenomenology of Spirit*, tr. A.V. Miller, Oxford: Oxford University Press 1977, §§90–110.

17. See §§213, 251, 321, 524, 534, 539, 559, 568, 606, 609, 610.

18. '((Bermerkung über das reflexive Fürwort "dieser Satz".))'

19. This would be confirmed by analysing everything Derrida says about the sun throughout his work.

20. *Philosophical Investigations*, §219.

Index

Adami, Valerio 182, 183
Adorno, Theodor 82, 102, 113
Allen, Woody 6
Alexander, Peter 124
Althusser, Louis 29, 65, 66, 69–70,
    77, 80, 90, 98, 246
Anderson, Perry 49, 53
Aristotle 263, 264, 265, 266
Artaud, Antonin 58
Austin, J. L. 18, 50, 145
Ayers, Michael 124–5

Bachelard, Gaston 24–5
Balzac, Honoré de 78, 81, 83
Barthes, Roland 6, 24, 69, 187, 194
Bataille, Georges 24
Baudrillard, Jean 82, 83
Belsey, Catherine 65, 73
Benjamin, Andrew 47
Benjamin, Walter 2, 6, 49, 57, 64,
    67, 70, 178
Bennett, Jonathan 136
Bennett, Tony 64
Bennington, Geoffrey 6, 7, 52, 53,
    54, 151, 193, 205–6, 226, 253,
    256, 290, 294, 295
Benveniste, Emile 279, 288
Berkeley, George 125, 126–8
Bernal, Martin 207, 218, 222–6
Bernasconi, Robert 47, 55, 60, 194
Bernier, Charles L. 275, 276, 278,
    279
Bernstein, Jay 47
Birault, Henri 59

Blanchot, Maurice 199
Bloom, Harold 23
Borch-Jacobsen, Mikkel 253
Borges, Jorge Luis 125–6, 133
Bouveresse, Jacques 253
Bowlby, Rachel 226
Brooke Boothby, Charles 237–8
Brooker, Peter 65, 73
Bryson, Norman 153, 154
Buren, Daniel 153
Burt, Ellen 236–9

Carroll, David 51
Celan, Paul 54, 199, 230
Certeau, Michel de 60
Clark, Timothy 57
Comte, Auguste 248
Condillac, Etienne Bonnot de 237–8
Conrad, Joseph 78, 79
Corneille, Pierre 155–71
Coward, Rosalind 63
Creech, James 239
Critchley, Simon 58
Culler, Jonathan 12, 13, 14, 20, 48,
    49, 50, 51, 53, 98
cummings, e.e. 155
Cutler, Anthony 85

D'Alembert, Jean le Rond 236
David, Louis 154
Davidson, Donald 5
Deleuze, Gilles 77, 82, 84, 99, 110,
    112

de Man, Paul 53, 97, 130, 142–51, 205, 213, 250–51

Derrida, Jacques 5–60, 62, 63, 65, 74, 77, 82, 84, 87, 88–96, 98, 99–116, 134, 141, 142, 146, 154, 171, 172, 180–95, 196–206, 207–27, 229–30, 231, 232, 250, 260–62, 276, 278, 284–95

Descombes, Vincent 22, 28, 50, 54, 103, 194, 225, 253

Dews, Peter 4, 47, 49, 99–110, 113, 115, 254

Diderot, Denis 234–5

Doubrovsky, Serge 161

Dunn, John 135

Durkheim, Emile 84–5

Eagleton, Terry 4, 12, 49, 56, 57, 58, 63, 64–5, 66–73, 84, 100, 178, 179, 180, 193, 254

Eisenman, Peter 183, 189–92, 194, 195

Eliot, T. S. 65, 184, 187

Ellis, John 63

Engels, Friedrich 65

Felman, Shoshana 50

Ferry, Luc 254

Fichte, Johann 21, 103, 104

Filmer, Robert 135

Flaubert, Gustave 36, 57

Foucault, Michel 51, 57, 82, 107, 108, 109, 110, 112, 199, 200, 203, 223

Frege, Gottlob 260–61, 272, 273

Freud, Sigmund 25, 32, 38, 48, 50, 51, 53, 207, 215, 216, 217, 218, 221, 223, 225, 226

Fry, Northrop 64

Fuller, Peter 173

Gasché, Rodolphe 12–15, 17–33, 37, 38, 40–7, 48–60, 150

Gissing, George 78, 81, 83

Gödel, Kurt 145

Godzich, Wlad 143–4, 147

Goldmann, Lucien 80

Goldschmidt, Victor 256

Goux, Jean-Joseph 253

Granel, Gérard 23

Greenlees, Douglas 133

Greimas, Algirdas 77

Guattari, Felix 77, 82

Habermas, Jürgen 6, 32, 57, 102, 109, 110, 113, 192, 254

Handelman, Susan 223, 226

Harvey, Irene 13–20, 24–6, 30–37, 40–42, 45, 47, 52, 54–5, 57, 58

Hegel, Georg 6, 20, 21, 22, 24, 38, 43, 49, 50, 54, 57, 58, 65, 79, 99, 108, 111–15, 194, 199, 200, 207, 210–13, 215, 221, 222, 259, 261–3, 267–73, 284–5, 290, 292

Heidegger, Martin 19, 20, 23, 25, 29, 30, 31, 35, 37, 38, 39, 43, 45, 49, 50, 51, 53, 58, 59, 60, 111, 112, 113, 154, 188, 192, 194, 196–206, 210, 213, 225, 226, 261, 267, 282

Hindess, Barry 85–6

Hirst, Paul 85–6

Hitchcock, Alfred 6

Hobson, Marian 53

Horace (Quintus Horatius Flaccus) 152–3

Horatius 153–171

Horkheimer, Max 82

Hume, David 48

Hussein, Athar 85

Husserl, Edmund 20, 22, 23, 26, 37, 40, 41, 42, 44, 49, 50, 53, 58, 102, 105, 197, 210, 261, 279, 284–6, 288, 293

Jameson, Fredric 4, 12, 49, 62, 64, 66, 67, 69, 74–87, 144, 175–80, 193

Jencks, Charles 173–80, 182, 193

Jefferson, Ann 60

Johnson, Barbara 14, 24, 25, 50, 51, 205

Joyce, James 47, 53, 58, 216, 221

Kant, Immanuel 6, 21, 24, 25, 26,
    31, 36–9, 51, 52, 54, 55, 57, 58,
    99, 103, 111–13, 116, 153–4,
    181, 199, 210–13, 215, 222,
    226, 230–34, 235, 251, 259,
    261–71, 273
Kipnis, Jeffrey 189–90
Kortian, Garbis 57
Krantor 218
Krell, David 47, 58
Kristeva, Julia 82, 184
Kuhn, Thomas 25

Lacan, Jacques 6, 50, 77, 82, 98,
    104–9, 199, 200, 203, 205, 230
Lacoue-Labarthe, Philippe 51, 105,
    169, 206, 254, 255
Laruelle, François 115, 116
Lecercle, Jean-Jacques 5
Leitch, Vincent 52
Lentricchia, Frank 257
Levinas, Emmanuel 39, 40, 45, 58,
    59, 105, 110, 210, 213, 219
Lévi-Strauss, Claude 46, 77, 85–6,
    171
Llewelyn, John 14–26, 28, 35–39,
    44, 45, 47, 51, 52, 53, 55
Locke, John 119–36
Lyotard, Jean-François 5, 6, 51, 52,
    57, 58, 59, 61, 74, 75, 77, 81, 82,
    83, 85, 86–7, 99, 107–10, 112,
    114, 138, 151, 152–71, 172–82,
    188, 192–4, 203–4, 206, 225–6,
    233, 241, 242, 254, 256, 257,
    261, 276–90, 292–4
Livy 154–5, 156–7, 159, 161

MacCabe, Colin 58
McLeod, Ian 53
Mallarmé, Stéphane 22, 58, 59, 199
Marx, Karl 50, 68, 85, 88–98, 108,
    263
Maurel, Jean 51
Mehlman, Jeffrey 67
Melville, Stephen 47, 50, 52, 53, 54,
    58

Merleau-Ponty, Maurice 102, 103,
    105, 153, 286
Montesquieu, Charles Secondat de
    244–8
Morgan, Diane 226
Morin, Edgar 240
Morris, Michael 55
Moses 5, 207–26, 257

Nancy, Jean-Luc 51, 105, 168–9,
    206, 253, 255, 256, 257
Negri, Antonio 97, 98
Nietzsche, Friedrich 14, 16, 30, 48,
    49, 50, 52, 54, 99, 112
Norris, Christopher 12, 14, 15, 18,
    28, 47, 48, 49, 51, 52, 55, 56, 58

Pascal, Blaise 6, 137–51
Peirce, Charles 15, 17
Plato 22, 23, 33, 57, 103, 111, 199,
    201, 207, 213, 216, 218
Ponge, Francis 199
Porter, J. R. 226
Poulantzas, Nicos 81
Pynchon, Thomas 255

Quine, Willard van Orman 15

Renaut, Alain 254
Richardson, Samuel 71
Rogocinski, Jacob 254
Rorty, Richard 6, 7, 11, 47, 48, 254
Rose, Gillian 47, 54, 99–100, 103,
    110–15, 198, 205
Rose, Jacqueline 50, 54
Roudinesco, Elisabeth 223
Rousseau, Jean-Jacques 6, 22, 33–6,
    45, 57, 58, 59, 84, 103, 111, 115,
    131, 143, 198, 199, 200, 201,
    205, 206, 218–22, 226, 235–9,
    248–51, 252, 264
Royle, Nicholas, 56, 195
Russell, Bertrand 145
Ryan, Michael 4, 63, 88–98

Sade, Donatien Alphonse François
    de 251

Said, Edward 12, 49
Saussure, Ferdinand de 56, 185–6,
    199, 229, 283, 286, 287, 293,
    294
Schelling, Friedrich 21, 103, 104,
    200
Searle, John 18, 47, 104, 200, 225,
    261
Serres, Michel 115, 116, 255, 281
Sharratt, Bernard 141
Simonides of Ceos 152–3
Spinoza, Baruch 264
Spivak, Gayatri 15, 35, 49, 51, 53,
    57, 58
Sprinker, Michael 72
Sraffa, Piero 95
Stendhal 60
Strauss, Leo 73

Thom, René 257
Titus-Carmel, Gérard 182–3
Todorov, Tzvetan 256
Tschumi, Bernard 180, 189, 191–2
Trakl, Georg 200, 201, 202, 204

Ulmer, Gregory 13, 15, 40, 50, 51,
    53, 58

Vaillé, Eugène 243–4
van Eyck, Aldo 188–9, 192
Venturi, Robert 183–9, 191, 192,
    194

Warburton, William 98, 207, 220,
    221, 225
Weber, Max 79
Weber, Samuel 17, 52, 53
Wheatley, Henry 274, 275, 276
White, Allon 58
Widdowson, Peter 65
Williams, Raymond 65
Wittgenstein, Ludwig 15, 208,
    260–62, 272, 274, 281–2, 288,
    290–91, 293–4
Wood, David 47, 55, 58

Young, Robert 50, 53, 58, 242–3

Žižek, Slavoj 6